///*Violence* in the Home

MULTIDISCIPLINARY PERSPECTIVES

Karel Kurst-Swanger
and Jacqueline L. Petcosky

2003

OXFORD
UNIVERSITY PRESS

Oxford   New York
Auckland   Bangkok   Buenos Aires   Cape Town   Chennai
Dar es Salaam   Delhi   Hong Kong   Istanbul   Karachi   Kolkata
Kuala Lumpur   Madrid   Melbourne   Mexico City   Mumbai   Nairobi
São Paulo   Shanghai   Taipei   Tokyo   Toronto

Published by Oxford University Press, Inc.
198 Madison Avenue, New York, New York, 10016

www.oup.com

Oxford is a registered trademark of Oxford University Press

Library of Congress Cataloging-in-Publication Data
Kurst-Swanger, Karel, 1961–
Violence in the home: multidisciplinary perspectives / Karel Kurst-Swanger, Jacqueline L. Petcosky.
    p. cm.
ISBN 0-19-516518-7; 0-19-515114-3 (pbk.)
1. Family violence.   2. Family violence—United States.
3. Family violence—Prevention.   I. Petcosky, Jacqueline L., 1962–
II. Title.
HV6626.K83 2003
362.82'92—dc21   2002010637

9 8 7 6 5 4 3 2 1

Printed in the United States of America
on acid-free paper

/// *Dedicated to our parents*
Michalyn and Robert Kurst
and Eleanor and Andrew Petcosky

Violence in the Home provides state-of-the-art information on the different types of violence pervasive in homes throughout American society. Family violence occurs in all socioeconomic, age, racial, and ethnic groups. This volume thoroughly documents the different types of abuse and neglect in all types of families and interpersonal relationships throughout the lifespan. This book offers a humanistic and multidisciplinary perspective, and a valuable analysis of how public policies and programs can be utilized to sharply reduce child maltreatment, intimate partner abuse, sibling abuse, animal abuse, elder abuse, and nursing home caregiver abuse. This is the first book to focus on the common themes and policy issues involved in the different types of family abuse throughout the lifespan. Kurst-Swanger and Petcosky have eloquently identified and discussed the critical issues, continuum of the duration and severity of violence in the home, social isolation and restricting victims' movements and social contacts, power differentials that place different types of relationships at high risk of violence, physical and psychological consequences, cultural factors and influences, legal issues and remedies, and economic and social conditions that contribute to an escalation of violence among family members.

This outstanding, reader-friendly, and exceptionally well-written book integrates theory and practice with clarity and a most engaging method. Most of the chapters open with reality-oriented stories of abuse and neglect. The most up-to-date trends, research, and policy issues are woven into each chapter in an understandable manner. The authors' objective is to improve the plight of families plagued by violence through expanded research and program developments, and by improving system-wide coordination of prevention and intervention programs. In my opinion, the authors have met and exceeded their objective.

This book is essential reading for all human service and criminal justice professionals. This crowning achievement represents a straightforward, pragmatic, original, and critically important synthesis of the sociological, psychological, medical, and public policy professional literature on family violence through the life cycle. This comprehensive volume should be required reading for every student, criminal justice practitioner, domestic violence advocate, victim assistance counselor, public health official, public policy or legislative analyst, health care professional, and social worker.

Albert R. Roberts, Ph.D.
Professor of Criminal Justice and Social Work
Editor-in-Chief, *Brief Treatment and Crisis Intervention* journal
(Oxford University Press)

*T*his volume brings together the scholarly research and professional experience of numerous disciplines on violence in the home. This book examines the complex, multidimensional phenomena of family violence, taking a unique approach to defining family. We take special care to include the most up-to-date research available from different perspectives. We draw on the empirical findings from many different scholarly perspectives, including medicine and public health, law enforcement, law, social work, psychology, counseling, public policy, human development, religious studies, sociology, and veterinary science. We balance theoretical perspectives with practical dimensions while documenting the struggles practitioners are faced with. Current debates in the field are highlighted. You will gain a comprehensive understanding of the dynamics of family violence and the challenges of the practitioner.

Many of the chapters open with real stories of abuse or neglect, told from unique perspectives. Our intention is to point out the social impact that violence in the home has on victims, offenders, and the entire community. Violence in the home affects all of us. This book will confront you in many ways, regardless of your personal experience with abuse or neglect. We hope your journey ends with a commitment to get involved and to become part of the solution.

This book is divided into three main parts. The first two chapters provide an overview of the problem of family violence and the theoretical explanations for the prevalence of abuse and neglect. Chapter 1 provides an overview of the problem of violence in the home, framing definitions of family and family violence. We include a discussion of multidisciplinary perspectives and introduce some common themes that have been identified in abusive families. We conclude this chapter with an exploration of the role of cultural factors in the reinforcement of abusive behaviors and provide you with some specific examples to stimulate your thinking about how important culture is to our everyday lives and behaviors. Chapter 2 documents some historical perspectives of the evolution of family violence theory and research. Theory is explored on the micro, meso, and macro levels.

The second part includes chapters 3 to 7. Each of these chapters reviews a particular form of violence in the home, as viewed across the life span. Each chapter investigates historical perspectives and current issues. Chapter 3 examines the problem of child maltreatment, including all forms of abuse and neglect. Current issues and the consequences of abuse and neglect are discussed. Chapter 4 presents a comprehensive discussion of intimate partner violence, including an examination of historical and social trends, different forms abuse takes within intimate relationships, and some of the consequences for victims and their children. Chapter 5 explores topics often excluded from the discourse on family violence. Sibling, parental, and animal abuse take center stage to draw attention to the profound effects each of these forms of violence in the home has on victims. Little public dialogue has occurred regarding these issues, and we hope professionals will use this information to improve current intervention and prevention strategies. Chapter 6 reviews the problem of elder abuse, looking at the elderly as a particularly vulnerable population, and covers risk factors for perpetrators and consequences for victims. Chapter 7 is devoted to a discussion of what we refer to as *pseudo family violence*, or the maltreatment of children and adults in out-of-home care. This type of chapter is unique to a family violence text, and we provide ample discussion of our rationale for including such topics in this book. We think you will find these pages especially meaningful, bringing a brand-new perspective to our understanding of violence in the home.

The third part includes a comprehensive discussion of intervention and prevention. Chapter 8 presents a thorough discussion of the myriad of intervention strategies currently employed in the identification of and intervention with abusive families. We emphasize the integration of the various intervention and service models—in which some models are used for specific forms of violence, whereas others are more generic. Chapter 9 focuses on systemic problems and potential solutions, the ideology of prevention models, the role of technology, and the unique potential of various community groups to prevent future violence. We end the book with a discussion of the important role each of us can play in preventing abuse and neglect in the home. We challenge you to get involved, whether or not your contribution is within the purview of a specific profession. Families and pseudo families deserve our support.

/// Acknowledgments

We are deeply grateful to the many people who contributed to this book and supported our efforts. In particular, we are indebted to Dr. Albert Roberts, professor of criminal justice, Livingston College campus, Rutgers, the

State University of New Jersey. He generously gave of his time and expertise to assist us in every facet of this project. He is a true mentor, role model, and inspiration. We would also like to acknowledge the professionals at Oxford University Press who helped bring this book to life, specifically Joan Bossert, Kim Robinson, Maura Roessner, and Robin Miura, and the copyeditor, Elaine Kehoe. Also, to the scholars who conducted anonymous reviews of earlier manuscripts, we thank you for your insight and attention to detail. We express special gratitude to our friends Patricia Huntington-Sigel and Melinda Kleehamer for taking the time to read the manuscript and for providing us with honest feedback.

Karel would like to personally thank her colleagues in the Department of Public Justice at the State University of New York at Oswego—Celia Sgroi, Rosalie Young, Margaret Ryniker, Michele Fischetti, Ed Thibault, and Dave Owens—for their support and encouragement. Also, this project would not have come to such timely completion without a grant award from the Dr. Nuala McGann Drescher Affirmative Action/Diversity Leave program offered by the United University Professionals (UUP). Jacqueline would like to acknowledge the support she received from her colleagues at New York State Electric and Gas Power Partner Program.

We would like to express our appreciation to our families and close friends who supported us in many ways throughout this journey. We appreciate your understanding while we worked long hours on researching and writing in addition to our other work responsibilities. Thanks to Karel's husband, Russ, and children, Lindsey and Brenna, and to Jacqueline's siblings, David, Kathy, and Belinda, and their families for their enduring patience and support. Thanks to our parents for creating and maintaining strong family ties, so that we as distant cousins could enjoy a wonderful friendship and scholarly partnership.

Also, we would like to acknowledge the many practitioners, victims, and offenders we have worked with over the years, for their experiences and insights are represented in the pages of this book. A final thanks to those special professors at the State University of New York at Brockport during the early 1980s who inspired us on many levels.

/// Contents

I /// Overview

1 /// *Violence in the Home* An Introduction

Violence in the home is one social issue that cuts across all socioeconomic, racial, ethnic, gender, and age boundaries. Abuse and neglect can be found in all types of families and interpersonal relationships, transcending the life span. It is a dynamic and complex phenomenon that violates the very nature of human organization. Family structures exist in all cultures, with the main task of rearing and caring for both young and old alike. Even out-of-home care environments, such as nursing homes or residential treatment facilities, in which pseudo families are formed are generally striving to improve the quality of life for residents. Abuse and neglect within the context of family represents a breach of sacred function and purpose. Therefore, family mistreatment has devastating consequences. Repercussions span physical, mental, and behavioral health, academic achievement, economic success, and longevity. At a minimum, violence in the home impedes the quality of life for family members and, in extreme cases, can result in death.

As we discuss in this text, mistreatment is represented in a number of ways and involves children, adults, and pets. Violence is perpetrated in the form of physical, sexual, and emotional abuse. Financial exploitation, self-abuse, and neglect are also considered forms of violence in the home. History reveals that mistreatment between family members can be documented across centuries, providing evidence of its pervasiveness throughout time and space. Evidence of abuse can also be found in many cultures and environments and, like other forms of violence, we may ultimately conclude that it is an inherent part of the complex human condition. Yet, because most families take on their prescribed role of caretaker with love and devotion, we continue the quest to understand why some family systems are unable to do so.

Abuse and neglect occur with enough frequency, in the context of a variety of home settings, that it has drawn considerable attention from many professional and scholarly disciplines. Public health, criminal justice, medicine, social work, mental health, education, and even veterinary science professionals have been confronted with the damaging consequences and have responded in a number of ways. Research has been conducted in a multitude of scholarly contexts, collectively addressing a wide range of issues—including the efficacy of public policy; treatment effectiveness; predictive factors; physical, mental, and behavioral consequences; and family systems—and has explored the core features of abusive relationships.

This book combines both theoretical and practical dimensions to provide readers with a comprehensive understanding of the dynamics involved in abuse and neglect and the issues surrounding intervention and prevention. We approach the subject matter in each chapter from a multidisciplinary perspective, integrating the most recent research from a variety of different fields of study and professional practice. We provide readers with the appropriate theoretical and scholarly foundation, coupled with the practical aspects of working with families in a professional capacity.

Each chapter places the issues in a historical context, providing readers with an understanding of the emergence of defining various forms of abuse as a social problem, the development of professional responses, and the evolution of pertinent public policy. Sensitivity to political, economic, and social forces is important to our understanding of how neglect and abuse are defined, identified, and treated. At the same time, many chapters explore the current struggles of contemporary family structures and the issues plaguing professional practice.

Although much of the subject matter in this book is traditional in nature, we have chosen to take a nontraditional approach in our definition of family. We believe our understanding of family violence will be enhanced through the examination of many types of family structures represented in modern American culture. This requires readers to suspend their traditional definition of what a family is and adopt a more diverse perspective.

Finally, we must caution readers regarding the sensitive nature of the material covered in this text. We acknowledge that the issues explored are difficult and reveal a painful side of the human condition. We also are aware that many readers may identify with certain aspects of the material and may find their own experiences represented somewhere in these pages. We recommend that readers attend to their reactions carefully and seek out support if necessary.

This chapter provides a basis of understanding for the chapters that follow. We begin this chapter with a discussion of how we use the words *family* and *family violence*. We frame the words we use throughout the text. We explore the importance of studying violence in the home, especially from a multidisciplinary perspective. We also introduce common themes identified in abusive families. Finally, we examine the influence of cultural factors in the commission and rationalization of acts of violence within the family and provide some examples. Each of these issues is explored in more depth in future chapters.

/// Defining Family

As we alluded to earlier, we take a nontraditional approach in our definition of the word *family*. We intend to be more inclusive of the variety of ways in which families and living arrangements are constructed in modern society. The traditional family, meaning married parents with their biological children, may arguably be the exception today, rather than the rule. Today, a variety of individuals are likely to live together in a household, including gay and lesbian partners, cohabiting adults, and nuclear, extended, step, adoptive, and intergenerational families. We include all in our definition of family.

Pseudo Families

We also consider *pseudo families* to include the millions of children and adults living in out-of-home care environments. We chose to use the term *pseudo family* to represent the fact that this type of family affiliation is essentially artificial, yet we pair the word *pseudo* with *family* to signify the important role that caregivers play in the lives of children and vulnerable adults living in out-of-home care settings. A *pseudo family* refers to group residential settings in which children, adults, or both are attended to by paid providers who are responsible for their individual care. Children and vulnerable adults are placed in out-of-home care environments because of specific needs that require professional assistance or because a biological family is unable to provide necessary care. Examples of such living environments include facilities for children and adults with mental illness or developmental disability, long-term care or skilled nursing facilities for vulnerable adults, and residential treatment programs for juveniles. We also consider the context of abuse and neglect in foster families.

Our rationale for including pseudo families in a text about family violence is, first, that abuse and neglect in out-of-home care is a serious social problem that should be addressed with the same fervor as violence in other interpersonal relationships. Second, because violence within a traditional family and in a pseudo family is markedly similar, we provide an opportunity to examine theoretical constructs in new ways. We believe that further attention to the dynamics and the factors associated with abuse and neglect in out-of-home care settings will ultimately be of value to our understanding of family violence. Our intention is to spur interest in pseudo-family violence as a dimension of future family violence scholarship Third, because so many Americans call such living environments "home," it only makes intuitive sense to include such caregiving environments in our discussion. Finally, it is also important to acknowledge the role that physical environments play in the developmental aspects of people's lives. Interpersonal relationships, living arrangements, and physical environments are equally important to our understanding of interpersonal violence.

Family Living: A Broad-Based Approach

Our definition of family also includes those who may not live together but have strong ties, such as intimate partners and blood relatives. Therefore, we approach the subject of family in the very broadest of terms, to include those who live together within the same household and those with traditional family ties and intimate partners who may not physically live together. The term *home* also serves this purpose. We also include animals in our discussion. The connection between the abuse of humans and of animals within the same household is substantial, and therefore we believe it is important to consider animals and pets as family members.

Viewing family in such a broad way more fully conceptualizes the function of families as social groups. Richard Gelles (1997; Gelles & Straus, 1979) describes the characteristics of the family as a social group, noting that the unique features of family living can be risk factors for abuse. These features include the following:

- *Time:* We spend more time with family members (broadly defined) than with others.
- *Range of activities:* Not only do family members spend more time together than with others, but also the interaction tends to extend over a wider range of activities and life events than nonfamilial interaction.
- *Intensity of involvement:* The quality and intensity of family interactions tend to be different from other social group interactions. We tend to share more of our most personal selves with family members.
- *Impinging activities:* Many interactions are inherently conflict structured and therefore have a designated winner and loser. For example, decisions such as what to watch on television or how to decorate the home may offer little compromise.
- *Right to influence:* Family membership assumes the right to influence the values, perceptions, and behaviors of other family members.
- *Age and gender differences:* Families as a social group are unique in that membership tends to span age groups and gender. Thus there is greater potential for conflict.
- *Ascribed roles:* The unique mixture of ages and genders in the family also is indicative of the types of prescribed roles and responsibilities assigned to family members. This may be unlike other social groups, in which roles and responsibilities may be prescribed based more on interest or competence.
- *Privacy:* Family life is generally enclosed in a veil of privacy. Family privacy is carefully guarded and protected by the larger society, and therefore social control may be low.
- *Involuntary membership:* The phrase, "you can pick your friends but you can't pick your family" rings true. Being a member of a family

involves personal, social, material, and legal commitments, and therefore it is difficult to resign membership from the family.

• *Stress*: Life is stressful; therefore, the individuals with whom we spend the greater amount of our time are likely to be involved in that stress, as stress initiators or coconspirators. Stress felt by one family member is likely to be transmitted to other members.

• *Extensive knowledge of social biographies*: We are more likely to reveal our true selves to those we spend the most time with, most likely family members. Our strengths, vulnerabilities, interests, fears, and so forth are likely to be known to family members and therefore can be used as fuel during episodes of conflict.

It is within this context that we derive such a broad definition of family in this book. Close living environments, such as in the case of out-of-home care placements, can create the very same violent-prone environment as the traditional family. Ironically, Gelles (1997) also notes that Murray Straus and Gerald Hotaling (1979) argue that these same features can function to make the family a warm and nurturing environment.

Our goal is to broaden the examination of maltreatment to reflect the reality and diversity of living arrangements and interpersonal relationships in contemporary society. However, it is important to mention that few states recognize such a broad-based definition of family or household; therefore, some of what we address in this book will come into conflict with traditional views of family violence. For example, some state policies may not recognize the abuse between gay and lesbian intimate partners as domestic violence. However, we believe that a deeper understanding of family violence can be found in the examination of home environments and interpersonal relationships, in addition to blood relationships.

/// Defining Family Maltreatment

There is no standard definition of family violence. Researchers, practitioners, and public policy makers generally all operate from a distinct definition of what constitutes maltreatment; however, there is no universal definition on which all agree. Just as there are differences in how family is defined by state legislatures and human service programs, the standards for determining family mistreatment also vary. So, in fact, may the terminology used. For example, many use the terms *family violence, domestic violence,* and *domestic abuse* interchangeably to describe family maltreatment. Others use the term *domestic violence* to refer specifically to the violence between intimate partners. The term *violence* is often used as a catchall phrase to include all forms of maltreatment, that is, abuse, neglect, exploitation, and physical violence. We use the term *violence* in this manner.

To help clarify, we use the following terms interchangeably: *maltreatment, mistreatment, violence* and *abuse*. We mean to provide the most inclusive definition of family violence possible, one that addresses all forms of maltreatment. When necessary, further clarification of these terms is provided in the chapters that follow. Our definition of family violence therefore includes both acts of commission (something a person does) and of omission (something a person fails to do) and takes the broadest possible view of family. Wherever feasible, we use the phrase *violence in the home* to incorporate our broad definition of family, home, and violence. We borrow Mildred Pagelow's (1984, p. 21) definition of *family violence*:

> Family violence includes any act of commission or omission by family members, and any conditions resulting from such acts or inaction, which deprive other family members of equal rights and liberties, and/or interfere with their optimal development and freedom of choice.

We have chosen to use the term *victim* to describe the individual targets of family violence, whereas others may prefer the term *survivor*. We wish to suggest the lack of responsibility that individual *victims* have for the acts committed or omitted against them. We acknowledge the fact that victims should be considered survivors and mean no disrespect with our choice of the term *victim*. In terms of the individuals who commit acts of family violence, the general terms of *abuser, batterer,* and *perpetrator* are applied. As we discuss, often both victims and perpetrators have extensive histories with victimization.

////   Why Is Violence in the Home an Important Issue to Study?

Violence in the home is an important issue to study for a number of reasons. First and foremost, the tragic consequences of family maltreatment warrant our full attention. Physical and psychological injury, developmental impairments, suicide, poor academic performance, aggression, substance abuse, criminality, and loss of economic stability can all be linked to a form of family violence. Obviously, other social problems may indicate the same consequences, yet research continues to confirm the association between family maltreatment and these effects.

Second, family mistreatment occurs with such frequency in the United States that it should be a center-stage concern, especially given the devastating consequences. It should be noted that the majority of families and pseudo families provide nothing but nurturing care for their members. However, a significant number of children and adults are abused every year by the very individuals who should be protecting their safety. Each chapter in this book explores the estimated frequency of the particular forms of abuse that we address and describes some of the challenges of measurement.

As you might imagine, measuring abuse and neglect has proven to be an arduous task for government officials and researchers. We must rely on a variety of sources to help us paint a picture of the actual prevalence of family mistreatment. National surveys, official reports of acts of abuse and neglect through police reports, protection agencies, hospital reports, research studies that investigate individual victims and/or perpetrators, and so forth guide our understanding of the nature and extent of maltreatment in various family structures. Although the actual magnitude of mistreatment will never be known, most experts would agree that family violence is a significant public health problem.

Family maltreatment touches the lives of all members of a family, both young and old, regardless of the form the mistreatment takes. Even family members who are not direct targets of violence suffer the consequences. This is surely true in the case of children who witness intimate partner violence or the torture of a family pet. Thus the number of actual victims is likely to exceed any official measurement currently available and is likely to extend the effects of such abuse to these secondary victims.

Additionally, family maltreatment is one social issue that simply knows no boundaries. It is a phenomenon that involves rich and poor, all racial and ethnic groups, men, women, children, adults, and animals. Family maltreatment endures from one generation to the next, demonstrating its ability to persevere throughout time. The phrase "you can pick your friends, but you can't pick your family" serves to explain some of the intergenerational aspects of abuse, implying that we have little choice as to our family members; therefore, we must endure them regardless of how they treat us. This logic seems to extend to other intimate partners with whom we have shared emotional bonds. Yet maltreatment does not exist in all family structures or relationships. Thus we continue to seek for understanding about why maltreatment occurs and how best to interrupt the cycle.

Finally, because each of us belongs to a family of some definition, we believe it is important for students of all courses of study to become educated about family maltreatment. Each one of us possesses the opportunity for prevention by becoming educated or changing our behavior in some way. Education and change are best accomplished by viewing the unique characteristics of each form of family mistreatment from a number of different perspectives. Regardless of your individual motivations for reading a book such as this, we hope your journey ends with a commitment to improve the lives of the families you come into contact with. Whether this commitment involves ending your own abusive behavior, assisting a friend who is caring for an elderly parent, advocating for your company to review its policies on domestic violence, getting involved in fund-raising activities for a local prevention or intervention program, or attending parenting classes yourself, knowledge is the root of social change.

////   Multidisciplinary Perspectives

Our best bet to improve the plight of abusive families is to tackle the issues in a multidisciplinary fashion, involving all segments of the professional and lay communities. In this book, we investigate the various forms of violence in the home through a multidisciplinary review of recent research and trends in professional practice. It is only through continued dialogue, expanded research, program development, and rigorous evaluation that the cycle of violence can be interrupted. Yet this goal cannot be accomplished without a reexamination of the professional boundaries that have fragmented the systems of intervention and prevention. These systemic barriers have led to a fractionalization in the research and in policy development, making it difficult to understand the complex dynamics and interrelationships of the various forms of family maltreatment. Multidisciplinary approaches are likely to be more successful in the long run. We discuss these issues in more detail in the final two chapters, with some attention to disciplines that are often on the periphery of family violence intervention.

What do we mean by multidisciplinary perspectives? Any problem can be tackled with a particular perspective in mind, and often scholars and professionals research an issue from the disciplinary perspective in which they have been trained. We drew research from numerous academic disciplines, including medicine, psychology, criminal justice, law, social work, public health, veterinary science, theology, and sociology. Each of these offers a unique lens through which to view the problem of violence in the home, spanning micro, meso, and macro levels of analysis. Micro levels of analysis study an issue on an individual level, meso level analysis considers the interplay between environmental factors and individuals in a group, and macro level analysis views social problems within the context of broader social, political, and economic forces. We discuss these different levels of analysis in greater depth in chapter 2. The following descriptions provide a cursory review of the different perspectives presented in this text. We have condensed the multitude of perspectives into four general categories: medical, behavioral health, legal, and sociological perspectives.

Medical Perspectives

The medical community, including physicians, nurses, and other health care staff, is generally interested in approaching the problem of violence in terms of the treatment of physical injury and illness associated with violence. Direct care to victims of violence involves diagnosing symptoms, treating and preventing diseases, providing comfort while relieving pain and suffering, and enhancing the capacity to function (Lasker, 1997). The medical perspective tends to approach the problem of family violence from a micro level of analysis. Public health professionals are concerned with influencing the health of communities by intervening in the causes of poor health rather than focusing on specific treatment. Public health officials are concerned with assessing health problems among populations, ensuring that appropriate policies exist to protect health and safety and that laws and regulations related to the health of the public are enforced. The mission of the public health field is to develop and maintain vital public health information systems to provide critical information to communities regarding a variety of health concerns. Public health professionals have categorized family violence as a public health concern because of the frequency with which it occurs and the health consequences associated with abuse and neglect.

We also include veterinary science as a medical perspective to acknowledge the role that animal welfare practitioners and scholars may have in linking animal abuse to other forms of violence in the home. Veterinary science is generally concerned with the physical and psychological health of animals and focuses on the diagnosis and treatment of injury and illness. Animal welfare professionals include veterinarians and their staffs, animal control officers, animal shelter workers, and animal rights activists. To date, animal welfare professionals have not been fully engaged in the family violence dialogue; therefore, we devote a section of chapter 5 to a discussion of animal abuse and its connection to other forms of family violence.

Behavioral Health Perspectives

The mental health perspective considers the emotional, psychological, and behavioral issues associated with violence in the home. This perspective generally focuses on micro and meso levels of analysis and is concerned with victims, offenders, and the family system. The professional and academic disciplines of social work, psychology, human development, counseling, criminology, victimology, psychiatry, psychiatric nursing, and so forth are concerned with the mental health issues surrounding violence in the home. Mental health professionals are involved in assessment of mental health problems, diagnosis of mental illness, and a variety of treatment modalities (see chapter 8 for a discussion of different types of treatment methods).

Legal Perspectives

The legal perspective provides an avenue by which violence in the home is remedied through governmental intervention. Laws, statutes, regulatory policies, and governmental mandates serve to set rules of conduct for citizens, organizations, and institutions, as well as specific sanctions to support such rules. The legal perspective includes civil and criminal remedies intended to intervene and prevent violence in the home. This macro level perspective spans the legislative, executive, and judicial branches of government. Such professional groups as criminal justice practitioners (police, corrections officials, etc.), court personnel (judges, lawyers), administrative bodies (federal, state, and local governmental officials), and public policy makers are entrenched in legal solutions to the problem of abuse and neglect. The academic disciplines of public policy analysis, political science, law, criminology, and criminal justice focus on the study of the interaction of law, politics, and behavior.

Sociological Perspectives

Sociological perspectives consider the interaction of groups of people with their environment, with an emphasis on the interplay between social structure and behavior. Social groups, institutions, roles, and the arrangements of society and their interaction with group behavior are of interest. Social, political, cultural, theological, and economic forces are examined to determine their influence on abuse and neglect behaviors. The influence of cultural and religious practices, social position (based on gender, sexual orientation, race, ethnicity, or social class), and institutional organization are also of concern. The academic disciplines of sociology, social psychology, criminology, and sociology of religion focus on such macro level investigation. In addition to the sociological perspectives found throughout this text, we provide some examples of cultural influences later in this chapter.

/// Common Themes Identified in Abusive Families

Many of the chapters in this book set out to describe, in great detail, the distinctive characteristics of the various forms of family maltreatment. The chapters that follow explore the unique features and issues of child, intimate partner, elder, sibling, parental, animal, and pseudo family violence. It may appear on the surface that these various forms of maltreatment are inherently different. Although some very important differences exist, and although one or all forms of violence can be present in a family, some features are remarkably similar across all families and forms of violence. We discuss each of these issues in more detail in other chapters; however, these similarities bear mentioning here.

/// Abuse Tends to Occur on a Continuum

Acts of family maltreatment tend not to begin with the most serious or deadly of acts. In other words, a family member is not likely to stab another family member completely out of the blue. To outsiders, such a situation may on the surface appear to arise out of the blue; however, close examination is likely to reveal a long history of abusive behavior prior to such a deadly attack. Many families experience abuse along a continuum that ranges from minor to more severe acts of abuse. Also, many experience time periods in which abusive acts subside. Although a number of psychological, environmental, and biological factors may be associated with the level of abuse any one person is likely to exhibit at any given time (for instance, substance use, mental illness, stress, financial insecurity, hormonal levels, genetics, etc.), maltreatment tends to begin with relatively minor acts and, over time, to become more oppressive and intense.

For example, if you were on a date with an individual for the very first time and your date became angry with you for being 5 minutes late and broke your arm, you would probably not date the individual again. Unless you have a long history of victimization, you are likely to find this behavior rather bizarre for a first date. However, if after 3 years of investment in the relationship and many experiences of your partner's anger at your lateness, your partner breaks your arm, you might well blame yourself for being late, knowing that it disturbs your partner. At this point in the relationship, you are emotionally bonded and have already experienced a range of abusive behaviors from your partner. This type of physical violence may prompt you to leave your partner, or it may not. The abusive factor becomes just one of many complicating factors in a relationship.

The continuum may, in some cases, have more to do with the motivation of the abuser than anything else. For example, abusive intimate partners tend to understand that if they break their partner's arm on their first date, there is the chance that a second date will not follow. Yet, if the abuser finds other behaviors through which to signal his or her displeasure without breaking an arm, there may be a greater chance that a second date will occur. Only over time and with a level of comfort in a relationship will abusers let their true colors show. In the case of child sexual abuse, perpetrators often use low levels of interaction to further groom a child for more advanced sexual activity in the future. Lower levels of contact might include kissing, game playing, games involving touching, and so forth. Child sexual abusers must overcome both internal and external inhibitors of such socially unacceptable behavior and must also overcome a child's resistance (Finkelhor, 1984). This grooming behavior may, in fact, serve to prepare both the child and abuser for more severe acts of sexual abuse.

We must also add that not all abusive patterns move along this continuum in a linear fashion. Take, for example, the recent finding of Albert Roberts (2002). This study of 501 battered women found varying levels of abuse in each relationship, indicating that there are different characteristics for the patterning of violence over time.

Isolation

Social isolation is another factor that tends to be present in abusive families. Physical, sexual, and emotional abuse, as well as the various forms of neglect, are more likely to persist in families that are isolated or alienated from others. Isolation from neighbors, associates, or other family members need not be geographic; social isolation is achieved when families pull away physically or emotionally from the community in which they live. Sometimes others, not wanting to get involved with neighbors who are abusive, may pull away. In either case, social isolation becomes a powerful factor in abuse and neglect.

Social isolation occurs for a number of reasons. Isolation may be a result of an abuser's assertion of power and control, restricting victims' movements and social contacts. Frequent relocation may also cause further isolation. Mobility may be a result of economic factors or the result of disclosure of abuse. In the case of elders, nonambulatory victims are likely to have limited social interactions outside of the home. In the case of out-of-home care environments, children and adult residents may have no social interaction outside the facility. Often their movements and social contacts are restricted or carefully monitored. Families may also want to isolate themselves from others to hide the shame of their interactions.

All families expect some level of privacy. It is easier to approach the outside world if there is an expectation that what goes in one's home can remain private. Most abusers count on such seclusion, and when it cannot be achieved under normal circumstances, they may create new boundaries of isolation to add an additional layer of protection. The difficulty, of course, lies in the fact that "where privacy is high, the degree of social control will be low" (Gelles, 1997, p. 125).

Power Differentials

As previously discussed, the fact that the family is a social group inherently means that each social group, or family, is likely to be structured with a unique mixture of ages and genders. Power may also be differentiated by physical size and health, economic power, and social position relative to the larger society. Power differentials, therefore, create an environment in which abusive behavior can endure. Finkelhor, Gelles, Hotaling, and Straus (1983) have argued that situations in which there is the greatest power differential are more likely to be situations that carry risk for abuse. This makes intuitive sense. It is within the context of power and control that abuse is created and sustained.

Although it may not always be clearly evident, power and control issues are usually at the heart of family maltreatment. This is true even in cases of neglect. Acts of omission that are found in situations of neglect and self-neglect are often the result of alcohol and substance abuse problems, health care issues, or mental illness. In these cases, it may very well be the perceived lack of power and control of the perpetrator that leads to the eventual neglect of the victim. Yet in other cases of neglect, the perpetrator deliberately neglects the victim's needs, thereby asserting power and control over the victim.

More recent research has begun to further define the role of power differentials in different types of interpersonal violence. We explore this in more depth later. For example, Renzetti (1997) points out that power is a multidimensional issue and may play a different role in different relationships. She raises the question: Is it an imbalance of power that places relationships at risk for violence, or are abusive acts responsible for creating a situation in which the power clearly shifts to the abuser?

Consequences of Family Maltreatment

Another similarity among the various types of family maltreatment is the consequences of abuse for victims. The ultimate effects of such abuse on victims is determined by a number of developmental factors, as well as the frequency, duration, and severity of abusive behavior. The relationship to the offender and the age of the victim are also factors. Although we cannot predict with any precision the exact effect various forms of abuse will have on a victim, we do know that victims, across a broad spectrum of abuse types, sustain extensive physical and emotional harm. Some even experience a secondary victimization from the very system that is responsible for intervention. For example, consider the young child-abuse victim who is removed from the home. This child, placed in foster care or some other out-of-home placement, may experience additional psychological harm as a result of being removed from his or her home.

Abused children are likely to experience devastating disruptions to normal patterns of physical, cognitive, emotional, and psychological development. In some cases, developmental damages are irreversible, whereas in other cases, consequences can be overcome later in life. Children are at risk of experiencing the most devastating effects of victimization because of the long-term effects on critical periods of development. When abuse or neglect occurs during a particular developmental period, that milestone is likely to be impaired. Brain injury, physical disfigurement, psychological and emotional impairments, sexual dysfunction, cognitive deficits, overwhelming mental health problems, and disruptive behavioral patterns are a few examples of the long-term effects of victimization on children. We discuss this in more detail in chapter 3.

Adults, even those not abused as children, suffer physical and psychological consequences. As is the case with children, the physical wounds may heal, yet the psychological trauma is likely to haunt all aspects of adult life. Work life, friendships, social activities, and intimate relationships are likely to be affected by victimization. Mental health problems often surface in the form of alcohol and substance abuse, suicide ideation and self-harm behaviors, eating disorders, and social withdrawal. Physical abuse can result in temporary or permanent injury. Neglect can result in serious illness or death.

Animals also experience profound consequences as a result of physical, sexual, or emotional abuse and neglect. Animals are injured, maimed, and killed. They are also susceptible to life-threatening illnesses and disease in cases of neglect. Although determining psychological damage is obviously an impossible task, behavioral cues such as overt aggression or extreme withdrawal may be indicative of victimization.

/// Cultural Factors

Violence in the home must be examined from a number of different perspectives. Individual psychopathology and family system dysfunctions cannot be fully understood without reference to the role of broader cultural factors. We must not assume that the dominant Anglo-American cultural boundaries are the ideal standard by which all others should be measured (Markward, Dozier, & Hooks, 2000). Yet, at the same time, we cannot underestimate the role society plays in the encouragement or reinforcement of abuse and neglect. Legal and social systems have altered the standards by which we define violence in the home, yet numerous examples of societal collusion remain. Here we introduce violent social models, religious tradition, cultural and ethnic heritage, and elements of social structure as important factors. In addition, we describe other social conditions placing families at risk for abuse and neglect.

We ask you to keep our discussion of cultural factors in the forefront as you navigate through the text. The worldviews held dear by individuals and families are unique reflections of upbringing, cultural values, and ideology. Examples are provided to illustrate how cultural factors affect perceptions, belief systems, and, ultimately, behavior. What may be considered abuse or neglect by one group of people may be revered by another. Thus sensitivity to the worldviews of others is a critical element in understanding the function of the family and abuse. The challenge for professionals is to create an intervention schema that is sensitive to cultural differences and can effectively balance liberty and freedom with an obligation to protect the individual rights of family members.

Violent Social Models

The broader social landscape includes a cultural approval of violence, which serves to reinforce abusive behaviors in the context of family. One does not have to look very far to experience violence in the United States. Mildred Pagelow (1984, p. 127) argues that our cultural approval of violence is "almost entirely approval of male violence. Females are expected to be nonviolent, but to admire and respect male violence, or at least view men's violence as natural and inevitable."

Examples of our fascination with violence and the use of aggression to solve our conflicts are abundant. Popular entertainment is overrun with examples of violent conflicts shown in movies, television programming, and video and computer games. Even G-rated movies, such those produced by

Disney, explore images of violence and aggression. Violence is often a theme portrayed in music lyrics and video images. Some sports such as wrestling, boxing, and hockey showcase violence as much as they do skill. Toys encourage violent play. The news media covers real-life examples of violence in the daily news. Visual images of war and violent crime are now available 24 hours a day.

These violent impressions often are fused with sexual images. One example comes to mind. A local department store near our home once had a window display featuring female mannequins wearing new spring bikinis. Each mannequin had a noose loosely affixed around its neck, with a large rope connecting the mannequins. The advertisement read: "Taming the Savages." Such a display is representative of the cultural approval of violence against women in our society. The store manager was more than happy to take the window display down once it was brought to his attention. However, the fusion of sex and violence in our culture is so ingrained that it never occurred to him that the image might send an inappropriate message.

Even young children are sexualized in a number of ways. The erotic portrayal of children and youth in advertisements, use of young children in beauty pageants, sale of provocative clothing and accessories, and pornography available via magazines and the Internet provide a few examples. The music industry also contributes to the sexualization of young people. Adolescent music performers clothed in seductive costumes are marketing their sexuality, often at the expense of their talent. Therefore, confusing messages about sexual behavior and children are present in popular culture. Such messages are received by child sex offenders and may ring especially meaningful for those offenders seeking external approval for their behavior (Finkelhor, 1984).

Obviously, all of us are influenced to some degree by such violent images. It is difficult to quantify the relationship between violent social models and actual family maltreatment. However, social learning theory would suggest that when such violence is imitated and then reinforced, it is more likely to be repeated in the future. We discuss this in more detail in chapter 2.

Religious Tradition

Religious freedom is a precious right guaranteed to us by the First Amendment to the United States Constitution. Our country was founded on the principle that citizens should be able to freely practice religion without government interference. We closely guard this right, yet at the same time, we must acknowledge that there is a price to be paid for religious independence. When encouraged or condoned, religious practices can play a significant role in the abuse and neglect of family members. It is not always clear whether religious tradition guides abusive behavior or whether abusive family members rely on religious tenets to rationalize their behavior. Social science research regarding the role of religion in abuse and neglect is limited; however, a number of important issues have been identified. Here we provide examples of medical neglect, forcing obedience through physical punishment, new religious movements, and polygamy to illustrate the influence of religion on family violence.

Medical Neglect

Withholding needed medical care for family members is generally considered medical neglect. Medical neglect predicated on religious beliefs has proved to be a challenging issue for social service and health care providers and the courts. The consequences of medical neglect can be tragic. Asser and Swan (1998) studied the cases of 172 children who died between 1975 and 1995 whose families practiced faith healing instead of accessing medical treatment for their children. Of the 172 children, 140 fatalities stemmed from medical conditions for which survival rates would have exceeded 90 percent had the proper medical treatment been accessed, and 18 others would have had an expected survival rate greater than 50 percent. Only three cases were identified in which medical treatment would not have improved the outcome. Asser and Swan (1998, p. 625) conclude: "When faith healing is used to the exclusion of medical treatment, the number of preventable child fatalities and the associated suffering are substantial and warrant public concern." Additionally, William Simpson (1989, 1991), in two different studies, determined that adults who practice Christian Science have higher mortality rates than the general population.

Religious organizations that are most notable for rejecting medical treatment include Jehovah's Witnesses, who do not believe in blood transfusions, and Christian Scientists, who choose prayer over medical treatment (Bottoms, Shaver, Goodman, and Qin, 1995). Asser and Swan (1998) identified 23 different denominations in their study of child fatalities, the majority of cases associated with the Church of the First Born, End of Time Ministries, Faith Assembly, Faith Tabernacle, and Christian Science.

Legal intervention into situations of medical neglect has been a difficult road to pursue. The courts have generally given permission to adults to reject their own medical care based on religious beliefs. The courts, however, have not ruled that the First Amendment provides a right to withhold medical treatment from children; yet the states continue to allow specific exemptions from medical care standards on religious grounds. Thirty-nine states permit religious exemptions from child abuse or neglect charges in the civil code, and in 31 states a religious defense is available for a criminal charge. Iowa, Ohio, Delaware, West Virginia, Arkansas, and Oregon have statutes that allow a religious defense in the case of a death of a child. State exemptions include such items such as immunizations, metabolic and hearing testing and prophylactic eyedrops for newborns, lead screening, bicycle helmets, vitamin K, and physical exams. Additionally, six states allow students to be excused from studying about disease in school (Children's Healthcare Is a Legal Duty [CHILD], 2002).

This issue continues to be debated. Child advocacy groups, medical associations, and other religious organizations have argued vehemently against such state exemptions and have brought forth lawsuits and amicus curiae (friends of the court) briefs to argue against religious exemptions in the case of children. For example, the Child Abuse Prevention and Treatment Act (CAPTA) is due for reauthorization during the 2001–2002 session of Congress, and several organizations, such as the United Methodist Church, the National Association of Medical Examiners, Justice for Children, the National Child Abuse Coalition, and CHILD are arguing that Congress readdress the exemption issue present in the current CAPTA statute. CAPTA currently mandates that the states require parents to provide medical care for their children; however, the statute also allows the states to give parents the right to withhold treatment on religious grounds (CHILD, 2002).

Obedience Through Physical Punishment

The use and encouragement of severe physically punitive child-rearing practices has its roots in biblical interpretation. Greven (1991) notes that more than 2,000 years of physical violence against children is rationalized based on the Bible. For example, he provides numerous examples of verses from the Book of Proverbs based on which corporal punishment of children is encouraged, including: "He that spareth his rod hateth his son: but he that loveth him chasteneth him betimes" (Prov. 13:24), and "Withhold not correction from the child: for if thou beatest him with the rod, he shall not die. Thou shalt beat him with the rod, and shalt deliver his soul from hell" (Prov. 23:13-14). Ironically, he notes that the New Testament offers little support for such violence. Yet, for many Christians and fundamentalist Protestants, corporal punishment is a necessary function of parenting. "The threat of future and eternal punishment has provided the ineradicable core of violence, suffering, and pain that has perpetuated anxiety and fear in the minds of vast numbers of people throughout the world for two millennia" (Greven, 1991, p. 55).

Religious tenets that espouse male domination and female subservience may also play a role in battering. Additionally, religious traditions that oppose divorce and stress the importance of family unity may ultimately place women and children in physical danger. For example, Alsdurf (1985) found that 26 percent of Protestant ministers in the United States and Canada affirmed that the subordinate role requires women to defer to their abusive husbands, trusting that God will ultimately protect them by ending the violence or giving them the strength to cope. Nason-Clark (1997), in her examination of evangelical responses to battering, found little evidence that clergy openly suggested that women return to abusive environments. However, she did find that clergy significantly underestimated the frequency of violence within their own church families and often viewed abuse as a spiritual problem with solely spiritual resolutions, thus creating a lack of referral to appropriate secular interventions. Additionally, evangelical clergy were less likely to identify power differentials reinforced through religious ideology as being a factor in domestic abuse.

New Religious Movements

New religious movements, often referred to as cults, are considered organized groups formed to conduct ritual, magical, or religious practices. Serving as pseudo families, they vary based on their membership, beliefs, and type of ritualized practices. Some practice devil worship, and others are considered derivations of other established religions. Cults concern law enforcement and other professional disciplines because of their reputation for deviant practices, violent episodes, and abuse and neglect of members, although the majority of new religious movements have enjoyed a peaceful existence. However, our attention is drawn to the tragedies found in examples such as the Branch Davidians, Heaven's Gate, and Aum Supreme Truth. Rush (2000) notes that on March 26, 1997, 39 members of the Heaven's Gate cult committed suicide by ingesting phenobarbital and vodka. In 1993, a standoff between federal law enforcement officials and the Branch Davidian cult led to the deaths of 86 members (including 24 children) and 4 agents (16 others were injured). A cult known as Aum Supreme Truth is linked to a bioterrorism attack of poisonous gas in a subway system in Tokyo, Japan.

In addition, a cult's behavior toward its child members is of special concern. Schwartz and Kaslow (2001) note that the birth of children to cult members raises important concerns about child safety. Children raised within these group settings are often physically and sexually abused and neglected. They are subjected to psychological abuse, medical neglect, and educational deprivation. Schwartz and Kaslow (2001, p. 16) argue that, in some cases, children have been "virtually enslaved, with severe deprivation or punishment if they did not meet whatever performance standard was set for them, including that for sexual activity."

Women and the elderly are also targets for abuse within cult design. Elderly individuals may be targeted for financial exploitation. Women are recruited for their reproductive and sexual abilities. Lalich (1997) notes that women in cults are commonly exploited sexually, often by the cult leader.

Polygamy

Polygamous families are also a concern to human rights advocates and law enforcement. The number of people who practice polygamy is estimated to be somewhere between 30,000 and 40,000 in the United States. Polygamy was a cornerstone of the Mormon faith until the practice was outlawed in 1890 by the church. The practice of polygamy itself is a violation of the law.

Two celebrated polygamy cases have brought attention to the abuses of polygamy practices. David Ortell Kingston, a practicing polygamist, is currently serving a 10-year sentence for incest and unlawful sexual conduct with his minor niece. John Daniel Kingston, David's brother, was convicted of child abuse for physically abusing his daughter when she attempted to flee the sexual abuse of her uncle. This case prompted the Utah legislature to hire a full-time polygamy investigator (Cart, 2001). Tom Green, a polygamist from Utah who flaunted his lifestyle, was convicted and sentenced to a prison term of 5 years in 2001. His case brought attention to a wide range of illegal behavior in the guise of religion. Aside from public debate regarding the utility of polygamy, professionals are concerned about child sexual abuse, wife battering, intermarriage, child marriage, reliance on welfare and Medicaid, high levels of child poverty, tax and welfare fraud, and educational deprivation. The secrecy and isolation of polygamist families makes law enforcement and social service intervention difficult.

Julie Cart (2001), in an article about polygamy in Utah and Arizona, notes the overabundance of children with special needs being born to polygamous families, some of whom are a product of intermarriage. One source claimed that Down syndrome children, in particular, are highly regarded for their docile nature and their ability to garner additional monies from the government for their care. "You see these young pregnant mothers rubbing their stomachs saying, 'I hope this one's a Down's' " (Cart, 2001, p.1).

In response, antipolygamy activists have joined forces to launch a legal campaign against polygamy in the United States and in other parts of the world. According to the Associated Press, a Colorado organization, Polygamy Justice Project, and the International Human Rights Clinic of New York University School of Law, with the Child Protection Project, are advocating for state and federal law enforcement officials to continue to investigate and prosecute polygamy-related abuses. In addition, they are calling for legislative change and ensuring that services are available to abuse victims (Associated Press, 2002).

Cultural and Ethnic Heritage

Aside from religious ideology, other cultural or ethnic traditions influence how families interact and treat each other. Therefore, sensitivity to cultural differences is especially important in understanding family violence. In some cases, what may appear to be an abusive practice by one culture is considered a rational act by another. Because cultural practices vary significantly across the globe and throughout divergent groups within a society, it is important to distinguish between cultural practices and standards of what constitutes abuse.

Sensitivity to culturally diverse populations is critical for practitioners in all fields. For example, an instrument called a Culturagram is available to social workers to improve their ability to assess abuse among immigrant elders (Brownell, 1997). This tool was developed to assess the impact of culture on family life and to assist the social worker in providing culturally sensitive services. The Culturagram assesses reasons for immigration, length of time in community, legal status, age at time of immigration, language spoken at home and in the community, health beliefs, special events celebrated by families, impact of crisis events, values regarding family, education, and employment, and contact with cultural institutions (Congress, 1994). Here we provide several examples of cultural practices and traditions that have received attention for their potential influence on abusive behavior and of how certain practices may be mistaken for intentional abuse.

Social Status of Women

One aspect of cultural and ethnic heritage that is shared by many societies is the inferior status of women. American society joins many around the world in subjugating the power of women. Research continues to demonstrate that male-dominant marriages have the highest rates of domestic violence, whereas more egalitarian marriages have the lowest rates of violence (Straus & Gelles, 2001). For example, Kim and Sung (2000), in a study of 256 Korean American families, found that male-dominant couples were four times more likely to experience severe spousal violence than egalitarian couples. Bui and Morash (1999) found similar results in a study of Vietnamese immigrants, among whom spousal abuse was associated with patriarchal belief systems. Patriarchal social systems within the United States are explored in more detail in chapter 4.

Folk Health Remedies

Health remedies practiced by some cultures have often been misinterpreted by American health and child welfare professionals as abuse. Karen Kirhofer Hansen (1997) provides numerous examples of folk remedies practiced by a number of different cultural groups and examples of how the consequences of these health treatments are often misinterpreted as intentional child abuse. *Coining* and *cupping* are two practices that leave bruises on the skin. She describes *coining* as a Southeast Asian practice in which a coin is rubbed in a downward fashion on the skin. The edge of the coin or other object is strategically placed to rid the body of "bad winds" that cause cold or flu symptoms, seizures, or other symptoms. *Cupping* is a recognized practice among many cultures, including Asian, Mexican American, and Russian cultures. Cupping involves the placement of a cup in a specific place on the body, depending on the symptoms, thus creating a vacuum in which the skin is drawn up. A circular-shaped bleeding mark is left on the skin. The cupping procedure is meant to provide relief for a variety of symptoms, including pain, fever, poor appetite, and congestion (Kirhofer Hansen, 1997).

Therapeutic burning, referred to as *moxibustion*, is a health remedy practiced in Asian cultures. Moxibustion is a yang therapy utilized to treat yin problems. The process involves the rolling of the moxa herb or yarn into a small ball or cone, placing it on the body in a strategic place, then igniting it until the patient experiences pain. Other cultures practice a similar process found in some Arabic and African cultures. The Skolt Lapp population in Finland refers to the practice as *toullmos*. Kirhofer Hansen (1997) also notes other practices that leave burn marks, such as chemical burns applied to the skin in the Hispanic practice of the hot-cold disease concept. In this case, a hot therapy is applied to an illness that has been classified as cold. Also, the application of garlic and rue (a material utilized to treat Hispanic folk illnesses) may cause skin burns.

Female Genital Mutilation

Female genital cutting (FGC), or female genital mutilation (FGM), is a prominent cultural practice in at least 29 countries, affecting an estimated 132,490 females (World Health Organization [WHO], 1996). Practiced predominantly in African countries, FGC or FGM refers to a wide range of procedures that involve partial or total removal of or injury to the external female genitalia, generally completed during childhood. The World Health Organization (1996) establishes four different types of FGM, each type indicative of exclsions that involve different parts of the genitalia. For example, the most extreme form, referred to as *infibulation*, involves the excision of part or all of the external genitalia and stitching or narrowing of the vaginal opening:

> Infibulation involves the complete removal of the clitoris and the labia minora, as well as the inner surface of the labia majora. The two sides of the vulva are then stitched together with thorns or by silk or catgut sutures so that when the remaining skin of the labia heals, it forms a bridge of scar tissue over the vagina. A small opening is preserved by the insertion of a foreign body to allow for the passage of urine and menstrual blood. (WHO, 1996, p. 3)

The purpose of the procedure is generally to ensure a woman's virginity prior to marriage, firmly establishing the role of women as chattel (Boyle, Songora, & Foss, 2001). Husbands are expected to slowly dilate the opening after marriage; if penetration cannot be achieved, the wound must be recut. The health consequences of such a practice are both immediate and long term. Immediate complications include bleeding, shock, infection, menstrual pain, urinary problems, injury to adjacent tissue, chronic pelvic infections, infertility, vulval abscesses, vicious scars, cysts, painful sexual relations and dysfunction, and problems in childbearing (WHO, 1996).

The practice was outlawed in the United States in 1996 as a part of a large Department of Defense Omnibus Appropriations Bill (1996), even though only a few cases have been identified nationwide. In addition, the act also provided financial incentives to countries taking action against the practice (Boyle et al., 2001).

Social Conditions

A number of broader social conditions contribute to the abuse and neglect of family members, including lack of affordable health care, deplorable housing conditions, single parenthood, substance abuse, mental and physical illness, lack of quality day care, educational deprivation, and so forth. These conditions place families at risk for maltreatment in many ways, and their role should not be underestimated. Central to these conditions is the lack of appropriate economic resources due to unemployment or underemployment. Therefore, because of economic stressors, appropriate housing, nutrition, clothing, medical and dental care, and other resources are difficult to access. Even in pseudo family environments, lack of appropriate funding is linked to gaps in regulation, quality staffing, and training.

Economic distress not only affects one's ability to provide the basic elements for living but also is likely to produce psychological anguish. Neither of these conditions affords the optimum climate for family living. No can dispute that abuse and neglect are found across all socioeconomic groups and therefore are not exclusively the problems of any one group; however, the risk of abuse among people of lower income levels has been well established in the literature (Gelles, 1997). Our professional practice confirms these findings.

Economic difficulties that come as a result of substance abuse, mental or physical illness, or disability serve to compound the risk of abuse and neglect. Financial success is also mitigated by racial, ethnic, and gender bias. Additionally, public policy choices may help or hinder the construction of these social issues. We explore these issues in greater depth throughout this book.

/// Summary

This chapter introduced the reader to the complex phenomenon of violence in the home. The conceptual framework from which we approached the subject matter was outlined. We provided our working definitions of family and family maltreatment, honoring the addition of *pseudo families* to the discourse on family violence. We explored the many reasons that violence in the home is an important issue to study, including the high prevalence rate, the tragic consequences, and secondary victimization.

The common features of abusive home environments were briefly described. Abusive behavior tends to fall along a continuum, with a full range of abusive and neglectful behavior represented. Not all families experience the entire scope of abusive behaviors, nor do they necessarily all progress in the same fashion. Social isolation, the existence of power differentials, and similarity in the effects of primary and secondary victimization on individual family members are also common attributes of abusive home environments.

Finally, we introduced the concept of societal collusion, drawing attention to the role of cultural factors in the encouragement or inadvertent reinforcement of maltreatment. We reviewed the broader acceptance of violence by American citizens demonstrated in virtually all facets of the entertainment industry and pop culture. Mixed cultural messages are sent regarding violence and sexuality, especially in reference to women and children. We explored the nexus between religious ideology and family maltreatment through the examples of medical neglect, physical punishment, cults, and polygamy. The social status of women, folk health remedies, female genital mutilation, and the relationship of other social conditions to violence were provided as additional examples. Whether by design or by coincidence, the role of cultural factors in family maltreatment should not be underestimated.

//// Recommended Web Sites

Children's Healthcare Is a Legal Duty (CHILD)
    www.childrenshealthcare.org
World Health Organization
    www.who.int/frh-whd/index.thml
Antipolygamy sites
    www.anti-polygamy.org
    www.childpro.org
Propolygamy sites
    www.truthbearer.com
    www.polygamy.com

2 /// Theoretical Perspectives

*W*hen one thinks of the term *family*, what comes to mind? For many of us it is a safe haven, a place in which we seek unconditional love and acceptance, a group of intimates whom we bond with and depend on. We depend on these people to meet all our basic needs when we are children and then to support us when necessary as we grow and mature. Family to many of us also means good times, celebrations, and traditions. We who view family in this way are the lucky ones. For numerous others, *family* means something much different. The words *family* and *home* represent feelings of fear, anger, disappointment, and danger. Unfortunately, for some, home may be a place in which they are regularly physically assaulted, neglected, or sexually molested. So, although some families are able to love and support each other, others are in continuous conflict.

- Why are families different in this way?
- Why do some families tend to commit harmful acts against each other, whereas others do not?
- What causes a mother to neglect her own children?
- Why does one father seek sexual fulfillment from his own daughter?
- Why does another father repeatedly use a belt to discipline his young?
- Why would an adult not provide an elderly parent with the basics to live?

These are only some of the pertinent questions that family violence scholars and other professionals in the field attempt to explain.

Over the years researchers and scholars have developed a number of models and theories to explain abuse in families. Why are theories important? Theories help us explain aspects of our world. It is a means by which we attempt to make sense of the inexplicable. Whenever we attempt to explain why things happen a certain way, we are theorizing. Researchers and scholars in the family violence field do exactly the same thing. They, however, go about theorizing in a more formal way by testing their theories using scientific methods.

This chapter, in exploring the theoretical perspectives of family violence, looks at three main areas of concern. First, we consider the history of family violence and its impact on family violence theory. Second, we look at the evolution of family violence theory and some of the growth of social programs and legal propositions. Finally, we examine the specific theoretical viewpoints that scholars use to study and explain family violence today.

/// Historical Roots of Family Violence Theory

Theories of family violence were not formed until the middle of the nineteenth century. Prior to this time, violence within the family was not recognized as a social problem and thus was not of interest to scholars. Recognizing the social context in which families existed is important to our understanding of how family violence theory has evolved.

First of all, the family was viewed as a private entity. Thus what went on within the confines of the home was not the business of the neighbors, the church, nor the state. The state did not attempt nor did it have the right to step in on family matters. Even today, we question the appropriateness of intervening in family matters.

Privacy concerns regarding family issues have been documented as recently as the 1965 Griswold v. Connecticut case (381 U.S. 479(1965)), as detailed in Box 2.1. In this case, the Supreme Court ruled that the "right to privacy" for family relationships was inherent in the protections of the Constitution. Therefore, the case reinforced a precedent that holds that, when a man uses his power, whether physical, emotional, or financial, to control the actions and behaviors of his wife, children, or both, society was not seen as having the right nor the desire to step in. The concept of privatization of the family was expressed in the text from the case:

> Marriage is a coming together for better or for worse, hopefully enduring and intimate to the degree of being sacred. It is an association that promotes a way of life, not causes; a harmony in living, not political faiths; a bilateral loyalty, not commercial or social projects. Yet it is an association for as noble a purpose as any involved in our prior decisions. (cited in Schneider, 1994, p. 36).

Thus marriage was seen as a harmonious and intimate association between two people that should be left as such. It was not intended as a social project for outsiders to become involved in nor a union that could be subject to the political convictions of the day.

Although policies are currently in place that allow interference in family affairs, the protection of privacy continues to be an important concept. As we discuss later in this text, family privacy, and the social isolation it often creates, becomes a factor in abusive homes. Box 2.1 describes a Supreme Court case that illustrates these issues.

Along with this veil of privacy went the fact that a patriarchal society had existed for centuries, promoting a tolerance for violence perpetrated by men. Violence was perceived as a necessary means for maintaining social order. Family violence endured under a male-dominated hierarchy of power. Thus it was accepted that "outsiders" were powerless to do anything about known cases. Consequently, two types of family violence prevailed—abuse against women and children (Berry, 1995; Gelles, 1993; Pagelow, 1984; Viano, 1992).

In the patriarchal family, the hierarchy of power meant that children were afforded an inferior status. Children were expected to be subordinate and obedient, especially to their fathers. Fathers had the right to ultimately decide whether their infants lived or died (Radbill, 1987). Therefore it was common for fathers, as the highest power within the family unit, to use violence as part of their child-rearing practices. Corporal punishment was frequent and exercised without due cause or concern. Children were also often victims of infanticide, an ancient custom of killing infants and children for economic or social purposes (Gelles, 1993). See chapter 3 for a more detailed discussion of the history of child abuse and early child-rearing practices.

Like children, women in the patriarchal society had less power in all aspects (e.g., material resources, financial resources, personal resources) of social and private life. The subordination of women was legitimized through the hierarchal structure of the family unit, as well as the institutions and social structure of society as a whole (Sigler, 1989). Individual needs and self-fulfillment were goals appropriate for men, not women (Carderelli, 1997; Gelles, 1993; Pagelow, 1984; Viano, 1992). Women were considered the "appropriate victims" (Dobash & Dobash, 1978). A further discussion

---

Box 2.1 /// Griswold v. Connecticut

A Connecticut statute made the use of contraceptives a criminal offense. The executive and medical directors of Planned Parenthood League of Connecticut were convicted in the Circuit Court 6th, in New Haven, for violating the statute by giving accessories, information, instruction, and advice to married persons as to the means of preventing conception. The United States Supreme Court reversed this decision. The Supreme Court held that the defendants had standing to denounce the statute and that the statute was an unconstitutional invasion of the right to privacy of married persons.

Supreme Court of the United States No. 496, 381 U.S. 479; U.S. LEXIS 2282; 14 L. Ed. 2nd 510.

of the history of partner abuse, including the reference to women as the victims and the role of women in society, can be found in chapter 4.

/// The Growth of Family Violence as a Social Problem

Though historically family violence is not a new phenomenon, defining it as a social problem worthy of public attention and collective action is. State intervention and public action for family violence did not begin to take shape until the middle of the nineteenth century, and the process was gradual and narrow, at best. The initial actions and concerns focused only on the welfare of children (Carderelli, 1997; Gelles, 1993; Pagelow, 1984). As we discuss in chapter 3, the 1866 landmark case of Mary Ellen Wilson was the catalyst for the state to begin to take responsibility for what was happening to some children in the confines of their own homes. Mary Ellen Wilson was a child removed from a neglectful and abusive foster home. In addition, after this case received notoriety, in 1874, the New York Society for the Prevention of Cruelty to Children was founded (Gelles, 1993).

Since the case of Mary Ellen Wilson, public and state action for the welfare of children has grown tremendously. It was not, however, until the1960s that child abuse was said to be "discovered" and the actual term *battered child syndrome* was coined by physician C. Henry Kempe.

Today, county, state, and federal agencies regulate the treatment of children, protecting their rights and welfare. These regulations extend to the public lives of children (i.e., day care, school, workplaces), as well as their private lives. See chapters 3 and 8 for a more detailed history of child abuse and specific mandates and regulations protecting children.

The other population that eventually evoked concern about familial violence was, of course, women. Violence against women has been an embedded cultural practice. Thus it was not until the 1970s that spousal abuse was recognized as a serious social problem and one that commanded legal protections. At this time, researchers and legal advocates were also beginning to report more and more evidence of spousal abuse (Carderelli, 1997; Gelles, 1993; Pagelow, 1984).

Many of the initial actions for the protection of women were the result of grassroots efforts by feminists. The women's movement of the 1970s brought the issues of intimate partner abuse into public view. The opening of the first battered women's shelter sparked additional attention. Erin Prizzey, credited with establishing the first women's center in 1972 in London (Roberts, 1996), which eventually housed battered women, served as a model for shelters developing in the United States. She also wrote the first book about wife abuse in 1974, titled *Scream Quietly or the Neighbors Will Hear* (Gelles, 1997; McCue, 1995).

During this same period, and in addition to these grassroots efforts, actions were being taken by state, legal, and social agencies in an effort to alleviate spousal abuse. For example, on a national level, in 1975 the National Organization for Women established a task force to examine wife battering (Gelles, 1993). In 1984, the U.S. Attorney General created a task force on family violence that included spousal abuse as an area of research and proposed legislation. This report offered recommendations and suggested that men who assault their wives be sanctioned (McCue, 1995).

In the late 1970s and 1980s, with the "discovery" of child abuse and domestic violence, scholars and professionals eventually began to take an interest in examining elder abuse. With the state demonstrating a willingness to intervene in family matters and the growing aging population of elders at risk for violence in the home, elder abuse has recently gained public and scholarly attention. However, many would argue that the attention to elder abuse issues pales in comparison to that given to other forms of family violence. Kemp (1998) argues that elder mistreatment research is lagging 20 years behind.

Now, as we enter the twenty-first century, violence in the home has been fully recognized as a social problem by our political, legal, and social institutions. Our inquiry has deepened to include more specific forms of family violence, such as sibling abuse, ritual abuse, and parental abuse, as well as to examine nontraditional family systems such as gay and lesbian relationships and pseudo families. We also are focusing efforts on examining racial and cultural factors. Keeping in mind the social evolution of the process of defining the problem, we can begin to understand how theory has developed in attempting to explain why such abuse takes place.

/// The Evolution of the Research

Despite the growing interest in domestic violence and some progress on many levels for both women and children, early research into family violence was limited in its quantity, validity, reliability, and scope. First of all, many researchers were hesitant to administer surveys and ask the important yet invasive personal questions. Thus child abuse and spouse abuse remained "unapproachable" research topics, and so little was done. Gelles (1997, p.19) has referred to the "selective inattention to the problem of intimate violence," seeing the lack of research efforts as an effect caused by fearful scholars.

Those who dared to broach the subject of family violence relied on simple and less reliable research techniques. The early research was mainly descriptive. As such it described the problem of family violence based on survey statistics; it did not offer any means by which scholars could make inferences about family violence. Much of the research was also based only on retrospective studies. This research method involves participants in recalling past events (such as childhood abuse). As memory does not always serve us well, this method leaves much room for error. Ultimately, the research lacks validity and reliability, making it difficult to replicate.

Moreover, the research that was being done was narrow, focusing on either one area or the other, women or children. Thus child abuse and spouse or partner abuse were viewed as unrelated entities with no significant correlations. Furthermore, as with the advances in legal protections and social programs, children's issues not only preempted women's but also dominated the scholarly world.

Finally, all the early research, whether on child or spouse and partner abuse, focused on only one theory of family violence. This prevailing theory is referred to as the psychiatric/psychopathological theory. This theory hypothesized that violence was the result of some aberration in the character of the offender. Thus the offender was seen as having some type of psychopathology, personality trait, or character disorder that caused that person to physically attack family members. This medical theorizing came mainly from physicians, who were routinely seeing the effects of abuse on children in their practices. This psychiatric/psychopathological model was used as the basis for many social programs and legal reforms and continues to influence the field of family violence today (Gelles, 1993; Pagelow, 1984). We show in chapter 8 that family violence intervention strategies tend to focus on the individual batterer.

Since the 1960s tremendous changes and advances have occurred in the field of family violence research. There has been more interest and a greater number of scholars researching the field; and the focus of this field research has expanded to include not only child and spousal or partner abuse but also other overlooked pertinent areas, including elder abuse, caregiver/institutional abuse, partner abuse with the male as the victim, sibling abuse, and parental abuse. Within these new areas of abuse research, specific topics and definitions for each area have also been developed.

Additionally, theories about the causes and correlates of violence in the family have broadened from the primary medical model centering on a psychiatric/psychopathological individual-based theory to theories that encompass the family group itself and the larger societal structure and all its facets. Only recently have scholars attempted to pull together numerous theories, incorporating many contributing factors such as family patterns and societal structures into a general theory (Gelles, 1979).

Finally, the research methods used to study family violence have developed. In the 1960s and early 1970s the literature was based on crude, uncontrolled descriptive studies of the problem. Thus the problem (i.e., child abuse) was identified and defined and the scope of the problem described. There were no studies that could explain why certain types of family violence were occurring in certain family systems.

It was not until the later 1970s and 1980s that the research, in a controlled and empirical manner, examined issues in the family, as well as different intervention strategies (Bersani & Chen, 1988). Research results then became more valid and thus testable and reliable. Moreover, scholars could make inferences from the results.

It was not surprising, in light of the research advances, that in the 1970s the psychiatric/psychopathological model took a backseat to more extensive theoretical reasoning and sociological models. We now take a look at how scholars analyze the problem of family violence today and at the models and theories that have developed as a result of their efforts.

/// Analyzing Family Violence

Over the past 30 years, research on family violence has evolved tremendously, and now scholars research and attempt to explain family violence from three levels of analysis that include micro level, meso level, and macro level. These levels of analysis can be applied to any social problem in an attempt to explain it or, at the very least, to gain a greater understanding of some of the factors that contribute to the problem.

Using the micro level of analysis, a social problem is studied on an individual level. That is, the researchers attempt to explain the social problem by analyzing the behavior of the individual(s) involved. This level of analysis has also been referred to as the *intraindividual level* (Gelles, 1993).

The meso level of analysis expands on the micro level by studying social problems from the group level. It explains a problem in terms of the group of people involved and the environmental factors that affect the group. A family system and the interactions within the family would be subjects for a meso level of analysis. This level has also been referred to as the *social/psychological level* of analysis (Gelles, 1993).

Finally, the macro level of analysis views social problems in terms of the larger societal structures and organizations that affect it. Thus family violence is understood through socially structured variables, including but not limited to cultural values of different societal organizations, differing socioeconomic status groups, and so forth. Gelles (1993) has referred to this level as the *sociological/sociocultural level*.

These three levels of analysis are used to examine the four major theoretical models that serve to identify specific explanations for different types of family violence. Though the three levels of analysis are distinctive, as we show, more than one can sometimes be applied within theories. Some theories are very simplistic and clear-cut and thus appropriately examined under one level of analysis. Other theories are more complex and comprehensive. These theories are therefore best understood by using more than one level of analysis. Now we look at the four theoretical models: (1) the psychiatric/psychopathological model, (2) the sociological/sociopsychological model, (3) the sociocultural model, and (4) the multidimensional model.

The psychiatric/psychopathological model involves theories about family violence that focus on the individuals involved and thus is a micro level model. The sociological/sociopsychological model, under a meso level of analysis, approaches family violence through an expanded version of the psychiatric/psychopathological model. This model looks beyond the individual and takes into account the relationships between the individuals involved in the violence and the environmental factors that affect the family and its organization, structure, and everyday interactions (Gelles, 1993). The sociocultural model, which is a macro level model, further enhances the other two research models by viewing family violence in terms of the cultural contexts in which it occurs. Thus the theory looks at socially structured variables such as gender inequalities and cultural norms and attitudes surrounding violence and family relations (Gelles, 1993). Finally, the multidimensional model, using all three levels of analysis, augments all the research by attempting to account for many of the other theoretical viewpoints and factors involved in the first three models (Gelles, 1993; Pagelow, 1984).

As you will notice, some of the theories may seem similar and have overlapping ideas and qualities. Additionally, as we mentioned earlier, some theories may be appropriately analyzed with more than one level of analysis. Moreover, whereas some theories are generalizable across the various forms or all forms of familial violence, others are more specific in nature. We now examine these theoretical models and the specific theories that have developed under the framework of each. Box 2.2 provides a chart that summarizes the theories discussed.

/// Current Family Violence Theory

Micro Level Analysis: Psychiatric/Psychopathological Model

The *psychiatric/psychopathological model*, often referred to as the medical model, developed during the 1960s with the "discovery" of child abuse. At that time, it was thought that family violence was a rare occurrence that could or would manifest itself only in circumstances in which an individual family member had a mental illness or some psychopathology. Thus only "sick" individuals would harm members of their own families. Overall, this theory focuses on the personality characteristics of the offender and includes personality disorders, character disorders, mental illness, and alcohol and substance abuse (Gelles, 1993).

Further theorizing attempted to identify abusers and neglecters based on specific skills, temperament, personality, histories, and physiologies that were different from those of so-called normal people. Some of the personality characteristics described included immaturity, impulsiveness, dependency, narcissism, egocentrism, demandingness, and sadomasochism (Pagelow, 1984).

Today, the theoretical framework of the model persists but has also been

Box 2.2 /// Theoretical Models and Specific Theories

Micro Level Analysis

Psychiatric/Psychopathological Model

Defined: Referred to as the "medical model"; views family violence as the result of the psychopathology of individual family members (e.g., mental illness, personality disorders, alcoholism, etc.).

Psychobiological Perspective: Biologically based; views family violence in terms of inherent personality characteristics or as a result of increased hormone levels, brain abnormalities, mental illness, etc.

Psychodynamic Perspective: Based on Freudian theory; views family violence as the result of internal conflicts and an abnormal death instinct and abnormal aggressive tendencies.

Victim Theory: Views family violence in terms of the victim's personality characteristics; "blaming the victim."

Meso Level Analysis

Sociopsychological Model

Defined: Explains family violence in terms of family interaction patterns and relationships between individual family members.

Traumatic Bonding Theory: Explains family violence in terms of the unique relationship that develops between victim and abuser.

Stress Theory: Explains violence in terms of the increased levels of stress within a family. Scholars look at family characteristics and issues that make a family prone to violent interactions (e.g., social isolation, alcoholism, too much time together, etc.).

Resource Theory: Based on the power theory, it explains family violence in terms of who has the most resources—social, personal, and economic—within the family unit.

Interactionist Theory: Explains family violence in terms of the family processes and member interactions. Specifically looks at the effect of the aging process on families.

Power Theory: Explains family violence in terms of the natural power differentials that exist within families based on gender and age.

Exchange/Social Control Theory: Developed by George C. Homans and built on by Gelles; based on an economic philosophy that explains family violence in terms of costs and rewards.

Sociobiological Theory: Based specifically on child abuse and infanticide; views abuse as a result of decreasing the probability of transmitting "bad" genes to future generations. Looks at the reproductive success potential of children and necessary parental investment.

Box 2.2 (continued)

Social Learning Theory: Referred to as the intergenerational theory and based on the work of Albert Bandura; explains family violence in terms of cognitive processes and demonstrates how violence is learned through modeling, imitation, and reinforcement.

Social Conflict Theory: Explains family violence in terms of the impact social isolation has on the health of the family: its bonds with each other and the community.

Macro Level Analysis

Sociocultural Model

Defined: Explains family violence in terms of socially structured variables.

Culture of Violence Theory: Explains family violence in terms of the larger cultural norms and values.

Cultural Approval of Violence Perspective: Explains family violence in terms of the level of violence accepted in the larger society.

Subculture of Violence Perspective: Explains family violence in terms of subcultures that value and use it at higher levels than thought acceptable in the larger society.

Patriarchal-Feminist Theory: Based on feminist thought, explains family violence in terms of how society is socially structured by gender and more specifically by male domination.

Environmental Stress and Strain Theory: Explains family violence in terms of structural inequalities within society: poverty, race, socioeconomic status.

Political Economy Theory: Based on the gerontological perspective; views family violence in terms of how aging is socially structured and how this predisposes the elderly to abuse.

Multidimensional Model

Defined: Explains family violence in terms of all the variables that could affect the situation.

General Systems Theory: Explains family violence in terms of the family system and its relationship to society; includes individual (psychological) variables, family interactions (sociopsychological) variables, and socially structured (sociocultural) variables.

Ecological Theory: Developed by Garbarino and Belsky; explains family violence, and specifically child abuse, under three levels of analysis: the relationship between the organism and the environment, the interacting and overlapping system in which human development occurs, and the quality of the environment.

expanded. The model been analyzed further to distinguish not only various abuser pathologies but also victim pathologies. Browne and Herbert (1997) have broken down the model into two different perspectives, the *psychobiological perspective* and the *psychodynamic perspective*, to identify the ways in which individuals become abusers.

The psychobiological perspective explains violence in terms of inherent personality characteristics. These personality characteristics are thought of as the "cause" and make the abuser prone to act in violent ways toward intimates. Scholars study these biological variables and measure these inherent qualities in terms of hostility, aggressive temperament, and anger expression. Some inherent characteristics that are thought to predispose one to violence are testosterone and other hormone levels, alcoholism, brain abnormalities, and mental illness.

The psychodynamic perspective, as described by Browne and Herbert (1997), considers the internal conflicts of the individual and is based on Freudian theory. This perspective considers that some people have an abnormal death instinct or an abnormal drive for aggressive behavior. Thus individuals are viewed as having abnormal aggressive tendencies. These tendencies are viewed as the result of internal conflicts due to adverse socialization experiences, but they can also be genetic or biologically based.

In addition to looking at the abuser as the "cause" of family violence, research proponents of the psychiatric/psychopathological model later theorized the role of the victim. Researchers attempted to identify characteristics of the victims that might "invite abuse," thus essentially "blaming the victim." Research on children included studies on failure to bond, failure to thrive, prematurity, physical and mental handicaps, listlessness, and fussiness (Pagelow, 1984).

Friedrich and Boriskin (1976) found that some children possess defects and personalities that may precipitate abuse. For example, a developmentally disabled child or a child with attention-deficit disorder (ADD) may increase the stress levels for parents.

Research on women also involved victim-blaming theorizing. This research has dealt mainly with women's perceived masochism. It has been postulated that women somehow enjoy and ask for the abuse. Though advanced, this theory has received little to no attention from the scholars.

Many researchers have debunked the claims made by the psychiatric/psychopathological model and have shown that it cannot explain family violence on its own but is only a part of a much bigger picture. In fact, no strong empirical support exists to substantiate its claims. Researchers, for example, were also unable to successfully categorize abusers into an "abuser profile." They found that there was no consistency in labeling abusers as psychotic or neurotic, as some abusers were found to be no more psychotic than the general public.

It seemed that this model was a simple explanation that brought some sense to a "hush-hush" social problem while keeping the problem away from the general public. It was easy to say, in denial, that family violence happened only in families with "sick" individuals. In this way, society could keep itself supposedly safe from the problem and not acknowledge its full scope nor feel obligated to do anything about it. Despite these shortcomings, the psychiatric/psychopathological model continues to be widely accepted in the field of family violence and with the general public (Pagelow, 1984). Though it may not explain family violence in total, this model offers explanations of contributing variables that can be built on.

Meso Level Analysis: Sociopsychological Model

It was not until the 1970s that the psychiatric/psychopathological model took a backseat to more extensive meso level theorizing. At this time, scholars were postulating family violence theories under a social psychological scheme. This *sociopsychological model* integrated family patterns and relationships between individual family members to explain family violence. The sociopsychological model takes into account not only the individuals involved but also the relationships and interactions between the individuals in the family and the environment. It examines the structure and organization of the family, as well as the environmental factors that affect the whole family system.

The sociopsychological theories that have been proposed in the family violence research include the following: traumatic bonding theory, stress theory, social conflict theory, power theory, resource theory, exchange/social control theory, symbolic interactions theory, sociobiological/evolutionary theory, and social learning theory.

Traumatic Bonding Theory

As a contemporary theory, *traumatic bonding theory* explains family violence in terms of the unique relationship and interaction that develops between a victim and the abuser. The theory has been used to explain and treat intimate partner abuse, as well as incest. Dutton and Painter (1981) defined *traumatic bonding* as "strong emotional ties that develop between two persons where one person intermittently harasses, beats, threatens, abuses or intimidates the other." Mary deYoung (1992) takes this a step further, arguing that the trauma of the abuse creates a strong emotional tie that is characterized by cognitive distortions and behavioral strategies that ultimately and unintentionally perpetuate the abuse and strengthen the bond. This tie is distinguished by mutual emotional dependency between the abuser and the victim. This emotional dependency, or traumatic bond, is said to develop because the abuse is characterized by *intermittent reinforcement*. Intermittent reinforcement involves the alternating of highly intense positive and negative abuser-victim interactions (Berglas, 1998). For example, a husband may be very abusive for a time and then replace that behavior with intense affection. This behavior not only strengthens the bond but also leaves the self-esteem of the victim in the hands of the abuser.

Both the abuser and the victim suffer cognitive distortions that involve blame, responsibility, power, and trust. For example, whereas a child who has been a victim of incest may blame himself or herself for the abuse, the adult may also blame the child.

Finally, the behavior strategies of both parties often place the victim at risk of revictimization and the abuser at risk of revictimizing. In the case of intimate partner abuse, a victim, in order to relieve the anxiety of impending abuse, may actually create a situation that escalates the abuse. The abuser, on the other hand, would do the same to relieve his or her own tension, frustration, and anxiety.

Stress Theory

Family violence has long been viewed as a problem for those families with increased levels of stress, whether economic, social, or personal. Skolnick and Skolnick (1977) found family violence to be the result of stressors that affect families at all levels. Other empirical investigations support these claims and demonstrate that an increase in stress and tension increases the risk of abuse between family members.

In addition to Gelles and Strauss (1988), in 1981 sociologist David Finkelhor also attempted to find similarities between violent families. Finkelhor made no distinction as to the type of violence that occurred in the family (child abuse, elder abuse, etc.) nor the extent of the abuse (neglect, physical abuse, etc.). Finkelhor found four common features of violent families: power differentials, social isolation, similar effects on victims, and alcohol abuse and chemical dependency (Finkelhor, 1981).

Social isolation, effects on victims and abusers, and alcohol abuse and chemical dependency can be viewed as factors contributing to the *stress theory*, namely the stress a family encounters in their daily lives. Power differentials may or may not cause stress, depending on the members' viewpoints and adaptability. Social isolation, as a common feature of violent families, involves the privatization of the family, as discussed earlier. Finkelhor (1981) postulates that because the family as an institution is isolated from the larger society, families are not obligated to explain negative situations such as abuse. Thus, when family violence occurs, it is often within the confines of the family. Individual family members, therefore, are not in a position to have to explain to anyone what goes on inside the walls of the home. This makes it easy for those who wish to keep family secrets.

This social isolation also precludes families from getting the help they need. Their limited or total lack of contact with resources outside the family makes it difficult to ask for help. Moreover, in order to maintain this social isolation, violent families have been found to move frequently (Pagelow, 1984). Thus they create a situation in which they have few opportunities to establish relationships outside the family unit. Such geographic mobility also helps to maintain family secrets.

Finkelhor (1981) also noted substance abuse within a family as a common feature of a violent-prone family. Though substance abuse has not been found to be a cause of family violence, it is definitely a contributing factor. The use of substances by one or more individuals within a family can cause added stress. It also may help keep the abuser from acknowledging his or her actions. The abuser truly may not remember his or her actions. Furthermore, he or she can more easily deny remembering violent incidences, using intoxication as an excuse.

Overall, social isolation of the family and alcohol or drug dependency contribute to increased stress levels. For those who are abused, the isolation leaves them feeling that there is no way out. Although the abuser may obtain some immediate gratification from getting his or her needs met, he or she may also feel shame and guilt. Without an outlet for these feelings, the stress increases, and the abuse is perpetuated.

Social Conflict Theory

Social conflict theory, proposed in 1991 by Retzinger, similarly deals with the results of social isolation on the family. Retzinger (1991) sees the bonds between community and family as essential to the health of the community, of families, and of individuals. Because social bonds are so critical to human functioning, individual family members are likely to suffer when bonds with the community are nonexistent or in conflict. As is the case in socially isolated families, individual members experience intense feelings of shame. These feelings of shame, when unacknowledged, serve to escalate family violence.

Power Theory

Power theory is based on the power differentials that exist within families. Power differentials, as described by Finkelhor (1981), naturally exist within the family through age and gender differences. Finkelhor stated that these differentials take form when those who are bigger and stronger and have greater access to valued resources exert their will on others who are smaller and weaker and have little or no resources. Thus, traditionally within the family, men are normally granted power over other members due to their social status, age, and physical size and strength.

Finkelhor (1981) also found that the most common patterns are for the most powerful to abuse the least powerful. Hence, he stated, "abuse gravitates to the relationships of greatest power differentials" (p. 3). Therefore, children are at an increased risk of being abused, especially those under 6 years of age. In addition, the sexual abuse of subordinate, younger females by older adult males in dominant, authoritative positions is a common form of abuse. Similarly, Finkelhor (1981) states, the less power a female has as compared with her husband, the more likely she will experience abuse.

Resource Theory

Resource theory, as an extension of power theory, contends that the more resources a person has, whether social, personal, economic, or all three, the more power he or she has in the family system. Consequently, this person has more decision making rights and responsibilities and therefore is in a better position to enforce his or her will or decisions on other family members. Such enforcement is said to involve the use of abusive tactics or the threat thereof (Gelles, 1997). Similar to the power theory, men are viewed traditionally as having been in this position. Men hold the majority of high-paying jobs, carry the most weight in the community, and therefore command the most power. Women and children are thus left in subservient roles, prone to possible abuse (Gelles, 1993; Viano, 1992).

Goode (1971), the author of this theory, recognizes that individuals with more resources are often less likely to use force. He sees men who have *limited* resources as having to establish their dominance through the use of threats, force, or both. In addition to Goode's varying conclusions, one could contend that the resource theory is outdated as women gain more social power.

Exchange/Social Control Theory

Exchange/social control theory was initially developed by social psychologist George C. Homans (1961). Building on theories of the social behaviors of animals, Homans saw social attraction as a function of costs and rewards. Thus we bring certain qualities or resources to a social situation (investment/cost), and we expect to reap some kind of benefit (reward). The reward may be approval or esteem from others. Accordingly, we should be attracted to those who hold us in high esteem. Homans also theorized that due to the interdependent nature of human beings and our dependency on others, we are often subjected to the power of others.

Building on Homans's (1961) theories, Gelles (1997) proposed that family violence was governed by the social exchange theory and the economic philosophy of costs and rewards. Gelles (1997) surmised that individual family members use violence to obtain desired goals such as those described by Powers (1986), which include getting attention, meeting one's own needs, gaining control over family decisions, avoiding the risk of intimacy, and protecting the self from harm.

Social norms and family structure increase the likelihood that the rewards of violence against or between family members will outweigh the costs. Gelles (1997) argues that the private nature of the family precludes it to violence. Therefore, if violence occurs, family members are reluctant to seek outside help. In addition, social and community services and social institutions are similarly reluctant to intervene in family problems. Thus there are no strong deterrents, and much of the abuse goes unreported and undetected. Family members abuse other family members because they can and because, in Gelles's terms, it is "inexpensive."

Symbolic Interactionist Theory

Symbolic interactionist theory, as described by social theorists Herbert Blumer, George J. McCall, and J. L. Simmons (as cited in Phillipson, 1997, p. 111), states that the "way social life is organized arises from within society itself and out of the processes of interaction between its members". Thus family violence is viewed as a result of family processes.

Symbolic interactionist theory specifically looks at the aging, both biological and sociological, of individual family members. Acknowledging how the aging process can change and threaten roles and identities, this theory views stress in these relationships as inevitable. For example, an elderly parent who loses friends, can no longer work, and suffers from some debilitating health problems is often left feeling a great loss of identity.

In addition, adult children who have the task of caring for these elderly often find it quite a difficult job. In some cases, the relationship becomes abusive. Many family members find it difficult to deal with the elderly due to their history with the person (e.g., a prior abusive relationship), their own fears about aging, and the general nature of the aging process (physical and mental decline).

Infantilization is one form of psychological abuse in which the adult child or caregiver treats the elderly person as if he or she were an infant because of his or her age and physical and mental condition (Phillipson, 1997). This attitude may lead to other, more severe forms of abuse. In addition, because the elderly person may have mental impairments, there may be little risk of anyone finding out about any abuse or of retaliation on the part of the elderly person. Thus the abuse is more probable.

Sociobiological/EvolutionaryTheory

The *sociobiological theory* focuses specifically on child abuse and infanticide. This theory has been applied to the animal world, as well as to human beings. The sociobiological theory hypothesizes that child abuse and infanticide are the result of individuals attempting to increase the probability that their genes will be transmitted to future generations (Daly & Wilson, 1981; Justice & Justice, 1990; Viano, 1992).

Daly and Wilson (1981) declare that "violence towards human or non-human off-spring is the result of the reproductive success potential of children and parental investment." Thus parents value offspring that are healthy and can reproduce and that will not "cost" them much in terms of energy and resources. As discussed earlier, and according to the sociobiology theory, children who have chronic illnesses, physical deformities, or handicaps of any kind (developmental or behavioral problems) are looked down on and are more likely to be the subjects of abuse and infanticide. This theory is likened to Darwin's *natural selection* theory.

In addition, when little or no attachment to the child exists, the risk of abuse increases. This may be especially true of large families in which there is not enough time nor energy for all the children. Thus, again, those children who pose the greatest problems or are the neediest are apt to be the ones neglected or abused.

Sociobiology theory also holds that both males and females are more likely to invest in offspring when paternity is highly certain. Thus illegitimate children are at risk of abuse. Similarly, stepchildren, adopted children, and foster children, being genetically unrelated, are also at an increased risk. They have not been afforded the natural bonds between a parent and child. This situation particularly holds true for younger children who cannot defend themselves and female adolescents who are at greatest risk of sexual abuse (Reiss & Roth, 1993).

Finally, sociobiologists have hypothesized that the circumstances of a child's delivery, as well as age and gender, can increase the risk of abuse or infanticide (Justice & Justice, 1990). In terms of the former, a difficult birth may predispose a child to abuse. A 2-year-old having tantrums or a rebellious adolescent may also be at increased risk. Moreover, depending on the culture, either males or females may be at greater risk. A good example of this is the status of female infants born in the People's Republic of China. Because females are not revered in the Chinese culture, many end up in orphanages and are often adopted out by people in other nations.

Along with these general hypotheses, Malkin and Lamb (1994) have studied and established five specific hypotheses that have been the focus of much of the sociobiological theory research (the relationship between child abuse and relatedness):

1. Nonbiological parents engage in more severe types of abuse than biological parents.
2. In two-biological-parent households, biological fathers maltreat their children more than biological mothers do.
3. Biological parents are more likely to abuse their children when the children are young, whereas nonbiological parents do not show a predictive age-related pattern.
4. Biological parents from poorer families who abuse their children are more likely to be male, whereas biological parents from affluent families who abuse their children are more likely to be female.
5. Female relatives past their reproductive prime are less likely to abuse their children than females relatives in their reproductive prime.

Malkin and Lamb (1994) used historical research data from 1984 from 10 states and the District of Columbia and found limited support for the sociobiological theory. Though there has been some support for all these hypotheses, their research supported only two of the hypotheses. First, the study found that biological parents tended to abuse younger children more often, whereas nonbiological parents did not show an age-related pattern. In addition, the research supported the hypothesis that female relatives past their childbearing years tended to abuse their children less severely than those in their childbearing years.

Though there are some problems with the research methods in this study (historical data, population limited to social services cases, etc.) and although it supports only two of the hypotheses, it proves to be a basis for further research. Further study is needed in these two areas to see whether these results can be replicated. Given the increase in the number of children living with nonrelatives, either in step situations or in other forms of substitute care such as foster care, adoption, and so forth, it is imperative that scholarship reach some sound conclusions in the sociobiological field. This is especially true with respect to the sociobiological theories that nonrelated parents are more likely to abuse their children and to abuse more severely than biological parents.

Social Learning Theory

Social learning theory is one of the most widely proposed theories. It is a behavioral approach based on the work of Albert Bandura (1973) that looks at a person's behavior as a result of his or her cognitive processes. It considers learning instead of inherent qualities, stimulating the nature versus nurture debate. Bandura states that "violence is learned, either directly or indirectly and reinforced in childhood and continued into adulthood as a coping response to stress or a method of conflict resolution" (as cited in Mihalic & Elliott, 1997, p. 21).

Straus (1990) claims that the family provides a "training ground" for violence and that physical punishment is a major mechanism for learning violence. Whether it is the family of origin or some other social system, this theory proposes that family violence is the result of behaviors learned in childhood that are carried into adulthood.

Social learning theory rests on two cognitive principles: modeling and reinforcement (Browne & Herbert, 1997; Hampton, Jenkins, & Gullotta, 1996; McCue, 1995; O'Leary, 1988; Pagelow, 1984). Modeling involves imitating. Children learn through role modeling: parent modeling and imitation. Thus, when a child witnesses a behavior, he or she is likely to imitate that behavior. In abusive families, therefore, children learn to use aggressive tactics because that is what they are exposed to. Further, children, as learners, are more apt to pay attention to models who possess or are perceived to have high status. Therefore, the behavior of this role model is more likely to be imitated (Pagelow, 1984). For example, if a male child witnesses a father having overall power within the family and using aggression against other members to get his immediate desire (e.g., dinner on the table, a child to stop crying), while at the same time maintaining a higher status in the family unit, this male child will attempt to do the same.

In addition to modeling, imitation, and attention factors, social learning theorists also see behavior that is reinforced as more likely to be repeated. Hence, aggressive responses to environmental cues or stressors are more likely to be repeated if these behaviors are reinforced by some desired outcome, but they are not likely to be repeated if they result in punishment. Therefore, if violence is reinforced positively and is an accepted mode of conflict resolution or of meeting one's needs, violence is likely to be repeated. Thus, as some theorists have stated, modeling and imitation have some functional value. The violence provides a functional value to the individual members and, at times, to the family as a whole. For example, a parent's spanking may get a child to behave and thus serve a purpose to the parent. Children will witness this outcome and may use this tactic later in life (Browne & Herbert, 1997; Pagelow, 1984; Viano, 1992).

Social learning theory has also been referred to as the intergenerational theory; it perceives abusive behavior as transmitted from one generation to the next. The research on intergenerational theory involves the effects of not only experiencing violence in the home but also witnessing it. The intergenerational theory states that violent and abusive adults learned this behavior as a result of witnessing or directly experiencing abuse within the family of origin. This theory views abusive parents as disciplining their children by physical means based on how they were disciplined as children (Justice & Justice, 1990). Consequently, their own children will grow up to do the same, and the "cycle of abuse" will continue (Hampton, et al, 1996; Kalmuss, 1984; O'Leary, 1988; Reiss & Roth, 1993; Viano, 1992).

Social learning theory research on domestic violence has focused extensively on marital violence. In particular, researchers have studied whether or not witnessing or experiencing violence as a child leads to perpetrating violence or being the victim of violence in adult intimate relationships. The research has attempted to confirm the idea that children who experience abuse are more likely to abuse or to be victims of abuse as adults. Straus, Gelles, and Steinmetz (1980) found that sons who had witnessed their fathers' violence had a 1000 percent greater battering rate than those who had not. Similarly, Gelles and Straus (1988) found that husbands who batter their wives are more likely to come from homes in which they themselves were abused or homes in which they witnessed their fathers abusing their mothers.

There has been widespread support for social learning theory. Extensive research has been done, and evidence suggests that violence between parents affects the children (Fagan, Stewart, & Hanson, 1983; Roy, 1977; Steinmetz,

1977; Straus et al, 1980; Walker, 1984). As the intergenerational theory proposes, research shows that once children learn aggressive styles to get their needs met, they continue to use this style as adults (Browne & Herbert, 1997). Straus and colleagues (1980) also found that adults who were abused as children were more likely to abuse their own children. Furthermore, research indicates that violence between parents adversely affects the children in the family in other ways. Children from such abusive families demonstrate behavioral and psychiatric problems that include truancy, home and school aggression, and anxiety disorders (Browne & Herbert, 1997).

Though social learning theory has been widely acclaimed, there has also been much criticism. The validity of much of the earlier research has been criticized because it is based on retrospective studies that require adults to recall events from their childhood. Several factors could impair memories, thus leaving the research ambiguous and inconclusive (Reiss & Roth, 1993). In addition, not all adults who are exposed to violence as children grow up to be perpetrators of violence or victims. A number of variables affect the outcome. In addition, it is not clear which is more predictive of later experience with abuse—being abused or witnessing abuse. The research, therefore, has yet to account for these problems and to determine exact intervening variables and pathways. Hampton and colleagues (1996) see social learning theory as too simplistic to explain human behavior and family violence.

Mihalic and Elliott (1997), in examining marital violence through social learning theory, expanded on the earlier work. In their longitudinal study, they attempted to remedy the validity issues involved in retrospective studies and to account for more variables that influence such a complex social problem. Mihalic and Elliott (1997) attempted to determine whether or not violence was transmitted from one generation to the next and whether the violence learned in the family of origin was generalizable to contexts outside the family. They found that violence was generalizable contextually, as many participants who had either witnessed or experienced violence in childhood had records showing adolescent felony assault charges outside the home.

Mihalic and Elliott (1997) were also interested in examining whether the intergenerational transmission of marital violence (for both offenders and victims) was different for males and females. They found that prior experience with violence affected females more than males during adolescence and adulthood, meaning that females experienced more incidences of abuse or violence later in life. Therefore, though social learning theory has its share of theoretical issues, it has contributed tremendously to family violence research and will continue to do so as scholars fine-tune research methodology.

Summary

The theories proposed under the sociopsychological model, though an improvement over the psychiatric/psychopathological model, are not without issue. As we have seen, some of the theories account for only certain types of abuse (i.e., symbolic interactionist theory for elder abuse, sociobiological theory for child abuse). In addition, these theories, like the psychiatric/psychopathological model, are too simplistic to account for the total problem of family violence. Regarding power theory, for example, just because one has power over another does not necessarily mean that he or she will abuse that person.

Furthermore, though each theory accounts for some of the factors involved in family violence, no single one can account for all the conceivable variables. Finally, the theories do not take into account the larger sociological issues that affect violence within the family. We now discuss the sociocultural model, which deals with these larger sociological issues.

Macro Level Analysis: Sociocultural Model

Sociocultural models are based on theories of domestic violence that center on socially structured variables. These theories explain violence in the home in terms of social structures, values, and norms that legitimize violence. These theories include the patriarchal/feminist, culture of violence, political economy, and environmental stress/strain theories.

Patriarchal/Feminist Theory

The *patriarchal theory*, as discussed earlier, is based on feminist thought. This theory holds that domestic violence is the result of the social structure of our society. Our society, as these theorists see it, is socially structured by gender—specifically, a long history of male dominance. Therefore, these theorists focus on wife abuse. The theory states that, because males have historically had greater access to resources, including property, employment opportunities, education, material possessions, community groups and services, and status, they have maintained power over women. Male social power and the complementary legal system enable men to use abusive tactics to maintain the status quo and resolve conflicts without consequence (Berry, 1995; Browne & Herbert, 1997; Carderelli, 1997).

Over the years, the women's movement, as well as the civil rights movement, has chipped away at the historical gender-based injustices. However, we are still plagued by the patriarchal structure that has existed for centuries. For example, though many more women are in the workforce today, pay inequities between the sexes continue to exist. Few women hold the high-paying executive positions afforded to men. Moreover, though the media have improved over the years, some ads, music, movies, and other forms of communication and entertainment continue to condone violence against women and to depict women in submissive and subservient positions. For example, some rap music denigrates women by referring to them as "bitches" and encourages violence against them. Furthermore, in some subcultures within our society, male aggressiveness is valued as proof that the perpetrator is a "real man" (Gelles, 1997).

Critics of the patriarchal/feminist theory argue that it is dated and does not explain why some men abuse their wives but others do not. Therefore, it fails to look at specific intervening psychological variables, as well as other variables that are important in the study of domestic violence. In addition, it fails to take into account the slowly changing social structure within society. Women have gained greater access to educational and employment opportunities and thus to material possessions, self-esteem, power, and other desirable attributes. Therefore, the theory may be outdated for the times. Despite these legitimate criticisms, it is still a widely accepted theoretical approach to domestic violence. It can be used as a historical base from which to analyze familial violence over the years.

Culture of Violence Theory

Culture of violence theory looks at violence based on the larger societal norms and structure. It views violence under this social structure in two perspectives: the *cultural approval of violence* and the *subculture of violence*.

The *cultural approval of violence* perspective attributes violence in the home to the level of acceptance of violence in the larger society. Thus, if violence is an accepted means of conflict resolution, goal attainment, or status quo maintenance, it will more likely play into family interactions. Furthermore, if society provides reinforcements (e.g., lack of social sanctions, media images) and if weapons are readily available, violence will become an accepted means of conflict resolution on both institutional/structural and personal levels (Browne & Herbert, 1997; Viano, 1992).

Most of us can probably agree that we send mixed messages about our approval of violence. Although certain acts of violence are deemed unacceptable or criminal, many acts of violence are tolerated. For example, violence is accepted, and in many ways encouraged, in video games, sporting events, movies, newscasts, toys, and television. Violence between family members is therefore a reflection of the broader culture.

The *subculture of violence* perspective rests on the tenet that cultural norms vary within society and that some subcultures value the use of violence. Wolfgang and Ferracuti (as cited in Viano, 1992, p. 8) explained this perspective as maintaining that "within a large pluralistic society, certain subcultures develop norms and values that *stress* and *justify* the use of physical force to a higher level than thought acceptable in the predominant larger culture." Wolfgang and Ferracuti, after studying homicide rates in Philadelphia, came to the conclusion that murder was an accepted part of life for certain groups of people.

The subculture theory has been widely criticized, mainly because Wolfgang and Ferracuti focused their work on the violence perpetrated by lower class African American urban males and did not explain why violence still occurs outside of defined subcultural groups. For example, many of us would agree that men as a group, or a subculture, tend to approve of violence as a way of dealing with conflict more than women as a group do. Because men and women both have access to the same ways of learning about violence, such as the media, this theory does not fully explain why some men are not violent and why some women are.

However, it does make sense to consider that if violence is accepted as normal behavior within any specific group of people—not unlike the use of specific jargon, dress, or status symbols—then it is likely that more members of the group will participate in the behavior, especially if the behavior is rewarded in some way.

Political Economy Theory

Political economy theory is a gerontological perspective that expands on the interactionist theory described previously. The political economy theory, as a macro level theory, looks at how society and societal structures affect the elderly (Phillipson, 1997). This theory asks questions about how we view and treat the elderly population and why. Specifically, the political economy theory sees aging as not only a biological but also a socially constructed phenomenon. As such a distinct division of labor and a structure of inequality exist for this population.

The political economy theory argues that the elderly are not treated equally. They are isolated from the rest of society not only by their age and health status but also by their perceived dependency, unemployability, and lack of productivity. Lenore Walker (1984) referred to this situation as the "social creation of dependency in old age." Socially created dependency has a political and economic function in society. This societal structure supports a strong and productive economy, keeping important work and positions open for the younger members.

It is evident in many ways that we favor youth and see aging as a negative attribute. Take for instance the media. The majority of our TV shows are geared for the younger generation. In addition, there are millions of advertisements of products or gimmicks to slow or stop the aging process. The market for these products is tremendous.

Because the aged may be physically challenged and thus considered a devalued group, the political economy theory views them as predisposed to abuse. Not only is it a difficult time in their lives, but it is also stressful for those who care for them. In addition, the theory sees their stigmatization in society as fostering a lack of viable services and opportunities for them, thus compounding the problem.

Environmental Stress/Strain Theory

Though stress theory has been analyzed on a meso level and discussed in terms of a sociopsychological model, stress can also be examined on a cultural level. The *environmental stress/strain theory* looks at the structural inequalities—poverty, socioeconomic status, and racial inequalities—in society. The groups that have fewer opportunities due to these inequalities are said to be predisposed to family violence (Straus, 1990).

Summary

The sociocultural model offers a more comprehensive understanding of the complex interactions at play in abusive homes; however, it is not without criticism. As discussed, there has been much criticism of patriarchal/feminist theory. Some of these same criticisms could apply to the sociocultural model as a whole. The sociocultural model theories fail to look at specific intervening psychological and sociopsychological variables that need to be studied in family violence. In addition, the theories cannot explain why abuse occurs in some families and not in others. Consider the social conflict theory and the culture of violence theory. They describe how violence occurs but cannot specify why violence occurs in one family but not another. Also, the theories do not address other issues, such as the reasons that women may be abusive or abuse in gay and lesbian relationships.

Though the larger sociological factors are important in the study of family violence, they cannot stand on their own as an explanation of family violence. Finally we look at multidimensional theories that attempt to alleviate this problem.

Multidimensional Models

Multidimensional models account for violence in the home by taking into consideration micro, meso, and macro level explanations. These models attempt to account for all intervening variables. In other words, these theories acknowledge that each level of analysis is important to our understanding of family violence. No one level of analysis can explain all instances of abuse. The theories that have been proposed under this model are general systems theory/global theory and the ecological theory.

General Systems Theory/Global Theory

First developed by sociologist Murray Straus in 1973 and later expanded by Straus and his colleagues and by others (Straus, 1973; Straus et al., 1980;

Hampton et al., 1996), general systems theory was the first attempt to bring together aspects of all the theories in order to get a more comprehensive picture of the causes of family violence. Straus (1973) argued that family violence was not the result of individual pathologies but a systemic problem. This theory is based on a multidisciplinary approach that takes into account psychological (individual), sociopsychological (family interactions), and sociological (societal) factors. General systems theory attempts to study all the possible interacting variables and how they affect each other (Bersani & Chen, 1988; Gelles, 1997; McCue, 1995; Viano, 1992). Therefore, general systems theory looks at both the complexity of interdependencies between parts, components, and processes within the family and at the interdependency between the family and its environment (Bersani & Chen, 1988). The theory examines the family as a system and the environment as a system and the ways in which the two systems interact.

Murray Straus (1973) and his colleague Jean Giles-Sims (1983) saw family violence as a systems product, wherein the family system can operate to maintain, escalate, or reduce violence within itself. Though the causes of violence are many (e.g., personality traits, normative structures, stresses, etc.), these researchers attempted to explain why violence occurs in some families and not in others (Viano, 1992). Straus (1973) and Giles-Sims (1983) found family violence to be the result of the ways in which the family system operated within its environment. Straus (1973) stated that a general systems theory of family violence must include three basic elements (Gelles, 1993):

- Alternative courses of action or causal flow
- Feedback mechanisms that enable the system to make adjustments
- System goals

Within these three basic elements Straus argued that it is important to look at the rules and boundaries that exist both within the system and between the family and the environment. It is also important to determine whether or not it was an open or closed system and whether or not the system received negative or positive feedback. Finally, one must also look at the goals of the family system.

As a system, both the family and the environment are goal oriented. Therefore, all the parts of the system operate or are expected to operate in accordance with its goals. Under the tenets of these goals are boundaries, rules, and norms that all family members are expected to follow. Thus if one family member challenges the established norms, in effect breaking the rules and testing the boundaries, a corrective action would be taken by another family member. Corrective action is intended to reinforce the distribution of power within the family structure and to ensure that family system goals are reached. Likewise, the larger society may assist in setting the rules and boundaries based on culturally accepted practices and norms.

In addition to the goals and boundaries of the systems, Straus (1973) and Giles-Sims (1983) defined whether or not the system is open or closed. Whereas in an open system the family and its environment interact, in a closed system no interaction occurs. Of course not all systems are totally opened or closed. In a closed system, however, with no outside interaction, a family operating in isolation is more likely to continue to use violence because of a lack of repercussions for the perpetrators and lack of support for the victims.

General systems theory asserts that role expectations, labels, or behavioral scripts develop as to how one should act (Bersani & Chen, 1988). In this instance, family members learn to be tough or to be victims. At this point, the system functions to promote negative self-concepts and advance what Merton (1967) termed the *self-fulfilling prophecy*. In Merton's (1967) terms, family members are encouraged to be violent or victims of violence, and, subsequently, each develops a negative self-image as a result of receiving negative messages. They therefore produce behaviors that parallel the labels and self-concepts, such as "perpetrator" or "victim" (Bersani & Chen, 1988; Gelles, 1993; Pagelow, 1984).

Furthermore, general systems theory maintains that incoming stimulus or input is mediated within the family and that a response or output is returned to the environment. If the output is less than some maximum, the feedback is positive, and if the output has reached a maximum level, the feedback will be negative. Straus (1973) states that, if the feedback is positive, the system violence is reinforced through social interaction, the mass media, or both (Bersani & Chen, 1988). Thus positive feedback regarding the violence produces an upward spiral or escalation of violence because the initial violence serves to create further conflicts and violence. For example, if the violence serves to create a stable environment, produces desired results, and is a culturally accepted means of dealing with conflict, the feedback will be positive and the violence will be reinforced. Eventually, the violence will escalate until the point at which change is sought.

This situation, in which positive feedback perpetuates the violence, is characteristic of what Berrien (1968) terms *morphogenesis* (Bersani & Chen, 1988). In morphogenesis, a set of system behaviors allows for change or adjustment. For example, the violence will continue to escalate until it reaches intolerable levels. At this point, system change is inevitable. Either someone, such as a battered woman, leaves the system, or adjustments are made to decrease the level of violence within the family system.

Negative feedback, on the other hand, maintains the level of violence within tolerable limits within the family. Berrien (1968) refers to this situation as *morphostasis (homeostasis)*, wherein the family system maintains a level of stability and does not seek change (Bersani & Chen, 1988).

General systems theory, though more expansive than the other theories, has received much criticism. Because the theory is so extensive, taking into account numerous variables and the processes between all of them, it can be too complex to decipher any meaningful conclusions from it. The task of operationalizing and scientifically testing and measuring the variables and all their multidimensional relationships is viewed as too overwhelming (McCue, 1995; Pagelow, 1984).

Ecological Theory

James Garbarino (1977) and Jay Belsky (1980) originated the ecological theory of family violence in order to explain child abuse. They asserted that abuse must be viewed under three levels of analysis:

1. The relationship between the organism and the environment
2. The interacting and overlapping systems in which human development occurs
3. The quality of the environment

In addition, they argue that a mismatch between any of the organisms can create abusive situations.

Mismatches can occur between a parent and a child or between a family and a neighborhood. Garbarino (1977) and Belsky (1980) view abuse as more likely to occur when the functioning—whether mental, emotional, physical, or social—of the parent, the child, or both is impaired. For example, children with developmental disabilities are at greater risk of abuse. Likewise, mentally ill parents are at an increased risk of abusing.

In addition to these mismatches, the abuse is heightened when the family faces other stressors (e.g., poor or stressful relations between parents, lack of financial resources or community support systems, etc.). Moreover, Garbarino (1977) found two necessary conditions under which child abuse would occur or was at a great risk of occurring: first, there is a cultural justification through a value system that legitimizes the use of force against children; second, the maltreating family is isolated from influential family or community support systems (Gelles, 1993; Viano, 1992).

Summary

Multidimensional theories attempt to explore the complexity of family violence by taking into consideration all or many of the intervening variables that are important to understanding why violence persists in some families. However, as with general systems theory, these theories can be too complex to render any comprehensible and valuable insight into the problem of family violence. The ecological theory offers a clearer view of how family violence can occur. Though it is intended to explain child abuse, it could easily be applied to other forms of abuse, as well.

/// Chapter Summary

Over the years, scholarly attempts to explain family violence have resulted in four major theoretical models, each with specific theories and appropriate levels of analysis. As we have seen, explaining family violence has been no easy task. There are not only many types of violence but also many intervening variables to consider.

Though each model and the corresponding theories can explain some types of family violence, most of the theories examine only certain variables and thus can explain only a part of the bigger picture. In addition, whereas some theories are generalizable to most types of family violence, others are more specific, dealing with only one type (e.g., child abuse). Moreover, whereas some theories can account for the reasons that violence in the home begins, they fail to explain why it prevails. Finally, although many of the theories have been valuable to the study of family violence, the research methodology used has often been weak, leaving the results invalid and inconclusive.

Given the magnitude and nature of the problem, it is no wonder that the task of explaining family violence has been a daunting one. Explaining human behavior, especially in the private confines of the family, will continually challenge scholars. A complex problem will invariably require multidimensional solutions.

Despite this ominous venture, scholars have developed important theoretical principles that serve as a tremendous foundation. Though each proposed family violence theory has inherent weaknesses, each offers some invaluable insight and impetus for further study. Our discussion of theory does not end here. We continue to discuss the role of theory in each of the subsequent chapters. We pay close attention to how institutions, laws, and services embrace these theoretical models.

II /// Forms of Violence in the Home

3 /// Child Maltreatment

*K*aren pulled into her child care provider's driveway at approximately
5:00 p.m., exhausted after a long day. Immediately to her left was a
small child, wearing nothing but a diaper, sitting next to the driveway. Karen
emerged from her car, her heart racing with fear at the thought that she
could have run over this child with her car had she not been paying attention. She approached Megan, who was standing on her front porch, and
asked if she knew who the child belonged to. Megan pointed to a house five
doors down. Then the young child ran up the street, attempting to navigate
with her bare feet and bulky diaper.

When she turned the corner on a neighboring street, Karen strutted
down the street to find one of the child's parents. She pounded on the door,
and a man answered. "Is Sara your daughter?" "Yes," the man responded.
"Well, she just took off up the street. You probably should go get her,"
exclaimed Karen. The man replied, "She knows better than to go past the
corner!" He took off after his daughter, retrieved her, and brought her home.

Karen spent about 15 minutes talking with Megan and learned that Sara
was often unsupervised outside. Karen then got in her car to go home and
found Sara sitting in the next driveway, with no father in sight. Karen decided to place a call to the Child Abuse Hotline, and a child protective
worker responded within 10 minutes.

One week later, Sara's parents approached Karen as she arrived to pick
up her daughter from Megan's house. Sara's father, Greg, began screaming
and yelling at Karen, posturing as though to assault her. Sara's mother, angry
and confused, confronted Karen about her call to the child protective
agency, saying, "How dare you call those people on us. You don't know us
and you don't know this neighborhood." Sara's father continued to rant and
rave in the background, and eventually his wife sent him home, fearing his
behavior was out of control. After he left, Sara's mother, Karen, and Megan
were able to discuss the matter calmly. Sara's mother discovered that her
husband did not closely supervise their daughter when he was at home with

her. Karen found herself explaining to this seemingly responsible parent the
dangers of letting a toddler roam the streets unsupervised. After much discussion, Karen finally said, "I hope someday you will thank me for caring
enough about your child to make that call." Sara's mother said, "I understand, thank you." Sara was never seen unsupervised in the neighborhood
again.

This story, perhaps not as compelling or problematic as other examples
found in this chapter, illustrates child neglect. Although Sara's parents may
be good parents in all other respects, their lack of supervision could put
young Sara in significant danger. She could be hit by a car, bitten by a dog,
cut by glass, drowned in a small pool of water, injured by older children or
other adults, or abducted. Why would anyone want to put a child in harm's
way? In Sara's case, her father did not supervise her properly because he
was uneducated about child development and did not have an understanding that 2-year-olds are not, under any circumstances, able to monitor themselves. In this case, child protective workers were able to educate the family
about proper supervision, bringing about an end to this type of neglect.
    Of all the forms of family violence that we discuss in this text, child
abuse is probably the most difficult to comprehend. American society at
least appears to revere children. Considering the commercial success of a
variety of products geared specifically for children, such as toys, furniture,
music, food, clothing, books, and entertainment, it is puzzling to consider
why a society would invest billions of dollars in child-related products and
services yet neglect to care for children's safety and overall well-being.
    In other words, we say we are a child-centered society, yet between
1,000 and 2,000 children die every year as a result of abuse, neglect, or both
(U.S. Advisory Board on Child Abuse and Neglect [USABCAN], 1995), and
an additional 2 million children are estimated to be abused and neglected
each year (Sedlak & Broadhurst, 1996). In 2000, based on reports from child
protection agencies, approximately 1,200 children died of abuse or neglect
and 879,000 children were found to be maltreated (Administration for Children and Families [ACF], 2002).
    In order to fully understand this contradiction, we need to consider a
variety of factors. First, the role children have played in society throughout
time is important to our understanding of cultural norms of disciplining
and caring for children. Second, how we define *abuse* and *neglect* depends
on those cultural standards, as well as on the political, economic, and social
conditions of the time. The long-term consequences of abuse and neglect
provide the supporting documentation that this paradox continues to persist
into the twenty-first century.
    This chapter is divided into three major sections. In the first section we
examine how the role of children in society has changed throughout history,
the importance of understanding the social, economic, and political environment of the times, and the early development of child maltreatment

policies. In the second section we define the various forms of child maltreatment and explore some of the issues that are currently plaguing the child welfare and legal fields. In the third section we uncover some of the individual and social consequences of child maltreatment.

/// Putting Child Abuse in a Social and Historical Context

Although many argue that contemporary American children still do not enjoy the same rights and treatment as adults, they definitely experience life in a different way than did children of the past. As we discuss in the next few paragraphs, children, if they lived at all, endured rather bleak, heartless, and cold lives. That is not to say that no children enjoyed the love and affection of warm, nurturing parents. However, many of the practices of the past would very clearly be considered child abuse today. The plight of children has improved over time with improved medical technology, economic conditions, birth control, and the development of child protection agencies.

Medieval Times

Although records dating back to medieval times are not available to us, researchers have attempted to piece together a picture of what the lives of children were like based on sources such as historical paintings. Works of art often provide us with clues about ancient cultures and societies. The legacy of medieval art suggests that children did not experience what we would call a "childhood" period; instead they went from infancy into adulthood. Early paintings depict children as miniature adults, sharing in all aspects of adult life (Aries, 1962). Children usually were seen wearing adult clothing, featuring adult expressions. Only infants were clothed differently (Plumb, 1972). Once children passed the age of dependence, they were promoted directly into all aspects of adult life (Aries, 1962). For example, in the Middle Ages, not only were young children expected to participate in the labor market but also teen marriages were the rule rather than the exception.

Other sources present children as being nothing more than bothersome. Aries (1962) describes one scene in which a mother who has just given birth to her fifth child wonders what it will be like with one more mouth to feed. A neighbor comforts her: "Before they are old enough to bother you, you will have lost half of them, or perhaps all of them"(p. 38).

Considering the fact that adults did not have access to birth control and medical advancements as they do today, families tended to be very large, and children tended to die very young. Parents must have felt as though they had no control over children coming into or going out of the world. The short life span of children is a plausible explanation for parents not being emotionally attached to their children. Parents may have avoided strong emotional attachments to lessen the pain of loss or may have been so busy raising their large families that it was difficult to form strong attachments to individual children.

Additionally, the extra burden of a new baby to an already over-burdened family gave rise to a variety of practices that resulted in fatalities among for young children. The practice of infanticide, or the killing of babies, was a relatively common practice prior to the fourteenth century (DeMause, 1976). Mothers would kill their babies in order to ease the financial and emotional burdens of caring for another child.

The practice of abandonment was also very common and grew to be a more accepted practice than infanticide. Abandonment appears to have been present even into the seventeenth and eighteenth centuries (Whitehead & Lab, 1999). Parents left their newborn babies in the streets or on the doorsteps of churches. Although the parents' intentions may have been good, the reality was that the majority of these abandoned babies died (Lefrancois, 1992). Even today, it is not unheard of that a parent would abandon an infant or a young child. In fact, as a response to the growing number of infant deaths, new legislation is currently being debated that would decriminalize abandonment of newborns. The goal is to provide new mothers with alternatives to killing their newborns by making abandonment legal.

Early American Society

In early American society the plight of children did not appear to be much improved over that we believe existed during the medieval era. Children continued to die at a very young age due to childhood illnesses and the lack of immunizations.

Also, because of the economic needs of families, children's educational needs were abandoned, and children were sent out to work (DeMause, 1976). Children were especially exploited during the industrial revolution, when they were put to work in the factories. Families were also known to place their children under involuntary servitude and apprenticeships (Whitehead & Lab, 1999), which in reality meant that children were bought and sold like slaves.

Religious practices in early American society dictated a harsh approach to child rearing. Children were deemed to be sinful in nature, and as a result physical punishment was an accepted practice of discipline. Children who misbehaved literally had "the devil beaten out of them." As Wiehe (1992) notes, "Calvinistic theology was preoccupied with the issue of infant depravity and damnation, emphasizing the inherent corrupt and sinful nature of children" (p. 26). The biblical dictum "spare the rod and spoil the child" provided the biblical justification for beating children, and consequently beating a child with a rod was regarded as an appropriate method of discipline (Wiehe, 1992).

In addition to economic conditions, the lack of medical care and birth control, and strong religious beliefs, the law did not protect children in early American society. For example, the first child labor law was not passed until 1887 in Alabama (Pagelow, 1984), and the first juvenile court was not established until 1899 in Cook County, Illinois (Whitehead & Lab, 1999). Although there is some evidence that criminal cases involving child abuse can be traced back to as early as 1655 (Wiehe, 1992), it was not until the infamous case of Mary Ellen Wilson in the late 1800s that a national dialogue began about child maltreatment and the lack of legislation to protect children.

The Rise of Child Protection Policy: The Mary Ellen Wilson Case

Most researchers mark the case of Mary Ellen Wilson as the beginning of the American movement to protect children. In 1874, Etta Wheeler, a church social worker, heard about the plight of 9-year-old Mary Ellen Wilson, who was suffering from abuse at the hands of her legal custodians, Francis and Mary Connolly. Attempting to find legal recourse to protect Mary Ellen, Etta Wheeler sought the assistance of the American Society for the Protection of Cruelty to Animals (ASPCA). The ASPCA brought charges against the Connollys, charging that because Mary Ellen was a member of the animal kingdom, she had a right to protection against cruelty, like other animals (Sagatun & Edwards, 1995).

Box 3.1 /// Mary Ellen Wilson

In 1874, 8-year-old Mary Ellen Wilson lived in New York City with non-blood relatives. A neighbor noticed that she was repeatedly beaten with a leather thong and permitted to be underdressed in bad weather. This neighbor reported the situation to Etta Wheeler, a member of St. Luke's Methodist Mission. Etta Wheeler reported the case to the New York City Police Department and a charity agency. Neither would get involved because of the lack of proof of abuse and the lack of statutory guidelines on such matters.

Legend has it that Henry Berge, the founder of the Society for the Prevention of Cruelty to Animals, heard of the case and intervened on Mary Ellen's behalf, arguing to a New York City court that Mary Ellen was part of the animal kingdom and thus deserving of protection like other animals. The court agreed to hear the case. Mary Ellen was subsequently removed from the home and placed in an orphanage. Her foster mother, Mary Connolly, was imprisoned for one year. In December of that same year, the New York Society for the Prevention of Cruelty to Children was founded (Gelles, 1997).

The case promoted the development of the New York Society for the Prevention of Cruelty to Children (SPCC) and other similar organizations nationwide (Wiehe, 1992). In 1881, the SPCC was authorized by statute to be the first child protection agency in the country, with the authority to conduct investigations, to recommend placements for children, and to bring abusers to justice (Sagatun & Edwards, 1995). The SPCC, and other private voluntary organizations like it, remained the primary protective service for children until the passage of the Social Security Act in 1935. Although many states had created their own state-administered child protective agencies prior to the passage of the Social Security Act, this act provided the federal funding necessary to fuel state-operated protective services (Wiehe, 1992). Slowly but surely, private protection agencies were replaced by state-administered government programs.

Medical Technology and Child Maltreatment

Another noted movement toward the identification of child abuse and the subsequent development of public policy is the development of diagnostic X-ray technology in the 1940s. The use of radiology made it possible for the first time to uncover injuries not apparent to the eye. In 1946, John Caffey, a radiologist, published an article regarding his observations of six infants who had multiple fractures of long bones and chronic subdural hematomas (Rathgeb Smith & Freinkel, 1988). Although Caffey did not propose that violence was the cause of such injuries, his work did promote additional research into their nature and potential causes.

In 1962, Henry Kempe and associates published an article in a medical journal that introduced the term *battered child syndrome* (Kempe, 1962). Kempe and his associates reviewed research conducted on 302 cases of abuse and concluded that some children were being victimized by their parents, caretakers, or both (Rathgeb Smith &Freinkel, 1988). The term *battered child syndrome* is still used today to refer to a child who has suffered repeated physical injuries that cannot be attributed to accidental means (Sagatun & Edwards, 1995).

Kempe and his colleagues played an enormous part in bringing the issues of child abuse to the top of the political agenda. Although child protection agencies had been in existence for a number of years, their article fueled a legislative movement that gave more credence and authority to the work of child protective agents.

Also, although they focused their attention solely on the psychopathology of the parents as a cause for child abuse (Rathgeb Smith & Freinkel, 1988), Kempe and colleagues' work proved to be a springboard for additional research into the nature and causes of child abuse. No longer could the battered child be ignored by the government, the medical profession, or other professions that interact with children.

Enactment of Child Protection Policies

By 1963 the U.S. Children's Bureau disseminated model legislation for a mandated reporting procedure to the states. The model law designated certain professionals to report suspected cases of abuse and recommended that states adopt similar legislation. By the end of the 1960s, legislation was enacted in every state that mandated the reporting of child abuse (Rathgeb Smith & Freinkel, 1988). This initial mandated-reporting legislation at the state level prompted Congress to follow with important federal legislation.

In 1974, Congress passed the Child Abuse Prevention and Treatment Act (CAPTA, Pub. L. No. 93-247), providing federal power to change the identification, treatment, and prevention of child maltreatment (Rathgeb Smith & Freinkel, 1988). This landmark legislation did a number of important things, including authorizing $85 million for child maltreatment programs and services (Rathgeb Smith &Freinkel, 1988).

First, the CAPTA created the National Center on Child Abuse and Neglect (NCCAN) and the National Clearinghouse on Child Abuse and Neglect Information (NCCANI) to serve as a resource for research, programs, and general information. The National Center continues to function at the center of child abuse policy (Rathgeb Smith & Freinkel, 1988) and serves as a major informational resource for professionals and community members alike (Wiehe, 1992).

Second, the CAPTA provided federal funding for child maltreatment programs for states that were able to meet federal requirements. The CAPTA provided incentives for the states to improve their policies and procedures on mandated reporting, investigating, processing reported cases, and training of personnel in return for federal funding. This funding served as a catalyst for states to improve their statutes and procedures in dealing with abused and neglected children. Third, the CAPTA provided federal funding for research and demonstration projects.

This bill was, however, not without controversy in its own right. CAPTA was originally introduced by Senator Walter F. Mondale in his role as chair of the Senate Subcommittee on Children and Youth. Debates regarding this bill focused on the definition of child abuse, with the dialogue centering on cases of brutal physical abuse. As Rathgeb Smith and Freinkel (1988) note, "the focus on the most horrific examples of physical abuse headed off challenges from conservative critics who might otherwise have opposed CAPTA as undue interference in the family and parental discipline" (p. 34). As we discuss later in this chapter, child neglect was especially underplayed as a form of child abuse. Additionally, debate came from the Nixon administration, which opposed the bill. The CAPTA created a new categorical spending program, going against the Nixon administration's goal of curtailing federal spending on local social problems (Rathgeb Smith & Freinkel, 1988).

Despite the debates prior to CAPTA's enactment in 1974, it was reauthorized in 1978 with little fanfare (Rathgeb Smith & Freinkel, 1988). In

1978 the Adoption Reform Act was added to the CAPTA, extending federal funding through 1982 and 1983. The CAPTA was again amended in 1984, expanding its original definition of child abuse. In 1984, the amendments expanded the definition of abuse to include medically disabled infants and the mandated reporting of medical neglect and maltreatment of children in out-of-home care; it also added sexual exploitation as a reportable form of child sexual abuse (Sagatun & Edwards, 1995). The amendments also authorized a nationwide study of the incidence and prevalence of child maltreatment (Wiehe, 1992). The National Incidence Study (NIS; see Sedlak & Broadhurst, 1996) is currently our only tool to estimate the scope of child maltreatment in the United States.

Since the Child Abuse Prevention and Treatment Act was originally enacted in 1974, a new child protection system has developed across the country. Child abuse is no longer dealt with by private voluntary organizations such as the Society for the Prevention of Cruelty to Children. Child protection has become the responsibility of state and local governments. Today, a number of national, statewide, and local organizations have formed to prevent child abuse and neglect. For example, the National Committee to Prevent Child Abuse (NCPCA), located in Chicago, Illinois, is a national organization formed to prevent child abuse (see *www.childabuse.org*). We discuss the current child protection system in more detail in chapters 7 and 8. We now explore current definitions and issues in child maltreatment.

///   Forms of Child Maltreatment

Child maltreatment is a catchall phrase that is inclusive of all the various forms of child abuse and neglect. Children are mistreated in a number of ways, including physical abuse, sexual abuse, psychological maltreatment, and neglect. Official definitions of child maltreatment vary from state to state; however, the Child Abuse Prevention and Treatment Act, as amended and reauthorized in 1996 (Pub. L. No. 104-235, §111, 42 U.S.C. 5106g), defines child abuse and neglect at a minimum as:

- An act or failure to act on part of a parent or caretaker which results in death, serious physical or emotional harm, sexual abuse or exploitation.
- An act or failure to act which presents an imminent risk of serious harm.
- Whereas a CHILD is defined as a person who is under the age of 18, or except in the case of sexual abuse where the age is specified by child protection in the State in which the child resides.

Although each state is responsible for providing its own definitions of the various forms of child maltreatment, the National Clearinghouse on

Child Abuse and Neglect Information (NCCANI, 1999) provides the following operational definitions of the four major types of maltreatment: physical abuse, sexual abuse, emotional abuse, and neglect.

Physical Abuse

Physical abuse is characterized by physical injury to the child that results from punching, beating, kicking, biting, burning, or otherwise harming a child. Common injuries that child victims endure include bruises, fractures, water or immersion burns, pattern burns, and head and internal injuries (Wallace, 1999).

The parent or caretaker may have not planned to hurt the child, yet the injury may have occurred as a result of physical punishment inappropriate to the child's age or condition or of overdiscipline (NCCANI, 1999).

Box 3.2 /// Physical and Behavioral Indicators of Physical Abuse

Physical Indicators of Abuse:

- Unexplained or inadequately explained bruises, welts, burns, lacerations, abrasions, or fractures.
- Frequent injuries that are consistently described as "accidental" or "unexplained."
- Patterned bruising or burns in the shape of an object, such as a cigarette, rope, iron, electrical cord, or belt buckle, or immersion burns that appear to be glovelike.
- Injuries that are bilateral (appear on both sides of the body) or on several different surfaces.
- Injuries that regularly appear after absences, such as weekends and vacations.
- Injuries that are in various stages of healing.
- Human bite marks: >3 cm. between canines.

Child Behavioral Indicators of Physical Abuse:

- Reporting injury by parents or reporting unbelievable reasons for the injuries.
- Exhibiting extreme changes in behavior: aggressive or totally withdrawn.
- Destructive to self and/or others.
- Frequently late or absent from school or coming too early and/or staying too late.
- Wearing long-sleeved or similar clothing to hide injuries.
- Flinching when other adults raise their voices or appear to be angry.

Source: Adapted from Broome County Child Abuse Council: Mandated Reporter Training Materials, Broome County, New York

Some parents choose to use physical punishment such as spanking or slapping as a disciplinary tool. However, if the punishment results in injury, it is likely to be considered abuse.

Even well-meaning, otherwise "good," parents may not realize the damage they inflict on their children, especially very young children, by practicing corporal punishment as a form of discipline. The research evidence is very clear that corporal punishment does not work to change the behavior of the child and also has long-term negative consequences for the child's development that may include aggressive behavior, juvenile delinquency, poor school performance (Cyan, 1987), and lower cognitive abilities (Straus & Paschall, 1998).

Additionally, findings from longitudinal studies suggest that lessening

---

Box 3.3 /// To Spank or Not to Spank?

The debate continues: Should parents use physical punishment such as spanking, paddling, or slapping as a means of disciplining their children? Although corporal punishment is still used by some schools and many parents, the research indicates that it has no long-term positive benefits, and, in fact, it is associated with many negative consequences such as delinquency and poor school performance (Cyan, 1987).

Consider the following issues when deciding whether or not spanking is appropriate (under any circumstance):

- Hitting children teaches them that hitting is an appropriate method of dealing with anger and frustration. It also suggests to the child that sometimes it is OK to purposefully hurt the people that you love (Epstein, 1999).
- Hitting children does not help children develop their own sense of internal control. It lets children know their behavior is wrong but does little to teach them what is appropriate. Spanking leaves the child with feelings of being hurt, scared, and frightened.
- There is a very thin line separating physical punishment from abuse. It is very easy for angry, frustrated parents to hit with more strength than originally intended.
- Slapping on the buttocks is a sexual violation. Being hit in an erogenous zone of the body can send mixed messages and confusion about sexual pleasure and pain (Ontario Consultants on Religious Tolerance, 1999).
- Corporal punishment is associated with a decrease in the cognitive ability of children (Murray & Paschall, 1998).
- There is some evidence that even witnessing physical punishment leads to decreases in learning, most likely due to the anxiety and stress created when aggression is used (Charlesworth, 1992).

Recommended Reading: Straus, M. A. (1994). *Beating the devil out of them: Corporal punishment in American families.* San Francisco: Jossey-Bass/Lexington Books.

the use of corporal punishment in society is likely to reduce juvenile delinquency, adult violence, masochistic sex, depression, and alcohol abuse. Also, decreased corporal punishment means an increase in the likelihood of completing higher education and earning higher income (Straus, 1994).

Current Issues in the Physical Abuse of Children

Of the many issues currently under investigation in the professional community regarding the physical abuse of children, two in particular have gained considerable attention in the research literature and in the field. Munchausen syndrome by proxy, a mental illness in which the caretaker induces illness in a child, and the pre- and postnatal use of substances by parents have gained the attention of the medical, legal, and child welfare communities over the past decade. These two potentially fatal forms of child abuse have taken center stage in medical and psychological research and treatment and have ignited a variety of legal debates.

Munchausen syndrome by proxy.   Munchausen syndrome by proxy is a severe form of child abuse in which the parent (usually the mother) or caretaker fabricates or actually causes the physical signs and symptoms of an illness or disease in a child; the child thus must endure needless and potentially harmful medical treatments and procedures (Smith & Killam, 1994).

The syndrome is named after Baron von Munchausen, an eighteenth-century German baron and soldier, who was famous for his tall tales (Schreier, 1992). Adult Munchausen's describes adults who chronically fabricate or inflict illness or symptoms of illness in themselves in an effort to gain medical attention, testing, and even surgery (Libow & Schreier, 1986). Roz Meadow (1977) was the first to write about a variation of Munchausen syndrome to describe parents who falsified illnesses in their children, thus subjecting them to invasive procedures and testing.

This potentially fatal form of child abuse involves the fabrication or inducement of such illnesses as infections, electrolyte imbalances, nonaccidental poisonings, immunodeficiency disease, bleeding, seizures, drowsiness, comas, respiratory problems, allergies, and near-miss or actual sudden infant death syndrome (SIDS; Smith & Killam, 1994). There have been numerous descriptions of mothers poisoning their children, injecting them with contaminating materials (e.g., feces), and suffocating them (Libow & Schreier, 1986).

Although this syndrome has often been reported as rare, it is not as uncommon as it has been characterized. Schreier and Libow (1993) surveyed pediatric neurologists and pediatric gastroenterologists (physicians most likely to have these types of cases) and found that there may be large numbers of cases presented, although not all of them may be properly diagnosed. Although children are likely targets for abuse, Pasqualone and Fitzgerald (1999) note that elders and disabled adults are also at risk.

Box 3.4 /// The Case of Kathy Bush

One of the most well-known criminal court cases involving child abuse charges is that of Kathy Bush, a case that stems from what is believed to be Munchausen syndrome by proxy. In October of 1999, Kathy Bush was convicted of two counts of aggravated child abuse and one count of fraud in Coral Springs, Florida. The prosecution charged that she deliberately induced and fabricated illnesses in her daughter Jennifer. The fourth district court of appeals affirmed her conviction on March 6, 2002 (809 So. 2d 107; 2002 Fla. App. LEXIS 2390; 27 Fla. L. Weekly D 539).

Since Jennifer was an infant, she had experienced many illnesses. In fact, over the course of several years, she endured more than 200 hospitalizations and more than 40 surgical procedures. The prosecution (and the jury) believed these to be the result of her mother's own actions. In addition to numerous surgeries, Jennifer had three tubes running into her body to medicate and feed her. Prosecutors argued that Kathy Bush did everything she could to keep Jennifer sick, including altering her medications.

After Kathy Bush was arrested in 1996, Jennifer was placed in protective custody, where she has been living with a foster family. In addition to the other evidence brought forth by the prosecution, the fact that Jennifer's health had improved greatly since she had been away from her mother added to the evidence against Kathy Bush.

News Sources: *Stuart News Company Press Journal*, October 8, 1999; *People* Magazine, October, 25, 1999.

Additionally, a recent study conducted in the United Kingdom presents a frightening picture of the prevalence of Munchausen syndrome by proxy. Southall, Plunkett, Banks, Falkov, and Samuels (1997) utilized covert video surveillance in the hospital rooms of 39 children with a history of life-threatening events (as reported by the parents). In 33 of the 39 cases, there was disturbing video evidence of physical abuse by the parent.

In terms of prevalence rates, Munchausen syndrome by proxy has been a difficult form of child abuse to measure. It has been estimated that approximately 10 percent of child victims will die as a result of their parent's actions and that 25 to 33 percent of cases involve more than one child in the family (Smith & Killam, 1994). We still have much to learn about Munchausen syndrome by proxy. Perrin, Theodore, and Runyan (1999) argue for a medical research agenda that includes the incidence and full spectrum of this syndrome. The potential implications of this hidden form of child abuse are enormous.

Prenatal Substance Abuse.   Drug use during pregnancy is a health problem with serious long-term consequences. Research estimates that about 11 percent of all infants born are affected by prenatal drug use each year (Lyman

& Potter, 1998). Drug use during pregnancy has become a child abuse issue because of the danger to the developing fetus from tobacco, alcohol, and illicit drug use. Of equal concern is the impact of drug use by the father and mother at conception and after birth. Although women tend to be blamed and punished for the consequences that substance abuse has on their children, both parents are responsible for protecting their children from harm.

Tobacco use during pregnancy has been linked to an array of negative outcomes, including fetal death late in pregnancy, infant death after delivery, and retarded fetal growth. The more the mother smokes, the more likely her baby will experience adverse consequences, such as abruptio placental, placenta previa, bleeding during pregnancy, preterm delivery, and death (U.S. Department of Health and Human Services [USDHHS], 1994).

Babies and children who live in environments with smokers are also in danger of the adverse effects of secondhand smoke. Exposure to secondhand smoke leads to increases in the occurrence of lower respiratory illnesses, the frequency of chronic respiratory symptoms, and the severity and onset of childhood asthma; to decreases in the rate of lung growth during childhood and adolescence, and to middle-ear effusion (USDHHS, 1994). Additionally, recent studies have confirmed the link between smoking and SIDS, the leading cause of death during the first year of life (Schoendorf & Kiely, 1992). SIDS is a term that is used to explain the death of an infant up to one year of age when no other cause of death can be identified.

Alcohol use during pregnancy is also a significant health concern. Although no amount of alcohol use during pregnancy is considered to be safe (Karr-Morse & Wiley, 1997), the probability of having a child born with fetal alcohol syndrome (FAS) or fetal alcohol effects (FAE) increases with the amount and frequency of alcohol consumed. FAS and FAE refer to a group of irreversible physical deformities and mental birth defects that result from a woman's drinking during pregnancy (National Organization on Fetal Alcohol Syndrome [NOFAS], 1999).

In fact, FAS is the leading known cause of mental retardation (NOFAS, 1999). Babies born with FAS or FAE suffer from problems with their central nervous systems and growth patterns and often have facial abnormalities, cognitive deficits (Charlesworth, 1992), and impairments to both gross and fine motor skills (Karr-Morse & Wiley, 1997). Additionally, it appears that tobacco use further advances the destructive effects of alcohol on the developing fetus, greatly increasing the chance of FAS (Dorozyaski, 1993). Early exposure to alcohol affects children in many ways that result in educational, social, and behavioral problems that haunt them for their entire lives (Karr-Morse & Wiley, 1997).

Recent research efforts have focused on the impact of the father's drinking on fetal development. Researchers know that there is a link between the father's drinking and their infants' outcomes, but the specific link is still unclear. It appears as though alcohol use by the father is linked to impaired sperm or damaged semen or that prolonged exposure to alcohol alters the selection process for sperm survival (Karr-Morse & Wiley, 1997).

It has been estimated that approximately 5,000 babies are born each year with FAS and that another 50,000 children show the lesser set of FAE symptoms (NOFAS, 1999). These problems incur an estimated cost of approximately $250 million each year (Brown et al, 1991). The cost of caring for children exposed to alcohol is so high because many service delivery systems are involved in their care. These children have great need for ongoing medical treatment, special education programming, and behavioral health services.

Although the two legal drugs, tobacco and alcohol, have the potential to cause severe damage to developing fetuses, illicit drug use by pregnant women has generated public hysteria, media attention, and legal debate. Research suggests that cocaine, heroin, and marijuana use by *both* parents before and after birth has grave consequences. In addition, many men and women who use illicit drugs also use alcohol, tobacco, or both, thus magnifying the damaging effects. Compounding prenatal toxicity is the environmental neglect that often accompanies substance abuse: leaving children for long periods of time with multiple caregivers, not attending to medical and nutritional needs, inadequate housing, and social and emotional deprivation, for example (Karr-Morse & Wiley, 1997).

Like babies born to alcoholic mothers, babies exposed to cocaine and heroin are born addicted at birth, placing them at additional risk for medical complications and death. Although it has been researched less, marijuana appears to affect verbal and memory domains of learning and attention (Karr-Morse & Wiley, 1997).

Prenatal and perinatal substance abuse has begun to gain the attention of prosecutors and child welfare officials over the past decade. Prosecutors have used their authority in a number of ways to charge women criminally under existing state drug laws (Parks, 1998). For example, prosecutors have used drug delivery statutes to demonstrate that women who transmit drugs to their babies via the umbilical cord are in essence engaged in drug trafficking. Prosecutors have also used pure-use statutes, as well as involuntary manslaughter statutes, to charge pregnant women who use drugs during pregnancy (Parks, 1998).

The prosecution of pregnant women raises a number of legal concerns. Many argue that the criminalization of prenatal drug use keeps women away from treatment and prenatal care. Many women who would otherwise seek treatment, prenatal care or both have feared arrest or the loss of custody of their children (Join Together, 1999). Additionally, constitutional questions have been raised: Does the prosecution of a woman for a medical illness such as substance abuse addiction violate the Eighth Amendment's cruel and unusual punishment clause? Does prosecuting only women when babies test positive for drugs violate the equal protection clause of the Fourteenth Amendment? Does testing for narcotics violate a woman's rights under the

Fourth Amendment, which guarantees protection against unreasonable searches and seizures? What rights under the Constitution do fetuses have (Parks, 1998)?

One such case has recently been argued. The U.S. Court of Appeals for the Fourth Circuit in July of 1999, in the case of *Ferguson v. Charleston* (1999), held that the policy of a South Carolina hospital of testing pregnant women for cocaine use did not violate the U.S. Constitution, the Civil Rights Act of 1964, nor the South Carolina common law. Under a South Carolina statute, a woman who tests positive for cocaine after 24 weeks of gestation is guilty of distributing a controlled substance to a minor. The drug distribution charge is warranted because a viable fetus (meaning a fetus that is capable of living outside the womb) is considered a "person" under South Carolina law (Dubin, 1999).

In *Ferguson v. Charleston,* 10 women who had been tested for cocaine under the policy of the Medical University of South Carolina brought suit against the hospital, the Charleston police, and nurses and doctors, arguing that the hospital policy (and subsequent criminal charges) violated their Fourth Amendment right to be free of unreasonable searches and seizures, their constitutional right to privacy, and the prohibition in Title VI of the Civil Rights Act of 1964 against inequitable discrimination of the basis of race. The women also claimed that the hospital personnel committed the South Carolina tort of abuse process by improperly threatening the women with arrest in order to get them to comply with drug treatment. The court considered all of these legal challenges in their decision (Dubin, 1999).

The court's decision to uphold the hospital policy was grounded in the following determinations. First, the court agreed that the urine drug screens used by the hospital did in fact constitute a "search"; however, the court determined that they were reasonable under the "special needs searches" doctrine. The special needs searches doctrine allows a warrantless search when the search serves the special need of the government beyond the normal need for law enforcement. The court ruled that in this case a special government need existed, which was to reduce drug use by pregnant women (Dubin, 1999). Second, the court concluded that a woman may in fact have a right to medical privacy; however, in this particular case, the government's strong interest in the safety of the fetus outweighs her right to medical record privacy. Third, the court concluded that the method by which the hospital employed the urine drug test was reasonable and less costly than other options. And, fourth, the court dismissed the women's claims that hospital personnel threatened them with arrest if they did not seek drug treatment (Dubin, 1999). The United States Supreme Court ruled on the case in March of 2001, overturning the ruling of the U.S. Court of Appeals for the Fourth Circuit. The court, in a six to three decision, ruled that drug tests conducted without consent or a warrant are unconstitutional. Whether any of the plaintiffs consented to the drug tests in this case will continue to be contested in the lower courts.

The legal questions raised by *Ferguson v. Charleston* and other similar cases will continue to be debated as we attempt to work toward rational policies that ultimately get women the medical treatment they need. It is a delicate balance to attempt to protect unborn babies without disregarding the rights of the mother.

Sexual Abuse

Sexual abuse is characterized by the use, persuasion, inducement, enticement, or coercion of any child to engage in, or assist any other person to engage in, any conduct or simulation of such conduct (for the purpose of capturing a visual image of the sexual conduct) that is sexual in nature. Examples of sexual abuse include fondling, sodomy, intercourse, rape, exhibitionism, and exploitation through prostitution or the production of pornographic materials (NCCANI, 1999). Simply put, child sexual abuse is defined as an adult's use of a child to achieve any form of sexual gratification (Wiehe, 1992).

The term *sexual abuse* is generally reserved for cases in which the child is abused by a person responsible for his or her care, such as a parent, grandparent, or day care provider, whereas the term *sexual assault* generally refers to acts committed against a child by someone who is not responsible for his or her care (NCCANI, 1999). Children can be manipulated into participating in sexual acts with adults, but they can in no way consent because of their inability to fully understand the significance and ramifications of such acts. Therefore, any sexual act or contact between a child and an adult is considered to be child sexual abuse.

The National Incidence Study of Child Abuse and Neglect (NIS; Sedlak & Broadhurst, 1996) estimates that more than 300,000 children nationwide experienced sexual abuse in 1993. This represents a 125 percent increase over the previous estimate. Girls are victimized by sexual abuse about three times more often than boys. Sexual abuse reports are likely to continue to increase as professionals, community members, and children are better educated on the issues and reporting procedures.

Keep in mind that these statistics are estimates of the problem and that we probably will never know the true prevalence rates of such a personal, insufferable crime. Many would agree that sexual abuse is the most underreported form of child maltreatment because of the silence of the victim (Faulkner, 1996). Victims are silent for a number of reasons. They often harbor intense feelings of humiliation, guilt, powerlessness, embarrassment, and inadequacy (Bagley, 1992; Courtois & Watts, 1982). These feelings, coupled with a fear that disclosure will bring about even graver consequences (Berlinger & Barbieri, 1984), leave victims suffering in silence. Silence is perpetuated because sexual abuse often does not leave the tangible marks of abuse such as are seen in child physical abuse; there may be no bruising, broken arms, burn marks, or other signs. Box 3.5 describes the physical and behavioral indicators of sexual abuse.

One of the confusing aspects of gaining an understanding of child sexual abuse is the variety of terms that are often used to describe this type of abuse. Following are some of the common terms that are used by professionals.

Paraphilia is a general term relating to a variety of sexually deviant behaviors, including *bestiality* or *zoophilia* (sexual behavior toward animals), *exhibitionism* (exposing one's genitals to strangers), *masochism* (sexual pleasure derived from receiving pain), *sadism* (sexual pleasure derived from giving pain to others), *sadomasochism* (sexual pleasure gained by giving and receiving pain), *voyeurism* (sexual pleasure gained by watching nonconsenting people undress or have sexual relations), and *pedophilia* (described later).

Intrafamilial or familial sexual abuse refers to cases of sexual abuse that occur between family members, including incest. This term generally considers family relationships in a broad context, that is, family relationships as they are defined by state law, or more broadly defined as being among

---

Box 3.5 /// Physical and Behavioral Indicators of Sexual Abuse

Physical Indicators of Sexual Abuse

- Child has difficulty walking or sitting.
- Child has torn, stained, or bloody underclothing.
- Child experiences pain or itching in genital area.
- Child has a sexually transmitted disease.
- Child is pregnant.
- Child experiences rapid weight gain or weight loss.
- Child is observed to have changes in his or her hygiene practices.
- Somatic complaints (e.g., headaches, stomachaches)

Child Behavioral Indicators of Sexual Abuse

- Child is unwilling to participate in physical activities or change clothes for gym.
- Demonstrates fear in physical contact with others.
- Reports sexual assault by parent or caretaker.
- Child "acts out" with sexually aggressive behavior.
- Possesses excessive sexual knowledge.
- Exhibits extreme changes in behavior: engages in delinquent behavior, appears withdrawn, depressed, or suicidal, and/or develops academic problems.
- Has poor self-esteem and poor peer relationships.

Source: Adapted from Broome County Child Abuse Council: Mandated Reporter Training Materials, Broome County, New York.

blood relatives, relatives by marriage, live-in intimate partners, and adoptive family members (Wiehe, 1992).

Whereas intrafamilial abuse often refers to a broader category of family relationships, *incest* generally is reserved to describe sexual abuse between blood relatives. Incest is considered a taboo in many cultures; however, in some cultures it is accepted as normal behavior (Wallace, 1999). Even in the United States, where incest is strictly prohibited both socially and legally, there are groups that believe that sexual activity with young family members (especially between fathers and daughters) is not only appropriate but also healthy and proper. One such organization, the Rene Guyon Society, has a slogan: "Sex before eight, or else it's too late" (Wallace, 1999).

Intrafamilial abuse and incest offenders are generally considered to be regressed offenders. Regressed offenders have maintained sexual relationships with adults; however, under the stress of personal problems, they may turn to a child for unconditional love and intimacy (Wiehe, 1992). The child then becomes a substitute for the adult sexual relationship (Groth, Hobson, & Gary, 1982).

Extrafamilial abuse refers to sexual abuse that is perpetrated by an individual who is outside of the family. The perpetrator may know the child (neighbors, babysitters, friends of the family) or may be unknown to the child (Wallace, 1999).

Pedophilia is a term that is reserved for offenders who prefer children. The *Diagnostic and Statistical Manual of Mental Disorders* (DSM-IV; American Psychiatric Association, 1994) defines pedophilia as sexual activity with a child who is generally under the age of 13, in which the offender is over age 16 and at least 5 years older than the child. They are considered fixated offenders because their sexual interests are fixated on children, generally children of a particular age. Whereas regressed offenders do have sexual relationships with adults, the fixated offender prefers not to have sexual relationships with adults unless the relationship will provide access to children (Wiehe, 1992).

Nicholas Groth and his colleagues (1982) contend that pedophiles' attractions to children are persistent and compulsive and are generally well established by adolescence. Pedophilic behavior is not triggered by stress or substance abuse. Groth and associates (1982) argue that pedophiles are developmentally immature and see themselves as being at the same level as the child. In essence, they see children as their peers. It is also believed that pedophiles have been molested themselves as young children and often fixate their interests on children the same age as they were when they were victimized (Groth et al., 1982). Lee, Jackson, Pattison, and Ward (2002) recently found the relationship between childhood sexual abuse and pedophilia to be of theoretical significance and the role of childhood emotional abuse to be an important developmental risk factor.

Current Issues in the Sexual Abuse of Children

Ritual Abuse. One controversy currently plaguing law enforcement, child welfare agencies, and therapists is the notion of ritual or ritualistic abuse. Ritual abuse, also known as satanic ritualistic abuse, is defined as the abuse of children through various rituals conducted for the purposes of cult religious worship, often referring to satanic worship. Satanic cults are defined as intrafamilial, transgenerational groups that engage in explicit satanic worship that includes the following types of illegal customs: ritual torture, murder for sacrifice, deviant sexual activity, and ceremonial cannibalism (Young, Sachs, Braun, & Watkins, 1991).

Finkelhor and Williams (as cited in Jones, 1991, p. 164) further define ritualistic abuse as "abuse that occurs in the context linked to some symbols or group activities that have a religious, magical, or supernatural connotation, and where the invocation of these symbols or activities are repeated over time and used to frighten and intimidate the children."

Central to the controversy is whether or not this form of child abuse actually exists. Although therapists and mental health professionals have documented detailed accounts of physical and sexual abuse as a ceremonial part of various religious cult practices, generally satanic in nature, law enforcement has had a difficult time substantiating such claims. Others claim that therapists may have induced false memories of ritualistic abuse in their patients' accounts of their past histories (Kemp, 1998).

Although the debate continues, the truth is that there are a number of patients, in locations all over the world, who claim to have endured torturous examples of abuse for the sake of religious worship. We have discussed similar examples in the first chapter. Equally troubling is the fact that these patients share similar serious mental health problems (e.g., dissociative disorders, posttraumatic stress disorder) with other individuals who have substantiated traumatic childhoods. Although reliability, verifiability, and credibility remain a challenge for therapists and law enforcement, there appears to be enough psychiatric evidence to warrant a continued investigation of such claims (Young et al., 1991).

Juvenile Sexual Offenders. Another current issue facing professionals in the child sexual abuse field is the proper diagnosis, assessment, and treatment of juvenile sexual offenders. Since the 1970s, a growing body of literature has developed that specifically addresses the problem of sexually aggressive behavior by juveniles. Increasingly, juvenile justice professionals have documented sexually abusive behavior by youths as being different from other delinquent behaviors. Coupled with the knowledge that the histories of adult sex offenders include sexually aggressive behaviors in childhood, a powerful argument can be made for early intervention and treatment. The prevention of child sexual abuse seems to be strongly linked with the early identification of sex-offending behavior.

As the child welfare movement continues to grow, we are learning more about the long-term consequences of family violence. Some children respond to their abusive home lives by being sexually aggressive. Studies continue to find that youths who demonstrate sexually abusive behavior have either been themselves victimized by child abuse (James & Neil, 1996; Ryan, Miyoshi, & Metzner, 1996) or have one or both parents who were victims of child abuse (Graves, Openshaw, & Ascione, 1996).

Emotional Abuse

Of all the forms of child maltreatment we discuss in this chapter, emotional abuse is the most difficult to pinpoint and measure. Yet we know that emotional abuse is almost always present in families in which other forms of maltreatment exist. According to the National Incidence Study (Sedlak & Broadhurst, 1996) an estimated 532,200 children met the endangerment standard of being emotionally abused in 1996. This figure represents a 183 percent increase over the estimate made in 1986.

Emotional abuse is characterized in several ways. Abuse may be in the form of overt acts of emotional mistreatment, including using psychologically damaging forms of discipline such as locking a child in a dark closet or in a basement. Other overt acts might include using negative verbal and nonverbal interpersonal communications—for example, belittling, name-calling, insults, put-downs, humiliation, rejection, or terrorization—in day-to-day interactions with the child. Additionally, adults who use children as pawns in their disputes or who allow children to participate in violent disputes are also considered to be perpetrating emotional abuse. All of these derogatory interactions have devastating impacts on the psychological and emotional development of a child.

Far more subtle are acts of omission, by which the parent fails to meet the emotional and psychological needs of the child. In cases of omission, often referred to as emotional neglect, children may be ignored or isolated. Parents may put both physical and emotional distance between themselves and their children. Emotional neglect, as we discuss in the next section, involves the lack of love, nurturing, and support that children so desperately need to become confident, psychologically healthy adults.

Neglect

Child neglect is defined as the failure to provide for the child's basic needs. Neglect involves the failure to provide minimal standards of care for the physical, educational, or emotional needs of a child (NCCANI, 1999). This form of maltreatment is considered an omission rather than a commission of abuse. Parents and caretakers do not do what they are supposed to do to meet the needs of their growing children. Ongoing, chronic neglect can be catastrophic for children. Children whose basic needs are not met are put at risk for a variety of long-term consequences that include cognitive, social, and physical developmental delays.

Physical neglect may include refusal or delay in seeking health, dental, or eye care; inadequate supervision and attention; failing to provide appropriate meals, adequate personal hygiene, or adequate housing; and failure to ensure the child's physical safety. Educational neglect includes permitting frequent truancy, failing to enroll a child of mandatory school age in school, and not taking care of special educational needs. Emotional neglect includes refusal or inability to provide for emotional and psychological needs (including providing love, nurturance, and acceptance); exposing children to acts of intimate partner abuse; and permitting drug or alcohol use by the child. Box 3.6 describes some of the minimal standards of care that are used as guidelines for mandated reports of child neglect in New York State.

Given the fact that definitions of minimal standards of care vary by economic status, cultural norms, geographic location, and child's age, it is not always easy to diagnose child neglect, nor can we always blame the parent or caretaker. In fact, a true examination of child neglect would require us to look beyond the parents and caretakers and toward the broader community. For example, we should question the responsibility of landlords who refuse to care for their properties, leaving tenants without appropriate, safe housing; of dental and medical providers who refuse to take Medicaid patients; of an economic system that does not provide health care insurance for all; and of school systems that are so overwhelmed that they cannot follow up on every child's absence from school. Child neglect is as much a problem of our social systems and institutions as it is of parents.

The neglect statistics in the United States are staggering. The National Incidence Study (Sedlak & Broadhurst, 1996) provides us with two different estimates of neglect. The harm standard estimates the number of children who have already experienced harm from neglect, and the endangerment standard estimates the number of children who have experienced neglect that puts them at serious risk for harm. Under the harm standard, in 1996 338,900 children experienced harm from physical neglect, and 212,800 children experienced harm from emotional neglect. Under the endangerment standard, an estimated 1,961,300 children are at risk of harm due to neglect (Sedlak & Broadhurst, 1996). Additionally, Perrin et al. (1999), using raw data from a 1995 Gallup poll, estimate that approximately 40 per 1,000 children, or more than 2.3 million children, are neglected each year.

Current Issues in Child Neglect

Child neglect is the most common form of child maltreatment, yet, ironically, it is the least researched. The paradox lies in our inability to raise a meaningful public dialogue about what the standards of care for children

Box 3.6 /// Minimal Standards of Care

Supervision

- Young children should not be left unattended (inside or outside).
- Children should not be left in the care of siblings who are too young to provide adequate care.
- Children should not be left with adults who are inadequate or unsafe.

Clothing and Hygiene

- Children should be dressed appropriately for the weather.
- Babies and toddlers need to have their diapers changed on a regular basis.
- Children should not be chronically dirty and unbathed.

Medical and Dental Care

- Children who are ill should receive proper medical care.
- Children should be seen by a dentist and have proper eye care.

Education

- Children should attend school on a consistent basis.
- Older children should not miss school to care for younger siblings.

Nutrition

- Children should have an adequate quantity of nutritious food to eat.
- Children should not continually complain of being hungry.

Adequate Shelter

- Housing should be structurally safe and free of exposed wiring.
- Housing should have adequate heat.
- Housing should be clean and sanitary.
- Housing should have running water and appropriate toilet facilities.

Source: Adapted from Broome County Child Abuse Council: Mandated Reporter Training Materials, Broome County, New York.

should be and what the role of government is in providing for such needs. Current discussion among scholars and professionals concerns the promotion of child neglect as a serious social problem.

We cannot continue to ignore the statistics. The most recent estimates of child neglect, based on the 1996 National Incidence Study (Sedlak & Broadhurst, 1996), indicate that there has been a 163 percent increase in the number of children who have been physically neglected and a 188 percent increase in the number of children who have been emotionally neglected since the first study was conducted in 1986.

These documented increases, coupled with the consistent findings that about half of all victims of substantiated child abuse cases have suffered from a form of child neglect (National Center on Child Abuse and Neglect [NCCAN], 1994), should be enough to draw attention to the plight of neglected children. However, our apparent lack of attention to neglect continues to prevail. In fact, Wolock and Horowitz (1984) coined the expression "neglect of neglect" to describe our lack of attention to the problem, and Dubowitz (1994) demonstrated that we continue to ignore this form of child maltreatment.

The irony is that early identification of child neglect may in fact be one viable way of preventing the physical and sexual abuse of children. Why have we neglected the neglected child? Some would suggest that the strong association between neglect and poverty is so politically charged that it prevents us from a national dialogue on the issue (Wolock &Horowitz, 1984). Nelson (1984) charges that neglect was purposefully left out of early definitions of child maltreatment as a "conscious strategy to dissociate efforts against abuse from unpopular poverty programs" (p. 15). When one considers the other political debates taking place on the periphery of welfare reform, such as universal health care, affordable housing and child care, and educational equity, confronting child neglect would mean that we would have to confront a whole host of other problems. The bottom line is that parents need adequate financial resources to provide adequate child care, health care, and housing for their children.

Additionally, neglect often lacks a degree of crisis or "drama", unlike other forms of child abuse (Dubowitz, 1994; Wolock & Horowitz, 1984). It is far more difficult to ignore a 2-year-old child's broken arm and black and blue eye than to ignore a 2-year-old child playing quietly and happily in his or her front yard without adult supervision. However, the reality is that both children are at serious risk for harm.

Or perhaps the issue goes deeper. Maybe the lack of social power and equity that children experience in the broader social, political, and economic landscape is responsible for our lack of attention to all of their needs. Children have no social, economic, or political power to influence the world around them. Like those who suffer from mental illness and disability, we expect children to suffer quietly, silently, and without interference from others outside the family.

/// Consequences of Child Abuse and Neglect

Children who experience child maltreatment are at risk of serious developmental consequences and, obviously, can even be at serious risk of death. This section explores the effects of child abuse and neglect on the natural developmental growth process of children. It also examines some of the potential dangers to the cognitive, affective, and physical growth of children and discusses the most destructive consequence, child death.

Child Fatalities

The worst consequence of child maltreatment is child death. *Child fatality* generally refers to children who have died as a direct result or from the effects of abuse, neglect, or both. Child fatalities, although relatively infrequent compared with the number of children at risk for death, occur with enough frequency to warrant concern. The U.S. Advisory Board on Child Abuse and Neglect (USABCAN, 1995) estimates that about 2,000 children every year, or about 5 children every day, die as a result of child maltreatment. A total of 1,200 children died in 2000 as a result of maltreatment (Administration for Children and Families [ACF], 2002).

The difficulty in accurately estimating the problem resides in the fact that some child deaths due to abuse or neglect are difficult to differentiate from accidental deaths. For example, it is difficult to distinguish a child who has been purposefully suffocated from one who has died as a result of SIDS, or a child who was thrown or pushed from a child who dies from an accidental fall. Additionally, it is often difficult to determine whether or not better adult supervision could eliminate child deaths due to fire, accidental poisoning, and drowning.

Children most at risk for death due to maltreatment are the very young (age 5 and younger), mainly because of their size and their inability to care for or defend themselves. They also lack the internal controls to be able to supervise themselves safely. For example, of the 1,200 children who died in 2000 as a result of maltreatment, 85 percent of the children were younger than 6 years of age (ACF, 2002).

Many communities have implemented Child Fatality Review Teams to better coordinate efforts to investigate child deaths. Review teams often are composed of a variety of members from different disciplines, such as physicians, child welfare workers, social workers, prosecutors, police, and medical examiners. They work together to uncover the underlying causes of child deaths in order to improve the child protection system and community supports (NCCANI, 1999). After careful review of child fatality cases, teams are able to determine how and why children die and identify ways in which communities can improve to save future lives. Developing prevention recommendations based on actual data can play a significant role in educating communities about keeping their children safe. The Houston-Harris County Child Fatality Review Team (2002) in Texas says it best: "a community that does not know how its children are dying cannot save them."

The National Center on Child Fatality Review (NCFR), originally funded by the U.S. Department of Justice, is housed in Los Angeles County, California, under the auspices of the Interagency Council on Child Abuse and Neglect (ICAN). The NCFR has been instrumental in the growth of review teams nationwide. Today, many states have embedded legislative statutes that require the review of child fatalities and have institutionalized review teams as a matter of course. For example, in Texas, 42 local teams are in operation, representing 139 counties and 80 percent of the state's child population, as the result of a statewide committee formed in 1994 to study the child fatality response system in Texas. In 1998 and 1999, the teams reviewed more than half of the 8,000 child deaths among Texas residents and were able to make specific legislative and preventive recommendations to reduce child death (Texas Department of Health [TDH], 1999). In Arizona, the Child Fatality Review Program has been reviewing child deaths since 1994 and has begun to see a decrease in preventable child fatalities since its first report, in 1995. In 2000, out of 893 deaths reviewed, 247 child deaths were considered preventable (Arizona Department of Health Services [ADHS], 2001).

Cognitive Growth

Cognitive growth refers to the process by which the mind develops and how the mind works as the child grows and learns (Charlesworth, 1992). Another way to define cognitive development is as the process by which the child acquires knowledge and the way in which the child goes about using the knowledge he or she has gained. Cognitive development involves growth and learning in the following areas: language development, concept development, intelligence, memory, perception, attention, information processing, and creativity.

At birth, the brain is the most underdeveloped organ in the human body; it continues to evolve as a result of both genetics and environmental factors. In fact, "while genetics do set the broad parameters, actual matter in the brain is built—or not—by sound, sight, smell, touch, and movement from the outside environment" (Karr-Morse & Wiley, 1997, p. 24). In other words, the brain is dependent on stimulation from the outside world in order to generate the connections necessary to perform all of its functions.

By the eighteenth week of pregnancy, the fetus has developed all of the 100 to 200 billion brain cells that it will ever have. However, the dendrites and synapses, the structures that connect the cells, only begin forming at birth. These connecting structures are critical for brain cell functioning and provide the network through which various regions of the brain can communicate. The dendrites and synapses depend on stimulation from the child's environment for their growth and maintenance. For example, seeing objects, colors, and people will stimulate the development of dendrite and synaptic growth in the visual cortex; hearing voices and music builds the auditory cortex (Karr-Morse & Wiley, 1997). If the newly formed dendrites and synapses are not used or stimulated, they are "pruned"(Lowenthal, 1999)—in other words, they die.

We now know that the first thirty-three months of life are the most critical to developing the highly sophisticated brain wiring system and that child maltreatment during this period has long-term effects on a child's neurodevelopment. Children who lack appropriate sensory experiences through sight, sound, smell, touch, and movement are likely to suffer life-long developmental delays (Karr-Morse & Wiley, 1997).

Additionally, children who experience chronic stress are likely to produce higher levels of a steroid hormone called cortisol, which, in high levels, can kill brain cells and decrease the number of synapses (Lowenthal, 1999). Children who chronically live in fear of maltreatment are continually placed in a "fight or flight" response pattern, with the brain being saturated with "fear" neurochemicals. This causes the brain to reorganize itself to survive, ultimately leaving these children at great risk for emotional, behavioral, learning, and physical problems (Terr, 1990). There is also growing evidence that the changes made to brain chemistry during this critical period of development may in fact become encoded in the genes and passed on to new generations (Karr-Morse & Wiley, 1997).

Children who experience trauma may also dissociate as a coping mechanism. Dissociation is a response to trauma in which children, who cannot fight back, separate their painful experiences from their conscious awareness (Lowenthal, 1999). We all dissociate from time to time. Have you ever been found daydreaming? Or driven your car several miles without recalling actually driving? These are examples of dissociation. The body is doing one thing, and the mind is in another place. The child who is powerless against abuse learns early on how to use dissociation as a mechanism to protect the self from the pain.

Dissociation also affects brain chemistry. In dissociation, blood pressure and heart rate decrease, and dopamine secretion increases. These changes produce a calming effect on the brain. This reaction in effect alters one's sense of time, space, and self (Karr-Morse & Wiley, 1997). Although dissociation is an effective tool for children in surviving trauma, when taken to the extreme, it results in serious long-term developmental consequences for the child, including problems with memory, personality, and identity. Common problems associated with dissociation from early trauma include various forms of amnesia, dissociative identity disorder (formerly known as multiple personality disorder; Kemp, 1998), personality disorders, and hallucinations (Terr, 1991).

Affective Development

Affective development refers to the child's developing emotions, personality characteristics, sense of morality, and social behavior. Development in the affective domain is very closely tied to cognitive development; therefore, child maltreatment affects not only neurological functions but also the social abilities of children.

One of the most devastating periods of time in which a child can experience child abuse or neglect is in infancy. Infancy is a critical period of development for children in forming bonds with their caregivers. These bonds, called attachment, ultimately promote a sense of security, trust, and self-esteem for the child, which will become critical to his or her ability to interact with others later.

The attachment process affects the child's ability to cope with stress, regulate emotions, and form loving relationships with others (Lowenthal, 1999). Attachment to adult caregivers also provides the child with the support to explore and learn from their environments. Children who experience disruptions in the attachment process are unable to develop safe, secure relationships with others. They often grow up feeling inadequate and angry (Lowenthal, 1999), are less independent, have decreased cognitive abilities relative to children who have secure attachments (Bjorklund & Bjorklund, 1992), and are hampered from attaining readiness to learn (Aber & Allen, 1987). Additionally, research evidence suggests that a poor mother-infant relationship is the primary process by which intergenerational transmission of maltreatment occurs (Morton & Browne, 1998).

Child maltreatment affects a child's ability to regulate his or her affect and emotions. Although maltreated children are capable of describing other people's feelings, they are often detached from their own. They attempt to find relief from their feelings by numbing, which may result in aggressive behaviors, self-mutilation, suicide, or other antisocial behaviors. Intimacy with others presents a threatening environment for the maltreated child, and he or she may go to extremes to avoid being close to others. They demonstrate their discomfort with social interactions by exhibiting inappropriate behavior, withdrawing, and avoiding eye contact (Lowenthal, 1999). Consequently, they are not accepted by their peers. Some research suggests that the greater the severity and chronicity of maltreatment, the greater the disturbance in peer relationships and self-esteem (Bolger, Patterson, & Kupersmidt, 1998).

As you can well imagine, children who experience these types of problems as a result of maltreatment have a difficult time in school. Their social behaviors and lack of self-esteem, coupled with their decreased cognitive functioning, put them at risk for a whole host of academic problems. As maltreated children grow older, the impact on affective development becomes greater. They appear less motivated to achieve at school and are at increased risk for dropping out (Lowenthal, 1999).

Physical Development

Physical development is the process by which the body and its parts grow and mature. Motor growth is also part of the physical developmental process. Motor growth refers to the development of skill in the use of the body and its parts (Charlesworth, 1992). Child maltreatment affects the natural progression of physical development in a number of ways, creating a myriad of short-term and long-term health risks for children.

Failure to thrive and *nonorganic failure to thrive* are medical diagnoses designated for infants whose parents fail to meet their nutritional requirements and fail to provide a nurturing parent-child relationship. *Failure to thrive* is often considered a misleading term because it can be caused by disease or by a nonorganic cause; therefore, many physicians are more readily using the term *nonorganic failure to thrive* to refer to children whose conditions are due to neglect (Wallace, 1999). Children exhibit low weight, height, and a small head circumference when compared with other infants their age. Children suffering from nonorganic failure to thrive are emaciated and pale, have decreased muscle mass and little subcutaneous fat, and are lethargic, dispirited, and inactive (Wallace, 1999). Although failure to thrive and nonorganic failure to thrive can be medically treated, long-term studies suggest that these children continue to be plagued by growth problems, school failure, and psychological problems as they grow older (Peacock & Forrest, 1985).

Child sexual abuse can affect the physical development of a young child by injuring the sexual organs, passing on sexually transmitted diseases, or both. Children who have been sexually abused may experience genital or anal itching, pain, swelling, burning, bruising, or bleeding. They may also experience recurring urinary tract or yeast infections and chronic sore throats. Sexual abuse can also result in pregnancy and the spread of sexually transmitted diseases, such as gonococcal or syphilitic infections and HIV (Wallace, 1999). Serious injury to the sexual organs and disease can also cause permanent infertility, genital abnormalities, or both. Sexual abuse also has been linked to enuresis (bed-wetting; Trickett & Putnam, 1991) and somatic complaints (e.g., headaches and stomachaches). Additionally, children suffer from acute and chronic stress symptoms, promoting stress-induced illnesses and psychological problems.

Child physical abuse causes injuries, such as bone fractures, burns, and head and internal injuries that result in both short- and long-term medical problems for the child. There is some evidence that child maltreatment results in delayed motor development in infancy (Lyons-Ruth, Connell, & Zoll, 1989) and lower physical competence in early childhood (Vondra, Barnett, & Cicchetti, 1990).

Differential Impact on Development

Not all children who are maltreated experience the effects on their development that we describe here. Some children experience only minor effects, whereas others have been profoundly damaged by abuse or neglect. Why are some children more acutely affected?

Although we cannot predict which children will suffer more damaging effects from child maltreatment, we do know that the severity of the abuse, the frequency of the abuse, the age of the victim, and the victim's relationships with other adults all are factors in child maltreatment outcomes. The more severe and frequent the abuse, the more likely the child will suffer devastating consequences.

/// Chapter Summary

In this chapter we covered a variety of issues and concerns relating to the maltreatment of children. First, we explored the social and historical context in which society views and treats children. Although children in contemporary American society are still at risk for maltreatment, they have a better chance today of living longer, healthier lives than was true in the past. We also considered the importance of viewing child treatment and policy in the context of the economic, political, and social conditions of the time. As times have changed, so has our treatment of children and our policies to protect them.

Second, we looked at the various forms of child maltreatment. We discussed the generally accepted definitions of the physical, sexual, and emotional maltreatment of children. In addition, we explored some of the issues that are currently being debated within the professional community regarding these different forms of child maltreatment. Third, we explored some of the short- and long-term consequences of child maltreatment. We looked at the variety of ways in which a child's development is affected by maltreatment, noting that not all children experience the same consequences.

We hope that this chapter has helped you to understand how very important being a parent is. Whether you currently have children or are planning to have children in the future, your behaviors as a parent are critical to the health and well-being of your children. Equally important is the role of the professional in identifying, treating, and preventing this form of family violence. Because we know that early intervention and treatment are critical to helping families heal, it is imperative that all professions recognize their responsibility in solving this social problem.

On a broader level, we hope that this chapter has inspired readers to more fully explore the economic, political, and social conditions that perpetuate child abuse and neglect. Other, bigger social issues have as great a part to play in child abuse and neglect as parents do. Issues such as poverty, lack of affordable health care, lack of affordable day care, lack of parent education, educational inequity, and the lack of social and political power of children should be examined as we move toward the future development of child welfare policy.

/// Recommended Web Sites

Child Quest International
    http://www.childquest.org
Child Welfare
    http://www.childwelfare.com
Child Welfare League of America
    http://www.cwla.org

Join Together Online
    http://www.jointogether.org
National Center on Child Fatality Review Teams
    http://ican-ncfr.org
National Center on Shaken Baby Syndrome
    http://www.dontshake.com
National Clearinghouse on Child Abuse and Neglect Information
    http://www.calib.com/nccanch
National Organization on Fetal Alcohol Syndrome
    http://www.nofas.org

4 /// Intimate Partner Abuse

Suzanne arrives home from the grocery store to find a desperate message on her answering machine from a woman named Debbie. Debbie is the adult daughter of one of Suzanne's tenants. Debbie explained that her mother, Cathy, has been gone for several weeks and has not made contact with Debbie. Cathy, whose husband is a truck driver, often goes on long runs with her husband, but she always touches base with her daughters to let them know where she is. Debbie is particularly concerned because she has not heard from her mother and because the bouts of physical abuse her mother has been enduring over the course of the past year have been getting worse. Debbie tells Suzanne that she would like to search her mother's home to make sure that her mother is not dead in the house and asks Suzanne to come to the property with the key.

Suzanne arrives at the property, greeted by Debbie and a police officer. The police officer takes the key and does a preliminary search of the home. Cathy is not found. The officer interviews one of the neighbors and confirms that Cathy was seen leaving in the truck with her husband approximately 2 weeks before. Cathy appeared to be leaving of her own accord. The police officer explained that apparently no crime has been committed, and he leaves the scene. Debbie and Suzanne remain at the house talking. Debbie confides in Suzanne that her mother's husband is a drinker and often beats her mother. She explains that his drinking has been getting worse in the past year and that she is in total fear for her mother's life. Her mother, disabled from a previous work injury, is living on disability and is economically dependent on her husband. Debbie has pleaded with her mother to leave Stan, and at various times Cathy has tried to leave him, but eventually he is able to sweet-talk her back into his life. Debbie believes the beatings are getting worse. Debbie and her sisters have tried to talk to their mother about the situation to no avail. Now Debbie is unable to sleep with worry that her mother's life is in danger and says, "My mother has no idea how her victimization is affecting the rest of the family." Suzanne refers her to the local crime victim assistance program and suggests that she at least get some assistance for herself.

Six days later, Suzanne finds another message on her answering machine from Debbie: "My mom is finally home, she is OK. She didn't call me while she was on the road because she did not want to deal with what I would say to her. She is alive today, but I still worry about tomorrow." Three months later, Cathy and her husband Stan moved out of the property without paying their last month's rent. When Suzanne went to the house to clean it for the next tenant, she found the home bruised. Windows were broken, and two doors had holes in them that seemed to be made by a fist. One whole wall was covered in a substance that appeared to be Coca-Cola, as if someone threw a whole cup of soda at someone else, draping the wall in liquid. Small amounts of blood appeared to dot the kitchen floor.

The case of Cathy and Stan is not unique. This couple seemed to be madly in love, yet were hiding a deep secret from the rest of the world. Stan physically and emotionally abuses his wife, especially when he is drunk. Cases such as this are common in intimate relationships, and they affect not only the primary victim but also other family members and friends and the community at large. Criminal justice, public health, and social welfare officials are keenly aware of the toll such abuse takes on victims and their children. Much of the attention given to domestic violence has concerned the social and political context of gender, whereby men have been given social permission to exert coercive control over women. Our understanding of battering must include a thorough acknowledgment of the role gender socialization plays in interpersonal violence (Eigenberg, 2001), especially because the vast majority of cases of interpersonal violence involve violence against women by their male partners. However, we would be remiss if we did not use a more inclusive approach to battering, exploring the multidimensional dynamics of abuse between intimate partners. Our intention is to look beyond men beating women and acknowledge the variety of ways in which intimate partners are paired in modern society.

Accordingly, our approach investigates interpersonal violence on a number of levels, including historical perspectives, current policy issues, the dynamics of power in intimate relationships, the various forms abuse takes within relationships, the context of social position in relation to a broad range of couple relationships, consequences of abuse, and the social conditions that perpetuate violence.

/// Putting Intimate Partner Abuse in Historical and Social Context

A thorough understanding of intimate partner violence requires us to examine social and political trends and their influences on family life and interpersonal relationships. Therefore, we begin this chapter with a discussion of the evolution of public policy and the many social and political forces responsible for the development of our current thinking on intimate partner abuse. Although intimate partner abuse continues to be a pervasive social problem in the United States, an ideological shift has moved us from embracing the belief that a man has a "God given right to control his woman" to a time in which we consider such acts criminal.

Early Policy

Although social changes have recently evolved, efforts to cope with battering have appeared throughout the history of the United States. For example, in the 1600s, the Puritans placed restrictions on violence toward women and children. The Puritans did not object to violence in and of itself, for men had the responsibility to ensure that the family remained disciplined. Although some level of violence was considered necessary, legislation was enacted to create boundaries for what was appropriate under the watchful eye of God. However, there is little evidence that many men were actually punished for such law violations (Pleck, 1979). Pleck (1987) notes that charges of domestic violence were often resolved with a visit from a minister. Additionally, the demonic beliefs of the time (in particular, the fear of witchcraft) placed a great deal of social power in the hands of abusive men, who could easily explain battering as necessary to combat the practice of witchcraft.

By 1700, the enforcement of Puritan policies regarding domestic violence was virtually nonexistent (Pleck, 1979). The following excerpt from an 1864 case illustrates the ideology of the courts:

> Unless some permanent injury be inflicted, or there be an excess of violence, or such degree of cruelty as shows that it is inflicted to gratify his own bad passions, the law will not invade the domestic forum or go behind the curtain. It prefers to leave the parties to themselves, as the best mode of introducing them to make the matter up and live together as man and wife should. (State v. Black, 60 N.C. 266, 267–268, 1864)

Men were allowed to chastise or "correct" their wives within certain boundaries until the courts overturned such rulings in Alabama and Massachusetts in 1871 (Gelles, 1997). A renewed interest in the appropriateness of such treatment of women is likely to have been influenced by the advocacy of the temperance and women's suffrage movements. The temperance movement was concerned solely with the evil influences of alcohol on family life, raising questions about the rights of women to live free of "drunkards." Although their focus on battering was purely based on the relationship between drinking and violence, temperance advocates ultimately were successful in the development of divorce reform (Eigenberg, 2001). Women's suffrage groups were also instrumental in eventually gaining women's rights in a number of areas, including the rights to vote, to own property, and not to be considered the legal property of their husbands.

By the end of the century, three states had adopted legislation outlawing wife beating: Delaware (1881), Maryland (1882), and Oregon (1886). However, as Buzawa and Buzawa (1990) so aptly point out, several recurring themes continue to present themselves as relevant to more recent legislative connections regarding domestic violence. First, although laws may exist on paper, there is little connection to how such laws are actually implemented in practice. Criminal sanctions were rarely imposed, and when they were, the cases were generally of such gross conduct that the court could not ignore them. Second, when official punishment was enacted, it was often disproportionately used against minority groups and the poor, perhaps as a means to place additional social control over "undesirable" groups. Third, the specific use of the whipping post was the typical punishment of the day. The use of public humiliation may have served as a precursor to modern-day mandatory-arrest policies.

However, this brief period of reform was slowly dissolved by the beginning of the next century. More salient political issues, such as women's right to vote, World War I, the Great Depression, prohibition, and so forth, took center stage. Additionally, concern over the coercive power of the police began to grow, helping to develop a social respect for family privacy (Rothman, 1980). Victims who did attempt to utilize the criminal justice system were often met by disinterested police officers and prosecutors unwilling to move domestic cases forward. Ethnic, religious, and cultural practices also took a "hands off" approach. Victims were left with virtually no legal recourse and little social support. Domestic violence, although no longer legally sanctioned, continued behind the veil of family privacy.

The Development of Contemporary Policy: The 1970s Through the 1990s

It was not until the 1970s that a renewed interest in domestic violence resurfaced. Several forces converged over the next several decades, facilitating vast changes in public policy and professional practice regarding domestic violence. Advocacy, research, and legal precedent connected to create what has been referred to as the "battered women's movement" or the "domestic violence movement". Although the movement began in Europe in the 1960s, it was only in the 1970s that feminist and grassroots groups began to develop in the United States to address the issue of battering (Pagelow, 1984).

Women's Advocacy Groups

The women's movement of the 1970s also brought violence against women to the attention of public. Women's-rights advocates rallied nationwide to educate the public about domestic violence and sexual assault. Pagelow

(1984) credits the movement's early start to the results of a small study administered in an affluent county in Maryland that indicated high rates of wife abuse. The study, reported to the National Organization for Women (NOW), spurred the creation of a special task force that was charged with taking the issue nationwide and promoting the establishment of shelters to protect women. As a result of feminist activism, shelters, hotlines, and battered women's advocacy groups were created in many communities throughout the United States by the end of the 1970s.

Advocates were relentless in their pursuit to develop specialized services for victims, to change the way in which the police and the courts dealt with battering, and to educate the public to the plight of abused women. Activists also called for scientific research (Pagelow, 1984). Proving the power of grassroots initiatives, the battered women's movement was set in motion by the end of the 1970s, generating dialogue and much public debate.

At the same time, crime victims' rights advocates were demanding that the criminal justice system attend to the needs of crime victims. Although the crime victims' movement is usually not credited as being influential to the early success of the domestic violence movement, we believe it is important to acknowledge the work of these advocates as well. Working parallel to the domestic violence movement, crime victims' advocates were instrumental in getting the police, courts, and state legislatures to reexamine the treatment of victims in the criminal justice system. Advocates and their political partners were successful in moving states to develop crime victim compensation programs (discussed in chapter 8), the later passage of the Victims of Crime Act (VOCA) of 1984, and other services for victims of crime, ultimately supporting the needs of domestic violence victims and their children. Crime victims' rights advocates provided another venue in which the rights and needs of battered women could be raised in many political and social domains.

Research/Data Collection

Gathering official statistics from the criminal justice system and the medical profession proved to be difficult for advocates. Del Martin (1976) wrote one the first known books on wife beating in the United States, noting that hospitals, police reports, court records, and such do not specify acts of violence toward intimate partners or family members as a specific category. Crimes and injuries, when they were documented, were counted as assaults, aggravated assaults, harassment, homicides, and the like in official records. Therefore, official records were unable to provide the type of documentation that advocates sought to cement their arguments that battering is a social problem, not a problem between individuals who suffer from some sort of psychological problem (Pagelow, 1984).

However, within a few years, the grassroots efforts of the advocates were validated by prevalence studies on domestic violence. For example, surveys conducted by Gelles (1988), Straus and Gelles (1986), and Straus, Gelles, and Steinmetz (1980) confirmed that domestic violence occurred with great frequency in the United States. A proliferation of research and scholarly writings also drew considerable attention to the issue (Fleming, 1976; Roberts; 1981, 1984; Walker; 1979, 1984).

Legal Precedents

Along with the advocacy of grassroots organizations and the development of research regarding battering, legal precedents set during this period also influenced the development of reform. *Scott v. Hart* and *Raguz v. Chandler* were class action suits brought by domestic violence victims against the Oakland Police Department (*Scott v. Hart*) and the prosecuting attorney (*Raguz v. Chandler*). These cases are the first to challenge law enforcement practices regarding domestic violence. The plaintiffs' claims were based in part on violations of the equal protection clause of the Fourteenth Amendment. They argued that there was no basis for not affording female victims of domestic violence full protection under the law simply because they were married to the assailant. Both cases were settled prior to trial by consent decrees (Hathaway, 1986), in which the departments agreed to make certain changes in their policies and procedures.

Bruno v. Codd (419 N.Y.S. 2d 901 1979) brought about similar charges by a group of 12 battered women against several city officials, including the New York City Police Department. The common charge by the plaintiffs included the customary practice by the police department of ignoring complaints of abuse made by women who had valid court orders of protection. The plaintiffs alleged that "police officers . . . uniformly refused to take acton even if the evidence of the assault is unmistakable and undenied . . . solely because the victim is the wife of her assailant" (Hathaway, 1986, p. 670). As in the previous cases, *Bruno v. Codd* was resolved by consent decree. The New York City Police Department agreed to respond to all domestic calls immediately when a victim stated that there had been a violation of an order of protection (Anderson, 1985).

These cases laid the groundwork for judicial review of police practice; however, the consent decrees agreed on do not have the same impact as a formal court decision, thus limiting the scope of influence across the nation. However, two landmark cases did subsequently surface, ultimately helping to bring about instrumental changes in the legal response to battering. Both of these cases illustrate the types of police response typical of the time. In *Thurman v. City of Torrington* (595 F. Supp. 1521 (D.Conn. 1984) and *Sorichetti v. City of New York* (492 N.Y.S. 2d 591 1985) the courts recognized the lack of policy and strength of custom in police response to domestic violence incidents and the unconstitutional treatment often given to victims by the police.

Tracey Thurman sued the City of Torrington, Connecticut, for damages inflicted by her husband Charles Thurman on June 10, 1983. Her suit included 24 officers of the City of Torrington Police Department for violating the equal protection clause of the Fourteenth Amendment. On that day in June, Charles Thurman approached Tracey at the home of one her friends, where she was staying. Tracey phoned police and requested that Charles be arrested for violating the court order she had received in May 1983. Prior to June 10, Tracey had filed many complaints against her husband, requesting the police to arrest him. The police repeatedly ignored her pleas. Believing the police were on their way, Tracey went outside to talk to Charles for fear he would force his way into the home and place everyone else in danger. He began to stab Tracey repeatedly in the chest, neck, and throat. When the police eventually arrived, Charles dropped the knife and ran into the house to get his son. As police officers watched, he put his son on Tracey and kicked her in the head. The police continued to stand by while Charles continued to kick and threaten her, and it was not until she was placed on a stretcher that the officers put Charles under arrest.

Tracey brought action for violations of the Fifth and Ninth Amendments, and the equal protection clause of the Fourteenth Amendment. The court chose to focus on the Fourteenth Amendment challenge. Tracey argued that the Torrington police had consistently protected persons who were abused by someone with whom they had no domestic relationship far more fully than they protected women who were abused by their husbands or boyfriends. The district court found that:

> a pattern or practice of affording inadequate protection, or no protection at all, to women who have complained of having been abused by their husbands . . . is tantamount to an administration classification used to implement the law in a discriminatory fashion. (595 F. Supp. 1527).

The court further agreed that Tracey had proven that a police "custom" had existed that showed complete indifference to domestic violence victims' needs for protection. A jury awarded Tracey $2.3 million. She eventually settled for $1.9 million when the city agreed to forgo an appeal. The Thurman case is the first reported case in which the court identified police practice regarding domestic violence as gender discrimination in violation of the equal protection clause (Hathaway, 1986). Charles Thurman was convicted and sentenced to a 20-year term in prison; he was subsequently released in 1991 after serving 7 years of his sentence. Today, Tracey Thurman Motuzick still struggles, with the right side of her body partially paralyzed and her vocal cords damaged (Canfield, 2000). Interestingly, Charles Thurman appears to have continued battering. Box 4.1 refers to a recent newspaper article that reports that Thurman was sentenced for the violation of an order of protection.

In the case of *Sorichetti v. City of New York*, the plaintiffs were 6-year-old Dina Sorichetti and her mother, Josephine. They sued the New York

---

Box 4.1 /// Thurman Sentenced for Violating Court Order

In January 2000, Charles Thurman was sentenced to 1 year of probation for violating a court order of protection. The woman had an order of protection because of her claims that he had choked her, sexually assaulted her, and threatened her life.

In November 1999, Thurman pulled his car up alongside the mother of his 6-year-old son in Massachusetts. He honked his car horn at his son and waved to him. The assistant district attorney sought the maximum allowable sentence for Thurman; however, the Northampton District Court Judge sentenced him to 1 year of probation.

Sources: *The Hartford Courant*, January 27, 2000; *The Boston Globe*, January 28, 2000.

City Police Department to recover damages for injuries inflicted by Dina's father, Frank Sorichetti, and for loss of service for Josephine. Despite Josephine's protective order and the police department's extensive knowledge of Frank's violent behavior, the police failed to take any action in November of 1975. The plaintiffs argued that the New York City Police Department failed to provide reasonable protection to Dina as required under New York state law.

In November of 1975, Josephine received an additional court order of protection from Family Court for another year. The protection order stipulated Frank's right to visit with his daughter but required him to pick up and drop off Dina for visitation at the 43rd Precinct. The weekend after the final order was issued, Frank picked up Dina and threatened to kill her mother. Josephine went back into the police precinct to notify the officers of his threat. They told her there was nothing they could do. At the end of the visitation period, Frank did not arrive as scheduled. Josephine pleaded with the police to send a car to Frank's residence. Lieutenant Leon Granello dismissed her order of protection as "only a piece of paper" that "means nothing" and told her to wait outside. As time passed, her pleas continued to go unnoticed. Even after the insistence of Officer John Hobbie, who had prior experience dealing with Frank, Lieutenant Granello rejected the suggestion to send a police car to Frank's home. At 7:00 p.m., the lieutenant told Josephine to leave her number and go home, and she did.

At about the same time, Frank's sister arrived at home to find Frank passed out, surrounded by empty bottles of alcohol and a pill bottle. She also found a severely injured Dina. Between 6:55 and 7:00 p.m., Frank had attacked Dina with a fork, knife, and screwdriver and had attempted to saw off her leg. Police arrived to find Dina in a coma. She was subsequently hospitalized for 40 days and remains permanently disabled (1985 N.Y. LEXIS 15925).

Frank was convicted of attempted murder. A jury awarded $3 million for Dina and $40,000 to Josephine. The award was modified by the Appellate Division of the Supreme Court in the First Judicial Department to $2 million for Dina. After appellate review, the court upheld the modified award based on two issues. First, the court determined that a special relationship did exist between the police, Josephine, and Dina. Therefore, the jury could properly consider whether or not the police had afforded Dina reasonable protection. A "special relationship" must exist between the individual and the police in order for police to be liable for negligence. This special relationship was evident in that Josephine had a valid court order of protection, that the police had prior knowledge of Frank's violent behavior, that Josephine pleaded with police to respond on the day of the assault, and that Josephine had a reasonable expectation of police protection. Moreover, the court affirmed that the city had breached its duty of care and that this breach of duty was the proximate cause of Dina's injuries (1985 N.Y. LEXIS 15925).

Cases such as the ones we have presented demonstrate a number of things. First, they clearly illustrate the blatant lack of attention on the part of law enforcement to the safety of women in battering relationships. Second, they provide the impetus for change. Since these cases, state legislatures and police departments have made vast changes in their customary practices and formal policies regarding domestic violence. We discuss some of these changes later in this chapter.

By the 1990s the movement was in full swing. Sweeping changes had occurred on many levels, including law enforcement policies, court practices, state and federal policy and funding, and victim and abuser services. For example, Roberts and Kurst-Swanger (2002a) note the growth of specialized domestic violence units, the use of technology to protect victims and to monitor offenders, and the evolution of coordinated community responses to intimate partner violence as important law enforcement changes. Keilitz (2002) reports the development of specialized court processes to draw special attention to the problem of intimate partner violence, including case coordination systems, specialized intake units, specialized calendars, and utilization of specialized judges. Barasch and Lutz (2002) describe innovative programming developed by the Pace Women's Justice Center, such as Project DETER, the Family Court Legal Program (FCLP), and the Center's Civil Legal Assistance Practicum and Public Service Announcement Agenda. These four programs provide unique legal support to battered women, including civil legal services that are available 24 hours a day, 7 days a week; partnering legal and medical professionals to assist women with medical concerns; and providing ongoing public service announcements regarding domestic violence.

Today, we view battering in a variety of contexts, beyond simply that of men beating women. Battering in gay and lesbian couples and the victimization of men are gaining the attention of researchers and service providers. The next section is devoted to a more detailed discussion of these changes and the issues that are currently being debated by advocates, public policy makers, and practitioners.

/// Contemporary Policy: The Era of Reform

As we mentioned earlier, the battered women's movement called for political, legal, and social change in reference to the way battering has been viewed and dealt with. A number of issues for reform have been raised. Although the resolutions of these issues are still being pursued, widespread changes have occurred in recent years. The following is a brief summary of some of the efforts currently under way to address the intervention and prevention of intimate partner violence. These include attempts to officially measure the prevalence of intimate partner abuse, the development of more formalized victim service systems and advocacy programs, changes in how the police and the courts intervene in violent homes, and the expansion of legislation to better protect victims and ensure accountability of offenders.

Official Measurement of Intimate Partner Violence

As has been mentioned earlier in this chapter, official measurement of the prevalence and extent of battering did not exist prior to the 1970s. A number of issues are responsible for our lack of knowledge in this area. First, crimes of domestic violence often go unreported by victims. For obvious reasons—fear of future attacks by the abuser and the inability of the system to adequately protect women—women often choose not to report incidents of violence to authorities. Gay and lesbian partners and male victims have been even more reluctant to call the police. Police did not consistently document such calls, and when crimes were officially documented, they were hidden in official crime statistics and counted as harassments, assaults, criminal mischief, and so forth. Additionally, in some instances, only women who were married to their partners were considered to be victims of domestic violence. Consequently, no reliable source of measurement has been available in the past to document the extent and severity of battering in intimate partner relationships. Compounding the lack of data available from crime statistics is the confusion that arises from disparate research findings regarding the issues. Recent changes in the way victimization surveys are administered, coupled with a change in how the Uniform Crime Report is collected, will provide us with a better understanding of just how prevalent battering is.

The National Incident-Based Reporting System (NIBRS) is a revised version of the Uniform Crime Reporting system that includes more detail regarding the characteristics of incidents known to the police. The NIBRS, although not currently available nationwide, provides the FBI with the ability to more closely examine the nature of violent crime, in particular family violence. To date, the volume of data collected by the NIBRS is too small to be considered an official measurement of crime. For example, the FBI conducted a small analysis using data submitted to the NIBRS in 1995 regarding incidents of family violence. A total of nine states that participated in the NIBRS system reported a total of 836,846 incidents of Group A offenses (that include 22 crime categories that are considered serious, frequent, and represented nationwide). These incidents, on further investigation, contained information on a total of 889,573 victims, with 925,812 offenses actually being committed, involving a total of 936,828 offenders (Federal Bureau of Investigation [FBI], 2000). These data illustrate the level of complexity inherent in incidents of crime, especially incidents involving family violence. This study did not examine incidents in which the relationship of the victim to the offender was that of a boyfriend, girlfriend, ex-spouse, or ex-boyfriend or -girlfriend; therefore, no conclusions can be drawn about the prevalence of battering in intimate partner relationships. However, the potential for future measurement appears attainable. The results of this small study found that 27 percent of all violence occurs in a family setting, with the majority of these offenses being assaultive in nature (FBI, 2000). However, as the NIBRS grows in scope, it will provide us the opportunity to more closely monitor specific crime trends, especially in reference to family violence.

The National Crime Victimization Survey (NCVS), conducted by the Bureau of Justice Statistics (2002), continuously collects data from a nationally representative sample of households in the United States and has redesigned the survey to better account for crimes between intimate partners. The NCVS defines intimate relationships as involving current or former spouses, boyfriends, or girlfriends and may involve individuals of the same gender. According to the NCVS, in 1998, about 1 million violent crimes were committed against persons by their current or former spouses or partners. Women were victims in about 876,340 violent crimes and men were victims in about 157,330 violent crimes by an intimate partner. Therefore, women were victims of intimate partner violence at a rate of about 5 times that of men. The majority of men (68%) and women (65%) were victimized by simple assault, the least serious form of violence. However, a total of 1,830 murders (1,320 were female victims) were attributed to intimate partners, which represents a significant decline from the 3,000 murders in 1976 (Rennison & Welchans, 2000).

The National Violence Against Women (NVAW) Survey, a national telephone survey sponsored by the National Institute of Justice (NIJ) and the Centers for Disease Control and Prevention (CDC), was administered from November 1995 to May 1996 (Tjaden & Thoennes, 2000). The survey was conducted with a representative sample of 8,000 U.S. women and 8,000 U.S. men. Respondents were asked about their experiences as victims of violence. For those respondents who had had victimization experiences, further interviewing was conducted to gather information regarding the characteristics and consequences of their experiences. Victims were asked questions regarding the police response, medical services, restraining orders, and use of the criminal justice system. The survey results indicate that intimate partner violence is a significant social problem. Survey estimates reveal that approximately 1.5 million U.S. women and 834,732 U.S. men are sexually or physically assaulted by an intimate partner each year. Victims suffer multiple attacks, often with significant injuries. Although men are clearly identified as victims, this survey mirrors the findings of the NCVS in that women were significantly more likely than men to report being victimized by an intimate partner (Tjaden & Thoennes, 2000).

These three examples can never tell us the full extent of intimate partner violence; however, they do provide us with documentation that this form of violence is pervasive and should be considered a top public health concern. We need to keep in mind that each time researchers set out to measure something like intimate partner violence, different definitions are used to define the boundaries of the research; therefore, research often yields different results. We may never know the full extent of such violence. However, the early voice of advocates who demanded research regarding the prevalence of battering in intimate relationships has finally begun to take shape. Research is now being conducted on a regular basis, allowing us to compare and contrast the findings and to track trends.

Institutionalization of Advocacy and Services for Victims

Another outgrowth of the domestic violence movement has been the institutionalization of services for victims of domestic violence. Services such as housing, legal assistance, counseling, and hotlines have been instituted in many communities across the United States. Chapter 8 provides a more detailed discussion of victim services. In addition, national advocacy and educational resource materials are available via formal organizations such as the National Network to End Domestic Violence, the National Coalition Against Domestic Violence, the National Center for Victims of Crime, the National Task Force to End Domestic and Sexual Violence Against Women, and the Battered Women's Justice Project. These national organizations have played a critical role in the development of services and public policy. States also have coalitions, task forces, and such that provide an advocacy role at the state level. At the end of this chapter we list available Web sites from national organizations that fight domestic violence.

Brownell and Roberts (2002) surveyed state domestic violence coalitions and found that coalitions have achieved a number of important accomplishments in the past 2 years, including successfully advocating for legal and legislative changes and for funding; implementing training initiatives; improving responsiveness of the health, legal and criminal justice systems; expanding and improving services for victims; promoting informational and educational campaigns; and improving the organizational structure and function of coalitions. They found that the average operating budget of a statewide coalition was $1.4 million, which represents a mix of public and private funding.

The vast array of services for victims and the various national advocacy and resource centers available are a real testament to the grassroots advocacy effort of the 1970s. However, gaps in service for victims still exist nationwide. For example, the National Network to End Domestic Violence (NNEDV, 2001) found in a survey of 25 states that more than 3,000 counties still lacked emergency shelters for victims. Every state in the survey identified areas in which victims had to travel 100 miles or more to reach the nearest shelter.

Funding for programs comes from a variety of federal, state, and local government funding streams. In addition, private foundations and local fund-raising efforts have continued to maintain victim services across the nation. Although great gains have been made in the institutionalization of victim services and advocacy, most advocates would argue that the domestic violence movement remains underfunded. Considering the pervasiveness of intimate partner abuse nationwide, funding should be brought more in line with the actual need. For example, a variety of national domestic violence organizations jointly prepared a document titled "Campaign for Full Funding of the Violence Against Women Act," in which they argue that in fiscal year 2001, Congress authorized approximately $677 million toward programs (NNEDV 2001); however, only $468 million was finally appropriated for spending. Consequently, programs such as the rural domestic violence and child victimization grants, transitional housing program, rape prevention and education program, and shelter and services were ultimately funded below the authorization level (NNEDV, 2001). Funding and service gaps demonstrate the continued need for vigilant advocacy.

Police and Court Responses

The battered women's movement promoted vast changes in the way the police and the courts handle cases of intimate partner abuse. As the Sorichetti and Thurman cases illustrate, the traditional law enforcement response to intimate partner violence has not been productive. Through liability litigation and the development of state and federal law, police departments and prosecutors have been prompted to examine their practices and policies regarding battering. In many ways traditional police custom regarding domestic assaults was further complicated by the fact that many police officers could not make arrests, even if they believed it was appropriate. Most state laws required the police to witness misdemeanor level crimes or to have a court warrant for arrest. Previous laws, therefore, required victims to further pursue the arrest warrant process and limited the legal power of the police at the scene of a battering incident. However, today all states have passed legislation to allow the police to make warrantless arrests in cases in which there is probable cause to believe a domestic crime has occurred (Miller, 1998). We discuss pro-arrest and mandatory arrest policies in greater depth in chapter 8.

Today, police departments across the country have reevaluated their response to cases of domestic assault. With the assistance of federal funding, some police departments have developed rather innovative responses. As Roberts and Kurst-Swanger (2002a) note, changes in the police response have occurred across the continuum, including more specialized law enforcement training and the development of specialized domestic violence units that are responsible for investigating and tracking domestic violence cases. Additionally, many police departments have also applied the use of advanced technology to assist in the development of their cases (e.g., surveillance equipment, DNA profiling, fingerprinting, forensic techniques, computer-aided dispatch and case management systems, etc.) and to guard victims' safety (e.g., electronic monitoring, cellular phones, etc.). Perhaps the most important evolution in the police response is its coordination with the broader community of service providers. Police departments in many jurisdictions have coordinated their response with local victim advocates, prosecutor offices, shelters, hospitals, and family violence prevention programs, among others. Community-wide coordinated interventions, in partnership with a strong, consistent police response, are likely to be the most successful approach to the early intervention of intimate partner violence.

Changes in law enforcement practices are only beginning to be realized and are far from being considered ideal. Two pieces of legislation have been critical in the development of rigorous crime-control approaches to the problem of battering. The Violence Against Women Act of 1994 has provided law enforcement agencies, through the STOP (Services, Training, Officers and Prosecution) grant, monies to develop innovative law enforcement practices for crimes against women. At the same time, many police departments have accessed funding through the COPS (Community Oriented Policing Services) grant program made available through the Violent Crime Control and Law Enforcement Act of 1994. Grant funding has enabled police departments to hire additional staff to more aggressively investigate and intervene in domestic abuse cases. At this time it is unclear how police agencies will address issues of domestic violence once such additional funding is no longer available. Littel, Malefyt, Walker, Tucker, and Buel (1998) maintain that the fundamental components of any law enforcement approach should first and foremost safeguard the victims and their families and promote the accountability of abusers.

Both criminal and civil courts have undergone a transformation in response to intimate partner abuse. Like the police, courts have historically been reluctant to get involved in matters between intimates and have subsequently not taken a forceful role in intervention. However, in the past decade, both criminal and civil courts have begun to review their policies and practices and, with the assistance of new state statutes, have been able to take a more rigorous role in intervention. Keilitz (2002) notes that a number of factors are responsible for the courts taking a more active role in domestic violence intervention. These factors include the development of specialized courts for drug offenses, the therapeutic justice movement, an increase in the number of domestic cases flooding the courts, and a changing philosophy of how courts can be utilized for problem solving. These issues have merged to promote the development of specialized courts, integrated case management systems, and more stringent prosecutorial practices.

A discussion of the role of the courts in intimate partner abuse becomes confused by the fact that one or two court systems may be involved in any given case of abuse. The criminal courts are responsible for prosecuting and sanctioning the offender on behalf of the state. Many criminal courts also have the ability to issue orders of protection, or restraining orders. With the advent of mandatory arrest and pro-arrest policies for law enforcement, many prosecutors have moved to mandatory or "no-drop" prosecutorial policies as well. Civil courts provide relief to victims by issuing of orders of protection and making decisions regarding divorce, separation agreements, maintenance support, and child custody and support. Chapter 8 further discusses specific court strategies.

Another area of reform that has resulted from the domestic violence movement has been the expansion of legal services for victims of intimate partner violence. Domestic violence victims often do not have the financial resources to hire attorneys to work on their behalf, and these programs enable victims to receive legal services at little to no cost. As Roberts and Kurst-Swanger (2002b) note, some law schools have established clinical practicum programs to provide legal services to assist victims of intimate partner abuse. Although prosecutors represent victims in criminal courts, victims often need legal representation in civil courts. Sometimes victims are arrested for an incident and are in need of a defense attorney. Legal services might include assistance with protective orders and custody, divorce and separation agreements. Some of the universities that sponsor such projects are Fordham University School of Law, Northeastern University School of Law, University of Minnesota Law School, University of Missouri School of Law, and Washburn University School of Law (Littel et al., 1998).

Laws

A proliferation of legislation has followed the domestic violence movement, addressing issues such as orders of protection, criminal penalties and procedures, victim compensation, victims' rights, abuser treatment, training mandates, and child custody. States have adopted a wide array of statutory options, demonstrating the complexity of domestic violence intervention.

Some states have taken an aggressive approach, whereas others are more middle of the road. Some states have chosen to revise existing statutes, whereas others have crafted new legislation. In any case, all states have begun to engage in a dialogue about the issues inherent in cases of intimate partner abuse.

The National Council of Juvenile and Family Court Judges (NCJFCJ), with funding from the Conrad N. Hilton Foundation, has continued to track the passage of individual state legislation since the early 1990s. As a result of a 3-year research project to analyze state legislation, the council developed a Model Code on Domestic and Family Violence in 1994 (NCJFCJ, 1999). The model code has served as a blueprint for the development of public policy for communities nationwide. Roberts and Kurst-Swanger (2002b) summarize some of the legislative trends published by the Family Violence Department of the Council during the years 1996–1999:

- *Confidentiality of identifying information.* Many states have acknowledged the risk to victim safety when abusers have access to information regarding victim whereabouts. For example, in 1998, Florida and California enacted legislation creating a special program whereby victims have the ability to vote by absentee ballot.
- *Restriction of access to weapons.* Many states have imposed restrictions on the ability of known abusers to have access to weapons, for instance, by giving police the authority to seize firearms when an arrest is to be made or during a consensual search of property, or by prohibiting the possession or purchase of firearms while protective orders are active, or by increasing criminal penalties regarding the use of weapons.
- *Insurance discrimination.* Most states have recently addressed issues of discrimination regarding various types of insurance for victims of family violence. Legislation has generally addressed discrimination against victims of family violence in health care insurance. However, in 1996 Delaware extended its statute to include homeowners' and motor vehicle insurance, as well.
- *Child protection.* States have acknowledged the role of child protection in intimate partner violence and have developed a variety of policies that address children witnessing acts of violence and the revised statutes regarding child custody and visitation.

Miller (1998) notes that the most significant advancement in criminal law in recent years includes the adoption of antistalking laws in 50 states (no such statutes existed in 1989); repeal of or the limitation of the use of exemption for spouses under state rape laws (historically a man could not be charged with rape if he was legally married to the victim); and the enactment of new spousal or domestic partner battery laws that provide criminal sanctions. In addition, the violation of civil protective orders is considered a crime in most jurisdictions, and most states have revised their definitions of "domestic relationship" to include nonmarried partners.

Legislation has slowly evolved to address the myriad of issues that surround the realities of intimate partner abuse; however, reform is still necessary. For example, as recently as July 2001, Legal Aid Services of Oregon and the Oregon Law Center, in partnership with attorneys from the American Civil Liberties Union's Women's Rights Project and the NOW Legal Defense and Education Fund, have brought a federal sex discrimination lawsuit against a property management company for instituting a policy of evicting victims of domestic violence. Box 4.2 describes this case and provides an illustration of the kinds of social barriers victims of domestic violence continue to face.

Box 4.2 /// Battered Woman Denied Housing: Alvera v. C.D.M. Group, Inc.

In July 2001 Tiffani Alvera, age 24, brought a federal civil lawsuit against the C.B.M. Group, Inc., the company that denied her housing solely because she was a victim of domestic violence. The case was originally brought by the U.S. Department of Housing and Urban Development (HUD), which determined that the company did in fact violate Alvera's rights under the Fair Housing Act. As is her legal right, she is demanding a jury trial in this sex-discrimination case for an injunction against such discriminatory practices, compensatory damages, punitive damages, and attorney's fees.

In August 1999 Alvera's husband, Humberto Mota, physically assaulted her in their apartment, which is owned by C B M Group, Inc. After the assault, Alvera sought medical treatment and secured a temporary protective court order. Mota was arrested and was eventually convicted of assault IV. Alvera notified the apartment complex, Creekside Village Apartments in Seaside, Oregon, of her active restraining order. Several days later, Alvera was served with a 24-hour eviction notice that stated:

> Pursuant to Oregon Landlord/Tenant Law, this notice is to inform you that your occupancy will terminate because: You, someone in your control, or your pet, has seriously threatened immediately to inflict personal injury, or has inflicted personal injury upon the landlord or other tenants.

The lawsuit charged that the defendants, C.B.M. Group, Inc., terminated her tenancy at the apartment complex, refused to take her rent payments, and denied her application for the rental of a smaller apartment because she had been the victim of domestic violence and because of her sex. This case has been settled by consent decree in favor of Alvera.

Source: Alvera v. C.B.M. Group, Inc., et al., Civil No. 01-857-PA: Retrieved October 12, 2002, from www.aclu.org/court/alveraconsentdecree.pdf.

Summary

The recognition of intimate partner abuse as a social problem has evolved over the past several decades, culminating in broad-based changes on a number of levels. The domestic violence movement has changed our perceptions about how intimate partners should interact with each other; changed policies and procedures of professionals such as the police, courts, and counselors; forced us to critically examine our legal policies; and institutionalized funding streams and victim services across the country. Although change has been widespread, many would argue that there is still reform yet to be realized. We now turn our attention to a more detailed discussion of intimate partner abuse, beginning with an exploration of who the victims and abusers are.

/// Abuse in Intimate Relationships

Who Are the Victims, Who Are the Abusers?

As we alluded to earlier in this chapter, the domestic violence movement was born out of the earnest advocacy efforts of early feminists who took a specific interest in battered women. As we began to conduct more research about domestic violence, it became clear that battering occurs in different types of partner relationships. During the 1990s the dialogue regarding battering was extended to include further research into the context of violence in a broader array of relationships beyond those of legally married couples. Findings have compelled us to reconceptualize our notions about intimate partner abuse and our theoretical assumptions about why such abuse occurs. It has become clear that violence between intimate partners is a far more complex dynamic than had been addressed during the early years of the domestic violence movement. The belief that domestic violence is a phenomenon that is solely perpetrated by young men on their female spouses has finally been debunked. Unfortunately, public policy and social services currently lag behind the realization that violence occurs in all kinds of intimate partner relationships. Here we address specific populations that are subject to intimate partner abuse, including gay and lesbian couples, elderly couples, and male victims. Refer back to chapter 1 for a thorough discussion on the role of race and ethnicity in violent relationships.

Gay and Lesbian Couples

Whereas estimates of the prevalence of domestic violence in heterosexual couples ranges from 12 to 33 percent (depending on how one defines abuse; Straus & Gelles, 1990), best estimates of prevalence of abuse in gay and lesbian relationships appear to be relatively consistent. Some research has suggested much higher rates among some homosexual unions (Renzetti, 1997). Yet the National Violence Against Women Survey found that intimate partner violence is perpetrated primarily by men, whether against a same-sex or opposite-sex partner (Tjaden & Thoennes, 2000).

Researching violence within the same-sex community continues to be a daunting task. Claire Renzetti (1997) notes that, given the stigma attached to gay and lesbian relationships by the heterosexual majority, developing nationally based, random sampling frames has been virtually impossible. Therefore, studies that have been conducted tend to focus on a self-selected sample of individuals. Additionally, due to the efforts of the women's movement, more attention has been paid to abuse within lesbian couples.

Considering the incidence rate of abuse within homosexual relationships, it is obvious that the traditional feminist perspective no longer serves to broadly define our assumptions about how and why violence occurs in some relationships. It is clear that more is at play than the gender inequities present in society. However, common themes have surfaced that appear to link violence in both heterosexual and homosexual relationships. First, studies with both populations suggest that abuse tends to be recurrent and becomes more severe over time. Second, high rates of severe abuse found in the gay and lesbian self-selected studies mirror those found in the heterosexual population in more clinical settings (Renzetti, 1997).

Third, some research has suggested that in some homosexual and heterosexual relationships, partners can sometimes appear to be "mutually combative" (Lie & Gentlewarrier, 1991; Marrujo & Kreger, 1996). Although there most certainly are relationships in which battering is equally distributed between both parties, it is probably far more likely that a great deal of mutual combativeness is the result of victims fighting back. Marrujo and Kreger (1996) have more appropriately captured this phenomenon as the role of "participant," which they define as lesbians who establish a pattern of fighting back against their partners with the intent to cause them harm. Renzetti (1992) raises an important distinction between the ways in which victims and perpetrators describe their abusive behaviors. Victims will often express intense shame and guilt for engaging in abusive behavior, whereas batterers tend to rationalize their behavior, blaming their partners for their own abusiveness.

Findings also suggest that the correlates of abuse are similar for same-sex couples and heterosexual couples. Correlates cannot be considered "causes" of abuse in relationships, but they should be looked at as issues that serve to facilitate or accelerate violence in some relationships. Issues such as drug and alcohol abuse, personality disorders (or mental illness) of abusers, dependency and power factors within a relationship, and past experiences with violence in the family of origin are examples of problems that tend to be found in violent families. Because these factors are not present in all abusive relationships and because they may also be present in relationships in which no battering occurs, they do not help us fully explain why abuse occurs in intimate partner relationships. However, they tend to occur with such great frequency in cases of interpersonal violence that the role they play in abusive behavior cannot be ignored. Although the research is not always consistent, these issues appear to be present in both heterosexual and homosexual relationships to some extent (Renzetti, 1997).

Features that appear to be unique to abuse in same-sex partner relationships may be associated with the influence of the external environment on the relationship. The Lambda Gay and Lesbian Anti-Violence Project in El Paso, Texas, notes that same-sex partners often experience domestic violence differently because of these external issues (LAMBDA Gay and Lesbian Anti-Violence Project, 2001). The general oppression that same-sex partners experience in the larger community plays a distinct role in how intimate partner abuse is experienced. For example, threatening to "out" a partner to other family members or employers is a tool by which abusers control their partners. Local resources that are sensitive to the unique position of same-sex couples are scarce; therefore, victims are more likely to have to lie about their orientations to get help or risk being "outed" by insensitive service providers. Many fear that disclosing battering to heterosexuals may result in a reinforcement of the myth that same-sex relationships are "abnormal." Additionally, because the gay and lesbian population in many communities tends to be small, victims may be further isolated from supportive networks (LAMBDA Gay and Lesbian Anti-Violence Project, 2001).

Complicating these social dilemmas is the fact that public policy does not recognize same-sex relationships as legitimate, and therefore homosexuals are not able to enjoy the same things that heterosexuals take for granted, such as adoption and marriage. Policy may even discriminate against homosexuals when violence occurs. For example, Box 4.3 highlights a recent investigation by the American Civil Liberties Union into practices in the state of Florida. A Florida judge refused to grant a restraining order to a gay man under the premise that homosexuals are legally not considered family and therefore are not entitled to the protection of Florida's domestic violence statute.

Although strides have been made to address the specific needs of victims of same-sex violence, the service system and public policy lag in comparison to what has been provided for heterosexual victims of violence. For example, Claire Renzetti (1996) surveyed service providers and found inconsistencies in the official policies of providers, what they claim, and the reality of the services provided to battered lesbians. The domestic violence "industry" has not confronted the issue, nor, in some respects, has the gay and lesbian community addressed the reality of intimate partner abuse. Compounding the issue is a lack of research regarding abuse in same-sex relationships.

> ### Box 4.3 /// ACLU Investigates: Florida Judge Refuses
> ### to Grant Restraining Order to Gay Man
>
> A Manatee County judge in Florida has refused to grant a gay man a re-
> straining order under the premise that the State of Florida does not recog-
> nize gay and lesbian relationships as families. The judge claimed that the
> domestic violence law did not apply to "roomates," even when the victim
> disclosed that he had been in a monogamous relationship with his partner
> for 18 years and provided the judge with photographs of his bruises. Judge
> Marc Gilner denied the restraining order based on Florida's law banning
> same-sex marriages (which are not legal in any state), as well as adoption.
> The ACLU, which has already engaged the State of Florida in a lawsuit
> over the ban on homosexual adoptions, will investigate such discriminatory
> practices in Florida. According to Judge Gilner, "they can't adopt and they
> can't marry . . . and I believe it was the intention of the Legislature (to ex-
> clude gays) when they wrote the domestic violence statute." Matt Coles, di-
> rector of the ACLU's Lesbian and Gay Rights Project, argues that this prac-
> tice is unconstitutional and unconscionable.
>
> Source: ACLU Newswire: August 4 and August 7, 2000. Retrieved August 18, 2001,
> from *www.aclu.org/news/2000/n080700b.html* and www.aclu.org/news/2000/w080400c.html

Elderly Couples

A common myth about domestic violence is that only young people engage
in controlling, abusive behavior toward their partners. Although intimate
partner violence appears to occur with less frequency in those over the age
of 50, abuse is still an issue for concern. According to the National Crime
Victimization Survey, the rate of violence by an intimate partner for those
over age 50 was less than 3 victimizations per 1,000 persons. The National
Elder Abuse Incidence Study, conducted in 1996, revealed that spouses were
responsible for approximately 19 percent of all substantiated cases of elder
abuse.

Intimate partner abuse among elderly couples involves a complex set
of dynamics, some of which mirror the abusive patterns found in younger
couples. Although many of the risk factors for abuse are similar to those
found in younger couples (Harris, 1996), the unique features of aging must
be considered. For example, an inability to cope with caregiving responsibilities, acting-out behavior associated with cognitive impairments, barriers to independent living, disability, and so forth may all have distinctive
roles to play in this form of elder abuse. Therefore, one could argue that
there are two different concerns when considering partner abuse among
the elderly.

The first concern is often referred to as "aging-out" partner abuse
(Brownell & Abelman, 1998), which identifies domestic violence that has

occurred over the life span of a partnering relationship. It refers to the long-term battering that has occurred in a relationship in which the partners are now aging.

The second concern is the type of intimate partner abuse that appears later in life, perhaps as a direct result of the stressors of the aging process. Neglect is an issue specific to the elderly. Neglect becomes an issue between intimate partners when the physical, medical, or emotional needs of a partner are not being met. The reality is that, if we live long enough, it is likely that at some point in our lives we may need assistance with daily living, such as dressing, bathing, feeding, and so forth. If one partner must rely or dependent on another partner for such things and the other partner is struggling with his or her own aging issues, neglect can occur. The additional consequences of acting-out behavior associated with dementia or the life changes inherent in retirement can also play a role in intimate partner abuse among older adults.

The domestic violence service system in many parts of the country has not adequately addressed the needs of older adults who have been victimized by a partner. For example, domestic violence shelters have historically excluded older battered women from services (Vinton, 1992). Lack of services may be the result of many factors, such as an assumption that abuse does not occur in older couples; a lack of professional connections to adult protective agencies; a reluctance to provide services to individuals who are disabled, ill, or have cognitive impairments; the inability of referral agencies to identify partner abuse, and so forth. In addition, the criminal justice approach to domestic violence, which by now is standard in most communities, is most likely to be inappropriate for older couples (Brownell & Abelman, 1998). This probability raises critical questions about how best to intervene given the complexities of intimate partner abuse among the aged. Adult protective service agencies (as discussed in chapter 8) are most likely to be the parties responsible for intervening in cases of domestic violence among the elderly.

Men as Victims

Is it possible for men to be victimized by their partners? The answer is a qualified yes. Male victimization has now been clearly established by many sources; however, the prevalence is uncertain. For example, both the National Violence Against Women Survey and the National Family Violence Survey find that men are abused by their intimate partners. However, the NVAW finds that women are at a significantly greater risk of victimization than men, whereas the NFVS finds women and men at equal risk (Trjaden & Thoennes, 2000). Part of the discrepancy may lie in the incidence of male-to-male violence. The National Violence Against Women Survey identified that men living with male partners were more likely than men living with female partners to be physically assaulted (Trjaden & Thoennes, 2000). Additionally, survey methodologies may need to be modified to better capture the male experience with intimate partner abuse.

The FBI's Uniform Crime Report, via the National Incident-Based Reporting System (discussed previously) found evidence of male victimization in family-related crimes reported to the police. However, when examining all types of family violence offenses, we find that the vast majority involve female victims. Yet we cannot ignore the fact that 18 percent of family violence offenses involve assaults in which both the husband and wife are charged (FBI, 2000).

Complicating our understanding of male victimization is the fact that many women have been arrested as a result of mandatory or pro-arrest policies. Some women may appear to be the primary aggressors or may be arrested along with their male partners in cases in which officers are required to arrest both parties because it is not clear who is the victim and who is the perpetrator. As you might expect, determining who is the victim and who is the offender at the scene of a highly emotionally charged incident, in which one or both parties may be using substances and in which neither party may welcome the presence of the police can be a difficult task. Kindschi Gosselin (2002) suggests that police officers take a purposefully nonbiased approach to identifying the victim and perpetrator. She suggests that officers not make such false assumptions as that the injured person is the victim, that the individual who appears to be more likeable is the victim, that the larger person is the offender, that same-sex violence is mutual fighting, or that women are always the victims. She recommends that police officers take the time to fully understand who has initiated an incident, what the history of abuse in the relationship has been, and who is the one truly in fear, without relying on the arrest of both individuals. Such nonbiased purposeful interviewing is likely to yield a clearer picture regarding the true victims.

Regardless of the actual prevalence of male victimization and whether or not the male victim is heterosexual or homosexual, the current victim-service industry has been reluctant to serve male victims, especially in shelters and support groups. The first program to serve men was established in 1993 in St. Paul, Minnesota, and housed more than 50 men in its first 6 months of operation (Karmen, 2001), signifying the need to further explore the needs of male victims of battering. Battered men are likely to have unique needs and different resources than their female counterparts do.

Characteristics of Abusive Relationships

Issues of Power and Control

The central feature that links all forms of intimate partner violence is the coercive nature of the abuser's behavior. Asserting power, through decision making, division of labor, access to financial resources, and so forth, has long been considered to be a characteristic of the batterer's motivation. Physical or emotional abuse serves as a way in which abusers can assert their control and dominance over their partners. In other words, the goal of threatening or harming a partner is ultimately to get the partner to "behave" in certain ways. Abusers, for whatever reason (personality disorder, mental illness, substance abuse, learned behavior, low self-esteem, etc.), have a need to dominate and control their partners' every move. This may mean whom they talk to, how they spend their money, what they wear, and where they work, for example. There is a continuum of abuse that runs from relatively minor or temporary to long-term and increasingly more physically harmful.

Renzetti (1997) points out that power in intimate relationships is a multidimensional issue that requires us to consider that power differentials may play a role in battering in different ways in different relationships. For example, is it an imbalance in power that places relationships at risk for violence, or are abusive acts responsible for creating a situation in which the power shifts to the abuser? What kinds of power are more influential in placing relationships at risk for abuse? Is it social power, economic power, physical power, or status? Confusing our understanding of the dynamics of power in relationships is the fact that many relationships are characterized by an inequitable distribution of power but not by abuse or violence. Although there might be a variety of explanations for how and why power becomes an issue in intimate relationships, most researchers would agree that issues of power and control are central to the problem of battering in intimate partner relationships. Recognizing that partner violence also occurs outside of the traditional feminist paradigm of male privilege, a variety of approaches to studying the role of power in relationships is warranted (Johnson & Ferraro, 2000).

Abusive Behaviors

Characteristic of intimate partner abuse is the surprisingly similar way abusive behavior is displayed across the broad spectrum of cultural, economic, religious, and racial groupings. Although wide variation occurs in the individual characteristics of abusers and victims, what appears to be a relative constant is the way in which behaviors are displayed by abusers. For example, the following is a list of typical behaviors used by abusers to control their partners:

- Denying the partner autonomy
- Isolating victims from friends and family
- Instilling fear through intimidation, threats, and actual acts of violence
- Manipulative behavior
- Forcing victims to live by the abuser's rules
- Placing sanctions on victims who do not "behave"

- Punishing victims for challenging the abuser's authority
- Unjustified jealously
- Controlling financial resources
- Using children in a variety of ways to hurt, control or manipulate

Although the behaviors listed here are typical, further research has suggested that there are different types or patterns of abusive behavior, and we cannot therefore lump all abusive behavior into one general category. For example, Johnson (1995) and Johnson and Ferraro (2000) distinguish four major patterns of violence:

- *Common couple violence (CCV)*. This pattern of relationship violence involves abusive episodes that are not tied to a history or pattern of control issues. This form of violence erupts as part of a single dispute in which one or both of the partners engage in abusive behaviors. Johnson (1995) notes that this pattern of abuse generally is not likely to be severe, nor is it likely to increase over time.
- *Intimate terrorism (IT)*. This pattern of relationship violence is centered on the abuser's need to control his or her victim. This form of violence is generally more likely to increase over time, to involve a higher frequency of episodes, and to involve more serious injuries. Also, this form of violence is less likely to be mutual.
- *Violent resistant (VR)*. This pattern of relationship violence involves abusive episodes perpetrated by the victim in an effort to resist the pattern of violence displayed by the abuser.
- *Mutual violent control (MVC)*. This pattern of relationship violence involves the full participation of both partners in abusive, controlling behavior. Although it is assumed to be rare, this particular relationship system is not well understood at the present time.

Roberts (2002) recently conducted research with battered women in New Jersey to document the duration, severity, and lethality of intimate partner violence to better understand the differences in violence patterns. The sample of women were derived from four subsamples: battered women who had killed their partners and were serving time in a state prison facility; women who had reported domestic assaults to three suburban police departments; women who were receiving services at three battered women's shelters; and a subsample of formerly abused women that was drawn with the assistance of students from a New Jersey university. The total sample of 501 battered women indicated that a continuum of five levels best defined the experiences of the women in the sample. Roberts (2002) describe these levels as:

Short Term (Level 1). Ninety-four women described experiences with battering as limited to between one and three misdemeanor incidents, with acts classified as mild to moderate in severity. Most of the women in this category were young (ages 16–25) and ended the relationship with the assistance of a parent or older sibling. Most of the women in this category were in the middle class and asked for help from the police or other family members.

Intermediate (Level 2). One hundred and four women described experiences with battering that involved 3 to 15 incidents over a period of time from several months to 2 years. Most of the women were living with their partners, and none of them had children. Many had sustained injuries and had often secured restraining orders. Many had ended the relationship with assistance from the police or friends and family after experiencing a severe battering episode.

Intermittent/Long Term (Level 3). Thirty-eight women defined their experiences as being much longer in duration (5–40 years), with severe battering episodes occurring in an intermittent fashion. Most women in this category were financially dependent on their partners, and many had religious objections to divorce chose to stay in the relationship for the sake of the children. These women, mostly from the middle or upper classes, have rarely sought hospital services and have often lied to medical professionals regarding their injuries.

Chronic and Severe/Regular Pattern (Level 4). A total of 160 battered women made up this category of abuse, which is marked by a long period of duration (5–35 years), with increasingly more violent episodes over time. Women experienced severe injuries as the battering became more extreme over time, with the use of weapons, forced sex, and threats of death. Over time, battering became more predictable, such as every other weekend, every Friday, and so forth. Sixty-eight percent of the abusers had serious alcohol problems; however, women acknowledged that they were abused even during their partners' sober periods.

Roberts (2002) created a subset of this category, termed *chronic with a discernable pattern/mutual combat,* to acknowledge the experiences of 24 women who engaged in abusive behaviors toward their partners in an effort to defend themselves or to retaliate. Fourteen of these women had chronic alcohol or drug problems (as did their male partners), and some had a history of aggressive behavior as young girls. Most were from a lower socioeconomic class.

Homicidal (Level 5). A total of 105 women in this category described experiences in which the battering relationship was of significant duration, on average 8 years or longer. Most women were in common-law relationships (meaning they had been cohabiting with their partners for 7 years or longer) or were married or recently divorced. A total of 65.7 percent of them disclosed specific lethal death threats in which the batterer gave specific instructions as to the time, place, and method of their deaths. Most of the women in this category were of the lower socioeconomic class, many without the benefit of an education or skills to earn a decent living.

As these researchers have found, although a great deal of similarity exists in the types of behaviors displayed during abusive episodes, there appear to be differences in the patterns of characteristics of violence over time. Research such as this is instructive for professionals who are working to assess risk and lethality and to provide appropriate interventions for victims and batterers. Additionally, we know that power and control are central themes in such relationships; however, further research is needed to fully grasp the dynamics that rule any abusive relationship.

Forms of Intimate Partner Violence

As we discussed earlier in this chapter, abuse in intimate relationships may take many forms, with power and control as a central theme. Abusive behavior takes various forms in intimate relationships.

Emotional Abuse

As we discussed in other chapters, emotional or psychological abuse is the most difficult to define. Behaviors that are generally considered to be emotionally abusive because of the negative consequences for victims include degradation; name-calling; and threats of physical harm to the victim or the victim's children, family, or pets. Emotional abuse may also include restricting the victim's freedom of movement by limiting access to transportation, social interactions, finances, employment, and so forth. Abusers may also exhibit unjustified jealously and excessive possessiveness. Ultimately, victims lose their independence, self-esteem, and self-respect.

Emotional abuse, like other forms of violence, lies on a continuum. Therefore, minor psychologically abusive behavior is likely to be found in many couple relationships at different times. We mean that even couples who have normally healthy interactions with no display of physical or sexual violence can engage in emotionally abusive interactions from time to time. Partners may rely on name-calling, degradation, and hurting their partners with words out of anger and frustration. Instead of using more effective communication tools, a partner or both partners may reduce a dispute to more immature, childlike responses in which one or both parties are left emotionally wounded.

At the other end of the continuum is a terroristic form of emotional abuse wherein abusers use tactics similar to the brainwashing used on prisoners of war, hostages, and cult members. Such tactics may include isolation, humiliation, making allegations about the victim and blaming her for things she has not done, as well as conducting rampages of physical violence in an unpredictable fashion (Mega, Mega, Mega, & Harris, 2000). Abusers may also use violence or threats of violence against children as a mechanism to instill terror, to coerce, or to retaliate against a partner (McCloskey, 2001). Victims suffer from "battering fatigue," not unlike the battle fatigue soldiers experience (Mega et al., 2000).

Although emotionally abusive behavior can occur without physical or sexual violence, it appears to have a strong link to other forms of abuse. The National Violence Against Women Survey found that women who experienced emotionally abusive and controlling behavior by their partners were significantly more likely to also be victimized by physical or sexual violence (Tjaden & Thoennes, 2000).

Physical Abuse

Physical violence may involve kicking, punching, slapping, pushing, grabbing, shoving, pulling out hair, or hitting. More serious forms of physical abuse may include burning, stabbing, shooting, or beating with objects such as a belt, baseball bat, or hammer. We often refer to the physical violence present in an intimate relationship as battering. Battering can cause: fractures, burns, bruises, cuts, welts, internal injuries, facial disfigurement, injury to unborn babies, head or spinal cord injuries, chipped or broken teeth, dislocated joints, and, in some instances, death. Battering in and of itself is both physically and psychologically damaging. Victims are generally emotionally harmed when they are physically beaten. We must also consider that many victims suffer the consequences of sexual assault and emotional abuse, in addition to the types of physical violence we have described here.

Although it is difficult to measure the exact prevalence rate, most lifetime prevalence estimates of intimate partner victimizations are between 9 and 30 percent for women and 13 and 16 percent for men (Tjaden & Thoennes, 2000). Most recently, the National Violence Against Women Survey found that 22.1 percent of surveyed women and 7.4 percent of surveyed men experienced some level of physical violence by a partner at some point during their lives. The survey also found that 41.5 percent of women who had been victimized were injured by their partners during the most recent episode of violence, whereas 19.9 percent of male victims reported being injured (Tjaden & Thoennes, 2000).

Sexual Abuse

Sexual assault within an intimate partner relationship may involve a number of sexual violations, including rape, sodomy, forced pornography, fondling or grabbing, or use of objects to penetrate. Often sexual assaults are committed with the use of physical force and/or threats of physical violence or psychological coercion.

Determining the prevalence of sexual assault in intimate partner relationships has been difficult to gauge. Although numerous studies have documented a variety of forms of sexual violence in battering relationships, often the crime of rape is the only form of sexual assault that is officially considered in survey data. Therefore, we have reliable data on rape, but it is unlikely that we truly understand the prevalence of other forms of sexual assault in relationships. The National Violence Against Women Survey found that 7.7 percent of all women and 0.3 percent of all men surveyed had been raped by an intimate partner at some point in their lifetimes, which is consistent with other localized research findings (Tjaden & Thoennes, 2000). The survey used a broad definition of rape as "an event that occurs without the victim's consent and involves the use of threat or force to penetrate the victim's vagina or anus by penis, tongue, fingers, or object or the victim's mouth by penis" (Tjaden & Thoennes, 2000, p. 5).

Historically, one of the dilemmas facing women and the courts arises from state legislation that has allowed marital exemption to sexual assault laws. This basically means that, legally speaking, a man could not be found guilty of rape if he was legally married to the woman at the time of the assault. Although most states have repealed their marital exemption to rape laws, 12 states still provide for a limited exemption in certain instances (Miller, 1998).

Stalking

The National Violence Against Women Survey and the National Institute of Justice's project to develop a model antistalking code for states define *stalking* as "a course of conduct directed at a specific person that involves repeated physical or visual proximity, nonconsensual communication, or verbal, written, or implied threats" (Tjaden, 1997). Stalking may involve a variety of behaviors, such as spying on the victim; following the victim; sending mail, notes, and gifts; making harassing phone calls to victims; making threats of violence against the victim or the victim's children, family or pets; and vandalizing property. Stalking is a serious crime that induces great fear in victims.

The National Violence Against Women Survey identified stalking as a significant problem; about 1.4 million people are victimized each year. The survey has identified a strong connection between stalking and other forms of abuse in intimate partner relationships, with women being victimized at a significantly greater level than men. Stalking behaviors tended to last approximately 1 year, and about 45 percent of the victims reported that overt threats to their safety were made by the stalker. Seventy-five percent of the victims reported being spied on or followed, and 30 percent reported having property vandalized (Tjaden, 1997).

Cyberstalking, a rather new phenomenon, refers to stalking that occurs with the use of electronic communication, such as the Internet and e-mail. Cyberstalkers can engage in harassing, threatening behavior anywhere in the world without having to physically confront the victim. Perhaps even more frightening is the ability of cyberstalkers to deceive other Internet users into harassing or threatening a victim through the use of bulletin boards or chat rooms. In these instances, cyberstalkers use a victim's e-mail address, name, and address to post inflammatory or controversial messages, arousing the emotions of other online users and stimulating them to respond to the victim directly. Other forms of cyberstalking might include sending junk e-mail or other e-mails on a regular schedule, sending viruses, electronic identity theft, and so forth.

State statutes have begun to address the crime of stalking. Following the lead of the State of California, which enacted the first stalking law in 1990, every state now has enacted legislation to address stalking. Some states treat stalking as a felony-level crime, whereas others may consider stalking a felony only when it is repeated. In addition, 26 states allow orders of protection to be issued in stalking cases, and violations of such orders may have criminal sanctions attached (Miller, 1998). As you might imagine, law enforcement agencies are particularly challenged by cyberstalking. Agencies are still developing the expertise and resources to combat electronic stalking (Reno, 1999).

Parental Kidnapping

Another form of intimate partner violence is the abduction of or custodial interference with children. Abductions of children by family members (most often intimate partners or spouses) account for the vast majority of cases of child abduction, ranging from 163,200 to 354,100 cases per year (Finkelhor, Hotaling, & Sedlak, 1990). Child abduction is usually referred to as *parental kidnapping*, and it is defined by the American Bar Association as the taking, retention or concealment of the child by a parent, other family member, or their agent, in derogation of the custody rights or visitation rights of another parent or family member" (Hoff, 1997, p. 2).

There are a number of reasons why a parent would abduct his or her own child. In some cases, abduction is an extension of the battering relationship itself. Abusers attempt to further control the victim or coerce a victim to stay in a relationship by threatening or by actually kidnapping the children. In some cases, abductors kidnap a child because they are not happy with the custodial determinations set forth by the court, even in cases in which no history of abuse exists. Additionally, some abuse victims may abduct their own children in an effort to protect them from an abusive parent. Regardless of the motivation, children are gravely victimized by such acts. The emotional and physical toll on children is so great that parental kidnapping is considered a form of child abuse (Hoff, 1997).

A number of laws have been enacted to combat the problem. For example, the Parental Kidnapping Prevention Act (28 U.S.C. § 1738A) was established in 1980 to remove the problem of interstate jurisdiction associated with child custody determinations. This "full faith and credit" legislation requires that a custody determination in one state must be upheld by another. The Hague Child Abduction Convention, held in 1988, was followed by the International Child Abduction Remedies Act (42 U.S.C. § 11601), which addresses international jurisdictional issues (Hoff, 1997).

Homicide

The most severe form of intimate partner violence is death. Although intimate partner homicide has continued to decline since 1976, a total of 1,830 murders in 1998 were attributed to an intimate partner. Females are far more likely to be killed by an intimate partner than males. In fact, about one-third of all female murder victims were killed by an intimate partner, whereas about 4 percent of male murder victims were killed by a partner (Bureau of Justice Statistics [BJS], 2001).

Homicides result from a number of circumstances. Men often kill their female partners as a result of a severe beating, often involving drug and alcohol use. Men also kill their partners during bouts of intense jealously or because the relationship has been severed. Women, on the other hand, usually kill their intimate partners because of previous physical attacks or as the direct result of self-defense. Separation is often a key factor; men often kill their partners in locations other than a shared dwelling, whereas women are more likely to kill their partners in a shared dwelling (Browne, 1997).

As we alluded to earlier, the rate of homicide by intimate partners has been reduced drastically in recent years. For example, in 1976 there were nearly 3,000 such murders (Chaiken, 1998). Concern over the high incidence of murder in the 1970s became an issue for law enforcement and the courts. This concern led to the development of state interventions such as mandatory arrest. Victim advocates, law enforcement, and the courts looked to strategies that could serve to provide early intervention into abusive relationships, with the goal of preventing additional violence, especially lethal violence.

Summary

In this section we examined intimate partner violence in a number of ways. We discussed a variety of couple relationships and hopefully dispelled the myth that only young, married women are victims of intimate partner abuse. Acknowledging domestic abuse in gay and lesbian couples and the elderly and acknowledging the fact that men too can be victims of such abusive behavior has enhanced our understanding of the dynamics of violence in interpersonal relationships.

Next we explored in more detail the context of abusive treatment in intimate relationships, considering issues of power and control and typical behaviors of abusers. We also noted the importance of understanding the various patterns abusive relationships appear to take. Acknowledging different patterns in abusive behavior may help clinicians and other professionals to further develop appropriate intervention strategies and to identify cases in which there may be a high degree of lethality.

Finally, we discussed the numerous forms of intimate partner abuse, including emotional, physical, and sexual abuse. Included in our discussion was stalking, cyberstalking, and child abduction. We also explored the reality that many abusive relationships end in homicide. The next section explores the consequences of abusive relationships.

/// Consequences of Abuse in Intimate Partner Relationships

Impact on Children

Although we have alluded to the negative consequences of intimate partner violence on children, it is important that we recognize just how damaging such violence is for children. Cognitive, emotional, physical, and social development is negatively affected by exposure to domestic violence for children of all ages. This is true even for unborn babies, because stress experienced by mothers is transferred to their babies in utero (Karr-Morse & Wiley, 1997). Additionally, because child abuse often accompanies intimate partner violence (Rumm, Cummings, Krauss, Bell, & Rivara, 2000), children are victimized on a number of levels. Not only must they witness the attacks and threats made against a parent, but they must also endure the fear that they too will be victimized. Fear and terror often characterize their lives. Exposure to ongoing fear becomes a chronic stressor that has multiple short- and long-term consequences for children, with the most profound effects experienced by children who are both witnesses to domestic violence and victims of child abuse. Children observe dysfunctional communication and conflict resolution, as well as inappropriate abuses of power within intimate relationships—environmental learning that is likely to play a role in their own lives as adults.

Exposure to domestic violence is associated with a number of psychological problems, including depression, separation anxiety disorder, oppositional defiant disorder, anxiety, and posttraumatic stress disorder (Pelcovitz, Kaplan, DeRosa, Mandel, & Salzinger, 2000; Silva et al., 2000). Children may internalize or externalize their responses to witnessing domestic violence (Carlson, 1996). Internalizing behavior problems means that children turn their emotions of sadness or anger inward toward themselves, leading to depression, anxiety, and withdrawal. Externalizing behavioral problems results in a child directing his or her feelings toward others, resulting in aggressive and uncooperative behavior. Some evidence suggests that girls internalize their feelings, whereas boys are more prone to externalize theirs (Hilberman & Munson, 1977-1978). Also, such emotional turmoil is also likely to affect social competence and academic achievement (Carlson, 1996). Future violence by a child is also likely to stem from witnessing acts of violence by his or her own parents or caretakers (Hotaling & Sugarman, 1986).

The consequences of domestic violence on children can be negated through appropriate parenting by the nonabusive parent. However, victims of intimate partner abuse suffer extreme stress themselves, making healthy parenting difficult (Carlson, 1996). Additional stressors such as separation, divorce, testifying in court, custody and visitation disputes, constant moving or lack of stable housing, financial hardships, and so forth are likely to affect the nonabusing parent, as well as the children.

Recognizing the negative consequences for children, the courts have begun to change their response to child custody issues when domestic violence is a factor. Because separation itself often precipitates additional violence and is considered one of the most dangerous times for victims (Jaffe, 1995), the courts must be particularly mindful of protecting the children during this period. In fact, some argue that the notion of shared or joint custody should not apply to cases in which a history of intimate partner abuse can be established, as the system should be assuring the safety of children above the rights of violent parents (Doyne et al., 1999). States have responded with legislation that requires judges to consider domestic violence as a factor in their decisions regarding custody and visitation. For example, in 1999, 13 states established such criteria (National Council of Juvenile and Family Court Judges [NCJFCJ], 1999).

Other states have proposed taking criminal action against individuals who allow children to witness acts of violence. For example, Utah established a new domestic violence crime for allowing a child to hear or see an act of domestic violence, and Delaware created provisions whereby an individual can be charged with endangering the welfare of a child (NCJFCJ, 1999). Additionally, child protective mandates may lead to court responses against nonabusive parents, charging battering victims with child abuse or neglect. These legal responses are likely to cause conflict between child welfare workers and domestic violence advocates, raising interesting questions about how best to protect children without punishing victims. Although legislative action is warranted, such policies may have unintended consequences for children and nonabusive parents and will require continued study.

Poverty and Homelessness

High levels of interpersonal violence are also likely to interfere with a victim's ability to maintain employment and enjoy economic security. Research has demonstrated that battering increases the likelihood that a victim will be unable to maintain employment (Browne, Salomon, & Bassuk, 1999), in some instances specifically because an abusive partner is subverting her efforts to remain working. Johnson and Ferraro (2000) note that many batterers undermine their partners' employment by withholding transportation, changing alarm clocks, assaulting her or him prior to job interviews, breaking promises to care for children and leaving them unattended, and harassing victims at work. Episodes of battering tend to erode self-esteem and ambition while interfering with concentration, making work and career growth difficult. Also, battering is likely to result in repeated absences from work. Therefore, it is reasonable to assume that abuse may be the cause of poverty for some victims and, at a minimum, serves as a barrier to increasing employment status (Johnson & Ferraro, 2000).

Loss of employment or an inability to gain employment places victims and their children at risk for homelessness, especially if the victim chooses to leave the relationship. In fact, economic security is one of the main reasons that victims stay in abusive relationships. Victims often have to choose between that relationship and being on the streets—not a fair choice. Complicating the situation is the lack of affordable housing and long waiting lists for various forms of assisted housing, including domestic violence shelters. For example, the U.S. Conference of Mayors (1998) estimated that 32 percent of requests for shelter by homeless families were denied in 1998.

Consequently, domestic violence victims and their children make up a considerable percentage of the homeless population in the United States (Douglass, 1995; Homes for the Homeless, 1998; Zorza, 1991). In addition, the U.S. Conference of Mayors (1998) found that 46 percent of cities surveyed considered domestic violence to be a primary reason for homelessness. The National Coalition for the Homeless (1999) reports that homelessness is found more frequently within the welfare population and that the absence of cash assistance, coupled with the lack of affordable housing, victims of domestic violence are at increased risk of homelessness. Related consequences of economic instability often mean that victims and their children lack proper health care and nutrition. Homelessness is also likely to affect school attendance and performance.

Physical and Behavioral Health

Research has established that both acute and chronic trauma events have many physical and psychological consequences for victims. In the case of chronic battering, victims may suffer long-term stress reactions from experiencing the ongoing trauma associated with abuse and are likely to experience severe physical injury. Not all victims of intimate partner violence experience mental health problems nor serious physical injury; however, the longer the battering relationship continues, the more likely it is that a victim will suffer from the consequences of chronic abuse. We do not mean to imply that battered victims (most often women) are pathological; on the contrary, they tend to display acts of courage and strength that many of us could not even imagine. In fact, many prefer the term "domestic violence survivor" to "victim" to better reflect the courage, determination, and resolve that are so often characteristic of women who have endured such violence. We must be careful not to blame victims for abusive relationships. We must appreciate the decision-making process of victims and realize that their "responses to abusive relationships are never static or unidimensional"

(Campbell, Rose, Kub, & Nedd, 2001, p. 193). Yet we must also understand that battering has serious consequences and takes a toll on survivors. Victims are often left with marred faces and stolen souls, robbed of their dignity, self-esteem, and freedom.

We first began to understand the psychological injury of battering from the work of Lenore Walker (1979), a psychologist. She coined the term *battered women syndrome* (BWS) to describe a set of psychological characteristics that battered women often share, enhancing our understanding of how and why women tend to stay in battering relationships. However, over time, the term *battered women syndrome* has come to have a second operational definition. The legal definition of BWS is often meant to characterize the victim's experience of trauma and the dynamics of the battering relationship itself (Walker, 1995), often with the purpose of explaining a woman's criminal actions as a reasonable response to battering. Gordon and Dutton (2001) note that the legal term has come to be used to reference the large body of scientific knowledge available regarding the psychological consequences of battering and the dynamics of the battering relationship.

Since the term BWS became popular in the late 1970s, considerable attention has been drawn to the consequences of intimate partner violence. We now know that battering has a broad range of emotional, cognitive, physiological, and behavioral consequences for victims. The magnitude of potential physical and psychological injury is cause for serious concern. Besides the obvious physical injuries, clinical diagnoses such as anxiety disorders, depressive disorders, and substance-abuse-related disorders are associated with battering. Some of the responses of trauma might include nightmares and flashbacks, avoidance of thoughts and feelings, inability to focus or concentrate, inability to sleep, suicidal ideation, anxious or depressed feelings, somatic complaints, withdrawal from normal social activities, alcohol and other drug abuse, dissociation, and irritability (Herman, 1992). Posttraumatic stress disorder (PTSD), a specific psychiatric diagnosis often associated with battering, refers to a set of symptoms characteristic of survivors of severe trauma such as those experienced by survivors of combat and natural disasters. A history of child abuse, specifically child sexual abuse, may be especially connected to a battering survivor's trauma responses and intensity of PTSD symptoms (Astin, Ogland-Hand & Coleman, 1995).

/// Chapter Summary

This chapter began with a discussion of some of the political trends that have guided the salience of domestic violence intervention throughout American history. We briefly discussed how early restrictions set some boundaries regarding the responsibility of men to properly discipline their families under the auspices of religious conviction. Religious and social beliefs were then replaced by court rulings that condoned battering. By the end of the 1800s, states began to outlaw the practice of domestic violence, yet the actual rate of enforcement of such policies is unclear.

During the 1970s interest in protecting women from their abusive partners was restored. We explored the various factors that converged during the period 1970–1990 to define domestic violence as a prominent public policy issue. The diligent work of grassroots women's advocacy groups, the proliferation of research, and the growth of landmark legal decisions advanced the domestic violence movement to major reform.

We focused on contemporary policy, examining the context of social and political reform. We discussed the ways in which policy reform has reshaped how we define and measure domestic violence and in which it is responsible for the development of formalized victim service systems. Federal and state governments, along with law enforcement and court officials, have been forced to rethink their approach to domestic abuse. Today our response to battering is more sophisticated, and we have begun to explore the context of violence in a variety of intimate partner relationships.

We examined abuse in intimate relationships in more depth, focusing on special populations. We set out to dispel the myth that only young married women are beaten by their partners by exploring the abuse that occurs between gay and lesbian couples and elderly partners and acknowledged that men too can be victims of such violence. Characteristics of abusive relationship were explored, identifying issues of power and control as a central feature of battering. We also discussed some new research that suggests that not all battering relationships are the same and that in fact there appear to be different patterns of violence in different relationships over time. We examined different typology schemes that several researchers are currently using to further define the battering relationship.

We investigated the different forms of violence often found in intimate partner relationships. These include emotional abuse, physical abuse, sexual abuse, stalking, cyberstalking, homicide, and parental kidnapping. The chapter concluded with a discussion of some of the key consequences of intimate partner violence. Children in particular are significantly affected by violence that occurs between the adults in their lives, and they are often placed at additional risk of being victims themselves. In addition, victims of battering are profoundly affected by the poverty, homelessness, and physical and psychological injury that often accompany violent relationships.

/// Recommended Web Sites

Antistalking
    www.antistalking.com
Battered Women's Justice Project
    www.vaw.umn.edu/bwjp

Center for the Prevention of Sexual and Domestic Violence
    www.cpsdv.org
Family Violence Prevention Fund
    www.fvpf.org
Feminist Majority Foundation
    www.feminist.org/default.asp
LAMBDA Gay & Lesbian Anti-Violence Project
    www.lambda.org/DV_intro.htm
National Network to End Domestic Violence
    www.nnedv.org
National Coalition Against Domestic Violence
    www.brsf.org/ncadv
National Center for Victims of Crime
    www.ncvc.org

osh slowly approaches the building. He catches a quick view of the small sign lettered on the front window: "Family and Youth Center." Filled with anxiety, Josh enters the building and tells the receptionist that he is here for his first group session. Josh is then greeted by Tom, the therapist, who brings him down a long hall and into a small but comfortable room, where four other boys his age are seated in a circle. In addition to Josh's joining the group, Tom has brought a visitor, his 5-year-old golden retriever, Trevor. The boys, all ages 12 to 14, are excited by the sight of Trevor and begin to pet him with loving care.

As the group session begins, the boys take turns introducing themselves to Josh, welcoming him to this treatment group for adolescent sex offenders. Tom asks each boy to tell Josh why he is in the group. Nick, age 13, is in the group because he had sexual intercourse with his 10-year-old sister; Ozzie, age 14, is in the group because he was found fondling one of his young cousins (he is not sure of the cousin's age); Javier, age 12, is in the group for attempting to rape an elderly aunt; and Samuel, age 14, has been accused of forcing his 8-year-old sister to commit sodomy. Josh cannot bring himself to tell the group why he is there.

Tom begins the group with a discussion of the reason he brought Trevor on this day. Tom asks the boys if any of them have ever had any pets. All but Javier say yes. After some talk about the pets, Tom asks the boys to share any memories they may have about hurting their own or someone else's pets or whether anyone else had ever abused one of their pets. Nick starts by disclosing the fact that he used to love to torture his sister's hamster by throwing a baseball at it and watching the animal scurry around the room to avoid being hit by the ball. Ozzie told the group about the time his mother's boyfriend threw her bird across the room into a wall, killing the bird, and the time his friend Harper was caught having intercourse with a goat. Samuel told a detailed story of how his older brother used to love to capture small animals, partially bury them in the backyard, and then run over their heads with the lawn mower. Josh remains silent, yet his mind wanders to the numerous times his father threatened to kill his dog. Tom engages the boys in a deep discussion of their thoughts and feelings regarding such acts of violence toward animals for the rest of the session. By the end of the session, Josh begins to feel a connection with the other boys' stories and tears begin to well up in his eyes, yet he remains silent.

The boys depicted in this story are lucky, for their sexually offending behavior has been discovered and reported to the appropriate authorities early enough to make a difference. The intensity of this specialized treatment program will require each of them to confront their behavior, motivations, and past history of victimization. The boys will need to take responsibility for their actions, come to grips with the suffering they have caused their victims, and search for a new way to cope with their own anger, frustration, and pain.

This chapter is devoted to the discussion of three forms of violence in the home that are often hidden from the public and professional dialogue on family violence issues. Sibling abuse, parental abuse, and animal abuse are issues worthy of continued research and intervention. Exploring these topics helps us shed more light on the complexity and multidimensional aspects of violence within the home. These three forms of violence are representative of perhaps the most silent of victims: children, parents, and animals. These forms of abuse are hidden from professionals, public-policy makers, and researchers. Little public discussion has occurred regarding these issues, and professionals have yet to link intervention strategies and prevention messages in a consistent way to protect victims and make perpetrators accountable.

We explore sibling abuse in a number of ways: We acknowledge the extent to which sibling abuse is likely to occur in the general population; we distinguish between normal childhood sibling rivalry and sibling abuse and the various forms sibling abuse takes; and we conclude with a discussion of the various factors related to the reasons that violence between siblings occurs and the consequences of such interactions. We investigate circumstances under which parents are victims of abuse by their young children. We explore the prevalence of parental abuse and the reasons that children abuse their parents, and we focus on the deadliest form of violence, homicide. This chapter also examines the missing link in family violence research and practice: animal abuse. We define animal abuse and give examples of the ways in which animals are abused. We also explore the links between animal-focused violence and other forms of violence in the home and the future role of prevention and intervention to protect both animals and humans.

/// *Sibling Abuse*

Of all the forms of family violence discussed in this text, sibling abuse is probably the most common, yet ironically it receives the least attention from researchers, public-policy makers, and the social service system. Why? We suspect that sibling abuse continues to be ignored as a form of family violence because it is so common and occurs with such frequency that we simply consider it a normal part of growing up. Therefore, acts that occur between siblings are often written off as ordinary child's play. After all, we probably all can recall at least one memory of some kind of physical conflict or name-calling between ourselves and our siblings.

Sibling abuse may also go unrecognized because it is shrouded in confusing perceptions about sibling rivalry and other normal child behaviors. Although conflict is normal in human interactions, how conflict is displayed at various developmental stages is central to distinguishing between normal childhood behaviors and behaviors that constitute abuse. Because many children cope with inner conflicts and stress by being aggressive, rude, and disrespectful, parents often ignore abuse complaints from their children. Research supports the idea that aggression is a normal characteristic of the sibling relationship that appears to be perpetrated by both males and females (Roscoe, Goodwin, & Kennedy, 1987). Therefore, parents tend to look the other way or to believe that a child's own behavior precipitated events. Some studies have found that parents view negative sibling interactions as an important mechanism by which children learn to negotiate conflict (Goodwin & Roscoe, 1990).

The difficulty, of course, is the fact that acts of abuse between siblings carries over into adulthood. Adults who have not learned other, more appropriate ways to cope or are unable to resolve their interpersonal conflicts (because of mental illness or substance abuse) may continue to rely on old familiar patterns of abusive behavior. There is evidence to suggest that children who engage in abusive behaviors with their siblings are more far more likely to engage in other violent behavior in familial relationships later in life (Gully, Dengerink, Pepping, & Bergstrom, 1981).

Additionally, abuse between siblings has likely been ignored because it often exists within a larger landscape of family dysfunction and violence. In our attempt to deal with other forms of family violence, we have ignored the resulting element of sibling abuse. For example, Whipple and Finton (1995) describe the way problems in a family trickle down to the youngest children in a family. They provide a case example of a family in which a multilevel pecking order existed. The wife was dominated by her husband and was left feeling helpless and unhappy. She displaced her unhappiness on her eldest daughter, who in turn displaced her feelings on the youngest child in the family. Other unresolved family issues were played out by the children in a number of ways, including language delays, recurrent illnesses, and acts of mistreatment of the youngest child and the family pets. A family systems approach is likely the only way to uncover and properly acknowledge the sibling abuse that occurs in the context of other family problems.

Although we have paid little attention to sibling violence, the research that has been conducted is enough to cause us concern. In a study of 57 intact families in Delaware, Suzanne Steinmetz (1977) discovered just how pervasive sibling violence is and how most parents dismiss such behaviors as being nothing more than annoying. Parents certainly did not define their children's combative behavior as being abusive. Straus, Gelles, and Steinmetz (1980) found in a study of more than 2,000 families that acts of violence between siblings occurred with great frequency. In their study, parents reported that 8 out of 10 children with siblings committed acts of violence against a sibling every year. Although the level of violence reported tended to be minor, such as slapping, hitting, or shoving, more serious levels of violence were also reported. For example, 3 out of every 100 children used a weapon during a sibling altercation, and 42 percent of the children kicked, bit, or punched a sibling during the year.

Following the research of Steinmetz (1977) and Straus et al. (1980), in which parents were asked about their children's behavior, Roscoe and associates (1987) researched the prevalence of sibling violence by asking adolescents about the issue. In their survey of 244 junior high school students, they found confirmation that sibling violence is the most frequent form of family violence, and because they reported behaviors acknowledged by the youths themselves, they found a higher degree of frequency of violence in sibling relationships than the previous research had. For example, the survey revealed that 88 percent of the males and 94 percent of the females stated that they had been victims of sibling violence during the past year. Additionally, 85 percent of the males and 96 percent of the females admitted that they had committed acts of sibling violence.

Although we have not conducted any broad-based estimates of sibling maltreatment, the National Crime Victimization Survey (Bureau of Justice Statistics [BJS], 1999) has begun to further identify the role of family relationships in crime victimization by surveying about 50,000 households. The survey was completed by individuals age 12 and over. According to the 1999 survey, more than 5.7 million incidents of violent crimes occurred; of these, 92,616 victims, or 1.6 percent, were assaulted by a brother or sister (BJS, 1999).

The Difference Between Normal Childhood Behavior and Sibling Abuse

Because sibling interactions are so often marked by hitting, slapping, punching, wrestling, and name-calling, you may be wondering why we would consider such actions as abuse. All kids fight with their siblings. Although such behaviors are very normal, there is a line that, once crossed, changes the circumstance from normal harmless sibling conflict to abuse. But how do we distinguish between the two?

When we refer to sibling abuse, we are speaking of a pattern of behavior that leaves children and youths feeling victimized and hurt. Hurts such as these can last a lifetime. Generally, abusive behavior involves a situation in which an unequal distribution of power exists between the siblings and in which one sibling is the main contributor to the conflict. In other words, one sibling is clearly victimizing another.

Vernon Wiehe (1997) suggests that parents and professionals consider the following questions when trying to separate abuse from normal childhood behavior. First, we must examine the age appropriateness of the behavior. Having an understanding of the developmental process can be important in distinguishing between normal behavior and abuse. For example, it is absolutely normal for two preschool-age children to physically fight over possessions; it is, however, inappropriate for siblings in their late teens to do so. The teenagers should have a repertoire of communication skills at their disposal and should have the ability to share their things with their siblings without the use of physical force. However, the preschooler is learning concepts such as sharing and is developing the patience to wait to play with a toy.

One of the critical periods of development occurs between ages 5 and 7, in which children begin to develop more complicated cognitive tasks. According to Piaget, children attain a cognitive ability he called *concrete operational thought*. By about age 7, children should be able to understand the concepts of right and wrong and should be able to think following the rules of logic (Bjorklund & Bjorklund, 1992). The legal concept of *mens rea* applies here as well. The term *mens rea* literally means "guilty mind." It is a generally accepted belief that children are not capable of having guilty minds much before the age of 7; therefore, they cannot be held responsible for their actions in a court of law. For this reason, most states do not begin to process juveniles for offenses until after age 7. For example, when a 3-year-old girl places a bag of M&Ms in her pocket while standing in line at Wal-Mart, she has not "stolen" the candy; she has merely taken it for herself. She has not yet developed the cognitive ability to know the difference between taking candy off the shelf at a store and taking candy off the table at home.

Some additional examples may help clarify these differences. Consider a 10-year-old boy who continuously destroys his 4-year-old brother's block creations. The 10-year-old is old enough to know that by destroying the tower of blocks, his brother will get upset, probably cry, and is likely to respond by hitting his older brother. The 10-year-old should have sensitivity and respect for his brother's feelings; therefore, we would consider this destruction of toys an act of abuse. However, if it were the 4-year-old who continuously destroyed the 10-year-old's projects, then it would be considered an age-appropriate behavior. In either case, conflicts between siblings that result in name-calling, shoving, fighting, and such should be addressed at any age. Young children need to learn appropriate ways to deal with their anger, jealousy, and boredom. These behaviors, albeit normal, can result in harm if unchecked.

We also suggest that behaviors that can be characterized as being normal for young children constitute abuse when carried on between siblings into adulthood. Even when it appears as though power between the siblings is evenly distributed, it is inappropriate, if not criminal, for adult siblings to physically assault, verbally attack, or engage in any kind of sexual activity with each other. For example, consider two brothers in their mid-twenties who continue to physically fight each other to settle their disputes. At a minimum, siblings who continue to engage in conflicts of this nature are demonstrating that they have been unable to mature out of childhood behaviors. We believe that such acts between adults are a cause for concern because of the inherent risks for serious injury and the obvious fact that such conflicts illustrate a long history of dysfunctional interaction. For example, it is unlikely that a sibling pair would begin physically attacking each other as adults if they did not attempt to resolve their conflicts that way as children. Problems such as mental illness and substance abuse are likely to increase the risks.

Wiehe (1997) contends that, in addition to determining the age appropriateness of certain behaviors, we must also consider the frequency and duration of behaviors to distinguish between abuse and normal childhood behaviors. He notes that when fighting, name-calling, teasing, and even sexual exploration continue over a period of time, the behavior that may have originally been considered "normal" becomes abusive.

We must also investigate the purpose of the behavior and determine whether there is an aspect of victimization in the behavior. If the purpose of the behavior is to cause the other sibling injury or hurt or to provide the perpetrator with sexual pleasure, then the behavior is likely to be abusive. Wiehe (1997) notes that if the perpetrator is able to victimize the sibling through the use of game playing, trickery, deception, coercion, or physical force, we should consider the behavior abusive. For example, a teenage boy convinces his 6-year-old sister to "play with his private parts" in return for her favorite candy treat. Such behavior not only contains an aspect of victimization but is also age inappropriate and abusive, even if it occurs only once.

Box 5.1 describes a recent case of sibling abuse. In January 2001 a 12-year-old boy was arrested and charged with attempted murder and two counts of aggravated battery for attacking his sisters.

Although a representative from the sheriff's office was quoted as saying, "It apparently was just a typical sibling dispute that escalated way out of control," the act (as reported by the media) was age inappropriate, and the use of weapons indicates the boy's intent to inflict harm. This incident is an example of abuse.

> **Box 5.1 //// 12-Year-Old Attacks Sisters**
>
> In January 2001, a 12-year-old boy was arrested for attempted murder and two counts of aggravated battery for attacking his two sisters in their home near New Orleans. The incident began when the boy hit his 8-year-old sister with a chain. His 10-year-old sister attempted to intervene and reprimanded the boy for attempting to hurt his little sister. The boy responded by lunging at her with the chain and, as the girl held up her arms to protect herself, the pair of scissors she had been holding caused a minor scratch to her brother's shoulder. This incensed the boy, and he grabbed a 12-inch knife from the kitchen and lunged at his 10-year-old sister. The girl placed a pillow against her chest for protection. The girls suffered minor cuts and bruises.
>
> The children's grandmother called their mother at work, and the mother dialed 911 to report the assault. James Hartmann, the Sheriff's Office spokesman, said: "It apparently was just a typical sibling dispute that escalated way out of control."
>
> Source: The *Times-Picayune* (New Orleans), January 23, 2001

Forms of Sibling Abuse

Emotional Abuse

As we have discussed in other chapters, emotional abuse, although it does not leave physical scars, creates wounds that often last a lifetime. In his survey on sibling abuse, Wiehe (1997) defined emotional abuse as comments made by a sibling that are intended to ridicule, insult, threaten, or belittle another sibling. In addition, some siblings taunted their victims by exacerbating their fears, destroying property, and mistreating pets.

Emotional abuse is likely to be the most common form of sibling abuse, although it is also the most difficult type for which to determine the prevalence rate. The reasons are that emotional abuse often accompanies the other forms of sibling abuse and that parent-based reports tend to minimize emotionally abusive interactions between siblings. In his survey of sibling abuse, Wiehe (1997) found that, out of 150 respondents, 78 percent of the adults surveyed reported that they had been the victims of emotional abuse. However, only 7 percent of these adults indicated that they had been emotionally abused only, indicating that the vast majority of incidents of emotional abuse occurred within the context of physical or sexual abuse or both.

Emotional abuse, as well as other forms of sibling abuse, can serve as a mechanism to release or displace feelings of being victimized by a parent or older sibling. For example, Crittenden (1984) found similarities between how older siblings victimized their infant siblings and how these older siblings were treated by their mothers. Therefore, victims of sibling abuse or parental mistreatment react by abusing a younger sibling.

Victims also respond to emotional abuse in other ways. Wiehe (1997) notes that some of the adults in his survey reported that they retaliated by fighting back against the perpetrator. Some survivors internalized the negative messages they were taunted with, growing up to believe they were true. For example, a young girl who is painted with a negative image by her sister's name-calling and degradation grows up with a picture of herself as being "fat, stupid, and clumsy." As you might imagine, internalizing such messages can have a devastating impact on self-esteem. Low self-esteem affects one's choices and approach to life and is linked to self-destructive behaviors such as drug abuse, suicide, self-mutilating behavior, and eating disorders.

The consequences of emotional abuse affect all areas of a child's development, not only self-esteem. For example, emotionally and physically abused youths are at risk for delays in the areas of cognitive, language, and motor skill development (H. M. Hughes & DiBrezzo, 1987). Additionally, some researchers have argued that emotional abuse is the central element in all types of child maltreatment, having the most damaging effects on the victim's self-esteem, interpersonal relationships, and psychosocial functioning in general (Brassard & Gelardo, 1987; Garbarino & Vondra, 1987; Hart & Brassard, 1987)

Sexual Abuse

Although we often think of the term *incest* as referring to the parent-child relationship, sexual abuse between siblings is also a serious concern. In fact, some researchers believe that sibling incest is actually more prevalent, occurring at an estimated rate of at least five times greater than parent-child incest (Canavan, Meyer, & Higgs, 1992; Cole, 1982; Finkelhor, 1980). However, as with other forms of violence in the home, we currently have no broad-based way to measure the actual prevalence rate of sibling sexual abuse. It is, however, probably safe to assume that the studies that have been conducted grossly underestimate the actual occurrence of such abuse because of the veil of secrecy that is created by the shame and embarrassment connected with these types of sibling interactions (Wiehe, 1997). Additionally, parents, even if they are aware of the sexual abuse, may be unwilling to report such incidents to the authorities.

For example, a survey conducted by Finkelhor (1980) of 796 college students found that 15 percent of the females and 10 percent of the males had reported some type of sexual interaction with a sibling (Finkelhor, 1980). The common sexual experience reported involved fondling, yet 25 percent of the incidents were characterized as being exploitative because of the forceful nature of the acts and the age disparity between the victim and the perpetrator. More recently, Wiehe (1997) found a high rate of sexual abuse in his study on sibling abuse. Out of 150 survey respondents who were victimized by a sibling, 100 of them reported being victimized by sexual abuse. Wiehe (1997) notes that such a high rate of reported sexual abuse may be indicative of the fact that many incest survivors seek treatment as adults, and therefore they may have been more able to access information to complete the sibling abuse survey.

In an effort to understand the dynamics of sibling incest, researchers have studied sibling incest offenders in a number of ways. O'Brien (1991) compared sibling incest offenders with juveniles who sexually assaulted children who were not family members, as well as with offenders who assaulted adults or peers. He found that sibling-incest offenders were more likely to abuse a higher average number of victims, reported an earlier introduction to abusive behaviors, and were more likely to have been victims of sexual and physical abuse themselves. In addition, youths who abused a sibling were more likely to be reported by clinicians as having come from a severely dysfunctional family environment.

In attempt to improve reliability and validity, Worling (1995) conducted a similar study, examining 32 sibling-incest offenders in comparison with 28 offenders who had committed nonsibling sexual abuse. He found similar results. Sibling-incest offenders reported experiencing significantly more negative relationships within their family environments. They experienced more physical punishment and rejection from their parents, witnessed higher levels of marital friction between parents, and were more likely to have been victims of childhood sexual abuse. In addition, they were more likely to have younger children in their families than were nonsibling sexual offenders.

Adler and Schutz (1995) studied a small group of sibling-incest offenders ($n = 12$) who presented to a hospital-based outpatient psychiatric clinic for treatment. Although this study did not involve a comparison group, Adler and Schutz (1995) were able to provide an in-depth examination of a group of white, middle-income sex offenders from intact families (a group traditionally ignored in the research). The majority of participants were mandated by court to participate in treatment. They ranged in age from 13 to 19. These male offenders had all sexually abused a sister during the period of time in which they were between 11 and 14 years of age and their sisters were between 5 and 11 years. The mean age difference between the offender and his sister was 5 years. Results of the study confirmed previous results; these young incest offenders had a history of being victimized by child physical abuse by one or both parents. Although all lived in what appeared to be intact, functional families, family problems were evident. Parents tended to minimize and deny the abusive behaviors of their child. One area of concern was that 58 percent of the sample had a parent who had a history of being a victim of sexual abuse.

More recently, Rudd and Herzberger (1999) employed a different research strategy to enhance our understanding of dynamics of sibling incest.

Their study compared a group of women who had been sexually abused by their brothers with a group of women who had been sexually abused by their fathers. Their goal was to identify the distinct characteristics of each type of abuse and the differing impact each had on adult survivors. Surveys completed by 62 incest survivors revealed that 14 women had been abused by brothers and 15 women had been victimized by their fathers. In comparison, both groups of women endured very lengthy victimizations in which the use of force was evident. In all 14 cases of sibling incest, the absence of the father played a contributory role in the sexual abuse. Both groups of women also reported a high degree of overall family dysfunction, including substance abuse, mental illness, and extensive family-wide violence, and both groups of women experienced equally serious consequences as a result of being victimized.

These studies, although limited in number, beg our attention to the issue. They demonstrate the pervasiveness of sibling sexual abuse and indicate how connected and interrelated the various forms of family violence are. Although public policy and researchers often segregate the various forms of violence as distinct and singular, in reality, any form of violence within the family results in the potential for further levels of violence. Families that exhibit physical, sexual, or emotional abuse often perpetuate the abuse in a number of ways; sexual violence between siblings is certainly one of those ways.

Physical Abuse

The nature of physical abuse between siblings involves a continuum of violent behaviors, from minor incidents to more severe levels that cause physical injury and even death. Common forms of abuse include pinching, slapping, hitting, biting, shoving, punching, scratching and hair pulling. Perpetrators may also jump on victims, throw them to the floor, and pin them down. Abuse can become more serious with the use of weapons, such as broom handles, brushes, coat hangers, baseball bats and other toys, knives, razor blades, scissors, or BB guns. In Wiehe's (1997) survey on sibling abuse, he found that a number of respondents mentioned tickling as a form of physical abuse that was most unbearable. Tickling can be considered torturous when it becomes painful and the victim's cries for it to stop go unheeded. For example, Wiehe (1997, p. 18) notes the story of one woman who disclosed that her sister would tickle her to the point that she would vomit.

In Goodwin and Roscoe's (1990) study of adolescents, they found that 65 percent of the females and 64 percent of the males admitted that they had perpetrated some form of physical violence on a sibling during the previous year, and 64 percent of the females and 66 percent of the males experienced being victims of such acts of abuse. The most common forms of abuse reported were being pushed, shoved, or pulled, having an object thrown at them, being hit with a fist, and being hit with an object. The study found that both boys and girls played relatively equal roles in perpetrating violence or in being victims of violence. They also found that abusive behaviors tend to dissipate over time, suggesting that children often mature out of such behaviors. As we discussed earlier in this chapter, the great majority of children who experience such abusive interactions with their siblings do not continue to be victimized by such behaviors into adulthood. However, for those who do, the risks of serious injury increase as the sibling pairs grow into adulthood.

In a study conducted by Sandra Graham-Bermann, Susan Cutler, Brian Litzenberger, and Wendy Schwartz (1994), the researchers found that high rates of physically abusive behavior between siblings were recalled within the population of undergraduate college students. However, they concluded that birth order and gender differences were related to the experience of abuse. Older siblings were more likely than younger siblings to be perpetrators of conflict, with younger siblings the victims. Males were more likely to perpetrate conflict with a younger female sibling.

As these two studies indicate, the role of gender in sibling violence needs further examination. However, regardless of whether males or females perpetrate the same amount of violence, females tend to be more affected by physical violence. Saunders (1986) notes that women are more frequently injured by men during episodes of violence than men are by women. Graham-Bermann and associates (1994) found that female victims of sibling violence tended to experience anxiety as adults. Other emotional outcomes for victims included anger, resentment, and difficulty in expressing emotions. As they point out, this may be due more to social conditions that teach women to internalize their conflicts yet do not permit males to connect with emotional reactions to similar events.

Fratricide and Sororicide

The most serious form of sibling abuse is fratricide and sororicide, or the killing of one's brother or sister. Unfortunately, one of the most devastating consequences of sibling conflict results in the loss of lives every year in the United States. In a study of homicide statistics in 75 urban cities, Dawson and Langan (1994) found that of the 8,063 murder cases that occurred in 1988, 123 (or 1.5 percent) were considered sibling killings. Of all the family-related homicides reported, siblings represented 9.4 percent of the total.

One of the interesting findings in this study was the fact that the majority of the victims and the offenders in these sibling homicides were adults (over the age of 19) at the time of the murder. This suggests that sibling killings may be the result of long-standing rivalries and unresolved conflicts and not the accidental result of children quarreling. Ewing (1997) notes that in many adult sibling homicides, the siblings are living together at the time. Therefore, unresolved issues over space and control resurface to a deadly end. Often other stressors, such as unemployment, divorce, substance abuse, and illness, contribute to such conflicts.

We all may have some unresolved conflicts with our siblings, yet few of us turn to murder as a way of bringing closure to the situation. Why, for example, would one adult brother kill another over a piece of chocolate cake? Why would an argument over a video game result in a deadly beating with a baseball bat? Why would a woman kill her sister over innocent flirtatious behavior? There is no clear-cut answer to such questions; however, by examining homicide cases involving siblings, we do know that mental illness and substance abuse, particularly alcohol use, has a substantial role to play in such cases. For example, among the 123 sibling murders in Dawson and Langan's (1994) study for the Department of Justice, 17.3 percent involved perpetrators with a history of mental illness. More than one-half of the perpetrators and over one-third of the victims had been using alcohol at the time of the incident. For example, Box 5.2 describes the recent case of a young man who, out on bond for the murder of a 13-year-old girl in Cook County, IL, killed his brother and raped his sister. In this case, the young perpetrator admitted to drinking and smoking marijuana prior to the assault on his siblings.

Box 5.3 illustrates the case of Larry Dame, who, at age 28, was convicted of murdering his sister and her family. He was sentenced to five consecutive life terms in June 2002.

In the cases of sibling homicide that involve juvenile perpetrators, we find that many of the young perpetrators live in abusive families. Many, but certainly not all, of these youngsters have psychological problems, and some exhibit behaviors consistent with conduct disorder or antisocial personality

---

Box 5.2 /// 19-Year-Old Kills Brother and Rapes Sister

On March 17, 1995, Steven Pfiel, while out on bond for the murder of Hillary Norskog, bludgeoned his brother Roger to death and raped his sister. During his confession, he reported that he and his brother had been celebrating St. Patrick's Day the night of March 16th from about midnight to 3 a.m. After his brother Roger went to bed, Steven "smoked a little grass." He then went into his brother's room and beat him with a baseball bat.

"I couldn't control myself," he said. "When I stopped hitting, he was convulsing, so I grabbed a cleaver from the kitchen and went to stop Roger from dying slow." He slashed his brother's throat and fled.

Pfiel plead guilty to the murder charge of both his brother and Hillary Norskog. The Will County Court in Illinois sentenced him to life in prison without parole.

Source: *Chicago Sun-Times*, October 21, 1995

> ### *Box 5.3 /// Minnesota Man Accused of Murdering His Sister and Her Family*
>
> In December 2000, a grand jury in Anoka County, Minnesota, indicted
> Larry Dame, age 28, on five counts of first-degree premeditated murder in
> the deaths of his sister and her family. On October 18, 2000, Donna Mim-
> bach, her husband, Todd Mimbach, and their children, John Mimbach
> (12), Amber Duval (9), and Daniel Mimbach (22 months) were stabbed to
> death in their home.
>
>   The jury rejected Dame's mental-illness defense and found him guilty of
> the murders. Judge John Hoffman sentenced him to five consecutive life
> terms of at least 30 years each, with a minimum of 150 years, for this hor-
> rific crime.
>
> Source: *Star Tribune* (Minneapolis, MN), December 22, 2000, and June 6, 2002

disorder (Ewing, 1997). In the cases of accidental killings by young siblings,
the major factor appears to be parental neglect—for example, keeping a gun
in the home to which the child has access, keeping fire-starting materials
within reach of children, and substance abuse (Ewing, 1997).

Understanding Why Sibling Abuse Occurs

As is true for all forms of violence in the home described in this book, there
is no one clear explanation for the occurrence of sibling abuse. As we described in chapter 2, understanding why violence occurs between siblings
requires an examination of the individual, the family system, and the social
conditions present within a given society. Because the varying forms of sibling abuse occur so frequently, we should explore some of the factors that
we know or suspect are associated specifically with abusive behaviors between siblings.

Issues of Power and Control

As we discuss elsewhere in this book, issues of power and control weigh
heavily in abusive relationships. When power differentials exist, the potential
for abuse exists. In the case of siblings, power may be determined by birth
order, gender, or size. Therefore, siblings who have more "natural power"
are in a position to victimize children in the family who have less.

    However, when it comes to children, another factor is also important
to consider. How power is distributed or utilized by siblings may be determined by parental behavior. For example, an older sister may be left with
the responsibility of caring for a younger sister. The authority granted to
the older sister through the designation of the title "baby-sitter" may create
a potential situation in which abuse can occur. Wiehe (1997) notes that

parents often have unrealistic expectations of their older children's ability to responsibly care for younger siblings, creating a circumstance in which normal conflicts can be played out in an abusive way. Some siblings are simply too young to be left in charge, and others, although arguably old enough, lack the appropriate "parenting" skills to adequately perform the necessary functions of baby-sitters.

Lack of Supervision and Nonintervention

Although all siblings, with the possible exception of some twin pairs, have some level of power inequality in that one of them has to be older, bigger, and so forth, power inequities combined with parental behavior may be the determining factors in how sibling interactions will ultimately be played out. The lack of appropriate adult supervision, or the lack of parental intervention, provides an opportunity for abusive acts to occur. For example, siblings who engage in more predatory behavior, such as sexual abuse, generally require adult absences in order to be successful in their attempts to victimize. When adults are not supervising sibling interactions, the inequitable distribution of power is more likely to be an issue in sibling relationships.

Additionally, parents who do not intervene in sibling acts of abuse when they witness or are told of such events are, in effect, reinforcing the inequitable distribution of power and the inappropriate behavior. For example, a study conducted by Kramer, Perozynski, and Chung (1999) found that parental nonintervention in the sibling conflicts between their children (who had a 2- to 4-year age differential) was highly associated with the continued occurrence of additional events. In their study of 88 two-child, two-parent families, they found that younger children, in particular, were far more combative when their parents did not intervene.

For example, Box 5.4 describes a case in which parental nonintervention was found to be a key factor in the sexual abuse of their young daughter. This recent case involved a young girl who was found to be abused and neglected by her parents because they did not protect her from sexual abuse by her older brother. Her older brother pleaded guilty of sexual abuse charges in criminal court, and her parents were charged with child abuse and neglect for not providing her with adequate protection from her brother.

Family Dysfunction

The research we have discussed in this chapter points to overall family dysfunction, family stress, and intrafamilial abuse as being common themes present in families with siblings who are abusive. These research findings are consistent with two main theoretical perspectives, attachment theory and social learning theory. In other words, how we interact with others is a result of our early experiences with human interaction.

> **Box 5.4 /// Parents Charged with Child Abuse and Neglect**
> **for Not Protecting Daughter from Sibling Sexual Abuse**
>
> In Nassau County, New York, parents of a 16-year-old girl are charged
> with child abuse and neglect for not protecting their daughter from being
> sexually abused by her older half-brother. Although the young girl told her
> mother and stepfather about her older brother's abusive behavior, her par-
> ents refused to believe her. The parents originally asked the brother to stay
> out of the house; he eventually began to gain entrance to the home, only
> to continue the sexual abuse of his sister. The abuse began when she was
> 12 years old.
>
> In January of 1997, the brother was arrested on a sexual abuse charge.
> The parents came to the aid of their son, claiming their daughter was a
> liar. They threatened their daughter, trying to force her to recant her alle-
> gations against her brother. The parents did nothing to get help for their
> daughter.
>
> The parents were eventually brought before the family court on charges
> of child abuse and neglect for not protecting their daughter. In November
> of 1997, the family court ruled that the parents were aware of the sexual
> abuse, allowed their daughter to be abused while in their custody and care,
> and failed to protect her from harm. The court further determined that the
> couple's other four children were neglected children.
>
> Source: *New York Law Journal*, November 4, 1997

Specifically, attachment theory examines sibling relationships as a result
of the internalization of interactions with a child's primary caregivers. Social
learning theory suggests that abusive behavior by parents is reinforced over
time and eventually is generalized to sibling, and perhaps even peer, relationships (MacKinnon-Lewis, Starnes, Volling, & Johnson, 1997). In either
theoretical perspective, a child's social behavior is related to the interactional
patterns within the family. Therefore, such interactions as resolving conflicts,
showing affection, discipline, sexual behavior, power distribution, and so
forth are exhibited, reinforced, and internalized by children as they grow.
Children then take what they have learned and apply it to other situations.
There may even be an additive quality to such behaviors. For example,
Garcia, Shaw, Winslow, and Yaggi (2000) found that young boys who experienced high levels of destructive sibling conflict and high levels of parental rejection were more likely to exhibit aggressive behaviors, both at home
and at school, than children who experienced only one of these predictors.

Therefore, families teach children about social behavior through modeling and reinforcement. Families who exhibit violent, abusive behavior are
likely to find siblings reacting in similar ways. Social behavior is learned
from a variety of influences; however, parents' interactions with each other

and with their children do provide young children with a foundation on which to build their repertoire of behaviors. Therefore, it is not surprising that research continues to find linkages between child maltreatment, intimate partner abuse, and child-perpetrated violence.

Another factor in sibling abuse may be the inability of the parent to provide adequate parenting due to some other level of dysfunction. Wiehe (1997) notes that sibling abuse often occurs in families in which the parents are overwhelmed with their own problems and therefore are unable or unwilling to intervene in the problems of their children. Problems such as drug and alcohol abuse, mental illness, marital discord, and financial stresses can overload parents, rendering them ineffective in areas of discipline and supervision.

Social Conditions

We must also include the role of various social conditions in the perpetuation of sibling abuse. First, given the general acceptance of acts of sibling abuse in the larger social structure, even young people who live in relatively healthy families can experience sibling abuse. As we discussed earlier, current social standards regard physical acts of aggression between siblings as normal sibling rivalry. Therefore, parents may receive little guidance from their social support network of family and friends to assist them in appropriate levels of intervention into destructive sibling interactions. Communities dismiss sibling violence as a natural occurrence that children ultimately grow out of; therefore, it is not considered serious. The lack of concern over sibling abuse is evident in the lack of public policy and social service response systems to intervene in such situations. However, although sibling violence does tend to dissipate over time, Goodwin and Roscoe (1990) point out that, when older youths are still engaged in destructive behaviors, there is a greater risk of serious injury due to their size and physical strength. Additionally, we cannot dismiss the consequence that behavior learned and reinforced in childhood is often continued into later adulthood.

Second, economic forces often create circumstances in which families become vulnerable to abusive behavior by siblings. For example, if both parents must work or choose to work outside the home, children may be left alone to care for themselves. Families may lack appropriate financial resources to provide adequate child care, housing arrangements in which siblings have a level of privacy, and the ability to access appropriate services for themselves or their children (Wiehe, 1997).

Consequences of Sibling Abuse

As with all other forms of violence in the home, sibling abuse has devastating consequences for the victim and the family. Recently, research has begun to explore the ways in which sibling relationships influence development, psychological functioning, and social behavior. However, only a handful of studies have focused on the effects of sibling abuse in particular.

In his study of survivors of sibling abuse, Wiehe (1997) found that victims suffered from many long-term problems as a result of acts of abuse by their siblings. Perhaps the most pervasive finding was the impact on the victim's self-esteem. As we discuss in other chapters, self-esteem is frequently affected by abuse. Victims are left feeling insignificant, degraded, worthless, and unloved. Additionally, survivors reported having difficulty with relationships with the opposite sex and others; repeating the victim role in other relationships; self-blame, anger, and resentment toward the perpetrator; sexual dysfunction; eating disorders; alcoholism and drug abuse; depression; and posttraumatic stress disorder.

Garrett and McKenzie (1995) found that victims of sibling abuse suffer the same type of long-term effects as do victims of other kinds of child maltreatment. Consequences included difficulties with other interpersonal relationships and sexual functioning and emotional problems. Victims also reported low self-esteem as a direct result of being insulted by a sibling regarding their appearance, height, weight, and personality. Additionally, Graham-Bermann and associates (1994) found that the emotional toll of sibling violence was greater for females than for males and was associated with feelings of anxiety in young adulthood.

These studies provide evidence that sibling abuse is a serious phenomenon with consequences as devastating as those of other forms of violence in the home. However, the public discussion of sibling abuse has not yet been realized as fully as it has for other forms of family violence. Therefore, little aid is currently available in terms of prevention and intervention. Child welfare workers are bound by state policies that examine only the abusive acts of adults in the home. Therefore, parents would have to step forward to report their children to the police or juvenile court to seek intervention. Given the general lack of public recognition of sibling abuse issues, it is unlikely that parents would seek the assistance of the police and courts in such circumstances unless the violence resulted in serious physical injury or was one among other inappropriate behaviors, such as running away, truancy, fighting with peers, substance abuse, or acts of delinquency.

/// Parental Abuse

Many of us can recall having fights or disagreements with our parents during our growing years. In fact, many us may even consider conflict with parents a normal "rite of passage" from adolescence into adulthood. However, the idea of a young person physically attacking or threatening violence against a parent seems incomprehensible. As parents have more control and power by virtue of their age, size, and access to financial resources, how can they possibly be victims of family violence? However difficult this may be for us to imagine, the truth is that some children do abuse their parents (and as we discuss in chapter 6, many adults are abused by their adult children). In this section we restrict our discussion to children and adolescents who abuse their parents.

Although the research and experiences of juvenile justice professionals clearly documents the existence of parental abuse, measuring actual prevalence rates has been difficult. As you might imagine, parents do not often report such incidents to authorities due to embarrassment and fear of getting the child into trouble or of the child retaliating. Parents may actually go to great lengths to protect their abusive children and keep up the appearance of a happy family life (Harbin & Madden, 1979). Gelles (1997) describes the social disapproval of children using force against a parent as being a factor in parents' reasons for not routinely disclosing such behavior.

Although parents may not openly discuss such behavior, often young people who are abusive to their parents also exhibit other behavioral problems, such as running away from home, difficulties at school, alcohol and drug use, delinquency, and so forth, and thereby come to the attention of the juvenile justice system. Thus probation officers, family court personnel, and social service workers routinely come across youths who are abusive to one or both parents.

Outside the experience of juvenile justice professionals, the measurement of violence against parents has not drawn the attention of researchers in a broad way, as other forms of family violence have. Cornell and Gelles (1982) found that in a nationally representative sample of families who had a teenager living at home, 9 percent of the parents reported that at least one act of violence had been perpetrated by their child against them. Gelles (1997) argues that although this 9 percent may sound like an insignificant percentage, it translates into 2.5 million parents who are assaulted at least once a year by one of their children. Additionally, Peek, Fisher, and Kidwell (1985) estimated that 8 percent of fathers and 6 percent of mothers have been victimized by their children. More recently, Browne and Hamilton (1998) found similar results, with 8.5 percent of mothers and 6.1 percent of fathers experiencing violence by a child. According to the National Crime Victimization Survey (Bureau of Justice Statistics [BJS], 1999), of the more than 7 million crimes of violence reported by victims, 68,150 were perpetrated by a child against a parent.

Why are children abusive toward their parents? The answer seems to lie in the complexity of violent families themselves. Children who are violent toward a parent often have had a past history of victimization by a parent, either directly or through the observation of intimate partner violence (Browne & Hamilton, 1998; Cornell & Gelles, 1982). Being part of a violent family teaches young people to use violence to mediate their conflicts (Straus et al, 1980), and observing such violence consequently leads to child behavioral problems (M. Hughes, 1988). We also know that adolescents who have friends who assault their parents, who find some delinquent behaviors reasonable, who perceive the risk of getting caught to be very low, or who have weak attachments to their parents are also at risk for being abusive to a parent (Agnew & Huguley, 1989).

Our understanding of other forms of violence between child and parent is even more unclear. To date, little is known about possible emotional or sexual abuse by children against a parent. Most of the research has focused on physical assault. However, children killing parents has gained more attention from researchers.

Parricide

Parricide refers to killing one's own parent. *Patricide* is the murder of one's father, and *matricide* is the murder of one's mother.

Parricide has recently come to the public's attention because of the highly publicized case of the Menendez brothers in 1989. In this case, Erik and Lyle Menendez were found guilty of murdering their wealthy socialite parents in Los Angeles. The defense argued that Erik and Lyle had suffered past physical abuse by their father and believed that they were in danger of death or imminent serious bodily harm. The prosecution, however, argued that Erik and Lyle killed their parents to gain control of their parent's wealth. The first trial ended with a deadlocked jury, but the second trial jury was not convinced of their reports of past abuse. In 1996, the jury found the brothers guilty of first-degree murder with a special circumstance of financial gain, which carried a mandatory life-without-parole sentence. Although the brothers have appealed the convictions, the state Supreme Court ruled to uphold their convictions ("High Court Won't Hear Challenge," 1998).

Some 300 parents and stepparents are murdered each year in the United States by their children or stepchildren (Heide, 1992). Approximately 1.5 to 2.5 percent of all homicides in the United States are parricides. Both adults and youths, particularly those in late adolescence, have been responsible for the death of parents. Box 5.5 describes a recent case in which a 44-year-old woman who had a long history of alcohol abuse and depression killed her 81-year-old mother and attempted to murder her 49-year-old sister.

Victims of parricide are typically white and non-Hispanic and are in their late 40s or 50s. Perpetrators tend to be white, non-Hispanic males, and more than 70 percent of them are younger than 30 years old (Heide, 1992). Although we have been unable to determine the exact number of homicides involving young offspring because of limitations in data collection, Heide (1992) estimates that as many as 65 natural parents (45 fathers and 20 mothers) have been killed by children under the age of 18.

In a review of the literature on adolescent parricide, Heide (1994) notes that the majority of studies conducted on the subject have found widespread evidence of child maltreatment and spousal abuse. Therefore, other forms of violence in the home are important to our understanding of the reasons

---

Box 5.5 /// Woman Kills Her Mother and Wounds Her Sister

In March 2001, Sue Ann Wieczorek, 44, was sentenced to 28 years and 10 months in prison for murdering her 81-year-old mother and wounding her 49-year old sister. She pled guilty to intentional second-degree murder in the November 2000 shootings. She also received an 8-year prison term for the attempted murder of her sister, which will be served concurrently.

She admitted shooting her mother and sister; however, she offered no explanation. Her sister, Jane, told police that they had been arguing prior to the shooting. Other family members report that tape recordings found after the shootings indicate that Sue Ann had planned to kill more family members at an upcoming wedding in December. Her brother, Dan Wieczorek, said that the killings were planned, Sue Ann had purchased two 9-millimeter handguns and learned how to shoot them.

In determining her sentence, Ramsey County District (Minnesota) Judge George Peterson noted that Sue Ann had a lengthy history of treatments for severe depression and alcohol abuse.

Source: *Star Tribune* (Minneapolis, MN), March 16, 2001

---

that a young person would kill one or both of his or her parents. As we discussed in chapter 3, child victims of abuse and neglect often suffer many consequences, including later violent behavior. In a study involving 40 women who were abused as children, Heide and Solomon (1991) discovered that half of them had seriously considered killing their parents to escape ongoing sexual abuse. Many of the women reported that they did not ultimately murder their parents for fear that they lacked the speed, agility, or strength necessary to complete the act.

In addition to finding evidence of family violence, Heide (1992) has identified several other characteristics that tend to be associated with adolescent parricide. These include easy access to guns, failed efforts by the adolescent to secure help or escape from the family situation, social isolation, alcohol abuse in the home, and increased feelings of helplessness and an inability to cope with stress. Also this crime often involves youths who have not had any prior involvement in the justice system. Heide (1992) also found evidence that family members have felt relieved by the death of the parent. This finding relates to the work of Sargent (1962) and Ewing (1990), who have observed that in some cases of parricide a conspiracy exists in which the adolescent more or less acts on behalf of the rest of the family by killing the parent. The adolescent responds to direct or indirect messages from other family members who wish the parent dead.

Fewer cases of adolescent parricide can be attributed to mental illness. Sometimes the parricide is preceded by a long history of psychiatric problems, and in some cases the parricide event become the first obvious sign of illness (Ewing, 1997). However, especially in the case of adolescents, often the perpetrator suffers from acute depression and suicidal ideation (Dutton & Yamini, 1995).

Even fewer cases have been identified in which the motive for killing is greed. Even when economic gain can clearly be established, often it is also associated with long-term child maltreatment, antisocial behavior, or both (Ewing, 1997).

/// Animal Abuse

The link between animal abuse and other forms of family violence has historically been ignored. The connection between cruelty to animals and interpersonal violence has only recently drawn the attention of researchers and practitioners. Because all forms of family violence have been systemically dealt with as distinct and separate events, perhaps it is not surprising that animal abuse would be handled in a similar manner. Animal welfare practitioners such as animal control officers, humane investigators, and veterinarians have long witnessed the devastation of abuse toward animals and have noticed that many of these animals live with problematic families. At the same time, child protection and domestic violence advocates have observed the neglect and maltreatment of animals in their clients' homes. However, practitioners from both disciplines have rarely engaged the other (Arkow, 1999). Little is available in terms of protocols and formal policy to bring animal welfare workers together with child welfare and domestic violence specialists. Arkow (1999) argues that practitioners may be reluctant to report other forms of suspected abuse for many reasons, including lack of training regarding the connection between family violence and animal abuse, inadequate resources to address the issues, absence of policy regarding cross-reporting, and the lack of a desire to become involved in such problems.

Compounding the issue is the lack of interest on the part of the criminal justice system in aggressively prosecuting incidents of animal abuse singularly or in conjunction with other family violence offenses. Although ample federal and state legislation has addressed the issue by creating statutes that protect animals from neglect and abuse (Beirne, 1999) and although a significant body of case law exists regarding the protection of animals, it is very difficult to actually recognize such acts and to prosecute and convict those who commit them (Silverstein, 1996). Arluke and Luke (1997) argue that the criminal justice system has been indifferent to violence toward animals because animals are less valued in society and because incidents of animal abuse are presumed to be a rare occurrences and are considered distinct, isolated crimes. Concurrently, Beire (1999) notes that the lack of interest in animal abuse by criminologists has left the connection between animal abuse and interpersonal conflict virtually unexplored.

Investigations of the connection between animal abuse and family violence have recently begun to identify animal abuse as a factor in families in which maltreatment occurs. Although the research to date is in the exploratory stage, a mounting body of evidence suggests that the association of animal abuse with violence in homes is a critical link worthy of continued examination. For example, in 1997, the American Humane Association filed a formal petition with the Department of Health and Human Services requesting a formal federal investigation into the link between family violence and the abuse of animals. The petition calls on the department and its relevant subagencies to initiate a broad-based study of the link (American Veterinary Medical Association [AVMA], 1997). Additionally, the American Humane Association has recently created a national resource center on the link between violence to people and to animals. The goals of the center are to provide training to professionals, to explore the protocols for intervention and treatment of animal and human abuse offenders, to conduct research, to educate public-policy makers, and to conduct public awareness campaigns.

Defining Animal Abuse

All kinds of animals have been subjected to cruelty by family members. Actual violence, threats of violence, and neglect have been perpetrated on family pets such as birds, cats, dogs, fish, and turtles, on livestock such as goats, pigs, sheep, turkeys, rabbits, and horses, and on wild or stray animals. However, the task of identifying animal abuse in the context of family violence requires a clear definition of *animal* and of what constitutes *abusive treatment*. The legal definitions present in animal welfare legislation often have specific language defining what an animal is or is not. For example, Delaware defines animals as "excluding fish, crustaceans, and mollusks," Kentucky refers to "four-legged animals" (Patronek, 2001). Additionally, the criteria used to determine what types of behavior are to be considered maltreatment must also be well established within statutes. Behaviors such as hunting, mercy killing, killing animals for food, using force or prodding instruments for training purposes, using animals in entertainment, and so forth are socially accepted practices. The motivation for animal mistreatment is an important feature of the family violence dynamic. The reasons behind such cruelty to animals, especially by children, are complex and varied (Boat, 1999).

When the intention to harm animals is purely a result of the dynamics of abusive family relationships, the context and definition of animal maltreatment should be explored further by legislators, veterinarians, animal welfare workers, criminal justice professionals, clinicians, victim advocates, and researchers. One of the first attempts to begin to categorize animal violence has recently been developed by Barbara Boat. The Boat Inventory on Animal-Related Experiences (BIARE) was developed to gain assessment information from children and adults about the role of animal-focused violence in their histories (Boat, 1999). The inventory examines the history of pet ownership, experiences of animals as a source of support, experiences of participating in or witnessing acts of cruelty, killing, or sexual interactions, and animal fears. Although the inventory has been utilized (Baker, Boat, Grinvalsky, & Geracioti, 1998) or adapted for use (Flynn, 1999, Miller & Knutson, 1997) in only a handful of studies, it provides the initial dialogue on animal abuse in the lives of individuals in need of mental health services.

Following are a variety of examples of the numerous ways in which animals have been abused by family members. However, standards for what kinds of circumstances actually constitute cruelty vary widely in state laws and local ordinances.

Physical Abuse

Like humans, animals have suffered injuries from being hit, kicked, thrown across the room, stabbed or cut, jumped on, lit on fire, blinded, stoned, trapped, strangled, and so forth. Physical abuse may involve acts meant to torture animals (and their human victims) or to tease them; however, the intention is to cause suffering and pain.

Neglect

The vast majority of acts of cruelty to animals involve neglect. As we discuss elsewhere in this book, neglect generally refers to a lack of proper provision of food, shelter, and reasonable medical treatment and the failure to euthanize an animal when medically indicated. However, the standards of care for various types of animals are not well established, making the diagnosis of neglect very difficult. Emotional neglect is one area in which such standards are not clear. For example, many would agree that keeping dogs isolated for long periods of time has a negative impact on dogs; however, statutes may not address inhumane restraint (Patronek, 2001). Neglect may be a deliberate act of an abuser to gain control over a victim or a passive act as part of an overall picture of neglect for family members.

Sexual Abuse

Animals are also sexually abused in numerous ways. Adults or children may be forced into acts of or witnessing bestiality by their abusive partners or parents. Abuse might include sexual touching of animals, inserting objects into an animal's orifices, sodomy, and actual intercourse.

Peticide

Peticide can be defined as the willful, deliberate, unjustified slaying of a companion animal, with the specific intent to intimidate, terrorize, or emotionally blackmail the animal's owner (Animal Abuse, 2001). Death is often of the most violent nature, including mutilation, being set on fire, decapitation, hanging, shooting, placing an animal in a microwave oven, tying an animal to railroad tracks, leaving an injured animal in the road, and so forth.

Signs of Abuse

Regardless of the form abuse takes, both animals and humans are profoundly affected by such maltreatment. Sherry Schlueter (1999, pp. 316–319) outlines standard signs of abuse, which include:

- Animals in poor physical condition.
- Animals that are excessively aggressive or submissive.
- Poor general sanitation of animal living area.
- Space, light, and ventilation deficiencies.
- Excessive numbers of animals for the space and other resources.
- Cruel confinement.
- Lack of necessary medical care or absence of appropriate food.
- Evidence of dead animals, buried or unburied, on the property.
- Having species in locations where they are not permitted by zoning regulations.
- Financial inability to properly feed or care for animals.
- Evidence of bestiality.
- Evidence of ritualistic sacrifice.
- Evidence of animal baiting and fighting.
- Humans and pets living in a state of isolation.
- Excessive matting of hair coat
- Parasite infestation.
- Abandonment of animals.

Typology

In an attempt to further define animal abuse, Andrew Rowan (1999) has developed a typology that takes into consideration human motivation in examining animal abuse. He acknowledges that there are a number of reasons for which animals are hurt by humans, including power and control, curiosity, sadism, and other psychopathological problems. His typology divides behavior into four categories: *cruelty, abuse, neglect,* and *use.* He reserves the category of *cruelty* only for those situations that involve the intentional causing of harm to an animal, while taking satisfaction from watching the animal suffer. Cruelty may result from psychological problems of the human actor or from a belief system that does not acknowledge the potential suffering of animals (and perhaps of humans as well). Family violence specialists should be most concerned with the categories of cruelty, abuse, and neglect.

The category of *abuse* refers to situations in which the abuse of power and physical force have led to an animal getting hurt. For example, abuse may result from the inappropriate use of force for disciplinary purposes. The actor gains satisfaction from successfully being able to dominate and control the animal. The actor, therefore, is interested in controlling the animal and may in fact severely hurt the animal in the process.

The category of *neglect* refers to cases in which the animal is harmed because of the inability of the caretaker to properly care for the animal. Rowan (1999) acknowledges that cases of willful neglect are likely to be considered abuse and therefore should be treated as such by law enforcement authorities. However, his category of neglect can be related to our discussions of passive neglect. The caretaker gains no satisfaction from neglecting animals; however, due to financial or mental health problems, the caretaker is incapable of providing proper care. He includes in this category individuals who "collect" or "hoard" animals in an effort to protect them from some real or imagined danger. Animal collectors, often neglectful of their own personal care (and neglectful of the care of their children), coexist with many animals, often in filthy, disease-ridden conditions. Animal collectors are generally in need of mental health services.

Rowan (1999) also includes the category of *use*. This category is reserved for those animals that endure suffering as a result of some socially accepted practice, such as animal testing, hunting, and so forth. Individuals who engage in such practices may enjoy the activity or deem the activity as having important functions to better mankind, and the fact that the animals are injured or killed is considered an unpleasant consequence. Individuals who engage in these activities do not enjoy making animals suffer; however, they understand that animals will be hurt in the process. Although socially sanctioned, these activities are still regulated by state statutes and local ordinances to ensure that proper methods and conditions are present to minimize the suffering of the animal kingdom.

Link Between Animal Abuse and Intimate Partner Abuse

Stories of women who have been abused by their intimate partners are often filled with examples of brutality toward pets. Although ample anecdotal information is available from domestic violence advocates and treatment professionals, little has been done to formally document the extent of animal abuse in violent homes. It is theorized that abusers use violence toward pets as a way of demanding control and further threatening intimate partners, and this violence may in fact be related to the batterer's lethality (Ascione, 1998).

In an effort to begin to document such abuses, the Center for Prevention of Domestic Violence developed a protocol to identify and categorize violence toward animals in three programs that serve both victims and batterers (Jorgensen & Maloney, 1999). During the years 1993 through 1996, these programs asked victims and offenders questions regarding animals being threatened, abused, and killed. Interestingly, 12 percent of the victims who were served in the advocacy program during this time period reported that their partners had threatened, abused, or killed a family pet, and 15.5 percent of the women residing in the safe house reported such abuses. However, only .09 percent of the batterers completing the MOVE (Men Overcoming Violent Encounters) program took responsibility for such acts (Jorgensen & Maloney, 1999). The center documented both direct and indirect forms of abuse toward animals. Examples of direct forms of abuse included kicking the dog or cat; throwing an animal across the room, shooting the animal (often in front of the victim), breaking the pet's legs or neck, hanging the pet, cutting ears or tails, and so forth. Indirect forms of abuse included abandoning the pet; neglecting to feed or water farm animals, threatening to take the pet away, euthanizing pets to retaliate against human victims, threatening to kill and cook the pet rabbit, overfeeding fish, and making an asthmatic woman live in a house with long-haired cats (Jorgensen & Maloney, 1999).

In a study of battered women who were residing at a shelter in northern Utah, Frank Ascione (1998) found that of the women who owned pets, 71 percent reported that their male partners had threatened, hurt, or killed one or more of their pets. Women reported examples such as threatening to put a kitten in a blender, burying a cat up to its head and mowing it, and starving a dog. Animals were slapped, shaken, thrown, drowned, lit on fire, and shot by their abusive partners. Additionally, 18 percent of the women noted that they did not seek help earlier for fear of what would happen to their pets if they left.

In a national survey of domestic violence shelters, Ascione, Weber, and Wood (1997) investigated shelter professionals' perceptions of the connection between battering and animal abuse. They found that, although the majority of shelters reported that their adult and child clients talked about incidents of pet abuse, few shelters routinely inquired about animal abuse in their intake interview processes. In addition, only 8 percent of the respondents reported collaborative arrangements with animal welfare professionals to provide shelter for pets.

Link Between Animal Abuse and Child Maltreatment

Examining the link between child abuse and animal abuse has also generated substantial evidence worthy of further investigation. Research has focused on the clinical connection between children who are cruel to animals and past victimization. Children who have witnessed domestic violence or have suffered directly through the hands of an abusive parent may respond by being cruel to animals. DeViney, Dickert, and Lockwood (1983) were the first to explore the relationship between child maltreatment and the abuse of pets. In this early study of 53 New Jersey families indicated for child abuse, 88 percent of the families who physically abused their children also had animals that were abused, as compared with only 34 percent of the families who abused their children in a different manner. In this study, both fathers and children were the perpetrators of animal-focused violence.

DeViney and colleagues (1983) suggested that children engaged in cruel behaviors toward animals as a way to scapegoat their problems toward a more powerless creature. Although this makes intuitive sense, the link between animal abuse and family violence may also suggest that children engage in aggressive acts toward animals as a way of modeling the behavior of an abusive parent or because of psychopathology. Understanding the complex dynamic of cruelty to animals by children is of serious concern, especially to mental health specialists. In fact, the American Psychiatric Association's *Diagnostic and Statistical Manual of Mental Disorders* (DSM-III-R; 1987) added physical cruelty to animals to the list of criteria to meet the diagnosis of conduct disorder (Flynn, 1999). Conduct disorder is defined as "a persistent pattern of conduct in which the basic rights of others and major age-appropriate societal norms or rules are violated" (as cited in Arkow, 1999, p. 23).

Clinical studies of violent adults and youths have acknowledged an association between childhood violence toward animals and later violence toward humans. Although the research has been limited, there appears to be a strong link between the experience of harsh physical punishment and to the commission of animal abuse in childhood, especially for males (Flynn, 1999). Aggressive acts toward animals by children serves as an important indicator of future mental health problems and human violence (Kellert & Felthous, 1985; Lockwood & Hodge, 1986). Flynn (1999) found a relationship between parent-to-child violence and animal abuse. He examined the connection between socially sanctioned corporal punishment and animal abuse. He found specifically that male-to-male violence (in the form of corporal punishment) had the strongest relationship to animal abuse, even among a nonclinical sample of college students. Aggression and dominance by males (exhibited by parents through corporal punishment) may be rehearsed by young males through aggressive acts toward animals.

Future Prevention and Intervention

Regardless of the forms that violence and aggression take in the home, animals are likely to be at risk for injury and suffering. In fact, Arkow (1999, p. 23) states, "It is rare to see cases of severe animal abuse and neglect in which other problems are not also extant." Therefore, it is imperative that child welfare workers, family violence specialists, criminal justice professionals, mental health providers, and animal welfare professionals join together to protect animals within the context of violent families. Animal abuse serves as a marker for family violence, and in the same vein, family violence serves as a marker for animal abuse. The mutual goals of human welfare workers and animal welfare professionals demand a collaborative approach.

Additionally, although there is arguably ample legislation to protect animals, veterinarians have been reluctant to report cases of animal mistreatment, let alone suspected cases of family violence. To date, no legislation exists that requires veterinarians to report such maltreatment, although the ethical guidelines set forth by the profession do direct veterinarians to do so (Patronek, 2001). Family violence specialists have not acknowledged the connection between animals and people and rarely consider family animals in traditional intervention systems. The bottom line is that animal abuse is a warning sign, one that begs our attention, not only for the future protection of animals but also for the future protection of humans.

/// Chapter Summary

This chapter was dedicated to the three types of violence most often ignored in public and professional discussions on family violence. We explored sibling abuse, parent abuse, and the maltreatment of family animals. As we discussed, these forms of violence often exist within a context of other forms of maltreatment within the family. Each serves as a worthy topic for continued dialogue within public and professional domains, as little formal attention has been paid to them by service providers or scholars.

/// Recommended Web Sites

American Humane Association
    www.americanhumane.org
American Society for the Prevention of Cruelty to Animals
    www.aspca.org
American Veterinary Medical Association
    www.avma.org
National Network for Child Care
    www.nncc.org/Parent/parent.page.*html*
Petabuse
    www.petabuse.org
The Zero by Andrew Vachss, Esq.
    www.vachss.com/help_text/pets_animals.html

6 /// Elter Abuse

*P*at peers out the front window of her ranch house. "What are you looking at now?" asks her husband, Scott. Pat replies, "Gina just pulled in
across the street. She's driving a 2002 Buick LaSabre. Now, where do you
suppose she got the money to purchase that car?" Scott says, "Pat, mind
your own business." "Well, I can't," Pat says. "That Gina is stealing her
father blind, can't you see that? You know Antonio [her father] is 76 years
old now, and after those strokes he suffered last year, he depends on Gina
to take care of him. You know Gina got laid off six months ago. How can
she afford a brand new car? And look at that lawn, it hasn't been mowed
since last year. I wonder how long she's going to let it grow? I hate to picture
how bad the inside of the house is. Martha told me she stopped all health
aid and cleaning services. I think she's hiding something!" Scott laughs,
"You've been watching too many movies!" "No, really, Scott, I am really
worried about Antonio. I haven't seen him since Gina moved in. But I've
heard her screaming at him a lot. You know Antonio used to hit his wife a
lot when she was alive, you know that, Scott, you've seen him hit her in
the front yard." Yeah, I guess maybe we should be concerned, but what do
you expect us to do about it?" said Scott.

It has been estimated that anywhere from 1 percent to 5 percent of our
elderly population will become the victims of elder abuse annually (Swagerty, Takahashi, & Evans, 1999; Tatara &Kuzmeskus, 1997; Young, 2000).
Some scholars estimate the figure to be as high as 10 percent (Brownell &
Abelman, 1998). Moreover, the National Center on Elder Abuse documented an increase in domestic elder abuse cases of 150 percent from 1986
to 1996 (Tatara & Kuzmeskus, 1997). Indeed, most of the cases of elder
mistreatment occur in residential rather than institutional settings (Marshall,
Benton, & Brazier, 2000). These figures are likely to represent only a fraction
of the actual prevalence of elder abuse and neglect. Many cases go undetected and unreported.

Whether reported or not, elder abuse crosses all socioeconomic boundaries. Families from every walk of life have been affected. In addition, it can occur in various forms. These forms may occur singularly or in any combination. In one case, a son may refuse to care for a bedridden mother and verbally assault her as she asks for help. Another case may involve a granddaughter who, having power of attorney although she lives out of state, launders her grandmother's money. In a third case, a daughter-in-law may give the silent treatment and make demeaning remarks to her live-in mother-in-law. Each case is serious, and each has its own devastating consequences. The effects may be seemingly short-lived, but they are actually long term. Elder abuse not only affects the health of our elders but also that of our families and our nation. Though we have begun to address it as a serious social problem, we have a long way to go in understanding it as part of the complex issue of family violence.

In this chapter, we first explore historical perspectives. Second, we discuss how the changing status of the elderly has affected elders and the field of elder abuse. We also examine the elderly as a vulnerable population, looking specifically at biological, psychological, social, and cultural risk factors. Next, we address the measurement of elder abuse, paying particular attention to incidence patterns and victim and perpetrator characteristics. Furthermore, we investigate the various forms of elder abuse, noting the estimated prevalence of each. Finally, we consider the consequences of each types of elder mistreatment.

/// Putting Elder Abuse in a Social and Historical Context

Over the years, the status of older family members has changed. Seemingly, earlier times afforded elders more reverence and respect. In the preindustrial society, families maintained value systems that forbid any kind of conflict or violence directed at the elderly. Many Eastern cultures also held strong religious beliefs concerning worshipping ancestors and honoring mothers and fathers. There is evidence that in the later Middle Ages in Western culture, elderly family members were treated with great respect. The elderly were seen as having the wisdom of experience. It was common for elders to be taken care of by their children. In fact, they often lived with their children until their death. During the eighteenth century, religious manuals promoted respect and obedience to the elderly (Stearns, 1986).

In addition, the elderly were not only afforded more respect but also enjoyed more power. In colonial New England, during the seventeenth and eighteenth centuries, the elderly held most public offices. The older members of the family also held the right to property. This right to property gave the elders great power over their offspring. Adult children had to be granted property rights by their parents, holding them back from starting families and achieving economic independence (Stearns, 1986).

Despite these cultural practices, evidence of abuse is present. Greek mythology has touched on parricide, the murder of one's parents, as a means to move the world forward. The Bible itself, though demanding that we respect, obey, and fear our fathers, talks of sons outsmarting their fathers (Reinharz, 1986). Finally, Frazer (1900) wrote about rites and ceremonies that included regicide, the killing of an elderly king, and the euthanasia of elderly priests.

In addition, there is some substantiation of elder abuse during our preindustrial period. Older women, for example, were burned at the stake as suspects of witchcraft, and physical violence was used against elderly men in order to ensure land inheritance (Stearns, 1986). There is also speculation that the elderly of some societies died voluntarily, by self-imposed abandonment or suicide, in order to secure scarce resources for other family members (Daly & Wilson, 1982). Moreover, fairy tales and literature of the time depict adolescents killing parents in retaliation for past physical and sexual abuse (Reinharz, 1986).

During the early twentieth century, concern for the welfare of the elderly population was evidenced by the social welfare movement and the Social Security Act of 1935. The enactment of Title I of the Social Security Act required states to provide social support and financial assistance to indigent elderly who were not capable of protecting themselves from abuse and exploitation (U.S. Department of Health and Human Services, 1982). This act provided guaranteed federal subsidies for indigent elderly wishing to live and remain in their communities. At this time, state and county social workers and social service workers had the responsibility to protect the frail elderly who were receiving public assistance benefits (Axinn & Levin, 1997).

Discovering Elder Abuse and Neglect: The Twentieth Century

Overall, however, the recognition of elder abuse subsided in the late nineteenth and early twentieth centuries. Though many elderly people were probably abused during this period, elder abuse was not a salient public issue. Some interest in the elderly population in general arose during the 1960s, as is evidenced by the development of the Older American's Act of 1965. The act required a range of services for older Americans. It addressed those in the community who were in danger of losing their independence. The act also created the Administration on Aging, an office of the U.S. Department of Health and Human Services (Administration on Aging [AOA], 2001). It was not until the 1970s and early 1980s, however, that elder abuse was said to be discovered. This "discovery" occurred mainly as a result of increased attention to child abuse and domestic violence. The issue became popular first within professions such as social work and health care. Professionals began seeing an increased number of abused and frail elderly (Wolf, 2001). Interest extended to the scholarly world and scientific research (Block & Sinnott, 1979; Rathborne-McCuan, 1980; Steinmetz, 1978). In fact, a British medical journal first used the term *granny battering* during this same era (Swagerty et al., 1999).

Later, elder abuse became the focus of attention in the government. At this point, abused elders told their stories at congressional hearings that served as change agents for action (Wolf & Pillemer, 1989). In 1974, the federal government passed amendments to the Social Security Act that mandated states to provide protective services, still known today as adult protective services. States were required to meet the social, psychological, medical, and legal needs of all individuals with physical or mental limitations who were at risk of being neglected or exploited or who simply could not take care of their own affairs (Wolf, 2001). Consequently, the needs of elderly who are indigent were included in mandates that encompassed all adults in similar situations. *Parent battering* was an actual term used to describe elder abuse at congressional hearings in 1978 (U.S. House of Representatives, 1978).

At this point in the history of elder abuse, the concepts of the *perpetrator* and the *victim* were simple. Elder abuse was thought to occur as a result of the demanding caregiving duties of a family member who cared for a frail elder. The perpetrator was depicted as overworked and stressed, and the victim was depicted as very old, physically or cognitively impaired or both, and, more often than not, a woman (Wolf, 2001).

It was not until the late 1990s, however, that Congress finally passed legislation dealing specifically with elder abuse as an amendment to the Older American's Act. In 1992, Title VII, the Vulnerable Elder Rights Protection Title, was created as an amendment to the Older Americans Act. This amendment was developed out of the recognition that many older Americans were vulnerable and indigent and were denied their basic rights. Thus Title VII sought to protect the rights of older Americans and developed advocacy programs on their behalf, one of which was the Programs for the Prevention of Abuse, Neglect and Exploitation (American Society on Aging, 2002).

Decline in Social Status

Though elder abuse has been recognized as a social problem worthy of attention, many would argue that the social status of the elderly has declined during the past century. In a society in which youth and independence are favored, American elders are no longer revered for their wisdom. The aging process is feared and viewed negatively. Aging is no longer a cause for celebration, but a dreaded reality. *Ageism* is a term that aptly illustrates current attitudes toward the elderly. Old age is seen as a time of illness, despair, limited activity, and a decline in mental acuity. Most fear aging as a time during which independence is lost and death is imminent.

In light of these fears, we attempt to delay and deny the aging process.

These fears are explicit and are played on in various aspects of our culture, including marketed products and media representation. Numerous products on the market claim to delay the aging process. Exercise gimmicks, vitamins, herbs, and growth hormones are marketed to promote youth. In addition, plastic surgery and cosmetic enhancements are intended to hide the effects of aging.

Most television shows today are geared for youth. The *Golden Girls* situation comedy was a breakthrough representation for our aging population; however, there has not been a show like it since it went off the air in 1995. Few shows highlight the lives of elders as contributing members of society. When older actors are utilized, they are often put in supporting roles (e.g., Tyne Daly on *Judging Amy*, Dixie Carter on *Family Law*). Popular entertainment provides few opportunities for the lives of older Americans to be central to the story line.

The magazine market, though also geared toward youth, has been much more generous in their efforts to cater to the elderly. More than 20 magazines are published specifically for the elderly. Many of these magazines are written for an older population that is still able to maintain its independence. For example, *Today's Senior, Grand Times, My Generation, Modern Maturity, Senior Lifestyle*, and *Vintage Magazine* are geared to active older adults. Some magazines and newsletters published for seniors deal specifically with current issues faced by our aging population. *Off Our Rockers* is a magazine designed specifically for older Americans who are raising grandchildren. *Today's Caregivers*, published quarterly, seeks to inform, educate, and offer support to elderly caregivers. These magazines not only address contemporary issues of the American elderly population, but many have also dealt with the issue of elder abuse. *Modern Maturity* and *My Generation*, published by the American Association of Retired Persons (AARP), have featured many articles on elder abuse. The AARP itself, a nonprofit, nonpartisan organization for those older than 50 years, provides information and resources through its bulletin and two magazines, researches topics specific to this population, and advocates on legislative, consumer, and legal issues.

Despite the marketing success of certain products, elders in Western society are not afforded the respect that elders in other societies receive. In fact, it has been noted that the elderly in underdeveloped nations are more revered and command a higher status than those in more economically developed countries such the United States (Kosberg & Garcia, 1995).

The decline in social status is a direct result of cultural change. Families are no longer made up of a working father, a stay-at-home mother, and children, with grandparents and extended family close by. Though this structure still exists, it is no longer the norm. Many younger families have two working parents or a single parent. Thus, if there is an elder in the family who needs care, many families are often financially unable to provide it. Contributing to the problem are divorce rates that hover at 50 percent.

In addition, the concepts of self-development and independence are so ingrained in our culture that our younger generation is often not willing to take on the responsibility of caring for the elderly. Career fulfillment, job opportunities, and mobility have moved both the younger and the older generations to different work settings or climates. Consequently, many elders no longer live near their children. As our society encourages and almost requires independence, many elderly live alone. Although some stay in their homes, many live in senior housing or in nursing facilities. They are separated from the family, often by great distances.

And yet, although some adult children are moving away from their aging relatives, others are staying at home. America has seen a shift in the age at which young adults go off on their own. Adult children are increasingly remaining with their parents or moving back in with their parents or other relatives well into their 20s and 30s, if they ever leave at all. This shift is partially the result of a depressed economy that fosters few opportunities and low-paying jobs, as well as of our changing cultural values (e.g., postponing marriage). Often, however, it is the result of an adult child's impairment at some level, whether physical, psychological, or social. These types of impairments, economic stress, teen pregnancies, and climbing divorce rates have all contributed to a situation in which many of our elderly are raising grandchildren or other family members.

In addition, medical and technological advances have had an impact on our changing family structure and on the risk of elder abuse by increasing the expected life span. For example, in 1900, life expectancy was 47 years; today it is approximately 79 years for women and 72 years for men (U.S. Bureau of the Census, 1998). The traditional medical field, through advancements in research, surgery, and medications, has increased the expected life span; in addition, holistic and preventive medicines have also contributed. Since the 1970s, there has been a huge movement toward exercise and better nutrition, partly from the large vitamin and herb industry. Moreover, advances in economics, technology, and agricultural practices have improved nutrition. All of these advances have contributed not just to prolonging our lives but to prolonging them with less physical and mental decline. Therefore, we are all living longer, healthier lives.

These advances have promoted a demographic shift in the population. The twentieth century has witnessed an elevenfold increase in individuals older than 65 years. Whereas in the 1900s those over age 65 numbered 3.1 million, or 4 percent of the population in the United States, the figures rose to 33.2 million, or 12.6 percent, in 1994 and continue to increase. The percentage is expected to reach 21 percent by 2050, with the most rapid growth occurring between 2010 and 2030, as the "baby boomers" become elderly. Thus, by 2050, one in five persons, or 80 million people, living in the United States are expected to be elderly. This demographic shift has been referred to as the *graying of America* (U.S. Bureau of the Census, 1993, 1998).

The graying of America is not just a general demographic factor. Specifics about this graying population are important considerations in elder abuse. First of all, those over age 85 are the fastest growing segment of this elderly population. This population grew 274 percent between 1960 and 1994, reaching 3 million people. Again, this number is expected to increase by 2050, reaching 19 million (U.S. Bureau of the Census, 1998). Thus, as greater numbers of elderly live to more than 85 years, the numbers of people who will require care and who are at risk for elder abuse will increase.

As our culture has become more self-oriented and mobile, more and more elderly people are living on their own. According to the U.S. Bureau of the Census, 9.9 million noninstitutionalized older persons (31 percent) lived alone in 1998. The majority of those living alone were women. In 1998, 7.9 million women lived alone, whereas only 2.6 million men did. Though many elderly prefer living alone, some require much assistance due to failing health. Furthermore, it is the oldest old who are more likely to live alone, as the number who do so increase with age. Although 32 percent of women and 13 percent of men ages 65 to 74 lived alone in 1993, 57 percent of women and 29 percent of men over age 85 did (U.S. Bureau of the Census, 1998). Those over age 85 are at greater risk for abuse in greater numbers. With old age comes decreasing health and increasing dependency. As more people live into their 70s, 80s, or older, many encounter chronic, debilitating conditions, including arthritis, osteoporosis, diabetes, senile dementia, and Alzheimer's disease. Consequently, many elderly are increasingly at risk for abuse.

Along with an increase in the older old in general, most of the elderly are and will be women. As men generally have shorter expected life spans and higher death rates at every age, the number of elderly women exceeds that of men. In 1994, women over age 65 outnumbered men in that age range by a ratio of 3:2. Moreover, as one would expect, this ratio increased from 3:2 to 5:2 for those over age 85 (U.S. Bureau of the Census, 1998). In light of these statistics, it is evident both that more women than men live longer and that consequently more elderly women presumably are living unmarried and alone. It was found in 1993 that although 75 percent of noninstitutionalized elderly men were married and living with a spouse, only 41 percent of elderly women were. Elderly women in this group were three times more likely to be widowed, and 8 out of 10 elderly women were living alone (U.S. Bureau of the Census, 1998).

Finally, the elderly population as a whole is becoming more diverse. There are increasing numbers of minorities within the elderly population. In 1994, 1 in 10 elderly persons were of a race other than white. This number is expected to rise to 2 in 10 by 2050, with the greatest increase occurring among Hispanic people (U.S. Bureau of the Census, 1993, 1998). Though seemingly not a drastic increase, this is one of the fastest growing segments of the elderly population. The implications, in terms of elder abuse, are evident. A large group of elderly will be living alone who represent a wide range of cultural backgrounds. Cultural differences and language barriers may serve to inhibit service provision.

In many ways, the elderly are the forgotten generation. This group, however, as the fastest growing segment of America, represents a larger and larger proportion of our general population. As a society, it behooves us to not forget them.

/// The Elderly as a Vulnerable Population

The elderly are a vulnerable population for abuse for many reasons. As we have touched on, the elderly are more likely to be living alone, more likely to have chronic and debilitating health problems, and more likely in general to be more dependent on their families or on service providers for help in the aspects of daily living. In thinking about them as a vulnerable population, we first consider how we define *elderly* and how the aging process affects their lives and those around them.

Many terms are used to describe the elderly, including elderly, aged, senior citizens, older adults, and so forth. At what age do we define someone as being elderly? For our purposes, we have defined *elderly* as those over age 65 years. In addition, we have defined a subgroup of this population as the "oldest old," those over age 85. We have not, however, defined exactly what this elderly person may look like. Although in the field of family violence and elder abuse we focus on that segment of the elderly population who are more dependent and have more health problems, it is important to remember that no matter the age, a person may be dependent or independent, healthy or unhealthy, mentally aware or mentally unaware, and so forth. The elderly population is a diverse group. Each elderly person is an individual with his or her own unique characteristics. It is also important to note that good health does not safeguard an elderly individual from abuse. Many elderly people who have all their faculties have become victims of abuse because of other factors. In fact, as mentioned, most older adults are not frail and dependent. Nevertheless, the physical limitations that occur as a result of the aging process can become risk factors that are associated with different types of elder abuse.

Physical Changes and the Implications of the Aging Process

The aging process involves the deterioration of the physical body. The age at which the body begins to decline varies individually. It depends a great deal on self-care and genetics. Many elderly maintain good health throughout their later years. In fact, even as far back as 1981, the National Center for Health Statistics (2001) estimated that 78 percent of those over age 65 years were able to continue to participate fully in normal daily activities, that 81 percent had no limitations in daily activities, and that only 5 percent were institutionalized. One would expect at least the first two figures to be even higher today. Despite these statistics, normal biological changes make the elderly vulnerable. These changes and some common illnesses affect their abilities, often leaving them victim to another's abuse. Common biological changes include the deterioration of the senses (vision, hearing, taste, touch, smell) and of physical strength, mobility, and cognitive abilities (Forst, 2000).

As a person ages, his or her vision becomes less acute, and he or she becomes more susceptible to specific eye diseases. The four main diseases that cause visual impairment in the elderly are cataracts, glaucoma, diabetic retinopathy, and age-related macular degeneration. Cataracts can be effectively treated through lens replacement surgery. There are also treatments, if detected early, for glaucoma and diabetic retinopathy. These treatments can alleviate some symptoms and slow the process. There is not, however, any treatment for macular degeneration (National Center for Health Statistics, 2001).

All visual impairments increase with age and can cause blindness if not treated. Recent studies estimate that 20 percent of the elderly age 70 years and over suffer from a visual impairment (National Center for Health Statistics, 2001). Certain elderly populations are affected more severely. Although macular degeneration is more common overall in white elderly persons, it is most common in white women specifically. Moreover, glaucoma has doubled in the black population over the past 20 years. Today, glaucoma is two times more prevalent among the black population than among the white population (National Center for Health Statistics, 2001).

The aging process also takes its toll on hearing. It is estimated that about one-third of elderly Americans between the ages of 65 and 74 are hearing impaired. This impairment increases with age, as 50 percent of those over 85 years are hearing impaired. Further, elderly men, as opposed to women, at all ages are more likely to be hearing impaired (National Center for Health Statistics, 2001). Hearing loss thus is part of the normal aging process. Hearing loss, however, can also be brought on or compounded by infection, a head injury, a heart condition, a stroke, tumors, or certain medications (Devons, 1999).

Hearing loss occurs on various levels and takes on various forms. In terms of the former, an elderly person may have minimal loss and may make minor adjustments, such as moving closer to the TV or to an individual to hear what is being said. On this continuum, another elderly person may need the TV volume increased as loud as possible in order to hear. Moreover, whereas an elderly person may be able to function well in a quiet setting, a noisy environment may make it difficult for him or her to hear well. Elderly hearing loss can include the inability to hear certain frequencies, trouble differentiating between certain consonants (z, s, sh, f, p, k, t, and g), and constantly hearing hissing or ringing noises (Forst, 2000)

Though there is treatment for the hearing impaired, many elderly do not take advantage of it. First of all, it is easier for the elderly to compensate for a hearing impairment. Second, many elderly people do not realize that they are hearing impaired. Although older people normally have their vision checked and do in fact wear glasses, they are less likely to have their hearing checked by a doctor (National Center for Health Statistics, 2001). Furthermore, hearing aids can also be problematic. For instance, hearing aids increase all sound levels. Therefore, background noise can become annoying, and loud frequencies become even louder. There is also a stigma attached to wearing a hearing aid. Unlike glasses, which one may need at a very early age, hearing aids remind the elderly of the aging process and their decreasing abilities.

Along with hearing and vision changes, many elderly individuals experience a decrease in their ability to discriminate tastes and smells, as well as their ability to feel pain. Although these may be seemingly trivial, these changes can increase the likelihood that the individual will be at risk of abuse.

A decrease in the sense of taste occurs due to the natural aging process and is also the result of medications that some elderly people are prescribed. Elderly people experience a decrease in the taste sensation due to the aging of their taste buds. The aging process also affects their oral health. Many elderly experience dental problems; they may need to wear dentures and may develop dental caries and periodontal disease. One-third of those over age 65 years have untreated dental caries, and 40 percent have periodontal disease. Antihistamines, diuretics, and antidepressants can also affect the oral health of the elderly when taken over long periods of time (National Center for Health Statistics, 2001). Therefore, the elderly are likely to lose their appetites because they cannot taste, and eating may aggravate their teeth or gums. Consequently, they may not get enough of the nutrients they need to sustain their health and may eat foods that are easy on their teeth and gums but promote disease (high-fat processed foods that clog the arteries). These changes may promote self-neglect.

The ability to smell also deteriorates as we age. This problem makes food seem less appetizing and can be extremely dangerous for an elderly person living alone. . For instance, an older person may not smell the gas of a furnace that has gone faulty or a gas stove left on with the pilot light out. This fact may contribute to self-neglect and can promote physical abuse in the form of gas being left turned on purposely.

Moreover, many elderly individuals also lose their sense of touch or the ability to feel pain and pleasure. The latter affects the quality of their lives, but the former puts them at risk. For example, if an elderly person cannot feel that a pan is hot, he or she may sustain burns. Likewise, if someone is physically abusing the person, he or she may not feel the physical pain, thereby minimizing the problem.

Finally, as we age, our strength and mobility decline. Elderly people cannot move as fast and may need aids to get around, such as walkers and wheelchairs. The ability to lift heavy weight also declines with age. This not only diminishes the quality of their lives but also puts them at risk for abuse. For example, if an elderly individual is being physically assaulted by a family member, he or she often can neither fight back nor get away from the abuser.

Mental and Cognitive Changes and Implications of the Aging Process

Most adults experience a decline in their cognitive abilities as they age. They start to experience memory loss and they forget more easily and find it more difficult to calculate figures and to move from one task to another. Although the elderly seem to retain their long-term memories, many lose short-term memory skills as they age. Moreover, the loss of memory increases with increasing age. The Administration on Aging (2000a) reported the following rates of memory decline: 4 percent (of those ages 65–69 years), 8.5 percent (70–74 years), 14 percent (75–79 years), 21 percent (80–84 years), and 36 percent of those over 85 years. Moreover, the agency reports that a greater number of men experience memory loss in all age groups. Memory loss often means that the elderly require some level of care, which increases the risk of abuse.

Age-Specific Illnesses

In addition to the normal or common biological changes that accompany the aging process, many illnesses specific to the elderly population put them at greater risk for abuse. Illnesses that affect physical functioning, mental health, and cognitive abilities are most commonly associated with elder abuse and neglect.

Physical disabilities include chronic illnesses and conditions that limit the ability of the elderly to actively care for themselves, as well as to participate in such instrumental activities as driving, working, and enjoying recreation. The Administration on Aging (2000a) reported that in 1995, of those individuals older than 70 years, 58 percent suffered from arthritis, 45 percent from hypertension, 21 percent from heart disease, 19 percent from cancer, 12 percent from diabetes, and 9 percent from stroke. These figures varied by age and race or ethnicity. These conditions in general are irreversible.

These debilitating illnesses affect every aspect of living and often make it difficult for the elderly to remain independent members of their communities. Great financial and caregiving burdens go hand in hand with these chronic illnesses. Consequently, this population is at increased risk of abuse.

Mental Health and Depression

Depression is a common illness in old age. Depression often comes as a result of the physical and social changes of aging. Increased isolation, coupled with a lack of social supports and debilitating physical illnesses, is often associated with depression. Depression is said to be the most common mental disorder in the elderly. It affects a significant proportion of that population, and depression increases with age. According to the Administration on Aging (2000a), 15 percent of each age group (65–69, 70–74, 75–79) suffered severe depressive symptoms, whereas 21 percent of those ages 80–84 and 23 percent of those over 85 years did. Women in particular are at risk. Women also are at greater risk of severe depression from ages 65 to 84 years.

Depression is characterized not only by mood changes and the inability to concentrate but also by changes in weight, appetite, and sleep patterns, by decreased interest in grooming and personal hygiene and activities once enjoyed, by the use or misuse of alcohol or drugs, and by talk of or fascination with death or suicide (Forst, 2000). All of these factors put the elderly at risk for abuse in different forms. They can cause increased stress on a caregiver relationship, which may lead to physical or psychological abuse, and can also put the elderly person at risk for financial abuse, self-neglect, and possibly suicide.

Substance Abuse

Substance abuse has been found to be a major risk factor in all types of elder abuse on many levels (Kosberg & Nahmiash, 1995). Substance abuse may be by the victims, the perpetrators, or both. Research has shown that abusive partners are more likely to be violent when using alcohol or drugs. It is not clear whether alcohol and drugs are associated with elder abuse because they decrease a perpetrator's inhibitions or whether perpetrators use alcohol, drugs, or both to justify their actions. In addition, caregivers may begin to use or abuse alcohol or other drugs as a response to the stress of caregiving (Bradshaw & Spencer, 1999). Further, it has been noted that many elderly begin to abuse alcohol or substances later in life to cope with isolation and loneliness (Kosberg, 1998).

Elderly people themselves may also develop a substance-abuse problem in response to the aging process. The abuse of substances by an elderly person leaves him or her at greater risk of abuse and exacerbates a potentially abusive situation. The elderly who are immersed in self-neglect often have substance abuse or alcohol problems. Elderly people who abuse substances sustain more cognitive losses and physical disabilities, which make them easy targets for all types of abuse. These individuals also usually do not have good relationships with their families. A family member who has lost respect for an elderly person is more likely to abuse him or her. Moreover, an elderly person may even be forced to use or abuse alcohol (Bradshaw & Spencer, 1999).

Cognitive Dementia

Dementia is an illness caused by a change in brain function. Dementia can be the result of nutritional deficiencies, metabolic disorders, or prescription drugs. Thus, in these cases, dementia is reversible. Dementia that is non-organic (that is, no known cause can be identified) is said to be irreversible. In this case, only the symptoms of irreversible dementia can be treated to reduce their effects on the elderly person's life (Forst, 2000).

Dementia is characterized by a change in personality, memory loss, disorientation, inability to follow directions, unstable sleep patterns, neglect of personal hygiene, hoarding, and wandering (Forst, 2000). In addition, many dementia sufferers can become aggressive (Paveza et al., 1992). Reissberg, Franssen, Sclan, Klugar, and Ferris (1989) found that 57 to 67 percent of dementia patients display some level of aggressive behavior: verbal outbursts, physical threats, and violence.

Alzheimer's Disease

Alzheimer's disease is the most common form of irreversible dementia. Alzheimer's disease is a progressive and degenerative disease that attacks the brain and results in impaired memory, cognition, and behavior In addition, it is said to be distinguishable from other dementias by microscopic brain changes that can be determined only at autopsy (Forst, 2000; Mayo Clinic, 2000).

More than 4 million Americans suffer from Alzheimer's disease, and this number is expected to triple over the next 20 years (Mayo Clinic, 2000). Not only does the disease get more severe with age, but also the incidence of Alzheimer's disease increases with age. Although less than 1 percent of 65-year-old Americans are affected, 3 percent of those ages 65 to 74 have the disease, and nearly 50 percent of those more than 85 years old are affected. Moreover, women are more likely than men to contract Alzheimer's disease (Mayo Clinic, 2000; National Institute on Aging, 1991).

Some common symptoms of Alzheimer's disease include increasing and persistent forgetfulness; difficulties in abstract thinking; language and communication problems such as the inability to adequately express oneself or deferring to a first language; disorientation; loss of judgment; difficulty doing routine tasks; and personality changes that may involve stubbornness, mood swings, depression, social withdrawal, anxiety, and aggression (Forst, 2000; Mayo Clinic 2000).

In light of the symptoms that accompany dementia and Alzheimer's disease, the risk of abuse is high. In fact, family violence seems commonplace in families who are caring for an elderly relative with dementia or Alzheimer's disease (Steinmetz, 1988; Paveza et al., 1992). Steinmetz (1988) found cognitive impairment to be associated with a higher risk of abuse and violence. Thus the caregiver job itself is exceedingly stressful, which may lead to abuse in some form; moreover, the elderly relative may also become abusive. Steinmetz (1988) theorized that, if we are to understand, treat, and prevent the abuse that can occur within these family situations, we cannot separate the caregiver's role in the abuse from the aggressive behaviors of the patient. Instead, it is imperative that we look at the interactive nature of the relationship between the elderly person and the other family members and at the mutual violence that can occur. The family member who provides the caregiving support may become abusive as a response to frustration and stress, and the elder, as a result of his or her disease and situation, may also initiate abuse (verbal, physical, or both).

Paveza and associates (1992), in their study of the occurrence of severe levels of abuse in families who care for a member with Alzheimer's disease, also found significant levels of violence. Although patient-caregiver violence was found in 17.4 percent of the families, caregivers reported that 15.8 percent of the patients exhibited severe violent behavior toward the caregiver, 5.4 percent of the caregivers reported being violent toward the patient, and 3.8 percent of the families reported mutual violence. Paveza and his associates (1992) determined particular risk factors associated with this particular patient-caregiver relationship, including high levels of depression among caregivers and patients who live with family but without spouses. Alzheimer's patients were at the greatest risk of abuse. Stressors for family members are illustrated in Box 6.1, including time commitment, psychological losses, physicality of the job, financial costs, and role changes.

Social Changes and the Implications of the Aging Process

The physical changes of the aging process go hand in hand with the social changes that elderly people experience. The aging process means not only a decline in their physical and mental abilities but also a diminishing of social

---

Box 6.1 /// Major Stressors for Family Caregivers of Alzheimer's Patients

- *Time Commitment*: Caregivers who live with the patient spend an average of 100 hours per week providing care, whereas those who work outside the home spend an average of 40 hours per week.
- *Psychological Losses*: Spouses or relatives of patients with Alzheimer's disease lose the relationship they once knew and must deal with the patient's personality changes.
- *Physical Effort*: The patient needs help bathing, dressing, and so forth.
- *Financial Cost*: It can be very expensive to care for the family member with Alzheimer's disease.
- *Role Changes*: Spouses and relatives must take on greater responsibilities for the patient and thus neglect their own priorities.

life and the inability to care adequately for themselves. Social living arrangements, whether alone or with others, influence the risk of abuse for the elderly.

Isolation can become commonplace for the elderly. Though isolation does not cause abuse, it provides an opportunity for it to occur easily and without detection. Isolation is the result of many social factors that can occur singularly or in varying combinations and that are affected by the physical and psychological changes of the aging process.

Physical deterioration is one factor that increases social isolation. Physical deterioration impedes the mobility of elderly individuals. They may find it difficult to walk or to continue driving. Thus many elderly are confined to their homes.

Memory loss is another factor. When they cannot remember what they had for breakfast or where the new grocery store is located, they may begin to lose confidence in themselves. Thus they tend to avoid situations in which they are required to use these skills, and social interaction becomes limited.

The loss of employment in older age is another factor that can predispose an elderly person to isolation and that may lead to depression. The losses associated with unemployment for the elderly include income, coworkers and social supports, and meaning, identity, or the feeling of fulfillment. Dependency on others may also result. Consequently, the loss of employment places the elderly at greater risk for abuse

As mentioned previously, changing social structures create situations in which the elderly are frequently living alone. Again, not only are they increasingly living alone, but they are also increasingly living alone without relatives nearby. Geographic isolation increases the risk of abuse, especially self-neglect.

Finally, as our elders age, they lose their friends and older family members to illness and death. A dwindling social network puts them at greater risk of abuse for two reasons. First, they may need to rely more and more on younger family members or strangers to meet their daily needs. This caregiver–related patient relationship can be extremely stressful for both parties. Living arrangements that involve some level and form of caregiving may provide more opportunity for abuse (Wolf, Godkin, & Pillemer, 1986). Second, a declining social network often leaves the elderly isolated. Isolation both increases the risks of abuse and affects the elderly person's health, which can lead to malnutrition, depression, and substance abuse.

//// Other Risk Factors

Numerous factors precipitate maltreatment. We have already touched on some of these: the health of the elderly person (including physical, mental, psychological, and social), the age and gender of both the victim and the perpetrator, and caregiver stress. Many other factors have been studied. We explore further the role of caregiver issues of stress, ignorance, impairment, and power differentials, the role of intergenerational abuse, intimate partner abuse, and culture. We also discuss screening tools that have been developed to identify and predict future elder abuse cases.

Caregiver Stress, Ignorance, and Impairment

Caregiver stress as a causal factor for elder abuse has been widely documented and studied (Anetzberger, 1987; Bradley, 1996; Mui, 1995; Wolf, 2000). An overburdened caregiver is often an adult child or a spouse. As noted in the section on Alzheimer's disease, the physical, psychological, and social implications of the aging process and the diseases that accompany it often cause insurmountable circumstances. Not only may the elder become abusive to the caregiver, but the demands of the caregiving role may also precipitate abuse. The role of caregiver may be taken on begrudgingly, leading to resentment.

Ada Mui (1995) studied the physical, emotional, and financial strain associated with caregiving among spouses. She also looked at caregiver stress in terms of role strain, role demand, and role conflict. She found that, overall, role strain was prevalent at similar levels physically, emotionally, and financially for both husband and wife caregivers, with financial strain being the least prevalent. On the other hand, Mui (1995) found that gender mediated the difference between the two groups in terms of role demand over load and role conflict.

In terms of role demand overload, or the lack of adequate time and resources to fulfill all of one's roles, including caregiver responsibilities, husbands were affected both emotionally and financially, whereas wife caregivers were not. Mui (1995) concluded that husband caregivers may generally have been less experienced in a caregiving role and thus felt more strain.

Mui (1995) also determined that role conflict, defined as the differing expectations of social roles that conflict, was also mediated by gender. Again, husband caregivers were found to experience greater strain in all three areas: emotional, physical, and financial. Thus husbands could not easily balance their personal and social lives with their caregiving roles, indicating that they continue to enjoy rich social and personal lives.

Finally, Mui (1995) found that caregiver role strain was mediated by race and ethnicity. Nonwhite wife caregivers experienced lower levels of stress than did white wife caregivers. Mui (1992) suggested that this fact may be attributable to the varying cultural meanings of caregiving. Whereas in the white culture it may be considered burdensome and not the responsibility of spouse or family, other, nonwhite cultures may have stronger senses of family obligation.

Ignorance also contributes to elder abuse. Sometimes caregivers are not aware of the care needed to maintain an elder's health. A caregiver may not understand the aging process and the changes that are required, such as changes in nutrition, handling an elderly person in a gentler manner, making sure an elderly person gets out of bed, and so forth. Further, the caregiver may have unrealistic expectations about what elderly people can and cannot do for themselves (Reis & Nahmiash, 1998).

Caregivers may themselves have some form of impairment or disability. Many caregivers who abuse the elderly, whether adult children or others, suffer from mental and emotional problems or from alcoholism or other substance abuse.

Elderly as Caregivers

Some of the elderly population may need to be cared for, but many are themselves the caretakers. An elderly person may be responsible for an impaired adult child, an ailing spouse, or a grandchild, which can make them vulnerable to abuse.

Some research has shown that abuser characteristics are more predictive of elder abuse than victim characteristics (Pillemer& Finkelhor, 1989). It has been noted that, in many elder abuse cases, a dependent adult child is responsible for the abuse. The child may be emotionally, socially, or financially dependent on the elderly person. Oftentimes the dependency stems from an impairment of one form or another. For example, the adult child may have a mental illness or emotional problems, alcohol or drug problems, or a physical disability (Bradley, 1996; Elder Abuse Center, 2001; Greenberg, McKibben, & Raymond, 1990; National Center on Elder Abuse [NCEA], 1997).

When an elderly person is ill, it is often his or her spouse who assumes his or her care. Many times the ailing spouse becomes dependent. This puts the caretaker spouse at risk for abuse. The ailing spouse may be unintentionally abusive, as is the case in dementia, or may have difficulty in accepting the limitations of his or her aging and take it out on the caretaker.

Finally, it is becoming increasingly common for grandparents to be raising their grandchildren. Parents with impairments, such as drug or alcohol addiction, mental illness, AIDS, or chronic illnesses; early death; financial instability; increases in divorces and single-parent households; child abuse and neglect cases; and parent incarceration can all be reasons for this situation (Brown-Standish & Floyd, 2000; Wallace, 2001). Many elderly people in these situations are often left with a grandchild who is in crisis and who has severe developmental, emotional, or other problems (Wallace, 2001). Given the age of the elderly caretaker and the issues at hand, this situation creates an atmosphere ripe for abuse. Jarde, Marc, Dwyer, and Fournier (1990) found that out of 55 cases of elder abuse, 19 were directly attributable to a grandchild.

Power Differentials

There is no doubt that power differentials exist in all elder abuse cases. Dependency, mental capacity, consent, and undue influence play major roles. More often than not, it seems that the elderly family member is dependent on a child or other caregiver. This dependency is created by the deteriorating physical, psychological, mental, and social health of the elderly person, as discussed previously. This dependency puts the elder at great risk for abuse (Choi-Namkee & Mayer, 2000). As we noted, at times the dependency role is reversed. For example, abuse often occurs in family situations in which an adult child is dependent on the elderly parent, emotionally, financially, or both. An adult child or caregiver may abuse an elderly person to get his or her need met, whether financial, emotional, or sexual.

An elderly person's mental capacity has much to do with dependency. *Mental capacity* is characterized by the everyday skills we use to make decisions and direct our lives. Often elderly people lose these skills due to aging and illness. The skills needed for us to be self-directing individuals include memory, logic, flexibility of attention, and the ability to calculate perceived outcomes. As the elderly lose their mental capacity, they become increasingly dependent and thus at risk for abuse (National Committee for the Prevention of Elder Abuse [NCPEA], 2002).

Abuse of the elderly is sometimes characterized by *undue influence*. This term, often used in the field of elder abuse, refers to a situation in which an individual who is perceived as having more power is able to get a "weaker" person to conform to his or her will. The more powerful person may use abusive and manipulative techniques to gain power and get the person to comply. Undue influence is common in financial abuse cases (NCPEA, 2002).

Intergenerational Abuse

Adult children are the main perpetrators of abuse and neglect (Administration on Aging [AOA], 1998). Adult children normally take on the role of caregivers for their elderly parents. Thus they are in a position to become abusive. Social learning and the intergenerational transmission of abuse (as described in chapter 2) may also play a role. Violent and abusive adults have often learned abusive behavior as a result of witnessing or experiencing abuse as youngsters. Consequently, when the tables are turned, the adult child has the opportunity to reciprocate abusive behavior (Reinharz, 1986).

Intimate Partner Abuse

Many reported cases of elder abuse are actually cases of intimate partner abuse, which has been largely ignored. Abuse between intimate partners is not something that occurs only in younger generations. Though the National

Crime Victimization Survey (NCVS) indicates that younger women experience higher rates of intimate partner abuse than older women, this does not absolve the elderly from intimate partner abuse (Gesino, Smith, & Keckich, 1982; Harris, 1996; Rennison, 2001). In fact, abuse that starts early in a relationship can carry over into the later years, or abuse may begin in the later years. Pillemer and Finkelhor (1998) found in their random sample survey that whereas 24 percent of the acts were committed by children, 58 percent were committed by a spouse. The authors attribute this in part to the fact that the majority of the elderly live with spouses. Nevertheless, spouse abuse in the elderly population is a social problem that warrants our attention.

Homicide-suicide incidents are one consequence of intimate partner abuse in elderly relationships. Homicide-suicides are typically deliberate acts of violence, directed mainly at women. These incidents are characterized by a male perpetrator with a very controlling personality, a male's perception of impending separation or a threat to the stability of the relationship, and a woman being an unknowing and unwilling participant who is shot either awake or in her sleep (Cohen & Eisdorfer, 1999).

It has been found that incidence rates of homicide-suicide are higher for the elderly than for the other segments of the population. Eisdorfer and Cohen (2001) estimate that every year, approximately 200 homicide-suicides occur among people over 55 years of age. In addition, there is evidence that this number is increasing (Eisdorfer & Cohen, 1999; Rennison, 2001). Box

---

Box 6.2 /// Three Types of Homicide/Suicides in the Older Population

Dependent/Protective: Accounts for approximately 50 percent of all cases. Characterized by a husband or male who is 2-4 years older than a wife or female and who is caring for the chronically ill female. There is evidence of untreated and undetected severe depression in the men: feelings of helplessness, hopelessness, and exhaustion.

Aggressive: Accounts for approximately 30 percent of all cases. Characterized by a male perpetrator who is 10 years older than the woman and a situation in which a history of verbal and physical discourse or domestic violence exists. Triggers of the incident include talk or threats of separation or divorce. Evidence suggests that the homicide in this case is typically an extremely violent, surprise attack in which the victim is stabbed or shot multiple times.

Symbiotic: Accounts for approximately 20 percent of all cases. Characterized by a relationship in which the male is a few years older than the woman and both are ill. Both parties are described as feeling overwhelmed by their illnesses and see death as a viable solution.

Source: Cohen & Eisdorfer, 1999

6.2 illustrates three homicide-suicides, as defined by Cohen and Eisdorfer (1999). Chapter 4 explores further the issue of intimate partner abuse and the elderly.

Role of Culture

As we have discussed, the status of the elderly in our population affects how they are treated. Different cultures or subcultures have their own unique systems of beliefs and values, which affect treatment of the elderly. Thus, whereas in some cultures the elderly may be revered, in others they may be seen as burdensome. In addition, some behavior directed toward an elder may be seen as abusive in one culture but not in another. Moreover, other factors may intertwine with cultural factors that put elders at risk for abuse.

Incidence reports of abuse and neglect demonstrate that blacks were the victims of abuse in comparatively greater numbers, whereas reports from sentinel agencies did not show any significant findings in regard to race (AOA, 1998). Lachs, Berkman, Fulmer, and Horwitz (1994) also found that minorities were referred for abuse investigations more frequently than non-minorities. Both studies raise the question of whether elder abuse in minority populations is reported more frequently or whether there is an actual incidence difference.

Some studies in the late 1980s and 1990s also presented some cultural variation with regard to abuse. Anetzberger (1987) also found differences with regard to elder abuse and culture and ethnicity. Among the Appalachian culture exists the idea of "abusive enculturation," in which behaviors commonly used would be seen by the general population as abusive. In addition, Moon and Williams (1993) found cultural variation in elderly women's abuse perception. In this study, African Americans and Caucasian Americans perceived certain elder mistreatment scenarios as abuse more frequently than did Korean Americans. Korean Americans revealed that they would be less likely to report abuse so as to avoid shame and conflict. Moon and Williams (1993) note that this attitude reflects the Korean values of community and family harmony.

Finally, studies on Native Americans have found that their cultural beliefs of harmony with nature, strong family interdependence, and responsibility to community may actually predispose them to abuse. In attempting to maintain these values, other factors intervene with these that can create abusive situations (e.g., disintegration of family ties due to assimilation, limited resources, poverty, unemployment, alcohol and substance abuse, etc.; Carson, 1995; Krassen & Maxwell, 1992).

Cultural factors are mitigated by the socioeconomic and political structure of the United States. Thus minority groups facing economic struggles, educational discrimination, and language barriers are less likely to use the intervention system and more likely to suffer the consequences of abuse and neglect associated with such factors. For example, Montoya (1997, pp. 15–

16) argues that "conditions that have been found to be associated with family abuse are circumstances that the Hispanic struggles with too frequently due to America's socio-political economic system."

Predicting Elder Abuse

Although the factors discussed herein are associated with elder abuse, they cannot singularly identify an elder abuse case or predict future risk. Screening measures attempt to create sets of factors that do just that. Various valid screens have been developed. The Sengstock-Hwalek Questionnaire is completed by seniors, and the Caregiver Abuse Screen for the Elderly is completed by caregivers. Other screens are completed by practitioners. Reis and Nahmiash (1998) attempted to validate and further develop one such tool, the Indicators of Abuse (IOA), by determining which items on a checklist of 48 problems and 12 demographic variables would form a subset that would discriminate between abuse and nonabuse cases and which variables would not be strong predictors.

The researchers validated the IOA and found 29 out of the 48 variables that formed a subset valuable in discriminating abuse versus nonabuse cases. Overall, they found that caregivers' characteristics and problems were more salient predictors of elder abuse than were elders' characteristics or problems. Results indicated that primary predictors of elder abuse included caregiver interpersonal problems; marital and family conflict; caregiver intrapersonal problems; mental health and behavioral problems; and past abuse of the care recipient. In addition, other strong predictors on the part of the caregiver included having poor current relationships, not understanding the medical condition, reluctance to give care, having alcohol and substance abuse problems, unrealistic expectations, inexperience, financial (but not other) dependence, and inability to take responsibility for a situation. Strong care-recipient predictors were lack of social support and a poor caregiver–care receiver relationship (Reis & Nahmiash, 1998).

Reis and Nahmiash (1998) also determined variables that did not readily discriminate abuse from nonabuse situations. These variables were the care recipient's physical or cognitive impairment or need for help with daily living skills, financial problems other than financial dependency, a caregiver's desire to institutionalize an elder, and caregiver stress.

/// Measuring Elder Abuse and Neglect

The National Elder Abuse Incidence (NEAIS) (NCEA, 1996) study, a 4-year study funded by the U.S. Department of Health and Human Services in 1996, attempted to estimate the number of cases of neglected and abused elderly living in their own homes that would have gone undetected. The study examined reports of elder mistreatment as documented by adult protective service agencies and reviewed reports from other agencies (sentinel reports). Overall, the study found that about 450,000 elderly over 60 years old were abused, neglected, or both in domestic settings in 1996. This number did not include self-neglect. When self-neglect was added in, this number rose to 551,000.

There has been some documentation that men are more frequently victims (Pillemer & Finkelhor, 1998); however, the NEAIS found that women were disproportionately represented as victims in both adult protective services (APS) reports and sentinel reports. Sentinel reports include statistics from local service providers that deal with the elderly population. Sixty to seventy-six percent of APS reports described women who were subject to all forms of abuse and neglect except abandonment, whereas sentinel reports documented that 67 to 92 percent of those abused were women, depending on the type of abuse. Moreover, the APS reports found the difference between abuse rates of men and women to be greatest in the area of emotional and psychological abuse: 75 percent of those who experienced emotional abuse were women. The sentinel reports found the greatest gender discrepancy in financial abuse, with 92 percent of the victims being women (Administration on Aging, 1998, 2000b).

Victim age is also a factor. The NEAIS found that those 80 years and older, the oldest old, were abused two to three times more often than those under 80 years of age. Furthermore, the oldest old were more often subject to physical, emotional, and financial exploitation (Administration on Aging, 1998, 2000b).

Along with gender and health status, the NEAIS also looked at the role of race and ethnicity as a factor in elder abuse. Although the sentinel reports did not show any significant findings in regard to race, the APS reports demonstrated that blacks were the victims of abuse in comparatively greater numbers (Administration on Aging, 1998).

It was speculated at the time of the "discovery" of elder abuse that adult male children were generally the perpetrators of elder abuse. However, during that same time, it was found that adult female children were often the perpetrators. Nevertheless, according to the NEAIS, the majority of the perpetrators continue to be family members. Ninety percent of the cases studied in the NEAIS involved family members as alleged perpetrators. The APS reports found that adult children of the victims composed the largest category of abusers across all types of abuse.

The stereotypical gender of the alleged perpetrator as male is not fully supported by the NEAIS. The APS reports found the alleged perpetrators to be generally males only when neglect—which accounts for the majority of cases—was controlled for. Otherwise, there was equality between the genders. However, in all other types of abuse cases reported to APS, males were more likely to be perpetrators at a ratio of 3:2. In the sentinel reports, males were more likely to be perpetrators at a rate of 1.8:1 (Administration on Aging, 1998).

The NEAIS also found that the majority of alleged perpetrators were younger than the victims. In fact, most perpetrators were under 60 years old. Of more concern is that this situation is especially true in cases of financial abuse. Whereas 40 percent of the perpetrators were between the ages of 41 and 59 years, 45 percent were 40 or younger (Administration on Aging, 1998).

Finally, the NEAIS supports the "iceberg theory" of elder abuse (AOA, 1998). This theory is widely accepted and holds that only the most obvious types of abuse are reported and that there are many more cases that are not. Thus we are aware of only the "tip of the iceberg." The NEAIS found that, although 70,942 cases were reported, investigated, and substantiated by APS, approximately 378,982 cases of abuse and neglect were reported to sentinels but not to APS and thus were not investigated. Furthermore, many more cases do not come to the attention of any legal entity.

/// Forms of Elder Abuse

Elder abuse or mistreatment is defined by the American Medical Association as an act or oversight that results in harm or potential harm to the health and well-being of an elderly person. *Abuse* includes intentional infliction of physical or mental injury, sexual abuse, or withholding of necessary food, clothing, and medical care to meet the physical and mental needs of an elderly person by a person who has the care, custody, or responsibility of an elderly person (Council on Scientific Affairs, 1987). Elder abuse or mistreatment as a form of domestic violence can occur in different degrees, at different levels, and with different participants. We now explore how elder abuse has been defined to include all forms, look at the varying situations in which it occurs, and consider the prevalence rates of each.

The 1987 Older Americans' Act offered the first federal definitions of elder abuse, intended to be used in identifying the problem. Under this act, elder abuse is first defined in three broad categories: domestic elder abuse, institutional elder abuse, and self-neglect/self-abuse. *Domestic elder abuse* refers to any form of maltreatment of an elderly person by someone who has a close or special relationship with that elder (e.g., spouses, siblings, children, friends, at-home caregivers). *Institutional elder abuse* refers to abuse that occurs within a residential facility for the elderly (e.g., nursing home, foster home, group home, board and care facility). This type of elder abuse is explored in chapter 7. *Self-neglect* involves the failure of the elderly person to provide appropriate care for himself or herself. Because elders have a constitutional right to make decisions regarding their own lives, delineating self-neglect can be an arduous task.

In addition to these broad federally defined categories, elder abuse has been classified into as many as eight different categories by various scholars, legal entities, and other interested professional parties. These eight categories include: physical abuse, neglect, self-neglect, emotional abuse, sexual abuse, economic abuse, abandonment, and violation of rights (Collins, Bennett, & Hanzlick, 2000; Swagerty et al, 1999). Each form can occur singularly or in combination with any of the other forms. It is important in combatting the problem of elder abuse that we define these terms accurately, that these definitions are uniform across disciplines, and that we have a sense of where abuse occurs and of the prevalence of each form, as well as the prevalence of the combinations that occur.

Physical Abuse

Physical abuse of the elderly has been defined as the infliction of pain, injury, impairment, illness, or coercion, such as confinement against one's will (Brownell & Abelman, 1998; Swagerty et al, 1999). Indicators of physical abuse can include bruises, welts, cigarette burns, cuts, lacerations, broken bones, scratches, and punctures. In addition, the definition of physical abuse also often includes sexual abuse. However, we consider sexual abuse as a separate category.

A lack of sound research and valid data has limited our ability to get a concise prevalence rate for physical abuse. Many researchers have documented physical abuse as the most prevalent form of elder mistreatment (Bradley, 1996; Pillemer & Finklehor, 1998). Pillemer and Finkelhor (1998) found in their Boston study that 32 in 1,000 of those over 65 years of age were abused and that 20 in 1,000 were physically abused.

Because physical abuse is seemingly the most detectable form of abuse, it has been thought to be the most prevalent form. However, other studies have found that it is not. Studies done in 1990 and 1991 in 29 and 30 states, respectively, indicated that only 20 percent of all the abuse cases were physical. Neglect occurred with more frequency, at a rate of 45 percent of all cases studied (Dobrin, Wiersema, & Loftin, 1996). Furthermore, the National Center on Elder Abuse (NCEA; 1997) found neglect in domestic settings to be more prevalent than physical abuse. The NCEA statistics are based on surveys of state adult protective service agencies and state units on aging. Whereas neglect accounted for 55 percent of all abuse cases in 1996, physical abuse accounted for only 14.6 percent. The NCEA (1997) also reported that, whereas elder neglect had increased between 1990 and 1996, physical abuse of the elderly actually decreased, from 20.2 percent to 14.6 percent, in that same time period.

Although physical elder abuse appears to be less common, researchers have also hypothesized that physical abuse in the elderly may be more difficult to detect, especially as compared with the physical abuse of children. This may account for the lower prevalence rates. Some of the health issues of the aging process discussed earlier play into this. For example, an elderly person may suffer bruises and may not remember their origin; or the bruises may be the result of bumping into something. A broken bone may be the result of a fall and osteoporosis, not abuse. Therefore, being able to separate the accidents from the abuse is essential.

Sexual Abuse

Often falling under the category of physical abuse, sexual abuse of the elderly involves any nonconsensual sexual contact of any sort and any sexual contact with a person incapable of giving consent. This includes unwanted touching and all types of sexual assault or battery: rape, sodomy, coerced nudity, and sexually explicit photography. Signs or symptoms of elder sexual abuse can include bruising around the breast and genital area, unexplained venereal disease, genital infections, vaginal or anal bleeding, and torn, stained, and bloody undergarments.

Sexual abuse of the elderly in institutions is on the rise. This is especially true for institutionalized elderly women who suffer unwanted touching during bathing, feeding, or dressing or at bedtime (Hodge, 2001). There are few statistics on sexual abuse of the elderly in domestic settings. The NCEA did find that of all the types of abuse reported in 1996, sexual abuse accounted for 0.3 percent of the cases (Tatara & Kuzmeskus, 1997). Thus it seems further study of domestic sexual elder abuse is warranted.

Neglect

Neglect has generally been defined as the failure of the caregiver to provide the necessary care to ensure optimal health and safety and to avoid harm (Brownell, 1996; Collins et al., 2000; Swagerty et al., 1999). Signs of neglect may include weight loss, dehydration, malnutrition, hypothermia and hyperthermia, bedsores, depression, social isolation, oversedation, and untreated medical problems (Young, 2000). This type of neglect has been referred to as *physical* neglect.

Neglect as a form of abuse may be intentional or unintentional. *Intentional neglect* occurs when a caregiver is educated about the needs of the elderly person and fails to take the necessary actions to ensure the well-being of that person. For example, if the caregiver fails to provide necessary medical care or fails to provide hygiene and clean clothes, he or she is intentionally involved in neglect. *Unintentional neglect* can occur when a caregiver is not aware of what the elderly person actually needs. This is especially true in the case of an elderly person with dementia. Because an elderly person with dementia may be coherent one moment and incoherent the next, it is difficult for family members to understand what the elderly person can and cannot do for himself or herself (Young, 2000). In addition, the stress of a caregiver-elder relationship may prevent a caregiver from seeing exactly how he or she is neglecting the elderly family member or patient. A caregiver who is mentally or developmentally impaired or who has a drug addiction may also unintentionally neglect an elderly person

(Brownell & Abelman, 1998). Moreover, neglect is more likely to occur if there is no defined caregiver. In such a case, a person may assume that the elder is being cared for when in fact he or she is not.

Like physical abuse, prevalence rates of neglect are not precise. Again, many cases of neglect go unrecognized and unreported. Karl Pillemer and David Finkelhor (1998) found the rate of neglect in their Boston study to be 4 in 1,000 persons over age 65 years. Dobrin, Wiersema, and Loftin (1996) found 45 percent of all the abuse cases from 1990 and 1991 in two states to be neglect. This figure represented the majority of the cases studied. The NCEA (1999) also reported that neglect made up the majority of abuse cases (58.5 percent) in 1994. In addition, the NCEA (1997) reported that the incidence of neglect increased from 47 percent in 1990 to 55 percent in 1996.

Self-neglect of the elderly occurs when the elderly individual cannot or will not properly care of himself or herself. It is defined as acts that threaten their health and safety. This form of elder abuse is more likely to occur if the elderly individual is living alone or with another impaired family member. Signs of self-neglect, similar to those of neglect, can include dehydration, malnutrition, failure to take medications, inadequate medical attention, poor personal hygiene, inappropriate clothing, lack of needed medical aids (hearing aids, eyeglasses, dentures), and living in conditions that prove to be housing or health violations (Marshall et al., 2000; Young 2000).

Unhealthy living conditions may involve improper wiring, lack of indoor plumbing or functional toilets, lack of heat or proper ventilation (air conditioning), lack of electricity, broken windows, holes in the roof, or uncleanliness (excess garbage, animal or insect infestation, fecal or urine materials or odors etc.; Young 2000)

As this type of abuse is often unrecognized and unreported, it has been difficult to establish prevalence rates. Most neglect prevalence rates exclude self-neglect cases. However, it has been stated that self-neglect is the most prevalent form of elder abuse, and nearly half of the cases reported to adult protective services involve self-neglect (Deets, 1993; Salend, Kane, Satz, & Pynoos, 1984; Sharon, 1991). The NEAIS revealed that there were 139,000 new cases of self-neglect in 1996. Most of the cases involved women (60 percent) and those elderly over age 80 (45 percent; Administration on Aging, 1998).

Self-neglect is said to be the most controversial type of elder abuse. Adults have the constitutional right to make choices for living; thus an elderly person has the right to accept or refuse help. In addition, adult children are generally not legally required to provide for their elderly relatives unless there is a specific legal relationship such as trusteeship, guardianship, or other fiduciary agreement or unless the adult children are providing caregiver services for elderly family members. If an elderly person does not have the mental capacity to make healthy decisions for himself or herself, society, under certain circumstances, may intervene. However, a court must declare the elderly person incompetent or mentally incapable before intervening (Salend et al, 1984).

Emotional Abuse

Elder psychological or emotional abuse is defined as an act that causes mental anguish to an elderly individual. Emotional abuse is characterized by threats, social isolation, demeaning remarks or insults, menacing, or giving harsh orders (Brownell & Abelman, 1998; Marshall et al, 2000; Young, 2000). Signs of emotional abuse include insomnia, depression, anxiety, fearfulness, memory loss, and feelings of helplessness and hopelessness (Young, 2000).

The prevalence rates for emotional abuse of the elderly have been inconsistent. Some are relatively low comparatively. The NCEA (1997) reported a decline of emotional abuse cases, from 11.7 percent in 1990 to 7.7 percent in 1996. Other scholars, however, recognize that emotional abuse is common and rank it among the top three forms, along with physical abuse and neglect (Marshall et al., 2000).

Financial and Economic Abuse

Financial abuse or exploitation of the elderly involves the unlawful or inappropriate use of the elderly individual's money, property, or assets (NCEA, 1997; Young, 2000). Indications of financial abuse may not be as blatant as signs of other forms of abuse. Financial exploitation can be recognized by the following signs: an elderly person's bills are no longer being paid; the person is losing amenities (phone, utility, television, food, or clothing); the person is being isolated from others; unusual activity is taking place in the person's bank account or with credit cards; new signatures appear on the person's bank transactions; new powers of attorney are created; the person no longer takes prescribed medicine or seeks necessary medical attention or does not eat right, if at all (Federal Bureau of Investigation [FBI, 1997]; Hodge, 2001; Young, 2000). Crimes associated with financial abuse involve larceny, burglary, embezzlement, forgery, issuing false checks, using false documents, destroying wills, or breaching fiduciary duties (Hodge, 2001).

It is questionable whether the prevalence of financial abuse of the elderly has increased over the years. There is no national reporting center to track reported cases. Moreover, financial abuse is often combined with other forms of elder abuse. Neglect and physical abuse are often present (Young, 2000). The NCEA (1997), however, reported that elder financial abuse actually decreased, from 17.3 percent of all abuse cases studied in 1990 to a rate of 12.3 percent in 1996. The FBI (1997), however, estimates that only about 1 in 10 cases of elder abuse is actually reported and that financial abuse is less likely to be reported than physical abuse. This may be the result of the crime being less evident and less threatening. Financial abuse often goes on for an extended period of time before a victim realizes, if he or she ever does, what has happened.

Whether or not it is on the rise, there is no doubt that the financial exploitation of our elderly population is occurring. Wolf (1986) found that financial abuse cases made up one-third of all elder abuse cases. A study in Forsyth County, North Carolina, found financial abuse to be the most prevalent form of elder abuse reported, making up 46 percent of the total reported elder abuse cases (Shiferaw, Mittlemark, Woffard, Anderson, & Walls, 1994).

Much of the financial abuse discussed here is perpetrated by someone the elderly person knows. Though we do not like to implicate family members, national law enforcement data indicate that family members are the most common perpetrators. This makes sense, as family members have developed a level of trust with the victim and have easy access to an elder's assets and as children or relatives of the elderly are most often in a caregiver role or have power of attorney (Hodge, 2001).

Finally, this population is increasingly being exploited by people to whom they are not related but with whom they have developed a trusting relationship. Caregivers can be health care professionals, such as home health aides, nursing home or hospital personnel, nurses' aides, administrators or support staff, and physicians and nurses. Fiduciaries are also guilty of exploiting the elderly financially. Such individuals might include lawyers, notaries, accountants, real estate brokers, stockbrokers, guardians, conservators, investment advisors, and others with power of attorney (Hodge, 2001). We discuss financial exploitation in more depth in chapter 7.

Violation of Rights

Violation of rights refers to the inalienable rights of all individuals (Collins et al., 2000). Some of these rights, as outlined in 1948 by the United Nations General Assembly in the Universal Declaration of Human Rights, include the right to personal liberty, the right to adequate and appropriate medical care, the right to own property and not to be arbitrarily denied of such, and the right to security in the event of widowhood, old age, or lack of livelihood beyond one's control (United Nations, 1948). Other recognized rights include freedom from sexual abuse, the right to freedom from verbal abuse, the right to privacy, and the right to a clean and safe living environment (U.S. House of Representatives Select Committee on Aging, 1981).

Abandonment

Abandonment has been defined by the NCEA (1999) as the desertion of an elderly person by someone who has the responsibility to provide care for that person or by someone who has physical custody of the elderly person.

Abandonment of an elder can occur in many situations. An elderly person may be left at an institution, such as a hospital or nursing home. In addition, some elderly people have been abandoned at malls or shopping centers. Finally, an elderly person can be abandoned in his or her own home.

/// Consequences of Elder Abuse

The consequences of elder abuse are many. The consequences of abuse and mistreatment for the elderly are unusual in two ways. First, the increasingly debilitating effects of the aging process often mean that elders are easily injured and have longer recovery periods. In addition, another unusual and difficult factor in elder abuse is determining whether the illness, injury, or ill condition of the elderly person is actually due to mistreatment or whether it is due to the normal aging process and the illnesses that accompany aging. Moreover, as mentioned, it is often difficult to determine the elderly person's mental capacity. Although determining abuse is sometimes clear-cut, in many cases it requires more advanced investigation by trained professionals. In light of this fact, we explore the consequences of elder abuse, including fatalities and the physical, psychological, economic, and legal consequences.

Fatalities

The highest level of abuse results in death. It may be difficult to distinguish between the factors associated with aging and those associated with the abuse. These elements may work in combination to cause death. Moreover, there has been little research on mortality rates and elder abuse. Nevertheless, it has been documented that elder abuse has had a significant impact on the mortality rates of older Americans.

Lachs, Williams, O'Brien, Pillemer, and Charison (1998a, 1998b, 1998c) implemented a study over a 13-year period of elderly adults in a community dwelling in New Haven, Connecticut. Of the 2,812 individuals studied, 173 were seen by adult protective services for allegations of abuse, neglect, or self-neglect. The researchers determined that of those elderly who died, 73 percent suffered from self-neglect, 17 percent from neglect, and 6 percent from abuse. After controlling for other mortality factors (e.g., demographic characteristics, chronic diseases, functional status, social networks, cognitive status, and symptoms of depression), these elderly adults were found to have mortality rates three times that of other elderly adults in the community. In fact, whereas 40 percent of those who reported no abuse or neglect were still alive, only 9 percent of those who were physically abused or neglected were. Thus it was concluded that mistreatment can cause severe interpersonal stress, which may predispose one to death.

In addition to this study, in its National Crime Victimization Survey

(NCVS), the U.S. Department of Justice (Klaus, 1999) has included statistics that, though they do not accurately measure elder abuse as a crime, provide some insight into elder abuse and mortality rates. Included in the NCVS of 1992 through 1997 were statistics on violent crimes committed against those age 65 and older by a relative, intimate, or person well known to the victim. The NCVS found that 36,290 individuals over 65 were injured by a relative or someone well known to them. Of the 36,290 elderly people, 15,040 were injured by their relatives. Thus, in light of the previous study by Lachs et al. (1998a, 1998b, 1998c) and given the numbers in these studies, one could infer that there may have been mortality related to this physical abuse.

Moreover, the NCVS reported that a total of 500 elderly people were actually murdered by a relative or someone they knew well. Out of these 500 cases, more than half (260) were murders committed by a relative. Furthermore, the NCVS found that these people were two times more likely than their younger counterparts (< 65 years) to be killed by a relative or intimate.

Physical Effects

The physical effects of elder mistreatment are devastating. Blatant effects, such as cuts, bruises, burns, and so forth, may be apparent; however, some effects may be less obvious and need the trained eye of a physician to diagnose. Some of these physical consequences include malnutrition and dehydration, head injuries, and sexual abuse.

Malnutrition and dehydration are common among the elderly. As the aging process erodes their abilities to care for themselves and affects them socially and physically, the elderly are continually at risk. Thus malnutrition and dehydration may be secondary to other factors (e.g., depression, isolation, decreased taste acuity, fixed incomes, medications, etc.). Some indicators of malnutrition and dehydration are weight loss, anemia, high sodium in the blood, mental confusion, fatigue, poor wound healing, and increased risk of infection (Quinn & Tomita, 1997). It may be difficult to distinguish whether malnutrition and dehydration are due to the aging process and illnesses that accompany it or to mistreatment. Autopsies can uncover the role of malnutrition and dehydration in death (Hood, 2001). Thus, in addition to other substantiating factors, a physician may determine the malnutrition and dehydration to be the result of mistreatment, whether it be neglect or self-neglect.

Abused elderly may sustain head injuries, or subdural hematomas, that may mistakenly be attributed to normal aging. In addition, they may suffer a traumatic abusive event that sets off a series of aggravating factors that eventually lead to death. This has been referred to as "delayed death" and can be easily overlooked. Sexual abuse injuries may be less obvious because some may occur inside the body (Hood, 2001).

Psychological Effects

The psychological effects of elder abuse may or may not be obvious. Some research has shown that victims of elder abuse suffer depression in greater rates than do elders who are not abused. There is evidence that victims of elder abuse also suffer other psychological distress or disorders (Bristowe & Collins, 1989; Comijs, Penninx, Knipscheer and van Tilburg, 1999; Pillemer & Prescott, 1989). These studies indicate that victims of abuse tend to exhibit increased depression, posttraumatic stress disorder, anxiety disorders, and other psychological conditions. It is difficult to determine whether or not individual victims exhibit such psychological distress prior to victimization; therefore, researchers are concerned about the validity of such findings (Wolf, 2000). Physicians have documented other psychological effects of elder abuse, including learned helplessness, alienation, guilt, shame, fear, anxiety, denial, and such disorders as PTSD (Booth, Bruno, & Marin, 1996). Isolation and alcohol abuse can also be attributable to mistreatment and can compound the psychological effects of victimization. Further, suicide is a concern. Suicide rates for the elderly increased 36 percent between 1980 and 1982 ("Suicide Rates," 1996).

Economic Effects

Elder abuse and neglect has financial repercussions. Financial exploitation can drain the financial resources of the victim, which may mean the loss of savings and assets. Physical, emotional, and sexual abuse may require medical care, thereby placing additional financial burdens on victims. This financial burden may extend to other family members, depending on relationships and living arrangements.

The cost of elder abuse and neglect is also passed on to the health care industry through the need for increased medical care. Government and nonprofit agencies, responding to elder abuse and neglect, must invest resources to combat the problem. Increased government spending includes prevention education and programs and community treatment programs. These programs may be based in social services agencies, numerous other human service agencies, law enforcement agencies, and the courts.

Legal Consequences

Types of elder abuse that are considered crimes vary from state to state. Although most states prosecute for physical, sexual, emotional, and financial abuse and for neglect, self-neglect is not embedded in many state statutes. The adult protective service units of most states handle abuse reports. Area offices on aging or county departments of social services handle elder abuse in other states. These units investigate the reports and provide treatment and protection for victims and their families. However, other public and private entities (e.g., law enforcement, hospitals, human service agencies, etc.) are involved in reporting, investigating, protecting, and treating abused elders. Consequently, many agencies and many professionals get involved in elder abuse cases. We discuss intervention strategies in chapter 8.

The legal concepts of mental capacity and undue influence become important in determining consent. For example, if an elderly person agrees to give power of attorney to an adult child, the elder needs to have the mental capacity to make that decision and to do so without undue influence. Additionally, intervention agencies are responsible for distinguishing abuse and neglect from the natural aging process.

/// Chapter Summary

Elder abuse and neglect are not new. They have existed in various forms, in various levels, and in different cultures for centuries. The status of the elderly, however, has wavered. Whereas in some cultures the elderly are still revered, in American culture they are not. We do not appreciate the old. Our culture and society are rampant with indications that we value youth and fear death. We have forgotten the keys to life that our elderly hold. We no longer celebrate them nor acknowledge their wisdom. Our fast-paced world does not allow for this. Yet, as we have seen, the number of older Americans is rapidly increasing. Many more of us will be elderly by the year 2050. In addition, there will be increases in the number of elderly women, the number of people over age 85, the number of elderly people living alone, and the number of culturally diverse elderly.

Although many of the elderly are at risk of abuse and neglect, some groups appear to be more susceptible. Women in particular seem to be at increased risk. Women live longer than men, live alone more often than men, and become more frail. Thus there will be more elderly women over 85 years, more women living alone, and more minority women in each of these categories. It also appears that women suffer more frequently from more serious compounding risk factors, such as depression and Alzheimer's disease. This is not to say that men are not at risk; we must investigate gender factors further. In addition to women, the poor will be at risk. Though many of us will enjoy healthy later years, many will not. Advances in technology, medicine, and economics are not distributed equally. Thus those with fewer resources will be at risk for not only poor health but also abuse and neglect in greater numbers. Moreover, our oldest old, the frailest of us all, are and will be at increased risk.

Hence, large numbers of American elderly individuals will be at risk for and subject to the types of abuses identified. As we have seen, the consequences of abuse can be devastating. The consequences can be short term, but many have long-term effects. We are not even close to understanding the full scope of this devastation. It is not characterized simply by the failing health and increased mortality of our elderly. Its impact is far reaching, affecting our families and the society as a whole.

It is our obligation to care for our citizens and for each member of our families. We owe it to our elderly, ourselves, and our nation to celebrate the elderly. Disregarding the issue will only serve to eat away at the fabric of our society. We must be willing to recognize elder abuse and neglect as a serious public issue worthy of further understanding and investigation. It is only in this way that we will be able to work on prevention and treatment modalities.

/// Recommended Web Sites

American Association of Retired Persons
    www.aarp.com
Federal Interagency Forum on Age-Related Statistics
    www.agingstats.gov
Alzheimer's Disease Education and Referral Center
www.alzheimers.org
Administration on Aging of the Department of Health and Human Services
    www.aoa.dhhs.gov
American Society on Aging
    www.asaging.org
National Center for Health Statistics, Centers for Disease Control
    www.cdc.gov/nchs
National Center on Elder Abuse
    www.elderabusecenter.org
Modern Maturity: AARP Publication
    www.modernmaturity
National Institute on Aging
    www.nia.nih.gov
U.S. Department of Justice, Office of Justice Programs, Bureau of Justice Statistics
    www.ojp.usdoj.gov
National Committee for the Prevention of Elder Abuse
    www.preventelderabuse.org
Senior Pages: Publications
    www.seniorpages.com
United Nations
    www.un.org

7 /// *Pseudo Families* Caregiver/Institutional Maltreatment

*I*t was a hot summer day when the call came in. Marsha could not believe that someone could have sexually abused her mother at a nursing home. Emma, Marsha's 94-year-old mother, had been in a nursing home for the past 5 years. Unable to speak, Emma had to rely on staff from the nursing home to care for her. During a routine sponge bath on this hot day, Joyce (a health care aide) found Emma's underclothes soaked in blood. Concerned that Emma was hemorrhaging, Joyce immediately called in the nursing supervisor. Emma was immediately examined. They discovered that the bleeding had subsided, but there was clear-cut evidence of sexual abuse. Emma was transported to the local emergency room so a trained physician could conduct a rape exam. Bruises had started to form on her inner thighs, buttocks and back, and her insides were ripped and torn. Semen was found. The staff members were beside themselves. Who could do such a thing to sweet old Emma? They called in the police.

After an intensive investigation, the police arrested Joseph Dilly for rape in the first degree. Joseph Dilly (age 45) was a janitor at the nursing home. Joseph had worked at the facility for only about 6 months and disclosed to police that he liked "rough" sex and had had "relations" with at least seven female residents since he began his employment. After a thorough investigation of his story, he was additionally charged with the rape of three other women.

Marsha was relieved that her mother passed away shortly after Dilly was arrested. She prayed that her mother never really knew what was happening to her. Emma seemed to retreat inside herself most days, and Marsha was never sure what her mother was really conscious of. Marsha, however, had trouble sleeping and eating since that first call came. Her mind was filled with thoughts of her defenseless mother being brutalized by this man, and she found herself having difficulty concentrating or focusing on any kind of task. She decided to contact the woman from the rape crisis center who visited her and her mother in the emergency room. Marsha expressed concern that she was "going crazy."

Emma and Marsha's experience serves as a horrific example of the type of maltreatment that residents of out-of-home care facilities may endure at the hands of nonfamily members. This chapter is devoted to a discussion of such abuses in what we refer to as "pseudo families." We define *pseudo families* as any out-of-home supervised setting in which individuals live and must rely on others for their daily care. The pseudo family is the core of staff and administrators who are responsible for the well-being of their residents.

You might be asking yourself, Why would we consider abuse taking place outside of the family to be relevant to our understanding about violence in families? Our response is fourfold. First, we believe it is important to draw attention to the issue. As out-of-home care has grown to be a commonplace setting for children, vulnerable adults, and the elderly, it is important that we recognize the problem with as much attention as we pay to violence in other interpersonal relationships. With the advent of modern medical technology and an aging population, we can expect that more older adults will need to rely on some form of institutional care in future years.

Second, as we will discuss, some of the same factors that are involved in abuse within a family are also at play in out-of-home settings. Therefore, this chapter may shed some additional light on the role of abuse and neglect in interpersonal relationships. Although out-of-home care is markedly different from family life, many of the basic daily living functions and communication issues are very similar. Also, other living environments provide us an opportunity to examine theoretical constructs in a new way.

Third, we tend to define *home* as the place in which we currently reside. So, although we may live in many places throughout our lifetimes, we consider the place in which we currently dwell as "home," even if we know our stay will be temporary. Therefore, individuals who live in settings other than their family home often come to think of their living space as home. In fact, one of the biggest ironies in institutional care is the fact that the facilities, although they are home to many, rarely resemble home environments in terms of their physical layout, furniture, decorating, activity, and meals. Individuals who are abused and neglected in these environments are also victims of violence in the home.

Fourth and finally, it is important to recognize the role that the physical living environment plays in relation to the developmental aspects of people's lives, particularly for children (Rivlin & Wolfe, 1985). Because a large number of children and adults are reared in settings other than their family homes, it is especially important to acknowledge the impact these settings may have on their development, especially when neglect and abuse are factors.

/// Defining Pseudo Family Abuse: Caregiver and Institutional Abuse and Maltreatment

Now we define what we mean by pseudo family abuse and maltreatment. We borrow from Mildred Pagelow's (1984) definition of family violence, as we discussed in chapter 1:

> *Pseudo Family Abuse* includes any act of commission or omission by individuals responsible for the daily care of others in an out-of-home setting, and any conditions resulting from such acts or inaction, which deprive individuals of equal rights and liberties, and/or inter- fere with their optimal development and freedom of choice. (p. 21)

Some may disagree with this definition, especially in reference to the restriction of freedom of choice, as freedom of choice is inherently void in out-of-home care settings. However, we would argue that freedom of choice is as important, if not more so, in out-of-home care settings as in family life. It is often the restriction of choice that makes out of home care so unbearable for residents, rendering them helpless, hopeless, powerless, and victimized. We include the issue of freedom of choice in our definition to highlight the fact that risk of maltreatment is greater in organizational cul- tures that restrict personal freedoms to a detrimental degree.

Our discussion is limited to children, vulnerable adults, and the elderly who have been placed in private or public agencies for their care and treat- ment. Out-of-home care, for our purposes, is defined as 24-hour group care provided by paid staff who are biologically unrelated to the residents. We also include foster homes in our definition. Abusers are the individuals responsible for providing the care, whether they are administrators, super- visors or direct-care staff, or foster parents. We focus our attention on the types of mistreatment that occurs, the consequences for victims, and various policy efforts.

This chapter is divided into four main sections. The first section is devoted to historical perspectives on out-of-home care. History suggests that out-of-home care has continued to thrive as an option for children and vulnerable adults. Unfortunately, out-of-home care has a historical foun- dation built on mistreatment. The second section explores what life is like for individuals living in out-of-home care settings. Here we discuss some of the consequences of living in such environments, even when mistreatment is not an issue (some would argue that placing someone in an institution is, in and of itself, a form of mistreatment). The third section covers the various forms that mistreatment may take in out-of-home care settings and examines several relevant case examples. Finally, the fourth section explores the various systems that are currently in place to investigate and prosecute pseudo family abuse.

/// Putting Out-of-Home Care in a Historical Context

What is "out-of-home" care? We use the term *out-of-home care* to describe a variety of settings in which individuals receive daily care and treatment. Although the settings vary greatly, their purpose tends to be similar: to care for and treat individuals who, for a variety of reasons, can no longer be cared for in their own homes. Out-of-home care settings might include psychiatric hospitals, group homes, foster care, developmental centers, detention centers, residential programs, and long-term care facilities. As we discuss, out-of-home care has a long history riddled with abuse.

Out-of-home care developed as a community response to deviance. In other words, when we have become uncomfortable with a particular social condition, we have often responded by isolating those who are different from the rest of society. Society's misfits have historically been shut away from plain view. These misfits have included such groups as orphans, the elderly, disabled, delinquents, the sick, and the poor. If we do not have to see "these people" every day, we do not have to acknowledge their presence, nor do we have to take responsibility for their plight. Koocher (1976, p. 7) says it best: "Children who are different or who are considered defective in some way have long been institutionalized as a kind of 'sanitizing' service for society."

The history of out-of-home care in the United States can be traced back to colonial times, when "public homes" and asylums lodged a variety of socially disadvantaged people (Mercer, 1983). The philosophy of these facilities was centered on a mixture of true charity and a strict adherence to the moral principles of the time. The hope was that residents could be molded into becoming more acceptable members of the community.

By 1712, the concept of the "almshouse" was developed (Mercer, 1983). The term *almshouse* is derived from the word *alms*, meaning relief given out of pity to the poor. Almshouses were commonplace for the next hundred years as an appropriate way to house the socially disadvantaged. The almshouses boarded both children and adults who suffered from a variety of social ills. Central to providing boarding services was the idea that the poor could be retrained to become productive members of society. Although we no longer use the term *almshouse*, some contemporary homeless shelters and missions provide a similar service.

By the early 1800s, the American Revolution, and the War of 1812 (Rivlin & Wolfe, 1985), the rise of industrialization, coupled with the development of the belief that deviance was caused by environmental forces (Whitehead & Lab, 1999), culminated in the development of asylums to serve as a solution for a wide range of social deviants, such as the insane, orphans, criminals, delinquents, and the poor. Rothman (1971, p. 18) notes, "the almshouse and the orphan asylum all represented an effort to insure the cohesion of the community in new and changing circumstances."

The asylum was initially developed to serve as a refuge by providing a serene setting, a regular schedule of activity, regular meals, and recreational activities in order to revitalize the patient back into the community (Rivlin & Wolfe, 1985). Initially designed to care for middle- and upper-income patients, the popularity of the asylum soon grew to include such "undesirables" as criminals and other deviants from other institutions. Eventually the refuge of the asylum became nothing more than an assembly line of custodial care.

Growth of Child Care Institutions

As we have previously mentioned, children and adults were usually placed in the same institutional settings. However, by the 1850s children were diverted from the almshouses into specific facilities often called "orphan asylums." Although the name *orphan asylum* implies services for orphaned children, the reality was that these institutions housed a variety of "deviant" children, such as children from single-parent families and children whose parents were poor, immoral, or incompetent to raise their children (Rothman, 1971). As with the previous generation of institutional settings, the central goal of the orphan asylums was to remove the child from an inappropriate home environment, often from growing urban centers, to retrain them to become proper citizens.

During this same period, houses of refuge—reformatories for children who misbehaved—emerged as commonplace settings across the United States. The houses of refuge were created by a group of activists known as child savers. The child savers, a group of well-to-do citizens and professionals, believed they could "save" children from their own parents and from poverty by placement in a controlled setting.

The first house of refuge opened in 1825 in New York City. The establishment of the houses of refuge served to remove children from the criminal elements of the workhouses and adult jails, in which delinquent children were often placed. The house of refuge was established to separate deviant youth from their deviant adult counterparts, while providing education, training, hard work, religious training, and strict discipline.

The philosophy included a strict regimen of discipline, enforced silence, wearing of uniforms, slavelike labor, and severe physical punishment. The military model was embraced as a tool to teach youngsters respect for authority (Whitehead & Lab, 1999). Rothman (1971) notes that the main differences between the orphan asylums and the houses of refuge were that the asylums did not usually lodge children in cells, as was common in the houses of refuge, and that the asylums spent more time on classroom instructions versus the hard labor of the houses of refuge.

Although the initial goals of the houses of refuge were commendable, in operation, instilling respect for authority meant severe corporal punishment (consistent with child-rearing practices of the time). Children were whipped, placed in solitary confinement, removed from recreational activities, and refused meals (Bremner, 1970). In addition, children often wore balls and chains (Rothman, 1971). An excerpt from an 1827 *Annual Report of the New York House of Refuge* illustrates the abusive tone of institutional life:

> It was found necessary to apply severe and continued punishments, in order to break the obstinacy of his spirit. The discipline enforced had a most happy effect. He became submissive and obedient. (as cited by Rothman, 1971, p. 215)

In reality, the operations of the houses of refuge were literally indistinguishable from those of the adult prisons. The children were treated no differently from the way the prisons and jails had historically treated their inmates. By today's standards, we can reflect back on such institutional settings with great disdain; however, these institutions were actually intended to be improvements over the traditional practices. We would consider such disciplinary practices as child abuse today, but at the time such methods were considered appropriate for proper child rearing.

Eventually, the Progressive movement (roughly 1865 to 1940) led to an era of reform. The Progressives consisted of a wide range of middle- to upper-class individuals who were not against institutional settings. However, with the growing contributions of sociology and psychology as developing fields of scientific research, the Progressives argued for more individualistic approaches to social deviance. New institutions were created to simulate a homelike environment, replacing cells with cottages and hard labor with vocational training (Rivlin & Wolfe, 1985). Institutional names were changed to reflect a change in philosophy, for instance, to "training schools" or "industrial schools." It was believed that institutions should be individualized to treat the specific problems of the residents.

However, these institutional improvements also proved to be indistinguishable from prison environments, contradicting the progressive rhetoric. Punishment was still utilized as a "training" method, including solitary confinement, rules of silence, and corporal punishment (Rothman, 1980).

Regardless of the outcomes of reformer policies, the reforms created during this era have had lasting effects on our current system of care. For example, the Progressive era was marked by the development of a separate system of justice for juveniles, with the first juvenile court being established in 1899 in Cook County, Illinois. The Progressive movement also helped to bring about such concepts as probation and the designation of the "emotionally disturbed" child, and it embraced the transfer of power from parents to the state (Rivlin & Wolfe, 1985). Perhaps the true legacy of the Progressive movement is the creation of a system of care for children that endures today.

Following the Progressive era, the 1950s through the 1970s saw a rapid growth in the mental health field, which contributed to the growth of mental health facilities geared to treat children. Although the first inpatient psychiatric treatment facility for children had opened in 1923 at Bellevue Hospital in New York and child guidance clinics were available at the time in many communities (Rivlin & Wolfe, 1985), this time period is marked by a rapid growth in mental health services. A number of factors are responsible for this growth. First, World War II brought about a new awareness of mental health, providing additional policy and research support for the growing fields of psychiatry, medicine, and social work (Rivlin & Wolfe, 1985). Additionally, the introduction of psychopharmacological drugs (Bentley & Walsh, 2001) and growing federal social welfare policies culminated in an expansion of programs and services to treat children with psychological, emotional, and behavioral problems.

During this period it is difficult to attain documentation on the treatment of children in institutional care. Some evidence suggests that children had been inappropriately placed in institutions (Koocher, 1976) and that institutions developed a growing dependence on treating problems only with psychopharmacological drugs. Child discipline methods have since relied on the use of drugs and token economy systems. Token economy systems are a form of behavior modification that utilizes rewards and punishments for appropriate and inappropriate behaviors. Rivlin and Wolfe (1985) point out that these "control" techniques have been used as therapy in institutions and are really no different from the types of treatment used by institutions of the past, particularly those espoused during the Progressive era.

Although institutions have progressed in the past several hundred years, a number of parallels can be drawn to connect our present with our past. First, our reasons for placing children in institutional and residential settings have not changed. We continue to place poor, disruptive, mismanaged children in settings out of their homes. At the same time, we continue to use institutions to assist in the daily care of emotionally and physically disabled children. In other words, we continue to utilize pseudo families to raise our socially deviant children.

Second, the progressive ideology that focuses on treating the individual based on diagnosis (Rivlin & Wolfe, 1985) is the paradigm that frames institutional life as we experience it today. Our current system of care no longer lumps a heterogeneous group of adults and children together; rather, specific institutional industries have developed that focus on distinctive social problems. For example, specific institutions house the developmentally disabled, the emotionally disturbed, runaway and homeless youths, or youths who break the law. Community-based residential settings, such as group homes, independent living quarters, children's homes, children's shelters, foster homes, residential treatment facilities, and so forth, have begun to replace the traditional institutional setting. We refer to these kinds of programs as *pseudo family settings*.

Third, the range of services available for children has expanded tremendously since the Progressive era. Today, children's services have evolved to include a continuum of care in which residential placement is theoretically used only as a last resort. The deinstitutionalization movement of the

1980s has challenged communities to create services for children without relying on continuous placement in residential settings. Examples of non-residential programs for children include outpatient clinics, day treatment programs, in-home parent aide programs, probation supervision, and alternative schools. These programs allow the child to receive appropriate care, yet often allow them to remain in their own homes or with extended family members.

However, as we discuss later in this chapter, children continue to be placed in pseudo family settings and thrown into traditional institutional settings at a high rate. The majority of children in substitute care today are currently in foster homes, yet many reside in group homes, detention facilities, developmental centers, and other residential programs. Additionally, it is unclear whether or not children have been inappropriately placed in such environments. Perhaps there is a disconnection between contemporary reform rhetoric and reality, much as in the past.

Fourth, it is sometimes difficult to distinguish the residential settings of the past from the programs of the present. The "get tough on juvenile crime" policies of the last several decades have been instrumental in cementing institutional punishment as an appropriate setting for delinquent children. State training schools, secure and nonsecure detention facilities, and other types of treatment facilities are still utilized to rehabilitate juvenile offenders. As public policy continues to take a crime control approach to delinquency problems, it is unlikely that this level of institutional living will be diminished any time soon.

It is unclear how these institutional settings differ from the asylums and houses of refuge of the past, and in many ways it is often hard to distinguish these facilities from adult prisons and jails. For example, one of the most popular new methods for "treating" deviance is the juvenile boot camp. Juvenile boot camps are short-term facilities (90 days to 6 months) that resemble military boot camps, with rigid scheduling, attention to discipline, physical training, and work. Although the educational and therapeutic programs in boot camps are stressed, the other central aspects of this modality do not appear to be so different from those that characterized the past.

Perhaps the most important parallel to consider is the fact that children continue to be mistreated and abused in these settings. Although the living conditions in out-of-home care have improved greatly since the 1800s, children are still at risk for abuse, mistreatment, and neglect and are subjected to the detrimental physical and emotional consequences of living in such settings. The painful irony is the fact that the children who are often placed in out-of-home settings are often the very same children who have already experienced some form of maltreatment in their family homes.

Growth of Institutions for the Elderly

As we discussed earlier in this chapter, elderly people who needed care, particularly those who were sick or poor, were placed in almshouses or asylums prior to the nineteenth century. By the late nineteenth and early part of the twentieth century, the Progressive era of reform led to changes in how the aged were to be cared for. Homes for the aged were created by churches and other private charitable organizations in an attempt to improve the plight of the elderly (Mercer, 1983). The aged, like children, were removed and placed in facilities that were theoretically geared to meet their specific needs; thus the birth of the nursing home. Unlike the boarding home model of the almshouses and asylums, the nursing home concept combined elements of a health care facility with those of a hotel (Stathopoulos, 1983).

Since the 1930s the growth of the nursing home industry has expanded to include a continuum of long term care that includes skilled nursing facilities, intermediate nursing facilities, and rest homes (Stathopoulos, 1983). A number of public policy initiatives coupled with social changes have stimulated the growth of the nursing home industry. The depression of the 1930s led to sweeping changes in social welfare policy that have persevered over the last 70 years. The Social Security Act of 1935 reduced the retirement age to 65 and provided old-age assistance for those 65 and older (Mercer, 1983). This change, prompted by the unemployment of younger workers, ultimately redefined the term *elderly*. Additionally, federal assistance for the development of nursing home care in the 1950s and the Kerr-Mills Act, which provided for Medicaid in 1960s, fueled the growth of the industry (Stathopoulos, 1983).

Additionally, the demands of industrialization led to changes in the way families lived and worked, often separating family members. Improvements in health and medicine have led to an extension of the life expectancy, altering the period of life that we define as "aged." Combined with these social changes was the growing need to find alternative solutions for patients in psychiatric facilities and general hospitals. In theory, nursing home care provided the right mixture of dedicated health services and supervised living arrangements, fulfilling the diverse demands of society (Stathopoulos, 1983).

Regardless of the popularity of nursing homes as an institutional model, nursing homes have historically been criticized for poor care and substandard living conditions. For example, the Subcommittee on Long-Term Care of the United State Senate Special Committee, chaired by Senator Frank E. Moss, documented widespread fraud and abuse in nursing homes during the 1970s (Halamandaris, 1983). The committee examined more than 23,000 nursing homes and found that more than half of them were below standard (Stathopoulos, 1983). Much of the substandard care can be attributed to widespread fraud committed with Medicaid and Medicare dollars. Instead of providing an appropriate level of care with government money, nursing home staff have defrauded the government in a variety of ways, many of which we discuss later in this chapter.

As a result of the Moss Report, legislation has been enacted to better monitor and regulate the long-term care industry. Today a system is in place for reporting, investigating, and prosecuting long-term care abuses. Problems of maltreatment persist in the industry for a number of reasons, including low staff-to-patient ratios, poor working conditions, low pay, and lack of adequate staff training. Also, the elderly, particularly the frail elderly, are especially vulnerable to all kinds of abuses and neglect.

With an increasingly aging baby-boom population, a continued examination of long-term care options for older adults is warranted. Given the social realities of changing demographics, economics, family mobility, and so forth, it is likely that long-term care facilities will continue to grow in popularity in future years. The challenge will be to provide settings in which older adults can live and heal without the threat of maltreatment and the detrimental effects of institutionalization.

/// Living Out of Home: The Process of Institutionalization

As we have previously mentioned, today specific out-of-home environments have been created to meet the specific needs of specific groups of people. We no longer group a heterogeneous mixture of adults and children who need care together in one residential setting. Therefore, a wide range of institutional and semi-institutional settings are available to care for children and adults. We have also noted the variety of reasons for an individual to be removed from his or her family home and placed in an out-of-home setting.

Living in out-of-home settings, although a necessity for many, is a departure from what is considered normal family living. For some individuals, out-of-home care means stability, regular meals, proper supervision, and a warm bed to sleep in at night—in other words, an improvement in their overall quality of life. Although placement in such a setting may be necessary and even welcomed, living out of home is not without its own set of problems. Living in an environment in which activities and choices are limited is an adjustment for both children and adults. The unintended consequences can be devastating to the developmental processes of both children and adults, and therefore they should be examined within the context of maltreatment. Although out-of-home care is a necessity in the modern world, we should recognize that placing someone in such an environment has its own set of consequences, which may in fact be worse than the problem that was originally to be treated. Also, the structure and organization of some out-of-home settings create a circumstance in which abuse and neglect can flourish.

As we alluded to earlier, out-of-home living is different from normal family living in many respects. Activities are limited and structured—for example, bedtime, rising time, bathing, television viewing, and recreational activities. Meals are often prescribed by the management and served at specific times of the day only. Adult residents often find restrictions in their ability to have sexual relationships and to partake in other kinds of adult activities, such as having a glass a wine with dinner or a mug of beer while watching the football game. Residents often have little say in the day-to-day decision making of the organization, such as staffing, meals, planned activities, building renovations, and so forth. In some instances, residents are not free to leave the grounds of the facility without permission. Privacy is often not guarded or considered to be a critical human factor in communal living. Residents often have to share bathing, toilet, and bedroom space with virtual strangers. Additionally, many out-of-home settings truly resemble institutions in their physical structure, layout, and interior design, and they are often isolated from the center of community life.

In many ways, the resident's entire life is controlled by the staff of the facility. The ability to freely decide what and when to eat, when to shower or dress, when to study or rest, and so forth is often restricted, and such decisions are often made by members of the staff. We are not describing a prison environment; however, many residents of nursing homes, children's homes, or psychiatric facilities often feel as though they are prisoners in such environments.

Erving Goffman, in his groundbreaking 1961 book, *Asylums*, describes this form of living as a "total institution." He describes the total institution as one in which individuals rarely are able to come and go freely and must eat, sleep, play, learn, and even worship together. Staff and residents live and work together under the same conditions and become excluded from the rest of society. He notes numerous examples of the "asylum," such as military camps, seminaries, convents, prisons, rest homes, and mental hospitals. He argued that individuals bring with them to the institutional setting a particular cultural heritage, which he refers to as the "presenting culture." Residents soon undergo a period of "disculturation" in which they must shed elements of their presenting culture and assume the culture of the institution. We often refer to this as the process of institutionalization (Goffman, 1961).

This process of institutionalization, also referred to as the social breakdown syndrome or the syndrome of psychosocial degradation (Yawney & Slover, 1973) can lead to feelings of helplessness, hopelessness, and powerlessness that induce profound changes in one's sense of self. These changes may lead to passivity, depression, and, in the case of the elderly, even death (Mercer, 1983). A disturbing example of the latter is indirect self-destructive behavior (ISDB). Conwell, Pearson, and DeRenzo (1996, p. 153) define ISDB as "an act of omission or commission that causes self-harm leading indirectly, over time, to the patient's death." Unlike overt acts of self-destructive behavior, such as burning oneself with a cigarette or carving oneself with a razor blade, as we often see with adolescents in psychological pain, ISDB involves more indirect harmful acts, such as refusing to take necessary medication, refusing to eat or drink, withdrawal from the social environment, and a disregard for or abuse of one's health (Nelson & Farberow, 1980).

Indirect self-destructive behavior appears to occur in long-term care settings on a consistent basis. Research conducted by Osgood and Brant (1991) reveals that the number of ISDB cases that led to death in nursing homes was 79.9 per 100,000 residents and that ISDB cases that did not ultimately lead to death numbered 227 per 100,000. Although ISDB is related to a number of factors, including psychiatric illness, physical health, coping style and personality, religious beliefs, and neurobiological influences, the institutional setting cannot be ignored as a major factor (Conwell et al., 1996). For long-term care residents, the only control they continue to maintain is over their own death.

For children, the institutionalization process can be even more damaging. Outcome studies have continued to demonstrate that children who live in group or institutional homes, especially very early in life, suffer life-long attachment and bonding problems (Bartholet, 1999). Although pseudo family care environments can provide a place to sleep, clothing, and a proper diet, institutional living generally lacks loving, nurturing relationships that are absolutely critical to a child's growth and development. Early brain research has been able to document the damaging effects of a lack of nurturing connections early in life (Karr-Morse & Wiley, 1997; Shore, 1997). Institutional living compounds the damage done to children who have already been maltreated by their families.

The psychological changes that result from being placed in out-of-home care are compounded by the conditions found in many facilities. For example, a study conducted by Dale Parent and associates (1994) found substantial and widespread deficiencies in facilities that house juveniles. The four major areas of concern were living space, security, control of suicidal behavior, and health care. They found that 47 percent of the facilities lacked appropriate living space for juveniles due to overcrowding, which often led to more incidents of aggression by juveniles. Staff and juvenile injury rates were higher in crowded facilities, and as the number of juveniles placed in large dormitory arrangements increased, so did the injury rate. Additionally, they found that suicidal behavior was a serious problem, with 970 juveniles committing 1,487 acts of suicidal behavior in the 30 days prior to the commencement of the study. Also, health care, specifically health care screenings and appraisals, were generally not completed in a timely manner. Nor were all issues of concern, such as sexually transmitted diseases and tuberculosis, tested for, making it difficult to control the spread of communicable diseases. Other overall deficiencies included obvious fire safety violations and further isolation of juveniles from the community by not permitting them to receive telephone calls.

As a result of the overwhelming evidence that institutionalization has negative consequences for many residents, a shift to move both children and the elderly into more personal levels of care, such as foster family care or kinship care, is generally a more appropriate option. However, as you might imagine, recruiting families, even extended family members, to provide such love and care is a difficult task. Although foster care is preferable to institutional care, it is not without its own set of problems. As we discuss later in this chapter, children and adults alike have also been abused and mistreated in this level of pseudo family care.

/// Caregiver and Institutional Abuse and Maltreatment

As we struggle to understand why family members abuse, neglect, and mistreat the very people they love the most, it is equally puzzling to consider why individuals who are paid to care for others would want to harm them. Why bite the hand that feeds you? Although there is obviously no clear-cut answer to such a question, clues are embedded in the organizational climate of the total institution, as Goffman (1961) described.

The total institution environment often creates loss of privacy, isolation from the outside world, and an organizational structure that perpetuates power differentials between staff and residents. Staff members are often overworked, underpaid, and not properly trained to work with the challenges of pseudo family care. In other words, isolation, power differentials, stress, and lack of essential skills, the very same elements that work to perpetuate violence in families, also play a role in pseudo family environments.

The Stanford Prison Experiment

Let us examine an extreme example of these principles in action. In the early 1970s, researchers Haney, Banks, and Zimbardo (1973) conducted the Stanford prison experiment. In the experiment, community members in Palo Alto, California, were enlisted to spend time in a fake prison. Volunteers were screened, and a total of 21 people were chosen to participate in the study based on their physical and mental stability. Of the 21 volunteers, 10 were randomly assigned to be inmates, and 11 were randomly assigned to be correctional officers. The experiment included as many real-life enactments as possible. For example, real police officers were enlisted to participate in the study and conducted typical arrests by handcuffing, searching, and fingerprinting the "offenders."

All interactions between the inmates and the officers were filmed and recorded by hidden camera. Although the experiment was scheduled to run a total of 2 weeks, the researchers had to shut the project down in only 6 days because of the behavior of the corrections officers. Volunteers, once granted the power and authority of a corrections officer, were negative and very hostile toward the inmates. Inmates were rendered helpless. The guards tormented the prisoners to such an extent that the researchers were concerned for the inmates' safety. Philip Zimbardo (1999) sums up the experience of the experiment:

> At this point it became clear that we had to end the study. We had created an overwhelmingly powerful situation—a situation in which prisoners were withdrawing and behaving in pathological ways, and in which some of the guards were behaving sadistically. Even the "good" guards felt helpless to intervene, and none of the guards quit while the study was in progress. Indeed, it should be noted that no guard ever came late for his shift, called in sick, left early, or demanded extra pay for overtime work.

The prison experiment provides us with a frightening vision of the role social power has in human interactions. Both inmates and guards modeled their behavior on preconceived notions of how they were supposed to act (Schneider, 1996), for in a matter of only a few days, inmates learned their helplessness and guards discovered unyielding power. Power differentials between inmates and guards were further highlighted by social isolation, use of power symbols (i.e., uniforms) and degradation ceremonies (stripping away of the personal identities of inmates), and the lack of professional correctional officer training.

Although prison environments present their own specific set of challenges, the results from the Stanford prison experiment suggest that the process of institutionalization has a powerful impact on all parties, creating an atmosphere in which mistreatment can flourish. All parties were well aware that this was "just" an experiment; however, the institutionalization process, whereby individuals dropped their "presenting culture" and adopted a new institutional culture, was quickly put into place. The participants quickly dropped their personal sense of self and fell into their prescribed roles. Isolation, loss of privacy, and designated power (reinforced by symbols of power) all played a role in the behavior of both staff and residents.

Although many out-of-home care settings have differing degrees of these elements, not all experience instances of mistreatment. Mistreatment appears to occur more frequently in settings in which staff members have little to no training, possess negative attitudes toward the clients they serve, and have little supervision from superiors. Compounding these issues are the effects of management practices that reinforce mistreatment or create environments in which mistreatment is more likely to occur.

Forms of Caregiver and Institutional Abuse

Pseudo family abuse and mistreatment occur in a variety of ways, as does violence within the context of family. Residents are victimized by financial, physical, emotional, and sexual abuse, as well as by physical and emotional neglect. Abuse serves to fracture and exploit the relationship of trust between the caretaker and the resident, thus compounding the effects of living in out-of-home care.

Financial Abuse

Financial abuse, in the form of fraud, has been a widespread problem in recent years, particularly Medicaid and Medicare fraud. Initially enacted in the 1960s, Medicaid and Medicare programs provide needed health care benefits to the poor, disabled, and aged and ultimately finance much of the out-of-home care in the United States.

As we noted earlier in this chapter, institutions have committed fraud in a variety of ways. Examples of fraudulent activities include billing for services never performed, billing for costs unrelated to patient care, billing for Medicaid and Medicare at the same time, and billing for food other than what was purchased. Other scams include placing relatives, or "ghosts," on the payroll and billing for the nonexistent staff person and collecting payments for patients who are no longer living or who have been discharged from the facility. Fraud has also been committed by failing to report auxiliary income from vending machines, beauty, gift, or coffee shops, and so forth although the initial costs for such services have been billed for. Also, some facilities use dummy invoices, completed by partner or parent companies, for services never performed (Halamandaris, 1983).

An example of Medicaid fraud is given in Box 7.1. This recent case of fraud was found in a nursing home called "Countryside" in Bristol, Connecticut, owned and operated by Barry and Dorothy Hultman. This case illustrates the variety of ways in which the Medicaid program is exploited. This case was originally uncovered by Union Tell, an accounting firm, which was responsible for preparing Countryside's 1994 and 1995 cost reports. Officials at Union Tell refused to sign off on Medicaid cost reports and referred the matter to the Department of Social Services for review ("Sovereign immunity," 2000).

In addition to fraud, financial abuse committed by out-of-home care facilities affects residents in a more direct way—for example, theft of residents' personal possessions bank accounts. In addition, residents' financial resources may be tangled with facility funds or used to pay for facility operations. In addition, some facilities have been prosecuted for what is referred to as "patient dumping." Patient dumping is the discriminatory practice of transferring, discharging, and preventing the readmission of residents who are Medicaid eligible in favor of the residents who have the resources to pay privately (Hodge, 1998).

Residents of out-of-home care facilities are particularly vulnerable to financial exploitation. Often they are unaware that they are being victimized. Residents suffer in immeasurable ways pertaining to the quality of their care

Box 7.1 /// Medicaid Fraud

State Department of Social Services v. Hultman and Hultman

In December of 1998, the Connecticut Department of Social Services adopted the ruling from an administrative hearing that Barry and Dorothy Hultman were guilty of committing Medicaid fraud through the operation of a Connecticut nursing home. The Hultmans were found to have charged the Medicaid program for goods and services not related to patient care. Among the 96 specific findings of fact, the hearing officer found that the Hultmans billed Medicaid for personal expenses such as a trip to India, meals at restaurants, purchases of guns and ammunition, and the cost of supplies and materials for their personal residence. In addition, the Hultmans were found to have failed to maintain time records for nursing home employees. Salaries paid to such employees were not supported by the documentation, and salaries billed to Medicaid were not related to patient care.

The hearing officers recommended that the Hultmans be required to pay restitution for the amount owed to the Department of Social Services for Medicaid expenses, reduced by the amount of payroll taxes due to the Internal Revenue Service, and that the Department of Social Services suspend them from the Medicaid program. The Hultmans appealed the ruling to the Superior Court of Connecticut, and in June 2000 Judge Robert Satter dismissed the appeal. In March 2001 Barry Hultman was sentenced to 27 months in a federal prison and 3 years' probation for embezzlement. He was ordered to pay $620,000 in restitution and a $6,000 fine.

The Hultmans also filed suit against Connecticut Attorney General Richard Blumenthal for statements he made on his Web site and to the press regarding the case. The Hultmans charged that the attorney general's comments that the Hultmans "cheated the state out of more than $1 million in Medicaid reimbursements," that "their luxury home in Avon was literally built on the back of taxpayers," and that it was "one of the most reprehensible and outrageous Medicaid fraud" cases amounted to defamation. However, the Connecticut Superior Court Judge Jon C. Blue dismissed the claim.

Defamation: Hultman v. Blumenthal. *Nursing Home Litigation Reporter* (2000, December 15),*3*(5), p. 54. *Hultman et al v. State of Connecticut Department of Social Services* (2000 Conn. Super. LEXIS 1587).

Associated Press. North Branford man sentenced in nursing home embezzlement. March 29, 2001.

and the loss of personal resources. Instances of fraud and financial mismanagement ultimately victimize all taxpayers.

Physical Abuse

Residents in out-of-home care facilities are also vulnerable to acts of physical abuse. Physical abuse includes assault, hitting, kicking, pinching, slapping, punching, pulling of hair, inappropriately applying restraints, and excessive corporal punishment. Children, the elderly, and vulnerable adults, such as those who are mentally retarded or mentally ill, are especially vulnerable to attacks of physical abuse, for they are often not able to fend off their attackers.

Additionally, due to the physical vulnerability of many residents, even the most seemingly "minor" aggression, such as a shove, a shake, or a push, could cause serious physical injury to the victim. For example, in 1995 Tera Eileen Jones, a direct care provider at Howell's Child Care Center in River Bend, North Carolina, pleaded guilty to one count of misdemeanor child abuse after investigators found records of her burning the back of a 7-year-old female patient who was confined to a wheelchair. The patient, who suffered from profound mental retardation and Down syndrome, experienced first- and second-degree burns to her back after Ms. Jones dropped an electric hair dryer between her back and the back of the wheelchair. Ms. Jones left the hair dryer to attend to a disruption with other patients and attempted to hide the incident by reporting red marks on the child's back 1 to 2 hours later (National Association of Attorneys General [NAAG], 1996a).

Whereas financial abuse is often perpetrated by administrative personnel, physical abuse is most often committed by individuals who are most closely associated with direct resident care. Certified nursing assistants, vocational nurses, aides, child care workers, and other direct care personnel, because of their direct and ongoing contact with residents, have the greatest opportunity to be abusive (Pillemer & Moore, 1989).

Understanding why such violence takes place by seemingly caring professionals involves a complex set of dynamics that is not yet fully understood. What we do know is that providing care for the physically or emotionally challenged is a demanding, exhausting job. The work that direct care staff engage in is often of the most personal in nature, such as bathing, dressing, and feeding, which often can be difficult and unpleasant tasks in and of themselves. Additionally, the behavior management responsibilities of caring for emotionally disturbed or cognitively impaired individuals can be very trying.

Compounding the intimate aspects of the job itself, direct care staff members are frequently exposed to attacks, both verbal and physical, by the residents. For example, Donna Goodridge and associates (Goodridge, John-

---

Box 7.2 /// California v. Gaylord

On August 23, 2000, licensed vocational nurse Gregg Gaylord was convicted of one count of misdemeanor elder abuse for emotionally and physically abusing residents at the Sierra Sunrise Nursing Center in California.
Witnesses testified that he swore at three residents, threatened to strike a
resident with his hand, physically assaulted three residents, and pushed a
resident into falling to the ground.

Gaylord was sentenced to 30 days in the county jail and 3 years' probation and was ordered not be employed by a such a facility. The court then
referred the matter to the Licensed Vocational Nurses (LVN) Board.

Source: Patient abuse: California. *National Association of Attorneys General Medicaid
Fraud Report*, August, 2000.

---

ston, & Thomson, 1996) found that nursing assistants in a long-term care
facility located in Canada could expect to be physically assaulted by residents
9.3 times per month and verbally assaulted 11.3 times per month. Additionally, 70 percent of the nursing assistants who participated in this study
reported that they had experienced physical aggression from residents during
the preceding month. Conflicts with the residents occurred most frequently
when residents wanted to go outside the facility or during personal hygiene.
Conflict was intensified with residents who were cognitively impaired and
nursing assistants who were inadequately trained to communicate with people with such impairments. They also found that aggression from residents
was rarely reported by nursing assistants in a formal incident report.

Caring for children in out-of-home care settings is equally as challenging. Considering that many children placed in out-of-home care present
with a myriad of problems, they are generally considered a challenging population to care for. For example, Parent and associates (1994) estimated that
6,900 incidents that resulted in injury to staff members by youths occurred
every year in juvenile facilities, whereas only 106 incidents involved staff
members injuring juveniles. Additionally, in any given year, 24,200 incidents
result in injury from acts committed by juveniles on other juveniles, and an
additional estimated 17,600 acts of suicidal behavior occur. These figures
provide an enduring frame of reference in which to explore aspects of physical abuse in institutional settings.

Our intention here is not to blame the victim but to highlight the
complexity of the dynamics that operate in out-of-home care settings. Many
of the situations we have just described constitute abuse by the residents
toward the staff members. Although these instances do not absolve staff
members of responsibility for the acts of physical aggression they commit
against residents, understanding environmental working conditions is im-

portant to our understanding of why some staff members are physically abusive to the residents in their care.

Emotional Abuse

Emotional abuse occurs when a caretaker makes verbal comments or subjects the resident to harassment by yelling, screaming, swearing, name calling, and so forth. Emotional abuse includes comments that chastise, belittle, degrade, or humiliate the resident, thereby contributing to a feeling of helplessness and incompetence. Emotional abuse can also be committed by the deliberate isolation of the resident from social contact with others, causing emotional or social deprivation (Manion, 2001).

This form of abuse leaves no visual scars, but it is equally, if not more, hurtful than other overt acts of abuse. Emotional abuse creates an uncomfortable, unsafe living environment for residents. Like physical abuse, emotional abuse is also most likely to be perpetrated by direct care staff members.

A typical example of emotional abuse comes from the state of Delaware, in which a nurse's aide was convicted of emotional abuse of an elderly patient. Although emotional abuse often accompanies physical abuse and neglect, this case is believed to be the first criminal conviction of its kind, charging the defendant solely with emotional abuse (Class A misdemeanor).

Crystal Robinson, a nursing aide at Layton Home in Delaware, was convicted of emotionally abusing an 85-year-old female resident and of conspiring with a coworker to commit such offenses. According to the state's witnesses, the incident began when Robinson and a coworker taunted the patient about some missing clothes. Knowing full well that the patient was rather possessive about her belongings, the aides knew they would upset her by telling her someone was stealing her clothes. Codefendant Yvette Jones threw towels at the wheelchair-bound resident, and Robinson used her fingers to throw drops of water on the woman, as if she were spitting on her. Arguing ensued between the aides and the resident. Robinson placed a flowerpot on the woman's head and laughed when it fell to the floor. Then the resident began to yell loudly, and Robinson told her to "kiss my butt," which prompted the resident to reply in the same manner. Robinson then lifted her nurse's uniform, shook her rear end, and placed it on the meal table of the woman's wheelchair (600 A.2d.356; 1991 Del. LEXIS 402).

Robinson appealed her conviction; however, the Delaware Supreme Court upheld the conviction, as well as the emotional abuse statute, and maintained that nursing home residents have the right to be treated with the same dignity and privacy to which one would be entitled in a private residence. As captive audiences, just like residential homeowners, they have the right to be protected from intrusive and offensive speech in the privacy of their residences (NAAG, 1992). This case serves as an important precedent for the development of emotional abuse statutes and prosecutions (Hodge, 1998).

Sexual Abuse

The least discussed form of victimization of children and adults living in out-of-home care settings is sexual abuse. Sexual abuse can involve a variety of acts, such as voyeurism, fondling, sodomy, sexual exploitation, and rape. Included in the definition of sexual abuse is the unpermitted touching of residents during personal hygiene routines.

In fact, any sexual contact between a resident and a staff member is considered sexual abuse, even if the parties agree that the contact was consensual. Due to the professional nature of the staff and resident relationship, even consensual sexual relationships are considered highly unethical, if not also illegal. Most residents are unable to legally consent to sexual contact because of their age or physical or mental conditions.

Residents in out-of-home care settings tend to be easy prey for perpetrators because it is easy to get to them. The personal nature of the caregiver and resident relationship often requires the resident to be placed in very vulnerable positions, such as when getting dressed, bathing, or sleeping in an unlocked room. Also, as the cases in Box 7.3 indicate, many residents are incapacitated because of physical or psychological conditions, and they are rendered defenseless against such assaults.

One of the most brutal examples of sexual abuse comes from Rochester, New York. John L. Horace, a certified nursing assistant at Westfall Health Care Center in Monroe County, was found guilty of raping a 29-year-old female patient. As a result of the sexual assault, the patient, who had been in a coma since 1986 from a vehicle accident, became pregnant. Although she was in a vegetative state, the victim carried the pregnancy to full term and delivered a baby boy in March of 1996. The boy is now living with his grandmother (Hodge, 1998, NAAG, 1996b).

Neglect

Neglect is a very dangerous form of mistreatment, and it is every bit as harmful as the other types of abuses we have described. Neglect, particularly "criminal neglect," requires that the prosecutor show that the perpetrator had a legal duty to the victim to provide care and that the neglectful act or failure to act was either intentional or constituted gross neglect or reckless conduct (Hodge, 1998). Neglect can result in injury, other serious health consequences, and even death. Examples of neglect might include failing to change soiled clothing in a timely manner or failing to provide adequate hydration, food, medicine, climate control, or proper supervision. Additionally, neglect may be evident when institutional practices, policies, and physical grounds of a facility violate the safety and security of the residents.

Box 7.3 /// Examples of Sexual Abuse

New York: In October of 1993 a female licensed practical nurse employed at Monroe Community Hospital's skilled nursing facility in Rochester was arrested for sexually abusing two incapacitated patients and physically abusing two other patients in 1992. She was accused of encouraging a 41-year-old female resident suffering from multiple sclerosis, seizures, and depression to touch the breasts of a 43-year-old female resident suffering from acute cerebral infarction and brain tumors. She was charged with two counts of sexual abuse in the second degree, three counts of endangering the welfare of an incompetent person, and four counts of willful violation of health laws (NAAG, 1993).

Arizona: In May of 2000, Edmundo Bartolo pleaded guilty to one count of sexual abuse, a Class 5 felony. Bartolo worked as a certified nursing assistant at Apache Junction Health Center. He sexually abused a resident who suffers from multiple sclerosis (NAAG, 2000).

New York: A woman sued the State of New York to recover damages for injuries her child allegedly sustained while a patient at the Bronx Children's Psychiatric Center. Her claim alleges that during 1993 a hospital employee sexually abused and physically assaulted her 14-year-old daughter (Hospital 'incident reports,' " 1999).

Maine: A 19-year-old certified nursing assistant was charged in juvenile court with having sexual intercourse with a severely retarded resident when he was 16. The patient, who became pregnant, had to have an abortion out of medical necessity. Because of his minor status, the nursing assistant was sentenced to only 30 days in the county jail, probation to age 21, and counseling (Hodge, 1998).

The consequences of such neglect include bedsores, dehydration, malnutrition, illness, and death. Serious injury can result from a lack of proper supervision or careless safety procedures. For example, Box 7.4 describes a case in California in which staff of a nursing care facility failed to properly care for residents on a hot summer day. The consequence of such neglect led to the death of at least one resident.

Direct care staff, supervisors, and facility administrators and owners are all responsible for neglect. According to a survey conducted by the National Association of Medicaid Fraud Control Units (NAMFCU) in 1997 (Hodge, 1998), the most common prosecutions for neglect in long-term care facilities involve situations in which caregivers fail to comply with a subscribed plan of care. to provide proper medications, and to notify appropriate emergency medical personnel or physicians. One of the worst cases of neglect reported was a Maryland case that involved a physician who was the owner, medical director, and personal doctor for residents in his nursing home in Baltimore.

Box 7.4 /// Wrongful-Death Suit

On August 14, 2000, family members of Hing Fai Wong filed a wrongful-death suit against Sun Healthcare Group (and others) for the neglectful care ultimately leading to her death in a nursing home in Burlingame, California.

The suit charges that on June 14, 2000, the temperatures inside the SunBridge nursing care facility rose to 108 degrees, and while the staff turned fans on to cool themselves, the patients were neglected. Nothing was done to prevent Wong's suffering except to place a wet washcloth on her face. The California Department of Health reports that paramedics found Ms. Wong with a 106.2 degree temperature and charges that the nursing care facility did not provide adequate hydration, ultimately leading to her death. The Department of Health fined the company $141,000 and issued two "AA" citations against the facility for the neglect of Wong and other elderly residents.

Source: Wrongful-death suit filed after heat wave in San Mateo County. *Nursing Home Litigation Reporter* (2000, October, 20), *3*(1), p. 5.

The doctor failed to provide the most basic care and refused to allow other physicians to treat the residents, leaving many of the residents to suffer from malnutrition, dehydration, and untreated bedsores that required amputations. He was convicted of criminal neglect, sentenced to 2 years in prison, and ordered to pay a $5,000 fine (Hodge, 1998). Box 7.5 describes a case in California in which a nursing home chain was charged with criminal abuse and neglect and ultimately pleaded no contest.

Maltreatment in Foster Care

Up to this point we have discussed mainly out-of-home care settings that are institutional in nature. Yet, because foster care has expanded as a preferable alternative to institutionalization for both children and adults, it is important that we discuss maltreatment in this particular out-of-home care setting.

Foster care is preferable over institutional placement because it more closely mirrors normal family living. Foster families take on the responsibility of providing care for children or adults who, for whatever reason, are unable to remain in their own homes. Some foster homes even have the capability to care for children or adults who have serious medical problems. Foster families open up their homes to take on the roles of provider and nurturer to complete strangers, often for little financial compensation. As Elizabeth Bartholet (1999, p. 86) states: "many foster parents qualify for sainthood."

Although many foster homes provide excellent care, there is a growing

---

Box 7.5 /// California v. Guardian of North Bay, Inc.

In 1999, the Santa Clara County District Attorney's Office brought criminal charges against Guardian of North Bay, Inc., for felony elder abuse and neglect. This was the first corporate nursing home chain to be charged with *criminal* elder abuse and neglect in the country. The allegations of abuse included evidence that residents developed infected bedsores or were left to lie in their own urine and feces after being unattended for days at a time.

On May 24, 2000, the company agreed to plead no contest to six of the eight counts of felony elder abuse and neglect. The company has agreed to divest control of two of its nursing homes and will pay $120,000 in fines. The company will be assigned a federal monitor as assigned by the Office of the Inspector General to oversee their long-term care administration. The no-contest plea establishes the guilt of the company, as would a guilty plea; however, a no-contest plea prevents the victims from establishing liability through the plea agreement in a civil case.

Source. Nursing home chain pleads no contest to felony elder abuse charges. *Nursing Home Litigation Reporter* (2000, July 27).2(19), p. 4.

---

concern regarding the overall quality of foster care in the United States. Concerns arise from the growing number of children and adults placed in care and the decrease in qualified foster parents willing to take on such responsibilities. States have had to reach out to families who, under optimal conditions, would not be considered appropriate foster families. Compared with the pool of eligible adoptive parents, the foster-parent pool is generally less well-off in economic terms and often live in neighborhoods that are plagued with violence, drugs, and failing public schools. Often foster families are recruited directly from the welfare system because the fostering stipends provide significantly more income than typical welfare benefits do (Bartholet, 1999).

Therefore, the foster care system has built in a financial incentive that may inadvertently attract potential caregivers because of money, not because they have the desire or the skills to be a good parent. The financial incentive may also overburden foster parents with too many children or adults to care for at one time. Bartholet (1999) gives a chilling example of the risks inherent in a foster system that is seen by some as a financially lucrative one. A lawyer from the Massachusetts Department of Social Services told of a case in which a woman earned a yearly salary of $38,000 from the six foster children she had in her care. The woman had three of the children for several years but made no effort to adopt them, nor did the state necessarily deem her fit to adopt them. The lawyer said that the women "seems to have thought of foster parenting as employment, but it was not a job she liked very much" (Bartholet, 1999, p. 88).

Compounding the recruitment issues is the lack of adequate monitoring of foster home environments. Supervising foster care placements is a monumental task, and an overwhelmed social services system has not been able to effectively monitor cases as closely as they need to be. Also of concern is the overcrowding of placements, the lack of adequate pre- and in-service training, and the lack of ongoing support. Therefore, the systemic issues, combined with the stresses of caring for a foster family member and personal life stressors, provide the backdrop for mistreatment to occur.

Susan Zuravin and associates (Zuravin, Benedict, & Somerfield, 1993) studied 296 foster homes in the city of Baltimore, Maryland, in an attempt to find the foster home characteristics that are more greatly associated with the maltreatment of foster children. Of the foster homes included in the study, 62 showed at least one confirmed report of maltreatment during the 5-year study period. Of the reported maltreatment incidents, sexual abuse was the most prevalent, with 48 percent of the homes having a documented sexual abuse report (about half of the incidents involved penetration). Physical abuse was present in about 39 percent of the foster homes, and neglect was present in 29 percent of the homes. The majority of the incidents of neglect resulted in at least one child being seriously injured or becoming ill. In comparing maltreating foster families with families who were not identified as being abusive, Zuravin et al. (1993) found four characteristics associated with maltreatment: younger foster mothers, homes in which children shared bedrooms with other members of the foster family, homes about which caseworkers had had previous concerns, and homes that were restricted for placement of certain children. Additionally, they found that kinship care homes decreased the risk of maltreatment (Zuravin et al., 1993).

In an effort to improve the plight of children in foster care, the Adoption and Safe Families Act of 1997 established requirements to further achieve safety (and permanency) for children in foster care. One of the new regulations requires states to conduct criminal record checks for prospective foster or adoptive parents or to otherwise be able to document the safety of a child's placement (Administration for Children and Families [ACF], 2000).

/// Combating Mistreatment

Measuring levels of violence and mistreatment in families has been an arduous task. However, we know even less about the actual prevalence of mistreatment in out-of-home settings. Currently, no national prevalence data are available that encompass all areas of out-of-home care. Therefore, we must rely on reported incidents of mistreatment to gauge the extent of the problem.

Compounding the issue is fragmentation of the systems involved in taking complaints of such abuses. Several general systems are involved in the investigation and resolution of cases that involve out-of-home mistreatment. Because these systems tend to operate independently of one another, there is little cohesion in examining the totality of out-of-home care mistreatment. Just as services have been developed to meet the needs of discrete populations of people, the data on mistreatment must be accessed through each service domain. In this section we discuss the current systems that handle reports of mistreatment.

Mistreatment of Individuals with Mental Illness and Developmental Disabilities

The Developmental Disabilities Assistance and Bill of Rights Act of 1975 established a special system to protect persons (children and adults) with developmental disabilities. The Protection and Advocacy Program (referred to as the P & A system), or Protection and Advocacy for Persons with Developmental Disabilities (PADD), was created in response to public outcry regarding the treatment of persons with disabilities who live in institutional settings. P & A is state administered and functions to pursue legal, administrative, and other appropriate remedies to protect and advocate for the rights of the disabled. State governors are responsible for designating an appropriate agency to administer the P & A program, and they must ensure that the agency remains independent of the service delivery system. Each state P & A program is mandated to investigate and follow up on reports of incidents of abuse and neglect (National Association of Protection and Advocacy Systems [NAPAS], 2001). In order to be eligible for the advocacy services of the PADD, clients must exhibit chronic developmental disabilities that are apparent by the age of 22, that are lifelong, and that result in limitations in three or more of the major life areas: self-care, language, learning, mobility, self-direction, and capacity for living independently.

According to NAPAS (2001), several specialized protection programs come under the general heading of P & A system. The Protection and Advocacy for Individuals with Mental Illness program (PAIMI) was created in 1986 and is administered by the Substance Abuse and Mental Health Services Administration (SAMHSA). The PAIMI program specifically advocates for and investigates incidents of abuse and neglect in mental health facilities. It addresses all issues within the time period that covers transportation to the facility, admission, and residency to 90 days following the client's discharge from the facility. Individuals who have been diagnosed with serious mental illness and who reside in out-of-home care settings, including homeless shelters, jails, and prisons, are eligible for the PAIMI program.

The Rehabilitation Services Administration (RSA) of the U.S. Department of Education administers the Protection and Advocacy for Individual Rights (PAIR) program and the Client Assistance Program (CAP). The PAIR program was created under the Rehabilitation Act of 1993. The program was established to protect and advocate for the legal and human rights of persons with disabilities. The PAIR program advocates on behalf of individuals who are not covered by the PADD and PAIMI. The CAP was established in 1984 to pursue corrective actions on behalf of persons receiving or seeking services under the Rehabilitation Act.

The Protection and Advocacy for Assistive Technology (PAAT) program, which was established in 1994 as part of the expansion of the Technology-Related Assistance for Individuals with Disabilities Act (also known as the Tech Act), provides funding to ensure that disabled individuals have access to technological devices and services. The PAAT program is administered by the Office of Special Education and Rehabilitative Services of the National Institute on Disability and Rehabilitation Research.

During the fiscal year 1999, P & A's were involved in serving a total of 27,747 (57 reporting agencies) individuals with disabilities who needed legal, administrative, or other advocacy services. The majority of cases involved young people. For example, a total of 674 clients were between the ages of 0 and 2 years, 1,227 were between the ages of 3 and 4 years, and 17,051 clients were between the ages of 5 and 22 years. A total of 8,752 adults over the age of 22 were served by the P & A system in 1999 (Administration on Developmental Disabilities [ADD], 2001). Although we currently have no statistical estimates of the prevalence of abuse and neglect within this population, considering the relatively small size of the population of children and adults who have substantial limitations due to a mental illness or developmental disability, these agency statistics should not go unnoticed.

Mistreatment of Adults

Measuring the prevalence of institutional mistreatment of adults, who do not fall under the rubric previously discussed, is also impossible at this time. We do not know the exact incidence rate, nor have we conducted any broad-based estimates. Instead, we must rely on reports from the state Medicaid fraud control units and the long-term care ombudsman programs, two of the main professional organizations that uncover and resolve issues of mistreatment. Agency reports can at least inform us about the number and types of incidents that have officially been reported.

Reports of mistreatment are funneled to state Medicaid fraud control units and long-term care ombudsmen in a variety of ways. Mistreatment may be reported through a designated elder abuse hotline, such as have been established in 42 states, through which adult protective services are likely to become involved (we discuss this at greater length in chapter 8). Licensing and regulation boards may report mistreatment during the course of their routine inspection and surveillance activities. Accounting firms may report fraudulent activity, and health care providers may report suspicions of resident mistreatment. Serious incidents may also warrant calling the local police department. In addition, family members and friends of the resident may bring their concerns directly to the ombudsman.

Agency statistics, coupled with additional research, paint a tragic picture of the plight of vulnerable adults living in out-of-home care settings. For example, a survey conducted by Pillemer and Moore (1989) found that, out of 577 nursing home aides and nurses, 10 percent admitted to committing physical abuse and 36 percent to witnessing at least one incident of abuse in the prior year. Many admitted to yelling, insulting, threatening to hit, using excessive restraints, and pushing many of the residents in their care.

By all accounts, it is fair to say that mistreatment of vulnerable adults is a significant problem in the United States, a problem that is likely to grow with the ongoing need for expansion of the long-term industry.

State Medicaid Fraud Control Units

Since 1978, Medicaid fraud control units (MFCU) have had the responsibility of serving as the primary law enforcement unit responsible for patient abuse investigations in nursing homes, group homes, and hospitals that receive Medicaid funds. The units operate at the state level, investigating and prosecuting instances of patient abuse and neglect. There are currently 48 units operating in 47 states and the District of Columbia. Many of the case examples we have previously illustrated in this chapter are a result of the work of the MFCUs in various states.

Nationwide, the MFCUs have been very successful at achieving convictions and recovering money from health care providers. Hodge (1998) notes that since 1978, the MFCUs have attained more than 8,000 convictions for health care fraud and patient abuse violations and have recovered millions of dollars from fraudulent activity. The most recent report from June Gibbs Brown (2000a), the inspector general, notes that during the fiscal years 1997–1999 the MCFUs recovered more than $318 million in court-ordered restitution, fines, and penalties and obtained 2,694 convictions.

In addition to law enforcement activity, the MFCUs have also been instrumental in the enactment of state and federal legislation pertaining to the protection of vulnerable adults. For example, the Minnesota MFCU spearheaded a statewide partnership of numerous stakeholders to update the reporting and responses to elder mistreatment, as well as the state's Vulnerable Adult Act. The New York MFCU introduced the need for background checks for nursing home and home health care staff, which became effective with the Elder Abuse Protection Act. This act also makes an assault on a "care dependent person" a greater felony (Hodge, 1998).

Nationwide, MFCUs have also been responsible for developing training curricula and conducting training to direct-care staff, ombudsmen, administrators, support staff, and other law enforcement agencies. In fact, the National Association of Attorneys General has designated the training programs of the Rhode Island MFCU as a national training model (Hodge, 1998).

Long-Term Care Ombudsman Program

Another critical force in the identification and resolution of institutional mistreatment of vulnerable adults is the long-term-care ombudsman program. The ombudsmen serve as advocates for residents of various adult care facilities. As of 1998, there were 587 local and regional ombudsman programs, located in every state, with approximately 927 paid staff and more than 7,000 trained volunteers. Trained ombudsmen identify, investigate, and resolve problems related to the health, safety, and rights and welfare of adult residents (Administration on Aging [AOA], 2001). The program has been established under the Older Americans Act and is administered by the AOA.

According to the AOA (2001), during the fiscal year of 1998, the ombudsmen investigated more than 200,000 complaints made by more than 121,000 individuals. The most frequently reported complaint from residents is the lack of proper care due to inadequate staffing ratios. Ombudsmen attributed labor shortages, coupled with the low pay and minimal benefits, as being the main issues for low staffing patterns in many facilities.

Nationwide, a total of 15,501 complaints were made of abuse, gross neglect, or exploitation in nursing care facilities, and an additional 3,548 complaints were made about board and care facilities during the fiscal year 1998. The five most frequently reported complaints involved unheeded requests for assistance, neglected personal hygiene, improper handling of accidents, lack of respect for residents, and incidents of physical abuse. When we consider that an additional 50,000 complaints were also made regarding overall care issues, the quality of care continues to be a significant social problem that warrants our attention. Families can play a critical role in the prevention of maltreatment by making frequent visits, monitoring care, and bringing potential problems to the proper authorities.

Mistreatment of Children

Children in out-of-home care are monitored by a different system than those we described previously. It is probably fair to say that children in care are more closely monitored by the government than are adults placed in out-of-home care environments. The reason is probably that children are often seen as more vulnerable than adults and have little social power; therefore, we have a greater responsibility to ensure their safety. This is especially true when the state is legally responsible for their custodial care.

The oversight of children in out-of-home care who are not designated as mentally ill or developmentally disabled generally resides with state child welfare agencies. As local child protection services (as described in chapter 8) investigate allegations of abuse and neglect of children living with their families, local and state child protection officials are also responsible for investigating reports of child maltreatment in foster care and other residential treatment programs. Because all states are required to have a mandated reporting system (discussed in chapter 8), suspicions of institutional abuse are generally handled in a similar manner. Most states have provisions containing specific criminal or civil sanctions or both for the failure to report suspected out-of-home maltreatment. Therefore, professionals who do not report instances of abuse and neglect may be liable for civil action or criminal penalty if they fail to report such incidents (Besharov, 1987).

State licensing specialists also play a role in overseeing the safety of children in placement. Because eligibility for federal reimbursement for out-of-home care requires states to justify the sites they place children in, all states have some system to approve facilities, usually in the form of a licensing procedure. In addition, ombudsmen programs have grown in popularity to assist the state in handling complaints regarding the treatment of their children while in care.

Child Protective Agencies

Child protective agencies are designated by state and federal law to protect children. Agencies are responsible for responding to reports of abuse, investigating the credibility of the reports, and providing the courts with a reasonable plan of intervention. Child protection officials work closely with state and local law enforcement officials in bringing cases into the courts for resolution.

According to statistics released by the ACF (2000) in 1998, 42 state child welfare agencies that reported 3,182 cases of maltreatment in which the perpetrator was a foster parent. An additional 1,459 reports were made of mistreatment by facility staff. In 1997, 37 states reported a total of 2,733 cases of mistreatment by a foster parent, and 1,714 reports were made of maltreatment facility staff.

State Standards

In order to be eligible for federal reimbursement, states must establish and maintain standards that address the health, protection, and safety of children in residential programs. In theory, licensing standards set a minimum level of care that must be provided and outline the facility's responsibility regarding the physical plant, staffing ratios, record keeping, care of children, use of restraints, and isolation.

June Gibbs Brown (2000b), U.S. Inspector General, recently conducted a study for the ACF that reviewed how states provide oversight for their residential children's programs. The scope of the inspection did not include an attempt to identify violations of state standards or procedures that may put children at risk; instead, it examined licensing processes.

However, the inspection revealed that there is no universally accepted set of licensing standards. Out of the 34 key standards examined by Inspector General Gibbs Brown (2000b), only 8 were addressed by all of the nine states in the sample. For example, two states do not require child abuse background checks of facility staff, and only three states require staff to have first aid training. The states varied the most in the areas of use of restraints and isolation. Box 7.6 highlights the variability in state standards regarding these two issues. The regulation of the use of restraints and isolation are important because the risks of child mistreatment are great.

Restraints are generally considered to be specific techniques used to subdue a child and prevent the child from hurting himself or herself or others. Restraints, if done improperly, can cause injury to the child, the staff member, or both. Isolating the child is another technique that should be monitored. Of the six states that regulate isolation, three prohibit the use of a locked room. Most of the states limit the time a child can be placed in isolation, usually ranging from 1 to 12 hours.

Another finding the inspection revealed was that state standards generally do not require licensing staff to evaluate the appropriateness of the placement of the child in the facility, nor do they address issues of quality of care. Additionally, the inspection found that most states monitor facilities on a yearly basis; however, rarely are licenses revoked, nor is license renewal generally denied for facilities that violate the state mandated standards.

An additional area of concern lies with the potential for conflict between the licensing process and the child protective process. Research conducted by Rindfleisch and Hicho (1987) found evidence of conflict between licensing officials and child protective officials. Central to the conflicts were ad-

---

Box 7.6 /// Variability in State Standards Regarding the Use of Restraints and Isolation in Residential Programs for Children

Licensing Standards	States								
	1	2	3	4	5	6	7	8	9
State sets standard	X	X			X		na	X	X
Facilities to develop standards				X		X	na		
Requires monitoring of restraints	X	X			X		na	X	
Limits time of restraint	X				X		na	X	
Uses under specific circumstances	X	X		X	X		na	X	X
Prohibits restraints							X		
Prohibits isolation			X						X
Sets standards on the use of isolation	X	X	na		X	X	X	X	na
Prohibits use of locked room		X	na		X		X		na
Limits length of isolation	X	X	na		X	X	X		na
Requires monitoring of isolation	X	1	na		X	X	X		na
Documents each isolation	X		na		X	X	X	X	na

1: Requires that isolated children be within hearing distance of staff; na = not available.
Adapted from Gibbs Brown (2000b, p. 11)

ministrative barriers such as the presence of a number of different licensing authorities in a given state, a diversity of licensing standards, and discrepancies between definitions of abuse and neglect by Child Protective Services (CPS) and licensing agents.

Ombudsmen Programs

Due to the successes of the long-term care ombudsman program, such programs are growing in popularity to assist in the protection of children living in placements. The American Bar Association Center on Children and Law has recommended the ombudsmen model as an effective tool to monitor the care of children in out-of-home care placements. The role of the ombudsman program is to provide accountability and independent review of facilities entrusted with the care of children (D'Ambra, 1996).

In a survey of all 50 states, Laureen D'Ambra (1996) found that in many states legislative action has led to the creation of state-funded ombudsman offices specifically to provide oversight for children's residential services. Most of the state agencies provided oversight of child placement facilities, investigated incidents of abuse, neglect, and fatalities, and provided troubleshooting of individual complaints in child placement facilities.

/// Chapter Summary

This chapter focused on the maltreatment of children and adults in out-of-home settings in which they are being cared for by *pseudo families*. We call such out-of-home care environments pseudo families because they serve, for all practical purposes, many of the same care functions "real" families do. Like biological families, pseudo families provide food, clothing, shelter, medical care, and social interaction. They serve, for all practical purposes, as surrogate family members.

We made the case that maltreatment that occurs in out-of-home placements is an appropriate issue to discuss in the context of violence in the home. Social isolation, power differentials, stress, and lack of appropriate training and communication skills provide the backdrop for maltreatment to occur in both living environments.

We then briefly discussed some of the historical developments of caring for "social deviants" by removing them from their homes and placing them in an institutional environment. We discussed the variety of contexts in which institutions of the past have been constructed and how often abuse has been central to the goals of "retraining." We explore the development of modern-day out-of-home care systems.

Next, we explored institutional life with and without the issue of mistreatment. We reviewed the institutionalization process and briefly discussed some of the consequences of living in an out-of-home care environment.

For adults, the principal concerns center on the loss of privacy, freedom of choice, and control. For children, lack of loving, nurturing care can have devastating consequences.

We then investigated the various forms of maltreatment that have been identified in out-of-home care settings. We discussed many the forms of pseudo family abuse, including financial, physical, sexual, and emotional abuse and neglect, utilizing numerous case examples. Finally, the last section of the chapter reviewed some of the current systems in operation that are responsible for intervening and protecting residents of out-of-home care. Families must take an active role in the lives of their family members who live in such settings. Frequent visits to monitor the care is an essential element in prevention and intervention.

/// Recommended Web Sites

Administration on Aging
  www.aoa.gov/
Administration for Children and Families
  www.acf.hhs.gov/
Administration on Developmental Disabilities
  www.acf.hhs.gov/programs/add
Centers for Medicare and Medicaid Services (formerly Health Care Financing Administration)
  http://cms.hhs.gov
National Association of Protection and Advocacy Systems
  www.protectionandadvocacy.com
National Long-Term Care Ombudsman Resource Center (National Citizens' Coalition for Nursing Home Reform)
  www.nccnhr.org/
Nursing Home Abuse Center
  www.nursing-home-abuse-center.com
Office of Inspector General, Department of Health and Human Services
  www.oig.hhs.gov/
Rehabilitation Services Administration
  www.ed.gov/offices/OSERS/RSA
Stanford Prison Experiment
  www.prisonexp.org

III /// Intervention and Prevention

8 /// Intervening in Violent Homes

*M*elissa arrives at the police department for the first night of her intern-ship. She is anxious yet excited. She is looking forward to discovering whether or not police work is really the career field for her. Her professors have prepared her well; at least, she thinks so. She meets a man in uniform at the front desk, and he refers her to Lieutenant Denise Donna. Lt. Donna is expecting her arrival and immediately makes her feel welcome. The lieu-tenant walks her around the department and then proceeds into the roll call room. The lieutenant asks Melissa to sit in the back and tells her that, after she has briefed the platoon on the day's events, she will assign Melissa to ride along with one of the patrol officers. The lieutenant reads off a long list of problems the section has experienced throughout the day, including burglary reports, car accidents, and alcohol-related problems at various "hot" spots around town. The group of uniformed officers cheer when Lt. Donna announces that the DEA has arrested Lorenzo Tomanicheck, a known drug lord. After roll call, Lt. Donna introduces Melissa to Officer Jothia David, the officer she will be spending this shift with.

Officer David and Melissa proceed to his car, which is parked and ready for the night's events. As they enter the car, a call comes in requesting David to go to a family disturbance at 12 Pine Street. "Oh no, not again!" exclaims Officer David. "What's wrong?" asks Melissa. "This is the address of the Sloggerts, they call us all the time. Sometimes it's Mrs. Sloggert making a report her husband has beaten the shit out her, other times it's Mr. Sloggert calling to report one of the kids missing, once even the 4-year-old called 911 to report his older brothers were in a bad fight. It's always something with this family. Can't seem to live together, can't seem to live apart. Drives this department crazy, no matter what we do, nor matter how many times we are called to the house, nothing seems to change. Going there will be a complete waste of my time," says Officer David. They arrive on the scene, and Melissa is taken aback to see Mrs. Sloggert with a bloody nose and three small children running around with barely any clothes on. The house is filthy, with garbage strewn about the living room. The home smells of cat urine, yet there is no cat in sight. Officer David talks with Mrs. Sloggert and finds out that her 18-year-old son punched her in the face after an argument. The son, Johnny, took off, and she has no idea where he has gone. Officer David attempts to calm her down, writes a report, and gives her a card with the number of the crime victim assistance center on it. They leave the scene.

"What happens next?" asks Melissa. "Well, nothing by me, I will refer the case to our family violence unit for follow-up. Since Johnny is not at the scene, and we have no idea where he is, I can't arrest him. Let the family violence investigators deal with it. They ought to lock up the entire family." Melissa is surprised to learn that the rest of the shift is spent going on similar types of family disturbance calls. She is distressed to learn how common such problems are and how Officer David seems to believe that he can have little impact.

This case illustrates the lessons learned by many new police interns, that is, that violence in the home is a significant social problem. It also illustrates the frustration that many practitioners experience when working with violent families, for this complex multidimensional problem defies short-term remedies. State-sanctioned intervention into the private lives of families is a relatively new dimension in the legal, political, and social service systems in the United States. It has been only within the past 30 years that the issue of violence within the home has risen to the forefront of the political agenda. We now know that abuse and neglect carry devastating consequences and result from complex relationships between the family and the environment.

Recognizing and defining family violence as a social problem, instead of just a personal one, requires institutions to address the issues in a formal way. Thus laws, policies, and systems have proliferated to address violent families. At the core of the development of legislation and services is the fine line between protecting vulnerable victims of violence and protecting the privacy of the family. On the one hand, we must strive to protect the sanctity of the family; yet on the other hand, the reality of family violence necessitates some kind of formal action by governments and service providers.

This chapter discusses the types of interventions currently being implemented. The system that has been created to protect family members and condemn abusers is not without controversy. We explore a number of debates that currently plague the professional community.

We also discuss the variety of ways different occupational groups are affected by policies and their individual roles in assessing and intervening in the lives of family members. Because family violence is a multidimensional problem that defies short-term solutions, a multidisciplinary approach is likely to be the best way to address the problem in the long run. Therefore, family violence prevention and intervention require the efforts of many different professionals, institutions, and community members.

Responding to family violence has required a variety of approaches. In this chapter we explore a variety of intervention strategies that are utilized on the national, state, and local levels. Although we have discussed the specific systems that are responsible for responding to the specific forms of family violence in other chapters, we explore intervention in greater detail here.

The family violence network of intervention strategies can appear to be a confusing maze of programs and services. Incidents of family violence sometimes come under the rubric of the family court (a civil court), sometimes are more appropriately dealt with within the criminal court setting, and at still other times are more informally handled through protective agencies that work in conjunction with local programs and services. Still other incidents of family violence are handled outside the formal system of intervention, with assistance from clergy, friends, neighbors, and social service agencies.

This chapter is divided into three general categories. First, we examine state policy interventions most widely used by state and local government officials to respond to violence in the home. Second, we look at the wide variety of programs available to assist victims of family violence. Third, we address interventions that focus on the abusers.

/// State Interventions

In this section we examine some of the more common state-mandated strategies utilized by government institutions to identify and intervene in cases of family violence. We discuss mandatory reporting laws, protective service agencies, mandatory and pro-arrest and prosecution policies, and protective orders. These policy interventions are embedded in state laws and are a relatively new force in the fight against family violence. As we discuss, interventions tend to be geared toward a specific type of family violence and are still being tested empirically.

Identification of Family Violence: Mandatory Reporting Mechanisms

Mandatory reporting has become one of the most commonplace strategies used by state governments to identify family violence. Mandatory reporting policies are those that require specific professionals to report suspected cases of family abuse. Once suspected abuse has been reported, an official investigation is prompted.

Although many different professional fields are subject to mandatory reporting laws, medical personnel fall under the rubric of policies that address the mandatory reporting of all kinds of family violence. Because victims of family violence, whether they are children or adults, are likely to seek medical assistance at some time during their victimization, health care providers are in a unique position to identify abuse. Theoretically, early identification of violence can lead to early intervention and treatment.

Medical providers are subject to a variety of laws that require personnel to report abuse to authorities. Most states have statutes that specify situations in which health care professionals must report incidents to the police or other protective agencies. Some require personnel to report injuries caused by firearms, knives, or other deadly weapons, and other states require physicians to report injuries that result from acts of violence (Mills, 1999). Most states have policies that broadly cover the array of injuries that victims of family violence suffer, whether they are children or adults. Therefore, unlike other professional groups, medical providers may be subject to reporting incidents to authorities under more broad reporting requirements than specific mandated reporting laws.

In addition to the reporting requirements of medical providers, every state in the United States has statutes that specifically address suspected child abuse. With the passage of the Child Abuse Prevention and Treatment Act (Public Law 93-247), all states must have a child abuse and neglect mandatory reporting system. These statutes outline who is required to report suspected abuse and what the specific standards are for reporting. Statutes generally require that the caller have "reasonable suspicion" that a child is being abused or neglected (Wiehe, 1992).

Those who are mandated to report child abuse include a wide range of professionals, including medical personnel. The broad net of mandated reporters allows for state intervention even if medical intervention is not required. For example, some laws require commercial film and photographic print processors to report any obscene materials being presented for film processing that involve children (Sagatun & Edwards, 1995).

Mandated reporters are generally required to receive specialized training and certification in the identification of abuse and neglect and in reporting procedures. Reports of child abuse and neglect are generally made to a state child protective agency, which then has the responsibility to investigate the validity of the report or to make a referral to law enforcement for immediate police intervention.

In the case of elder abuse, although all states and the District of Columbia have passed legislation creating a system to respond to elder abuse (Adult Protective Services; American Bar Association Commission on Legal Problems of the Elderly, 1999), not all states have specific mandated reporting statutes. Those states that have created a mandated reporting system did so by following the child abuse model (Wolf, 1996). Currently, 42 states have mandated reporting laws that require certain professionals to report. Reports of elder abuse tend to come from health care professionals, service providers that cater to the elderly, and relatives of the victims. Additionally, friends, neighbors, clergy, banks and businesses, and victims also make reports (Tatara & Kuzmeskus, 1996).

Mandated reporting laws have helped to create and sustain an ongoing system in which allegations of abuse and neglect within families can be dealt with. Therefore, because statewide hotlines are generally established to handle and triage such mandated reports, a system exists in which other members of the community can report the abuse and neglect of the elderly and children. Because the elderly and children are especially vulnerable to abuse, reporting hotlines provide community members with an opportunity to report such acts when it is unlikely that victims will be able to report such abuses themselves. Although a similar reporting system currently does not exist in the same way for victims of intimate partner abuse, medical personnel, bound by more general reporting laws, often have to summon the police.

In addition to the formal reporting system, anyone can call the police at any time to report a family violence incident. Therefore, acts of family violence may be identified by any number of individuals, including mandated reporters, other family members, neighbors, social service agency personnel, clergy, business owners, victims, and the general public.

Mandated reporting laws are not without controversy. First, false reports are a concern, and therefore all reports made to such hotlines must be handled with the utmost care. Harm is caused when innocent individuals are accused of abuse (Sagatun & Edwards, 1995). Besharov (1990) notes that the possibility of civil and criminal liability of mandated reporters who fail to report, coupled with the lack of knowledge that private citizens have about what legally is considered abuse and neglect, ultimately leads to the overreporting of minor situations that do not constitute the legal standards of abuse or neglect. Also, because the provisions of reporting statutes generally protect the confidentiality of the individual making the call, some people feel free to make false reports as retaliation for interpersonal problems with a neighbor, ex-spouse or partner, or a family member.

Second, critics of mandated reporting laws argue that these laws prevent battered women and abusive parents from seeking proper medical treatment for fear that a report will be made. Some critics argue that the reports themselves can generate additional violence (Mills, 1999).

If the reported abuser is subject to mandatory arrest and prosecution policies, reported incidents could precipitate a criminal investigation. The fear of involving the police and courts may keep some families away from seeking medical care, endangering their health and safety even further.

Third, a concern specifically of medical educators is that mandated reporting statutes are not being utilized fully to identify cases of elder mistreatment (Kitchens, 1998). A study conducted with an analysis of medical records from the state of Michigan found that medical providers reported only 2 percent of all suspected cases of elder mistreatment (Rosenblatt & Cho, 1996). Regardless of the laws currently in place in most states, further training of medical providers (and other professionals) to better recognize signs of abuse of the elderly is warranted.

Another concern calls for the reexamination of the assumptions that underlie such policies in reference to older adults. Some argue that the development of mandated reporting laws for cases of elder abuse, replicating the child abuse model, have not taken certain important factors into consideration. As the victims in elder abuse cases are adults and not children, these laws take away control from the elderly person to determine his or her own life. Wolf (1996) notes that mandatory reporting laws can infantilize the elder's position in society and reinforce negative stereotypes of older people. Discussion of the efficacy and appropriateness of mandated reporting laws in cases of elder mistreatment continues to unfold as more states examine the issues.

Protective Agency Service Laws

State laws designate and authorize various protective agencies to respond to cases of family violence. Along with local law enforcement, these protective agencies are mandated by state law to respond to reports of abuse, to investigate their credibility, and to provide the court with a reasonable plan of intervention. Protective services are generally reserved for the protection of victims who cannot, because of their age or ability, reasonably protect themselves. These agencies have the authority to remove children, adults, or both from their homes and to intervene on their behalf. Like the police, protective agencies are available 24 hours a day to respond to cases of abuse that require immediate attention.

As mentioned previously, investigating child abuse and neglect cases is the responsibility of child protective services agencies (CPS), typically part of local departments of social services. Cases of elder mistreatment are investigated by adult protective services agencies (APS). However, any abused adult who has a disability or impairment may be handled by APS.

Once an allegation of abuse or neglect has been made through the formal reporting network, an investigation is initiated. Once the investigation is completed, cases of abuse and neglect are considered to be either "indicated" or "unfounded." Cases that are considered "indicated" are those in which evidence is sufficient to indicate that abuse, neglect, or both have taken place. Cases that are considered "unfounded" are those ones in which no evidence was found to substantiate the claims of abuser neglect. Cases that fall outside of the child or adult protective laws are referred to local law enforcement officials for follow-up. For example, if a child is abused by a neighbor, not a family member, it is likely to be handled by the police, not CPS. Cases brought forward by CPS or APS are generally dealt with by a family court system rather than a criminal court, unless there is clear evidence that a criminal act has been committed. The lines are often blurry in terms of which court is the best one to bring about appropriate action in cases of family violence.

Protective agency staff members work independently from law enforcement officials; however, they generally work very closely with them. In fact, protective agency staff members often see their role as partly social work and partly law enforcement. A good working relationship between protective staff and the police is critical to investigating and intervening with violent families.

No protective agency is mandated by law to investigate cases of intimate partner abuse (other than laws that govern the police). However, often intimate partner abuse occurs in families in which a child is being abused or neglected. Therefore, CPS can intervene in battering situations in which children are put at risk. APS can intervene on behalf of adult victims of intimate partner abuse who are considered disabled or impaired. Other victims of intimate partner abuse rely on local victim services and court programs.

Criminal Laws: Arrest and Prosecution Policies

A growing strategy to combat family violence is to use laws that designate criminal penalties for various forms of domestic abuse. Mandatory arrest and mandatory prosecution policies have developed nationwide as a specific response to protect women from abusive partners. Most states have enacted some version of mandatory or presumptive arrest and prosecution policies. A mandatory policy directs the police or prosecutors to a specific action and limits discretion. For example, a policy may dictate that a police officer "shall" arrest any person for committing a domestic assault when there is probable cause. Presumptive policies (also referred to as pro-arrest policies) strongly suggest arrest and prosecution (Buzawa & Buzawa, 1990). In the case of pro-arrest policies, a statute might read that arrest shall be the "preferred" response to a case of domestic assault.

Whereas child abuse and elder abuse have been generally brought to civil courts for intervention, a criminal justice response to the problem of battering has evolved. As was discussed in chapter 4, using the criminal courts to intervene in relationships of intimate partners is a result of three major social influences (Buzawa & Buzawa, 1990). Beginning in the early 1970s, the women's movement demanded that the public take notice of the plight of battered women and of the blatant disregard of their needs by the police and the courts. Civil liability suits filed against police departments and prosecutors for their failure to provide for the equal protection of women resulted in the reexamination of both formal and informal policies related to domestic violence. Change was also spurred on by seminal research that investigated criminal justice responses to the problem. These factors, which served as a catalyst for policy reform, have resulted in policies that have removed discretion of the police and the courts and, perhaps more important, the decision-making power of victims. An example of Nevada's mandatory arrest policy is shown in Box 8.1.

Mandatory arrest or pro-arrest policies have grown to be widely accepted interventions and were intended to serve two purposes—to change

---

Box 8.1 /// Mandatory Arrest Law

Nevada law (NRS 171.137)

Whether or not a warrant has been issued, a peace officer shall, unless mitigating circumstances exist, arrest a person when he has probable cause to believe that the person to be arrested has, within the preceding four hours, committed a battery upon his spouse, a person to whom he is related by blood, a person with whom he is or was actually residing, or with whom he has a child in common, his minor child or a minor child of that person.

---

the behavior of abusers and of the police. Sherman and Berk's (1984) well-known Minneapolis experiment found that arrest in and of itself was almost twice as effective as other interventions in reducing battering. These policies have also intentionally limited a victim's input into the decision to arrest, thereby freeing her from the responsibility of having to be the one to send her partner to jail. Criminalizing domestic abuse therefore provides an opportunity to make abusers accountable for their actions, sending a message that domestic violence is a not a matter of male privilege but a crime against the state.

These policies have also attempted to change the historical "do nothing" approach of police toward intervention in domestic violence cases. Both mandatory arrest and pro-arrest policies have been intended to serve as a guide for police intervention and to limit liability. Although some evidence suggests that the police have been slow to embrace these policies, Mignon and Holmes (1995) found that mandatory arrest policies have in fact increased arrests, especially in cases in which a protective order is in force. They found that arrest was more likely to take place when a victim's injuries were more serious and when a witness was present during the assault.

A change in police response has also meant a need for change in the way prosecutors and judges handle cases. Historically, the courts required that victims sign formal complaints against abusers, obligating the victims themselves to bring charges. However, in all other types of criminal cases, prosecutors themselves signed complaints against defendants. Therefore, victims of domestic violence, unlike victims of other types of crimes, had the added burden of being responsible for having the defendant charged with a criminal complaint. Subsequently, the prosecution rates of domestic violence cases have been rather low (Dutton, 1988).

Since the advent of mandatory and pro-arrest policies, prosecutors' offices have moved to mandatory or proprosecution policies as well. For example, "no drop" policies have been established in many communities. No-drop policies reduce the ability of both prosecutors and victims to dismiss or drop criminal charges of domestic assault once presented to the court.

Intending to better protect victims and to improve the wasted costs associated with victims dropping charges, these policies reflect the change in ideology that domestic abuse is not just a crime against an individual party but a crime against the state (Buzawa & Buzawa, 1990). Victims then become witnesses for the prosecution and therefore are not responsible for the outcome of criminal charges. Many victim advocate programs have supported such policy reforms, arguing that such strategies protect victims from further abuse.

There is some evidence to suggest that prosecutorial no-drop policies have in fact increased the number of cases processed through the criminal courts. For example, in San Diego, California, and Washington, D.C., prosecutors have experienced a substantial increase in caseload and convictions since no-drop policies have been instituted. Additionally, San Diego has seen a substantial decline in the number of domestic-violence-related homicides, from 30 in 1985 to 7 in 1994 (Epstein, 1999).

These policies have promoted vast changes in institutional responses to the problem of intimate partner abuse. However, many argue against such strategies. Critics contend that further research into mandatory arrest policies indicates that the results found in the Minneapolis experiment have not been uniformly replicated in other cities. After further research, Sherman (1992) concluded that arrest is most effective when the batterer is married and employed; with unemployed abusers, arrest is actually likely to increase future violence.

Also, these strategies have literally flooded the courts with cases in which victims are uncooperative. Although prosecutors are routinely challenged by uncooperative victims and witnesses, they generally make up only a small portion of the caseload. However in domestic violence cases, the majority of victims are uncooperative (Davis & Smith, 1995), placing an added burden on prosecutors. Buzawa and Buzawa (1990) note that a lack of prosecutorial support from victims results in low conviction rates.

Some also argue that such stringent policies deter victims from reporting incidents in the first place. Victims come to understand that they will lose control of decision making when they involve the police. Mills (1999) argues that mandatory state interventions mirror the battering relationship itself, reinforcing a patriarchal system in which women have little power. She argues that these policies, although intended to help women, have in fact continued to place women in an oppressed position. She argues:

> Mandatory state interventions, even when sponsored by feminists, not only disregard these clinical concerns, but also are in danger of replicating the rejection, degradation, terrorization, social isolation, mis-socialization, exploitation, emotional unresponsiveness, and close confinement that are endemic to the abusive relationship. (p.551)

Additionally, Rosenbaum (1998) raises some interesting questions that are worthy of further research. His research, conducted in California, found that mandatory interventions produce less violence against the family member on whose behalf the arrest was made, but at the time it increased the level of violence perpetrated on other members of the family. He has labeled this finding the "substitution effect theory." His conclusions raise important implications for the safety and well-being of other members of the family, particularly children (Rosenbaum, 1998).

Significant policy reforms often result in unintended consequences. It is probably too early yet to tell whether or not mandatory state interventions are an effective tool in reducing violence in the home. The implementation of policy over time and further research will be our guide to future effective policy reform.

Protective Orders

Civil protective orders are intended to put an immediate stop to violence by restricting an abuser's behavior. Also called *restraining orders*, these protective orders dictate that an individual refrain from harassment, abuse, molestation, and contact with certain family members. States have granted the courts the authority to issue such orders, intending to provide a timely response to protect victims from further harm. Orders are generally granted by civil court judges; however, some jurisdictions have enacted legislation that gives similar power to criminal court judges. States have statutes that govern the procedural and eligibility requirements for obtaining protective orders, the length of time orders are in effect, and the consequences of violating orders (Davis & Smith, 1995).

Protective orders require a lower standard of proof than criminal proceedings and can be issued relatively quickly. Orders can be issued ex parte, which means that only one party needs to be present, raising constitutional questions about due process rights for the defendant. Orders can be issued on a temporary basis or can be granted on a permanent basis. Protective orders often include the following types of restrictions, intended to protect victims (Buzawa & Buzawa, 1990):

- Ordering the abuser to refrain from physical or psychological abuse.
- Restricting contact with the victim.
- Ordering the abuser to leave the home.
- Allowing victims the exclusive use of certain property, such as a vehicle.
- Ordering abuser to enter counseling.
- Orderings abuser to pay child support, restitution, or attorney fees.
- Restricting custody and visitation of children.

This is not a definitive list, for protective orders are intended to be crafted to individual situations and circumstances. Through protective orders, judges have the discretion to build a court order that specifically relates to the problems raised by individual parties.

However, without concurrent laws to punish individuals who violate protective orders, the orders themselves can offer victims little peace of mind. Many jurisdictions have enacted statutes that provide the courts with the authority to sanction individuals who violate protective orders. Sanctions may include contempt of court or criminal charges that may result in fines or possibly incarceration (Caringella-MacDonald, 1997). Currently 34 states have criminal contempt laws and at least 45 jurisdictions have made violating an order a crime in and of itself (Epstein, 1999). The 1994 enactment of the Violence Against Women Act (VAWA) has redressed jurisdictional issues of protective order enforcement. Section 2265 of VAWA, often referred to as the Full Faith and Credit section, requires states, Indian tribes, and U.S. territories to honor valid court protective orders issued by other states (18 U.S.C. § 2265).

Like other state-sanctioned interventions, protective orders should not be considered a quick fix to the problem of violent families and should be examined more closely. As Davis and Smith (1995) point out, recent research indicates that protective orders have not been effective in reducing violence, nor have the police consistently responded by arresting individuals who have violated orders. Additionally, some evidence exists that the issuance of protective orders has led to further violence, particularly for those with more serious prior histories of abuse.

Specialized Courts

As a response to the growing number of communities that have instituted criminal justice policy remedies for family violence matters, court administrators have recognized the need for enhancing the administration of cases once they have entered the system. Better coordination and communication, particularly between the civil and criminal courts, have been called for. Some communities have attempted to solve case coordination problems by creating integrated, specialized courts to handle all cases. An example of the Eleventh Judicial Circuit in Dade County, Florida's, Domestic Violence Division is described in Box 8.2.

Specialized courts have a number of advantages. First, they provide attorneys and social service systems an opportunity to work more closely together toward resolving family violence issues. Second, attorneys and judges are afforded the opportunity to develop a level of expertise about how best to handle cases. Third, victims are better served when case information, protective orders, and so forth are all centrally located. Fourth, specialized courts can plan for the unique physical safety issues involved hearing cases (Epstein, 1999).

Summary

In this section we explored a number of interventions that we refer to as state interventions. These are strategies that are currently utilized to identify

---

Box 8.2 /// Specialized Domestic Violence Court: Dade County, Florida

In 1992, the Domestic Violence Plan of Dade County was enacted to provide a Domestic Violence Division with concurrent jurisdiction for handling injunctions for protections, violations, contempts, and misdemeanors involving domestic violence. The plan calls for mandated punishment for the offender and emphasizes treatment for all parties. Court action is tied to batterer intervention, parenting classes, counseling, and educational classes.

Central to the plan is the guiding principle that active prosecutorial action and a responsive, active judiciary have an integral role to play in stopping violence and protecting abused adults and children. The Domestic Violence Plan falls on the 1991 enactment of Florida's comprehensive domestic violence law, which mandates that acts of family violence be treated as criminal behavior (F.S. 741.2901 and 741.30 1995).

All misdemeanors involving family violence are separated from general court dockets and are handled by the Domestic Violence Division of the Administrative Office of the Courts.

Retrieved Dec. 23, 2000, from www.fcc.state.fl.us/fcc/reports/courts/ctappe.html.

---

and intervene directly into the lives of families. With the development of these types of policies, intervention into family violence has been institutionalized through the formal channels of law enforcement and the courts. In addition, state laws have mandated the involvement of other professional groups to assist in the identification of family violence. Next we discuss interventions that focus on providing services to victims of family violence.

/// Services for Victims

In addition to the state interventions discussed herein, a variety of different programs and services have emerged to protect and assist victims of violence. In this section we explore some of the more common types of programs and services that are currently available in communities across the United States.

Victim services have evolved over the past 30 years to provide for the special needs of victims of family violence. As we discussed in other chapters, services for victims have evolved in a response to grassroots advocacy efforts, public policy, and research, as well as the overall crime victims' movement. Today, a rather sophisticated system of victim services exists in local communities that addresses the housing, financial, mental health, and safety needs of victims of violence. Box 8.3 illustrates an example of a comprehensive crime victim service agency.

Programs are funded by a variety of sources. Federal and state govern-

---

Box 8.3 /// Safe Horizon: A Comprehensive Victim Service Agency

Safe Horizon is a comprehensive victim service agency that provides services to crime victims and their families in New York City, New York. They offer a variety of services including:

- 24-hour hotline
- Safe Horizon Crime Victim Center: licensed treatment center for survivors of violent crime and domestic violence
- Free emergency lock changes or repair Advocacy
- 200-bed shelter
- 27-unit transitional housing shelter
- Batterers' intervention programs
- Family violence intervention project
- Staff availability at 24 police precincts
- Collaboration with other professionals to train doctors and other professionals to screen for domestic violence
- Law project that assists survivors in obtaining protective orders and pro bono legal assistance in divorce and custody cases

Retrieved from: www.safehorizon.org, Dec. 21, 2000

---

ment funding is available under a number of different legislative umbrellas. For example, funding for victim services is available through the Victims of Crime Act (VOCA), which created a fund that reserves the revenues from offender fines, penalty assessments, and forfeited appearance bonds. The VOCA funds are transferred to the states to provide direct compensation to crime victims and to support victim service programs. In addition to VOCA, victim programs may have access to funding that is available through other federal programs, such as the Family Violence Prevention and Services Act, Title XX Social Services Block Grant, and Emergency Assistance for Families (L. V. Davis, Hagen, & Early, 1994). In addition to public funding, victims' services are often funded by private sources such as community foundations, special events, community donations, and the United Way.

Services that address the needs of victims are found in a variety of different types of agencies. Police, prosecutors' offices, family courts, and departments of social services are a few of the examples of government-administered services. Other institutions, such as hospitals, schools, and not-for profit organizations, may also provide services to victims of family violence. Programs may employ staff to work directly with victims or may function with the strong support of community volunteers.

In addition to providing direct services to assist victims, organizations and advocacy groups exist to spur on social, political, and legal changes in the area of family violence. Advocacy efforts take a variety of approaches, such as educating the public about family violence issues, educating special populations of potential victims (e.g., children, the elderly), promoting legislation to protect the rights of victims, and pushing for continued funding to support the network of victim services. Advocacy efforts have long been instrumental in challenging the social ideology of the role that women, children, and the elderly play in the family, and they are responsible for putting family violence issues on the forefront of the political agenda.

Victim Compensation Programs

Victim compensation programs are state-administered funds to assist victims of crime in recouping their financial losses. Compensation programs have a long history, predating many other types of victim programs. Senator Ralph W. Yarborough (D-Texas) was the first to introduce a federal victims' compensation bill in 1965. He argued that "the right of the victim to compensation from the state arises from the failure of the state to protect from crime" (Yarborough, 1965, 258). This bill, although it died in committee, helped to generate political interest in the needs of victims. As the federal dialogue began about compensating victims, California was the first state to pass legislation to create a victims' compensation program in 1966 (Meadows, 1998), followed by New York (1967), Hawaii (1967), Maryland (1968), and Massachusetts in 1968 (Rathgeb Smith & Freinkel, 1988).

In 1984, the VOCA was passed, designating a federal victims' fund created from federal offender penalties. The federal fund provided the much-needed financial support to enable states to more appropriately handle the level of compensation being requested by victims and to develop compensation programs in states in which programs did not exist. By 1998, the fund had grown to $343 million per year to compensate crime victims and support victim services (Administration for Children and Families [ACF], 1999).

In most states, victims of family violence are eligible for some form of compensation from the state in which the violence occurred. Compensable losses include: medical expenses, mental health counseling, loss of earnings, rehabilitation, funeral costs, property loss, replacement services, and, in a few states, pain and suffering damages and attorneys' fees can be awarded (Parent, Auerbach, & Carlson, 1992).

Some basic criteria must be met for victims to be eligible for financial support: (1) they must be residents in the state in which they are applying; (2) they must be innocent victims of a crime, (3) they must have reported the offense to the police and cooperated with the courts, (4) they must file for compensation within a particular period of time, and (5) they must not have received financial reimbursement for losses from any other source. In addition, most states require that only victims of violent, physical crimes apply for funding (Meadows, 1998). However, in some states, such as New York, elderly victims of property crimes can be reimbursed for essential personal property such as eyeglasses, medications, and so forth.

Most states have created state agencies to administer the crime victim compensation program. Victims can generally access compensation information from local victim assistance programs, law enforcement agencies, prosecutors' offices, and hospital emergency rooms. Although compensation programs were not originally designed with the victim of family violence in mind, most states have gone to considerable effort to use language that includes compensable crimes such as child sexual abuse, child physical abuse, spouse abuse, and other domestic violence offenses.

Safe Housing

Shelters and other out-of-home placements provide safe housing for children and adult victims of family violence when it is no longer safe for them to remain in the home. A wide range of programs exists to ensure the short-term and long-term safety of victims. Domestic violence shelters, foster care, safe homes, transitional housing, residential treatment programs, skilled home nursing, and nursing homes function to provide for the basic living needs of abused persons. We discuss two of the most common services available in most communities: domestic violence shelters and foster care placement.

Domestic Violence Shelters

Shelters for women with abusive partners cropped up all over the United States during the 1970s as a result of the advocacy efforts of the feminist movement. The first shelters operated more like an "underground railroad," with an informal network of women volunteers who were willing to open their homes to women fleeing violence. These safe houses provided women and their children the comfort of a home as a temporary resting place until more permanent housing arrangements could be made. Over time, these shelters became institutionalized, supported by governmental and private funding, with full-time professional staff. Since the Violence Against Women Act of 1994, shelters continue to receive federal support. Overall, the Clinton administration allocated more than $350 million to support the 1,400 emergency shelters and safe homes nationwide (ACF, 1999). In 2002, Congress fully funded programs through the Department of Justice, appropriating more than $390 million for criminal justice programs. However, critical funding for shelters was only approved for modest increases from $117 million to $125 million, leaving it more than $50 million below the authorization levels (National Network to End Domestic Violence, 2002).

Shelters play a vital role in assisting women and children to make the transition from violent homes. Given the economic reality that many women face, women often feel they have to choose between remaining in a violent situation and being homeless. According to the United States Conference of Mayors (1999), 57 percent of the homelessness in U.S. cities can be attributed to domestic violence. Additionally, approximately 50 percent of the women who receive Temporary Assistance to Needy Families (TANF) cite domestic violence as the primary factor in the need to seek financial assistance from the government (National Coalition Against Domestic Violence [NCADV], 2000).

Although shelters serve only as a temporary refuge, they often provide other services to assist women in gaining self-sufficiency. Shelters often help women to gain financial assistance, such as TANF, and help with job training and employment, long-term housing arrangements, court advocacy, and child care. Shelters also provide women with emotional support and counseling. A study conducted by Tutty, Weaver, and Rothery (1999) concluded that shelter residents found the supportive climate, the safety of the setting, and child care resources to be particularly beneficial. In addition, Tutty and Rothery (2002) found that shelter services alone may be insufficient for victims. Support groups, shelter outreach programs, and follow-up are critical services to be offered in conjunction with safe housing.

Although shelters play a critical role in the continuum of care for survivors of family violence, they are not seen by all women as an appropriate option. First, women with financial resources or supportive family members may not seek the services of a shelter. Because many shelters often provide their counseling and advocacy services only for residents of the shelter, women who are not in need of shelter services are often not able to take advantage of such services, unless another victim service program exists in the community.

Second, lesbian women often believe that shelters are a potentially unsafe environment. They may believe that shelters are for heterosexual women only and may fear that they will be discriminated against. Additionally, some women may be afraid that, because their abuser is also a woman, she would have easier access to the shelter than the typical male abuser (Sullivan, 1997).

Third, women of color often face barriers to services. For example, Latina survivors of domestic violence, particularly those who are Spanish-speaking, find it difficult to access shelters with bilingual and bicultural services. A study conducted in New York State found that shelter services are inadequately prepared to serve Latina women, particularly non-English-speaking women. Although shelter services do exist to meet the specific needs of Latina women, beds are very limited, creating a disparity in the availability of services (Rivera, 1997-1998). Latina women are expected to wait until a bed opens up, or they may have to be transported to a shelter in another region of the state to find immediate protection. This situation undermines the entire mission of shelters, which is to provide immediate, emergency housing for women and their children who are fleeing violent relationships.

Fourth, age also appears to serve as a barrier to service, although at this time we can only speculate as to why. Studies have documented that women under the age of 20 or over the age of 60 are underserved by shelters (Sullivan, Basta, Tan, & Davidson, 1992). However, according to the National Crime Victimization Survey of 1998, young women ages 16–24 were victimized by an intimate partner more frequently than women in any other age category. Young women in this age range reported violence rates of 19.6 per 1,000 women for the years 1993–1998 (Rennison & Welchans, 2000), placing young women in high need for shelter and domestic violence services. Boudreau (1993) notes that emergency shelters for abused elderly that provided specialized support services for older adults would be beneficial.

Fifth, shelters overall remain underfunded and therefore cannot adequately meet the demand for services. It is common for shelters to have a waiting list or to have to refer survivors to a shelter in another region, particularly those in large metropolitan areas. Given the temporary nature of shelter services, often providing a safe home for only 30 days or less, a need exists for more long-term transitional housing for women committed to leaving their abusive partners.

Foster Care

Foster care provides a stable living environment for children who can no longer safely remain in their homes. Foster parents are provided stipends by local social service agencies to provide children who have been removed from their homes with a safe place to live. Children may remain in foster care until their parents are able to demonstrate that they have solved the problems that led to the out-of-home placement or, if the family cannot be reunited, until the child can be legally freed for adoption.

For children age 16 and older, who are too old for foster care, transitional services are available to help them to live independently. Independent living programs provide education and employment assistance, training in daily living skills, and counseling services (ACF, 2000). In 1999, President Clinton signed the Foster Care Independence Act of 1999, a law designed to prepare young people who are too old for foster care to live successfully on their own. The act invests $350 million more over the next 5 years in such services (ACF, 2000).

The number of children placed in foster care continues to rise each year. Petit and Curtis (1997) report a 74 percent increase in children in out-of-home care from the mid-1980s to the late 1990s. For example, more than 560,000 children were in foster care in September of 1998, 220,000 more than were in foster care placements in 1988 (ACF, 2000). It is difficult to determine what factors account for such an increase. One possible factor is the length of stay of children in foster care. Bishop, Murphy, and Hicks (2000) found that despite some improvements in the child protection system since the 1980s, the time frame for cases to be processed through the system in 1994 was very similar to the time frame for case processing in the previous decade. They noted that children still remain in the child protection system for an average of 5 years, with an average of 1.6 years in the court process. Children who have been permanently removed from the custody of parents were still floundering in foster care 4 years later. Considering that foster care is intended to be a temporary placement to ensure the safety of children, it is not encouraging that children are spending a good deal of their young lives in foster care placements.

Besides the difficulty inherent in providing long-term permanency planning for children whose parents are unable to care for them, the foster care system presents many challenges for children. Child protection agencies find it difficult to recruit and retain an adequate number of foster families. Some studies have provided evidence that children placed in foster care (and residential care) are at high risk for maltreatment by their foster families (Hobbs, Hobbs, & Wynne, 1999), thereby making the recruitment process a challenging one.

It is also important to keep in mind that children who enter the foster care system present with a variety of difficulties. As we discussed in chapter 3, children who have been abused and neglected have a variety of problems. Children who are placed in foster care often have academic, health, and mental health problems and difficulty interacting with others, problems that make placement in a "normal" family difficult. Finding foster families to provide support for children with disabilities is an even greater task. Additionally, the high reentry rate of children into foster care placements adds a further burden on caseworkers who attempt to place children in appropriate foster homes.

Although the foster care system is still in need of improvement, some evidence suggests that family foster care can provide the best possible alternative for children who need to be placed outside of the home. Wilson and Conroy (1999) interviewed more than 1,000 children placed in out-of-home settings between 1993 and 1996. They found that children rated their satisfaction with their living environments and with their caregivers as high, especially those children who had been placed with foster families.

Foster care is also a potential option for adult victims of abuse who have physical or mental impairments or disabilities that require supervision or personal care. Although not available in all communities, adult foster care is a growing alternative to nursing home care for those adults who are unable to live independently. Foster care can provide an opportunity for the elder to remain in a home environment and receive the care they need.

Research has demonstrated that family foster care can provide the same level of care as nursing homes at a reduced cost (Reinardy & Kane, 1999; Braun & Rose, 1986). Additional benefits for the elder include interaction with daily family living, children, pets, and so forth. This option is especially attractive to elders who have limited involvement with their natural families (Braun & Rose, 1986).

Crisis Intervention

Crisis intervention services are available to victims of family violence from a variety of organizations. Personnel from police departments, the courts, victim service programs, protective agencies, hospitals, and community groups often offer crisis intervention services to victims and families in crisis.

Crisis services generally provide immediate, time-limited counseling and advocacy services to family members shortly after an incident of family abuse. Intervention services are provided in a number of venues, including services for families in-house, at police stations, in hospitals, in family court, at protective agencies, or over the telephone. Depending on the role of the agency providing the service, crisis intervention can typically involve assisting the family member in establishing safety; ensuring that he or she receives appropriate medical care; validating her or his emotional experience; advocating for the victim with medical, law enforcement or court personnel; actively recruiting other family or friends to assist; arranging for immediate placement in therapeutic or residential services; and assisting the victim in developing short-term plans for the future. Roberts (2000, p. 11) presents a seven-stage model of crisis intervention and states that "the goal of effective crisis resolution is to remove vulnerability from the individual's past and bolster him or her with an increased repertoire of new coping skills to serve as a buffer against similar stressful situations in the future." In violent families, motivation to change the living environment is often fueled by crisis events; therefore, crisis periods can provide practitioners with an important opportunity to intervene (Roberts & Schenkman Roberts, 2002).

Hotlines

Hotlines are typically run 24 hours a day, 7 days a week, and provide crisis counseling, information regarding family violence and the court process, referrals to other agencies, and emotional support. Hotlines are often run by specially trained volunteers or by paid staff members of victim service programs. Hotlines are available at the national, state, and local levels. Some operate as specific hotlines to address a particular area of family violence, and some hotlines are more general in nature, providing individuals with crisis intervention in a broad array of topic areas such as suicide, drug and alcohol problems, school problems, and so forth.

For example, in 1996, President Bill Clinton launched a nationwide 24-hour domestic-violence hotline as part of the administration's fight against intimate partner abuse. Since its inception, the hotline has taken about 100,000 calls per year from all over the country. The hotline provides immediate crisis intervention, counseling, and referrals to local shelters and domestic violence programs (ACF, 1999).

Crisis Response Teams

In addition to hotlines, many communities offer in-person crisis response services. Staff or volunteers may provide crisis intervention services at the victims' homes, at police stations, in hospitals, or in court facilities. Crisis services may be located in a particular agency, or they may be mobile, with support staff reaching out to victims, whether in hospitals, police stations, or their own homes. In some communities, crisis services are offered by multidisciplinary teams. Teams made up of different professionals, such as protective workers, nurses, police officers, social workers, psychologists, and community volunteers, work with families. The National Organization of Victim Assistance (NOVA) is a national organization that provides crisis intervention teams to local communities that are experiencing difficulty as a result of traumatic events.

Therapy

Although many victim services are considered to be therapeutic in nature, psychotherapy is a counseling service that is generally of longer duration than traditional crisis intervention. Therapy can involve individual or group counseling or both and is generally provided by a professional with an advanced level of training, such as a psychologist or social worker.

Therapy services are provided in a number of settings, such as nonprofit agencies, private practices, mental health centers, and victim service agencies. Group therapy is often organized around specific types of victims, for example, adult victims of child sexual assault, battered women, elder victims, and so forth. However, because of the integrated nature of family violence, some group therapy is structured to include a mix of individuals with different kinds of abuse experiences. The support group model is particularly helpful to victims of violence and can provide an essential complement to other victim services (Tutty & Rothery, 2002).

The psychological consequences of victimization include a wide range of difficulties such as PTSD, depression, eating disorders, self-mutilating behavior, substance abuse, and suicide. Psychotropic medication may also be prescribed in conjunction with therapy. For example, survivors of abuse who suffer from depression may be prescribed an antidepressant drug such as Prozac or Zoloft.

Not all victims of family violence require long-term therapeutic intervention. However, for those individuals who exhibit symptomatology consistent with a psychological diagnosis, therapy is regarded as an important factor in facilitating recovery. However, it is often unclear if therapy alone is responsible for recovery. For example, Finkelhor and Berliner (1995), in examining 29 different studies that evaluated the effectiveness of treatments for sexually abused children, found that only five studies were able to demonstrate that recovery was not merely the result of the passage of time or some other factor.

Advocacy

Advocacy is an important component in providing services for victims of family abuse. Advocacy can be provided on a number of levels. On the individual level, victim advocates can ensure that victims are treated fairly by the police, the courts, and other institutions such as schools, hospitals, and insurance companies. Advocates often ensure that victims have access to appropriate services and have all the information they need to make decisions.

Advocacy can also take place on a broader level. Acting on behalf of victims and their families, advocates work to improve the way the system responds to cases of family violence, educating professionals and the community about family violence issues and ensuring that appropriate services are available to assist.

Here we discuss four different types of advocacy programs. Coalitions, which may also be referred to as task forces, associations, or alliances, advocate for victims on a global scale. Ombudsman programs assign a specific individual to serve as a client advocate. Court-appointed special advocates and child advocacy centers provide advocacy services to individual victims and their families.

Coalitions

Advocacy is also provided through networks of local, state, and national coalitions. Coalitions typically represent a cross-section of the community, involving professionals who respond to cases of family violence, leaders from business and industry, interested community volunteers, and survivors of family violence. Together, coalitions work to change legislation and improve the system's response and may provide training, education, and support services to agencies and victims.

Ombudsmen

Ombudsmen serve as intermediaries between clients and staff of various institutions in airing grievances and investigating allegations of abuse. Ombudsmen are found in many settings, including nursing homes, educational institutions, and prisons. We discussed the role of the ombudsmen in more detail in chapter 7; however, here it is important to recognize the critical role they play in advocating for children and adults who are receiving care in "pseudo families."

Long-term care ombudsmen, authorized under the Older Americans

Act, act on behalf of older citizens who reside in long-term care institutions. Both paid staff and volunteers serve in this advocacy role for older adults. It is their role to act on behalf of the elder with the administration and staff of the various institutions.

Although ombudsmen have historically represented older adults in long-term care settings, the ombudsman model is also gaining popularity in children's services. For example, the Michigan Office of Children's Ombudsmen was created to examine complaints concerning children in foster care, adoption, and child protective systems (Bearup & Palusci, 1999).

Court-Appointed Special Advocates

The court-appointed special advocate (CASA) movement has its roots in the 1970s with the 1974 Child Abuse Prevention and Treatment Act. The act provided support for the appointment of "guardians ad litem," or court-appointed special advocates, to represent the best interests of abused children. In the early days, attorneys were generally appointed to serve this advocacy role.

However, in 1976, Judge David Soukup, presiding judge in King County Superior Court in Seattle, Washington, developed a program to utilize specially trained community volunteers as an alternative to assigning overworked, undertrained attorneys.

According to the National Court-Appointed Special Advocate Association, Judge Soukup's program quickly gained support from judges across the United States and was followed by the development of similar programs. In 1990, the Victims of Child Abuse Act allocated federal funds to start and expand the volunteer-based CASA model. Today there are more than 950 CASA programs nationwide, utilizing the assistance more than 52,000 community volunteers to advocate for the special needs of abused children (Court-Appointed Special Advocates [CASA], 2002).

The CASA model utilizes volunteers to serve as advocates for children and to provide information for judges. Volunteers are assigned a limited number of cases and follow each case from the beginning to the end. Volunteers have the capability of putting in the appropriate amount of time and energy into properly investigating and advocating for the best interests of children.

Although the research is limited, CASA programs represent promising approaches to advocating for the needs of children in the family court system. Research suggests that children who have been appointed an advocate from CASA have significantly fewer placements, are more likely to find a permanent home, and spend considerably less overall time in the custody of the courts (Calkins & Millar, 1999).

Child Advocacy Centers

Child advocacy centers have developed across the country to improve the response of the system to victims of child abuse and neglect. Centers are based on a philosophy that change is required in the ways child abuse cases are investigated and the ways children are treated through the process.

Advocacy centers have a mission to provide services to children in a child-friendly facility, and they stress the importance of a multidisciplinary team approach to investigation and intervention. An advocacy center provides a comfortable, private setting for children that is physically and psychologically safe. The team of professionals, made up of representatives from protective agencies, the police, medical providers, mental health, and victim support agencies, coordinates its activities from the center. Having one central location, one that is especially designed to suit children, is meant to reduce the trauma that children often experience by being reinterviewed by many professionals and shuffled through different agencies (National Children's Alliance [NCA], 2000).

A research project conducted by the New York State Child Advocacy Resource and Consultation Center (NYSCARCC) in 1994 found support for the child advocacy center model in improving the system for young child abuse victims. The NYSCARCC interviewed 61 individuals and found that, on average, each child had to tell her or his story to eight different people and that, in one case, a child was interviewed by 27 different people. Additionally, families had to endure long waiting periods, had to race their children all over town for various appointments with professionals, were met by some insensitive and untrained professionals, and were not given all the necessary information (NYSCARCC, 1994). Children and nonoffending parents were in many ways victimized again by the system that has been created to protect them. Child advocacy centers are intended to solve these types of problems by providing a system that truly advocates for the needs of the children.

Summary

In this section we explored a number of different types of services that are available to victims of family violence. Although the types of services we discuss by no means represent an exhaustive list, they represent some of the more common types of assistance that are currently available in the United States.

/// Services for Offenders

In the past 30 years, we have struggled to develop institutional responses to the problem of family violence. We have focused our efforts on state mandates and criminal justice approaches, while directing our services toward survivors of violence. However appropriate these policy choices may be, treatment services for offenders are currently underdeveloped, and research on their effectiveness shows mixed results. Offender services are focused on changing the behavior patterns of the individual, not on addressing the larger social and political issues that also play a role in abusive and neglectful behavior.

As with victim services, programs for offenders are administered by a variety of different types of agencies. Programs may be located in settings such as not-for-profit organizations, hospitals, churches, police departments, courts, and protective agencies, as well as with private therapeutic practitioners and the like. Like services for victims, programs for offenders are funded by a variety of sources. Public and private funding, coupled with self-pay and insurance, provide the basis for the programs that are available to assist abusers.

Programs for offenders tend to center on psychotherapeutic models, focusing on counseling and educational approaches. In the case of elder and child abuse, some program models include providing respite and aid services for caregivers. In this section we explore several different service models for abusive family members.

Therapeutic Services

The most typical approach to providing services to offenders is to engage abusers in counseling. Both individual and group counseling are utilized as part of the rehabilitative process. Clinical interventions focus on alleviating the psychological and emotional factors that contribute to abuse while educating the offender. According to Jennings (1990), therapy should encourage the abuser to take responsibility for his or her behavior, assist the abuser in developing a repertoire of peaceful alternatives, and help the abuser to develop empathy and sensitivity.

Treatment Issues

Treatment issues cover a wide range of dimensions. In studies that compare abusers and nonabusers, research suggests that abusers employ a significantly lower level of moral reasoning (Buttell, 1999); have negative and unstable self-concepts (Ragg, 1999); differ in the cognitive domains of memory, learning, executive, and verbal functioning (Cohen, Rosenbaum, & Kane, 1999); and may have specific personality characteristics associated with abusiveness that are formed in early childhood (Dutton, Starzomski, & Ryan, 1996). Studies have also identified high levels of emotional disturbance, mental illness, and substance abuse among perpetrators (Anetzberger, 1987).

Given the wide range of treatment issues, it is likely that no one program model can be effective in treating all types of abusive individuals. A variety of behavioral health services are probably warranted to meet the needs of abusers in any given community. Substance abuse treatment, psychotropic medication, conflict resolution training, anger management programs, and psychoeducational groups all have a role to play in meeting the specific treatment needs of offenders. For example, batterer intervention programs have evolved nationwide as a treatment response to intimate partner violence and as a tool for the criminal justice system to merge court sanction with treatment. To date, such treatment models have not yielded standard protocols nationwide. Hanson (2002) notes that, although batterer intervention programs have grown as a popular method of dealing with male batterers, some states have not developed standards for such programs. Additionally, because most programs focus on heterosexual male offenders, treatment models are needed that consider race, class, and sexual orientation issues.

Self-Help Groups

Self-help or support groups have been found to be a complementary component to the counseling process. These groups are based on the self-help model that is popular in assisting victims of other types of violent crime or those struggling with drug and alcohol addiction or serious illnesses. Self-help groups provide much-needed support and guidance from peers who have similar experiences.

One such self-help group is Parents Anonymous. Founded in 1970 through the efforts of one mother seeking help to create a safe home for her children, Parents Anonymous chapters are located across the United States and assist parents in providing a nurturing home environment. Weekly support group meetings are offered by local chapters, and 24-hour hotlines provide immediate assistance for parents. Through Parents Anonymous, parents identify and build on their strengths, learn how to manage their stress, broaden their network of social support, and acquire realistic expectation about themselves and their children's behavior (Parents Anonymous, Inc. 2000).

Family Therapy

Family therapy, also referred to as *conjoint treatment*, is another counseling service available for violent families. This form of therapy is based on the premise that families need to understand their family patterns and improve their ability to communicate with each other, to set appropriate boundaries, and to develop family structures conducive to living without violence (Blau, Butteweg Dall, & Anderson, 1993).

Correctional Alternatives

Court-Mandated Treatment

Court-mandated treatment programs (mandated by both civil and criminal courts) provide offenders with a variety of services. Services may involve group therapy sessions, often with a mix of psychoeducational programming. They may also provide support through home visits from professionals or make referrals to other agencies for specific services such as alcohol and drug treatment. Court-mandated programs tend to be affiliated directly with the court system, although they may be administered by local nonprofit agencies.

Examples of court-mandated programs include programs for men who batter their partners, parenting classes for abusive parents, programs that provide a parent aide to assist in the home, counseling and respite care for caregivers, and so forth. These types of programs are intended to augment the authority of the court with a specific service that is geared to bring an end to abusive or neglectful behavior.

Some evidence suggests that court-mandated programs may be more helpful than traditional correctional options, such as incarceration or probation. For example, Babcock and Steiner (1999) conducted a study that compared men who were mandated by court to enter group treatment for men who batter with men who were simply incarcerated. They found that men who completed the domestic violence group treatment had fewer recurrences of domestic violence offenses at the time of follow-up, whereas the men who were incarcerated had a greater number.

Probation

Probation officials can play a critical role in family violence intervention. As a sentencing alternative, probation affords offenders the opportunity to remain in the community with supervision. Probationers are required by the court to abide by a contract that requires them to obey all laws and orders of protection, to maintain employment or educational programs, to attend substance abuse treatment or other treatment programs (e.g., child sexual abuse offender therapy or batterer treatment programs), and to pay all court-mandated fees or restitution. Offenders who do not fulfill their contractual obligations risk probation revocation and incarceration.

Respite Care

Respite care is a specific support service intended to provide relief to caregivers of the elderly or disabled or of ill children. Because the frail elderly and children with disabilities or illnesses are at particular risk for abuse and neglect, respite care affords caregivers the opportunity to take a break from

Box 8.4 /// ARCH National Respite Network and Resource Center

ARCH stands for Access to Respite Care and Help; it is a national resource center funded in part by the U.S. Department of Health and Human Services, Administration for Children, Youth and Families, Office of Child Abuse and Neglect.

The mission of the center is to support service providers and families through training, technical assistance, evaluation, and research. The center provides:

- a National Respite Locator Service
- a lending library of relevant books, journals, and audiovisual materials
- an informative Web site with downloadable fact sheets on respite
- training and technical assistance to professional respite staff

Retrieved from www.chtop.com/ARCH/ARCHserv.htm, Dec. 23, 2000

their caregiving responsibilities. Some respite care programs bring trained professionals to the home to provide care on site, and others provide a specific location at which respite care is provided.

The intention of respite care is to help reduce the stress associated with caring for an elderly parent or a disabled or seriously ill child. It is hypothesized that if the stress can be reduced, neglect and abuse rates will fall. Although utilization rates of such services tend to be rather low (Boothroyd, Armstrong, Evans, Kuppinger, & Radigan, 1998), it is widely believed that respite care provides an important support for stressed families. A study conducted in Arkansas interviewed 66 families with disabled children and found that overall the families gave positive ratings to respite care (Baltz, Kelleher, & Shema, 1995). Additionally, Boothroyd and associates (1998) found that respite care users tended to have younger children, children who had a greater number of impairments, fewer social supports, and a more difficult time managing their children's behavior.

However, some studies have indicated that, although respite care provides a supportive function, it does not result in clinically significant changes in stress-related concerns (Lundervold & Lewin, 1987, Flint, 1995). It is unclear at this point whether or not respite care is a viable treatment alternative for stressed families. The research is unclear as to whether or not this form of support has the ability to reduce abuse in families.

Summary

In this section we discussed some of the most common types of programs geared toward providing support and treatment to individuals who abuse or neglect family members. Most programs rely on changing abusive behavior through different therapeutic or educational approaches. A wide range of treatment problems exist with individuals who are abusive or neglectful. No one treatment method can realistically serve every offender and every form of family violence. An integrated approach, one that is tied to state interventions and victim services and that works toward changing social inequities, is likely to have the greatest impact on the overall health of families.

/// Chapter Summary

This chapter examined a number of intervention strategies utilized by communities to identify, intervene in, and treat violence in the home. We explored current state-level interventions that include mandatory reporting mechanisms, protective agency service laws, criminal sanctions, protective orders, and specialized courts. Through the proliferation of policies and laws centered on family violence issues, intervention into the private lives of families has been institutionalized and engages the involvement of many different professional groups.

We also explored a variety of services available to assist victims of abuse. Crime victim compensation programs, safe housing, crisis intervention, therapy, and advocacy are available to support and assist survivors. We also discussed different types of treatment programs available to offenders.

Although we cannot come to any conclusions on the best way to intervene in families who are struggling with abusive situations, it is clear that most of our effort goes toward working with individuals within a family system. Little energy is given to some of the broader social issues that place families at risk for abuse. Although we have recognized the macro level issues as being important to our understanding of the reasons that family violence occurs, current interventions do little to redress environmental factors such as poverty, patriarchy, ageism, and the cultural approval of violence.

/// Recommended Web Sites

Administration for Children and Families
    www.acf.dhhs.gov
American Law Sources Online
    www.lawsource.com
ARCH National Respite Network and Resource Center
    www.chtop.com/ARCH/ARCHserv.htm.
Crisis Intervention Network
    www.crisisinterventionnetwork.com
Court-Appointed Special Advocates
    www.nationalcasa.org

Feminist Majority Foundation
    www.feminist.org
Elder Abuse Law
    www.elderabuselaw.com
Findlaw
    www.findlaw.com
Justice Information CenterVictims of Crime
    www.ncjrs.org/VictimsOfCrime.asp
Men Against Domestic Violence
    www.silcom.com/paladin/madv
National Center on Elder Abuse
    www.elderabusecenter.org
National Children's Alliance
    www.nncac.org
National Organization for Victim Assistance
    www.try-nova.org
Parents Anonymous, Inc.
    www.parentsanonymous-natl.org

9 /// Preventing Violence in the Home

As discussed in the preceding chapter, intervention strategies have proliferated nationwide to respond to violence in the home. With the formidable task of meeting the myriad of needs of families and institutions, a rather sophisticated system of intervention has evolved. Previous chapters have described some of these unique legal and programmatic interventions. Given the fact that violence in the home is the result of a complex set of factors, no one program or piece of legislation is realistically considered a panacea by anyone. Many contemporary interventions appear to have some success in reducing acts of abuse within specific home environments; however, it is impossible to gauge the overall impact of such policies and services across communities. To date, evaluation research has provided us with only limited knowledge about the efficacy of specific interventions (Chalk & King, 1998). Evaluation studies have focused predominately on child maltreatment and intimate partner violence, with little to no evaluation of interventions in the areas of elder abuse, sibling violence, same-sex partner violence, animal abuse, and pseudo family violence. We know that substantial change has occurred in how we respond to instances of interpersonal violence, yet most scholars and practitioners would agree that violence in the home is still a significant social problem. So, the question then becomes: Are we doing something wrong? Well, not necessarily.

In this chapter we explore intervention from a different perspective. We provide few answers on how best to approach the prevention of violence in the home; however, our goal is to challenge our thinking about the issue. Can we prevent abuse and neglect? Because humans have yet to be able to maintain a peaceful existence, it is unlikely that we will be successful in eliminating violence in the home in the way that other public health threats have been eliminated (e.g., certain diseases and illnesses). Yet we may be on the verge of the type of cultural change that can substantially reduce the level and context of abusive environments in the long run.

This chapter looks beyond the specific interventions explored in previous chapters and focuses on the multidimensional levels of preventing violence in the home. We first explore some systemic issues and unintended consequences of specific policy choices. These barriers are embedded in many human service and health delivery systems and should not be considered unique to family violence remedies. Communities around the country have begun to address such systemic concerns. We explore some community-based models that are currently working toward systemic change.

Second, we examine the ideology of prevention and investigate several different types of prevention models. Third, we discuss the roles that various professional disciplines may have in prevention and early intervention. The role of technology in improving the ability of professionals to respond to violence is also examined, as is the role of the larger community in moving toward cultural change.

/// Systemic Issues

Solving social problems is a difficult, if not an insurmountable, task. Nonprofit and government agencies have grown in number and in strength since the early days of the New Deal, with the formidable task of meeting the myriad of human service needs of the public. As we have discussed in previous chapters, specific systems and services have developed to respond to various aspects of interpersonal violence. Systems such as criminal justice (police, courts, corrections), civil court processes, health care, mental health, long-term care, child welfare, and education all have distinct roles to play in responding to various aspects of violence in the home. Health care workers, animal welfare specialists, substance abuse treatment professionals, judges, lawyers, police officers, social workers, and victim advocates are just a few of the professionals engaged in issues of interpersonal violence on a continual basis.

An issue so complex cuts across all these various systems and must be researched from a variety of social science perspectives. A number of systemic issues have therefore surfaced and are worthy of continued exploration. Here we examine issues such as fragmentation across system domains, paradigms focused on secondary prevention and pathology, professional conflicts, and the critical need for a body of evaluation research to guide the future development of intervention practices.

System Fragmentation

Current interventions focus on dealing with discrete populations and specific types of violence. The result has been a fragmented system of intervention that tends to provide short-term solutions to specific problems. For example, separate intervention systems and what we would refer to as "bundles of services" have been created to respond to specific instances of child abuse and neglect, elder abuse, intimate partner violence, and abuse in out-of-home care. Professionals bound by regulations, legislation, and funding streams are often able to respond only to problems within their immediate service domains, preventing the resolution of the entire range of social issues facing families today. Diverse and often conflicting policy objectives have discouraged integration of the service delivery system.

In other words, service systems, although developed with the best of intentions, are generally linear by design and often address only the short-term, piecemeal needs of the individuals and families they serve. For example, some services are geared to assist only children, whereas others tend to the needs of adults; some focus on victims, others work with offenders. Chalk and King (1998, p. 50), on behalf of the National Research Council and the Institute of Medicine, argue: "the overall 'system' of family violence interventions is highly disjointed, loosely structured, and often lacks central coordinating offices or comprehensive service delivery systems."

Systems are generally large and cumbersome. Any one single system can present a difficult maze to work through, let alone many systems at once. For example, Box 9.1 represents a listing of some of the typical systems present in any given community in the United States. In effect, this represents a "human services industrial complex."

Box 9.1 /// Systems at Work: Examples of Human Service Systems

Mental Health

Mental retardation and developmental disabilities
Mental illness
Substance abuse treatment
Counseling/therapy

Criminal Justice

Police
Courts
Victim advocacy

Health Care

Emergency care
Home health care
Skilled nursing
Family medicine

Schools

Public policy makers

Civil court

Child Welfare

Child protective agencies
Foster care system
Child care facilities
Placement agencies
Youth development agencies

Animal Welfare

Corrections
Animal control
Veterinarian care
Animal rights advocacy

Adult Welfare

Adult protective agencies
Adult advocacy programs
Elder care institutions/housing

Financial assistance

Religious organizations

Private nonprofit agencies

Operating independently from one another, these systems do interact with each other regularly, yet they rarely have the opportunity to integrate or coordinate their efforts. Agency staff members often get bogged down with the day-to-day operations of serving consumers, so little attention can be paid to renovating system interactions. Attending to the broader social issues endemic to the dynamic environment in which families and out-of-home care placement operate is virtually impossible. Consequently, little connection between broader theoretical premises and actual interventions can be made.

System fragmentation has plagued the human services field since human service programming began to proliferate, and such fragmentation is not unique to family violence intervention. For example, Trist (1977) argued that a turbulent environment is created when many organizations, all functioning autonomously in many diverse areas, produce unintended and contradictory results in the environment they all share. After 30 or so years of developing intervention strategies to combat violence in the home, it should be no surprise that organizations, although arguably sophisticated in their responses, have inadvertently participated in the creation of discordant outcomes. The service delivery system is now challenged with the resolution of system issues.

Focus on Secondary and Tertiary Prevention

Current intervention strategies function predominately to respond to violence once it has occurred (Chalk & King, 1998). Preventing violence in the home is the central goal of most intervention strategies; however, most programs and services are reactive by design (we discuss different levels of prevention in the next section). Some form of abuse must be substantiated or suspected before most services can be invoked. Education and prevention programs do exist in some communities, and we highlight some of these later in this chapter. However, most of what is termed *prevention* is really better termed *intervention* or *early intervention*.

Other programs do attempt to serve populations that are marked by traditional risk factors, trying to provide specific families with supportive networks before incidents of violence occur. However, a true prevention effort has yet to be realized. Little is done to provide the community at large with the tools and supports necessary to raise healthy, functioning families. Out-of-home care environments need to commit resources to provide appropriate training and support for employees.

Paradigms Based on a Pathology Model

Despite our understanding of the ecology of violence in the home, present paradigms continue to result in interventions that are based on the pathology of individuals. Criminal justice and social service models are based on the identification and substantiation of abuse and the punishment and treatment of offenders. Consequently, services also focus on the deficits of individuals and families, rather than building on strengths. Strength-based ideologies do frame many human service programs; however, overall, specific intervention strategies tend to focus on "fixing" the problem of abuse through accountability and rehabilitative efforts.

Considerable research has been conducted in an attempt to understand the pathology of individuals and their interpersonal relationships. Granted, our knowledge of the pathology of violence in the home is rather extensive at this time. Risk factors and correlated problems are well documented in the literature. What appears to be missing is research that can demonstrate factors associated with abuse-free environments. All home environments are riddled with stressors from time to time; why is it that the majority of households function without abuse and neglect? What are the factors associated with healthy, nurturing climates? These are questions that are rarely asked, mainly because our interest in deviant behavior is so great. However, understanding the healthy home environment could be crucial to the development of prevention and early intervention programs. Helping to build strengths instead of waiting to punish inappropriate behavior should be central to our prevention approach.

Professional Conflicts

Another systemic issue that appears to be dominant in the interaction of various systems in the intervention and prevention of violence in the home is professional conflict. As we have mentioned earlier, conflict is likely to be inherent in implementing such divergent policy choices within the scope of numerous institutional settings. Professional conflict is also likely to exist at all levels.

The policy domain is often riddled with professional conflict, whereas scholars, public policy makers, and practitioners disagree on policy development. The provision of direct services may also include levels of conflict, whereas various professionals, fulfilling their professional obligations, find themselves at odds with other professionals who work with the same clients. Each system domain is framed by a different mission and different guiding principles, regulations, political realities, and sets of goals.

The following situations are examples of professional conflict we have observed. The criminal justice system, concerned with due process and procedural fairness, may be in conflict with victim advocates whose main concern is the safety and well-being of their clients. The child protective worker, in his or her role of protecting children from violence, may work to remove children from a battered woman. At the same time, the domestic violence advocate is working on behalf of the battered woman who wants to keep her children. The school district, concerned about lawsuits from parents, refuses to allow child protective staff members on school grounds to interview children. The health care aide who witnesses acts of neglect by his or her employer against elderly residents may do nothing for fear of reprisal. Government and private funding agencies are requested to fund specific intervention or prevention programs without empirical documentation that such programs are effective. Legislators create public policy without examining the potential consequences of such policy choices on the systems and clients intended to be served. Finally, we have observed that the discourse on family violence issues by scholars, advocates, and practitioners has been abusive in tone at times. Family violence work is passionate by its very nature, and therefore, at times, discussions and debates regarding policy issues have risen to the level of interpersonal conflict.

We are not necessarily arguing that such professional conflict is a system barrier. In fact, system conflict may ultimately produce desirable outcomes. As Wright (1999) argues, such conflict in the criminal justice system provides for a system of checks and balances in which a wide range of social interests can be represented. Yet, considering the fragmentation of the larger "human service industrial complex," professional conflict is an issue that communities should openly address and embrace. Unchecked, such conflicts can serve to undermine shared goals and accomplishments. Therefore, it is important that officials continue to meet and talk about systems issues to resolve conflicts that can unintentionally thwart system effectiveness. Understanding the unique role each system plays is crucial to the effective implementation of current strategies and the development of new interventions.

Need for Evaluation

Another systemic issue lies in the overreliance on programs and services without empirical evidence that such programs are effective. Some interventions have been studied with more rigor than others. For example, Chalk and King (1998) note that interventions such as mandatory reporting for child maltreatment, although they have been adopted by every state, have never been evaluated. Conversely, other interventions, such as mandatory arrest policies in cases of intimate partner violence, the use of home visitation services for child maltreatment, and crisis-oriented family preservation services, have been researched extensively.

The current mix of system interventions has not evolved from theory, research, or data collection (Chalk & King, 1998) but rather as a response to events and to address specific systems issues. The multidimensional dynamics of violence in the home are not easily addressed by a specific intervention, nor can they easily be assessed by research. However, the investment in more rigorous research designs, development of valid and reliable measurements, and attention to multidimensional aspects of intervention systems is needed to identify promising approaches and to verify the effectiveness of current strategies. Scholars and practitioners may benefit from examining the shared characteristics of family and pseudo family violence, as well as continuing to probe for more knowledge regarding sibling, parental, and animal abuse.

A Call for System Change

Recognizing the need for system change, many service providers have begun to analyze the challenges of the human services maze. Coordinated community approaches to family violence have sparked interest across the country. Multidisciplinary teams of professionals have gathered to improve the coordination and communication of various system responses to violence. Many coordinated efforts still are fragmented by the focus on improving system responses to specific forms of violence (e.g., child abuse, intimate partner violence, or elder abuse). Little has been done to address the broader social issues that link violence in a variety of home settings and the coexistence of other social problems (e.g., poverty, homelessness, substance abuse, discrimination, mental illness, etc.).

In an extensive review of the research literature, the National Research Council and the Institute of Medicine identified three different initiatives that have begun to address various systemic barriers; these are service integration initiatives, comprehensive services that address cross-problem interventions, and community-change interventions (Chalk & King, 1998). Many communities have initiated systemic change through coordination and collaboration within service delivery, policy, and planning domains. Although virtually no evaluation research has been conducted to date to analyze the impact of such system innovation, community-based models that work to relieve system barriers are likely to be a promising approach and are worthy of future evaluation.

Service integration generally refers to collaborative or coordinated services among various system agents. Integration of services at the local level is a critical component in reducing the effects of system fragmentation. Improved organizational communication, resource sharing, and attending to policy and service gaps are just a few of the advantages of service integration models. Some models work to integrate services across systems. For example, child advocacy centers centralize the validation, investigation, and treatment of child sexual abuse. Child advocacy centers merge health care, law enforcement, child protective agents, and treatment professionals in one central location. Other models work to improve the service integration within a system, such as police-prosecutor-victim advocate teams that operate within the criminal justice system to improve the response of the criminal justice system to cases of intimate partner abuse. For example, Davis and Taylor (1997) evaluated a joint law enforcement–social service team in two public-housing police areas in New York. The joint response appeared to have little impact on reducing violence; however, the follow-up approach by team members appeared to have increased citizen's confidence in the ability of the police to respond to domestic violence situations, resulting in a greater likelihood that new acts of violence would be reported to the police.

Another initiative aimed at improving systemic intervention is the development of comprehensive services for cross-problem populations. Integration at this level addresses the reality that many families struggle with a multitude of problems, including substance abuse, poverty, educational problems, mental disorders, and so forth. Communities work to integrate or coordinate services for families that cut across several systems. Integration at this level is intended to assist clients in gaining appropriate specialized services. Improving organizational communication and reducing the duplication of services are two benefits of this level of systemic change. Case managers are often utilized to better "manage" multiple-system clients. Examples may include substance abuse and domestic violence treatment programs (Chalk & King, 1998), specialized domestic violence courts (those that integrate treatment with court action), and multidisciplinary case review teams.

Community change initiatives seek to generate broad-based community change by engaging those outside the service network into partnerships for prevention and intervention. Social reform regarding violence in the home embraces a larger audience than the individual professionals working in the service intervention industry can reach. Social problems are embraced by a partnership between the service intervention industry, local business, clergy, educational system, neighborhood-based organizations, and so forth. The goal is to work together to improve the quality of life for community residents, often by taking a planning role. Examples of community change models might include task forces, family violence prevention councils, and coordinating councils on aging.

The cultural change necessary to teach parents, caretakers, and partners appropriate ways to care for others and to manage conflict will require the involvement of an entire community, and, therefore, we believe that such community change initiatives are critical to the prevention of maltreatment. We discuss the specific roles of various members of the community in achieving prevention goals later in this chapter.

/// Preventing Violence in the Home

Intervention and treatment strategies vary in their approaches and purposes. However, the central mission of any strategy is the prevention of abuse. Crime-control approaches seek to prevent further violence by sanctioning individual offenders, while at the same time serving as a deterrent message to others. School-based educational programs teach young people about dating violence and children about inappropriate "touches," intending to educate them to recognize abuse and the warning signs. Treatment programs for offenders and support services for victims function to prevent further violence. Family support programs assist parents in developing parenting skills to prevent child maltreatment. Media campaigns regarding violence prevention seek to reach a larger community audience.

Prevention Levels

As these examples illustrate, the term *prevention* represents a complex blend of methodologies and, as you might imagine, is very difficult to measure. Prevention generally is considered to be operationalized on three different levels—*primary*, *secondary*, and *tertiary* prevention. *Primary prevention* ventures to prevent abuse before it occurs and is often targeted toward the general public. *Secondary prevention* targets populations at high risk for abuse. Potential offenders and victims, by virtue of their social, economic, or emotional status or history, may be candidates for specialized programming geared to prevent maltreatment. *Tertiary prevention* focuses on intervention in identified cases of abuse and may target both victims and offenders with the objective of ending the abusive conditions.

As we mentioned earlier, current prevention efforts are focused on the secondary and tertiary levels of prevention. Primary prevention programs, although they do exist, are not currently invested in to the same extent. We believe this is due to a number of factors. As human service structures have developed, pathology models have dominated. Even the field of health care, which has the greatest motivation to invest in primary prevention, still only designates 1 percent of health care spending to prevention efforts (Bhalotra & Mutschler, 2001). Scarce resources, coupled with an ample number of identified abuse cases, compel decision makers to continue to fund programs that deal with identified problems. Little is then left to target a problem that may never come to be. Also, the benefits of primary prevention efforts must be maintained for the long term and are impossible to measure in the short term.

Prevention Models

Primary, secondary, and tertiary prevention goals are often implemented within the context of four different models, which we characterize as the *information, therapeutic, skill building,* and *social support* models. Prevention models can be categorized in a number of ways; we have chosen to summarize the majority of them within these four general models. These models are not mutually exclusive. Some interventions may provide elements of all four models, depending on the population being served. For example, many therapeutic programs may involve educational instruction and skills training as components of the therapy. In addition, the program may offer transportation to doctor's visits and referrals to other social support networks.

The *information model* provides the general community and specific at-risk populations with information regarding abuse. The information model supposes that knowledge will ultimately result in a change of behavior (El-lickson, 1995). Media campaigns and school-based educational programs that explore the dynamics of intimate partner abuse, child maltreatment, or elder abuse are typical examples. Information given to consumers might include definitions of and ways to identify abusive behaviors and where to get additional information or assistance. Training given to staff of out-of-home care environments that clearly delineates expectations of proper care and treatment and identifies specific behaviors that constitute abuse are con-sidered preventative. Additionally, training professionals in a wide range of disciplines in the identification of and protocols for responding to cases of abuse provides another example of the information model. Other programs might include information on nutrition, prenatal care, infant care, elder care, and so forth.

The *therapeutic model* incorporates secondary and tertiary prevention strategies that are therapeutic in nature and that are intended to prevent future abusive acts by offenders and to provide assistance to those individ-uals at high risk of victimization. We use the term *therapeutic* in the most general of ways, to capture a variety of intervention strategies that have some rehabilitative or restorative philosophy. Such preventative strategies may in-clude traditional group or individual therapy, crisis intervention services, multisystemic therapy, functional family therapy, cognitive restructuring, specialized treatment programs (e.g., batterer treatment programs), self-help groups, intensive family preservation programs, and so forth. Crime control strategies such as arrest, prosecution, and the use of sanctions and correc-tional alternatives may also be characterized as having therapeutic value. Offender accountability is viewed as a key element in preventing future abusive acts. The full range of victim services discussed in the previous chapter can be characterized as being therapeutic, whether the service is safe housing, advocacy, financial compensation, or counseling. Victim services seek to assist the victim in regaining stability and safety.

The *skill building model* may be implemented as primary, secondary, or tertiary prevention programming. The skill building model incorporates strategies that aim to develop specific skills, often assisting individuals in developing appropriate communication and coping skills to deal with a wide range of interpersonal and daily living issues. Personal safety programs such as Good Touch, Bad Touch (Harvey, Forehand, Brown, & Holmes, 1988) or Feeling Yes, Feeling No (Hazzard, Webb, Kleemeier, Angert, & Pohl, 1991) have demonstrated that even young children can be taught specific skills to prevent victimization. Typical skill building models address areas such as anger and conflict management, communication skills, appropriate disci-pline, stress reduction, parenting and child management, meal preparation, housekeeping, financial management, and so forth. Skill building and a commitment to continued training for out-of-home care staff can assist employees in developing appropriate professional skills to properly care for children and adults in a variety of out-of-home care settings.

An example of the skills building model is the Colorado RETHINK Parenting and Anger Management Program. An evaluation of this 6-week skill building workshop found that parents who participated in the program increased their knowledge levels, improved their attitudes and behaviors, and decreased their unrealistic expectations regarding their children (Fetsch, Schultz, & Wahler, 1999). More information regarding this program is given in Box 9.2.

The *social support* model acknowledges that many families lack the basic necessities and social supports, a lack that ultimately interferes with their ability to function in healthy ways. Prevention is achieved by assisting families in garnering the necessary resources to be successful. These resources may include transportation services, respite care, membership in recreational programs, homemaker services, financial assistance, referral to food pantries and the nutrition-based program, Women, Infants and Children (WIC), adequate health care, and so forth.

The social support model is illustrated by a program in the Cumberland Valley School District in Cumberland County, Pennsylvania. The school district created "security banks" that incorporate necessities such as safety, sustenance, clothing, transportation, and medical, dental, and employment services to provide students and their families with the means to meet their basic needs. According to Butch Bricker, Assistant Superintendent for Secondary Education, the security bank funds are raised by high school students

---

Box 9.2 /// Preventing Child Abuse Through Skill Building

Colorado RETHINK Anger Management Program

RETHINK is a Colorado State University Cooperative Extension parent education program that teaches parents how to deal effectively with their anger. The program consists of six 2-hour weekly sessions of skill training.

RETHINK teaches parents about child development, anger triggers, parenting strategies, and specific tactics to manage anger.

RETHINK stands for:

R   Recognizing when you are angry
E   Empathizing and seeing other's points of view
T   Thinking about what makes you angry
H   Hearing where others are coming from
I   Integrating anger with love and respect
N   Noticing what your body feels like when you are angry
K   Keeping the conversation in the present

Source: Retrieved Jan. 6, 2002, from www.tyc.state.tx.us/prevention/rethink.html.

or through a solicitation letter sent out by the district (Bricker, personal communication, January 15, 2002). Parents and community members are asked to contribute to the fund. Local physicians and dentists also volunteer their services.

Lessons Learned From Other Prevention Models

Preventative efforts to reduce the incidence rates of abuse and neglect may also be supported by the type of prevention programming that is targeted toward other social issues. Prevention programs that specifically address substance abuse, juvenile delinquency, pregnancy, and health problems (e.g., cancer and heart disease) share many of the components of the prevention models we have described. Yet, each field of prevention also has unique properties that may ultimately support the goals of violence prevention. Lessons learned about prevention programming in these other fields should be considered when developing family violence prevention programs. It is also important that we acknowledge how these various social ills are connected to each other and to other, broader social issues, such as poverty, unemployment, discrimination, and so forth.

For example, substance abuse prevention models are typically focused on three basic models: the information model, the affective model, and the social influence model (Abadinsky, 2001). These models provide information, affect personality development, and enhance skills in communication, problem solving, decision making, and resistance to peer pressure. Drug Abuse Resistance Education (D.A.R.E.) is perhaps the most widely adopted substance abuse primary prevention program in the country. A recent study conducted by Clayton, Cattarello, and Johnstone (1996) in Lexington, Kentucky, found that the D.A.R.E. program had no "sustained effects on adolescent drug use" over a 5-year period (p. 318), a disappointing finding considering the widespread application of the D.A.R.E. program in the United States. However, despite the research findings, communities are reluctant to abandon D.A.R.E. programs. Why? Perhaps there are benefits to such a prevention program that are impossible to measure or that have not yet been quantified, and therefore communities continue to embrace D.A.R.E. For example, the fact that police work side by side with school districts, parents, and community groups may have a valuable impact in and of itself, regardless of what happens in the classroom. D.A.R.E. may provide police departments with an opportunity to build positive relationships with young children that can be sustained for the future.

The lessons learned from D.A.R.E. suggest that we cannot consider a single curriculum to be the only prevention effort necessary in a social issue as complex as substance abuse. An overreliance on one strategy with the expectation that it can eradicate a social problem as pervasive and dynamic as drug abuse is obviously a mistake. Drug abuse, like violence in the home, requires examination of broader social conditions, such as economic structures, social position, political ideologies, and how social policy influences such social conditions.

The issues associated with abuse and neglect are far too complicated to be successfully eliminated by any one specific prevention or intervention program. A much broader range of prevention efforts is required. Institutions have changed the way in which they respond to cases of violence; now, we must promote change in the community at large. Communities must come to value and appreciate family life and quality care. The bar must be raised for what is to be expected of the average citizen in terms of parenting, caring for the elderly, and serving in supportive roles for young people. This requires the active participation of both professionals and lay people.

/// The Role of the Community in Prevention

The tasks of identifying and treating violence in the home formally reside with a myriad of professionals, making such abuse a multidisciplinary phenomenon. As we have learned in other chapters, violence within families and in out-of-home care environments has devastating consequences for victims and for our communities. Responses to the issue have cut across all kinds of professional occupations and service systems. We advocate for collaborative, coordinated, multidisciplinary approaches that comprehensively address violence in the home. Efforts to integrate systems and create partnerships between various professional groups will be critical to the future success of prevention and intervention. At the same time, we argue that professional conflict can be a positive force in initiating social change and therefore should be acknowledged and valued and that appropriate safeguards should be placed to ensure that it does not serve as an impediment to the service needs of family members.

Obviously, the police, the courts, the social service and health care agencies, and animal care specialists have their work cut out for them. The future of prevention and intervention will require these formal institutions to commit to systemic renovations, continued funding, ongoing training, and evaluation. Yet these institutions cannot and should not toil alone. Communities, neighborhoods, and local organizations need to make an investment in building strong, healthy families and quality out-of-home care facilities. The ancient adage, "It takes a village to raise a child," means as much today as it has in the past. A commitment is needed from all segments of the community to reduce the incidence rates of abuse and neglect.

In this section, we focus on the implications for professional and lay groups that are generally not considered responsible for abuse and neglect prevention yet that are in a prime position to promote social change. These include schools, public policy makers, business and industry, and the media. We offer some recommendations about how each group can positively influence the prevention of violence in the home.

Educators

Teachers, classroom aides, bus drivers, school social workers, and administrators all have a role to play in the prevention and identification of family violence. Although educators are generally considered mandated reporters of child abuse and neglect, often their involvement ends there. Schools are generally reluctant to get involved in issues outside the purview of education; however, the fact is that any issue children and young people are struggling with at home is likely to affect their ability to learn. Therefore, schools, although they are not responsible for intervening in formal ways into family life, can play a critical role in abuse prevention because of their central position in the community. We recommend that school districts take a five-pronged approach.

1. *School districts should invest in the type of professional staff, such as social workers and school counselors, who can respond to the emotional and psychological needs of young people.* Social work or counseling staff members who are present in or made available on a regular basis to every building in a district (including elementary schools) can provide a number of critical services, including furnishing counseling support to children and youths who have been victimized, providing linkages between the school and appropriate intervention agencies, and assisting families in accessing necessary support services to avoid abuse and neglect.

2. *Invest in ongoing training.* Typically, educators are mandated to complete training regarding child maltreatment and their specific role as mandated reporters. However, educators need to also understand the context of sibling violence, intimate partner violence, elder abuse, and pseudo family violence. All education staff members who have interactions with children or their families should be provided with ongoing training, including lunch servers and monitors, playground monitors, aides, bus drivers, administrators, and clerical staff.

3. *Support education and prevention programming.* School districts should encourage prevention and intervention specialists from the community to bring specialized prevention programs into the classroom. Partnerships with local community agencies, which have expertise in the areas of abuse and neglect, can often provide a wide range of prevention programs in such areas as child abuse and dating violence. Research has given us evidence that such programs can teach young people personal safety and proper actions to take if they experience victimization (Harvey et al., 1988, Hazzard et al., 1991), increasing the likelihood of disclosure and decreasing the self-blame associated with victimization (Finkelhor, Asdigian, & Dziuba-Leatherman, 1995). Programming aims to educate, prevent victimization, and promote the early identification of abuse.

For example, in Pittsburgh, Pennsylvania, the Women's Center and Shelter provides individualized school-based curricula for children and youths from kindergarten through grade 12. The center, in partnership with local schools, has developed a series of prevention programs that address a wide range of age-appropriate topics, including identifying feelings, nonviolent problem solving, safety planning, forms of abuse, dynamics of power and control, dating violence, assertiveness skills, self-esteem building, respecting differences, and decision making. The center provides training to all school personnel and informs parents of the programs. Follow-up services are provided for youths who disclose victimization (Fisher, 1998).

4. *Create partnerships with local intervention professionals.* School districts should actively pursue positive working relationships with local officials who are responsible for intervention, including police, prosecutors, child welfare agencies, victim assistance programs, court personnel, substance abuse treatment providers, family counseling agencies, and so forth. For example, in Jacksonville, Florida, the Department of Children and Families has staff members located in targeted school buildings throughout the district. Caseworkers work with children and their families to ensure that families have their basic needs met and that children are safe (Fisher, 1998).

Schools should also actively participate in violence prevention task forces or on planning councils such as family violence prevention councils, domestic violence task forces, and so forth. Participation in such planning activities provides schools with an opportunity to work toward the improvement of systemic issues and keeps them abreast of new research, policies, and other critical information. For example, in Broome County, New York, school officials regularly participate in the Family Violence Prevention Council (formerly the Child Abuse and Neglect Prevention Council), a standing county council for more than 20 years. Designated by the county executive, this council has forged partnerships with local schools in many areas, has developed a model school policy on child abuse and neglect, and has supported many school-based prevention initiatives.

5. *Create partnerships with the local community.* Schools are in an excellent position to serve the community in positive ways. Schools should open their doors to other local community organizations that work toward developing positive family structures. Youth development organizations (e.g., the Girl and Boy Scouts), sports and recreation organizations, elder organizations, food and coat drives, community outreach organizations, and so forth can benefit by partnerships with local schools. Violence prevention can be achieved through the conscientious development of assets and skill building. Other organizations can often provide programs and services for individuals and families, and schools are often excellent locations for such activities.

Parent-teacher associations (PTAs) should be engaged to provide specific violence prevention programming or activities that support child development and family asset building. For example, the Washington State PTA has initiated a domestic violence education campaign that places information regarding intimate partner violence and teen dating violence in the hands of local PTAs and parents (Fisher, 1998).

Public Policy Makers

As public servants, federal, state, and local legislators have an explicit responsibility to develop sound public policy and to utilize tax dollars effectively and efficiently. To this end, public policy makers are in a critical position to develop policies that can ensure that families and pseudo families have the appropriate tools. Although their role may be obvious, we believe it is important to highlight the level of responsibility that they bear in prevention. We make the following recommendations.

1. *Develop rational policies.* Public policy makers should be well versed in the issues, risk factors, and recent research on abuse and neglect in the home in order to fully understand the implications of their policy decisions. Understanding the impact that domestic public policy choices have on home life is also important. Economic, social welfare, health care, criminal justice, and mental health policies ultimately affect a family's ability to care for one another. Policies should support, not detract from, a family's ability to properly care for its members. Health care, adequate housing, sufficient pay, affordable child and elder care, adoption, and so forth are parallel issues to abuse and neglect. Changes in these parallel policy issues could render some families vulnerable to abuse and neglect, or, on the other hand, policies could ultimately support healthy family functioning. Additionally, policies should strive to create power balances instead of reinforcing power inequities. Legislators should consider all intended and unintended consequences of various policy choices.

2. *Provide adequate resources for prevention and intervention.* Policy makers have a responsibility to ensure that adequate resources are available to support prevention and intervention efforts. Public policy makers are faced with a divergent set of budgetary concerns; however, investments in preventive services are likely to yield enormous cost savings down the road. Programs cannot function without stable, predictable funding. For example, the landmark Violence Against Women Act, passed by Congress in 1993, authorized approximately $677 million in spending for prevention and intervention programs in 2001, yet only $468 million was appropriated in the final budget (National Network to End Domestic Violence [NNEDV], 2001). Funding shortfalls result in the underfunding of critical programs, and newly authorized programs receive no funding.

3. *Invest in research and program evaluation.* Prevention and intervention practices should be grounded in theory and supported by empirical research. Legislators should rally to support continued research and evaluation of intervention strategies to ensure that public policy choices have had their intended outcomes. Policy makers have a responsibility to ensure that public dollars are expended on programs and services whose efficacy can be demonstrated. When systems have been identified as being ineffective or dysfunctional, policy makers have a responsibility to see that systemic repairs are initiated.

Employers

The business community can contribute in a number of ways to the prevention of abuse and neglect. First and foremost, corporations must recognize the direct impact of such violence in their workplaces. Absenteeism, reduced performance, health care costs, and workplace security issues are real concerns for both small and large employers. In a survey conducted by Roper Starch Worldwide for Liz Claiborne's Women's Work Program, 66 percent of senior executives from Fortune 1000 companies reported that they believed that addressing domestic violence among employees would ultimately benefit financial performance (Fisher, 1998). Considering that 11 percent of workplace homicides can be attributed to relatives or acquaintances (Sygnatur & Toscano, 2000), the issue should be taken seriously. Corporate America can also play a pivotal role in assisting local communities in prevention. We make the following recommendations.

1. *Practice violence prevention.* Employers should evaluate their prevention policies to protect their employees from abuse while on the job. The Occupational Safety and Health Act of 1970 (amended P.L. 1010-552) mandates that all employers have a duty to provide their employers with a workplace free from recognized hazards likely to cause injury or death (Occupational Safety and Health Administration [OSHA], 1998) and therefore have an obligation to protect their employees while they are at work.

Workplace violence raises two separate concerns. First, employers need to acknowledge the reality of family violence, with the understanding that their employees may be victims or perpetrators. Second, employers in out-of-home care facilities must protect their employees from abuse by their clients. According to OHSA, more assaults occur in the health care and social services industries than in any other industry in the United States, with the majority of nonfatal assaults occurring in out-of-home care environments such as nursing homes and residential facilities (OHSA, 1998). Employees, therefore, may be subject to violence in the workplace by a family or a pseudo family member, and employers have an obligation to ensure that work environments are as safe as possible.

The Occupational Safety and Health Administration (2002) recommends that employers craft a written company workplace violence policy. In addition, threat assessment teams should be created to assess vulnerability to workplace violence by reviewing records, performing security analyses that evaluate security around the facility and work station areas and that inventory security equipment needs, and developing protocols regarding incident reporting, investigation, follow-up, and evaluation.

Administrative and work practice controls and standard operating procedures should be initiated to prevent violence, including the development of emergency response plans. A list of resources in the community should be available to employees at all times. Employers should comply with all court orders, such as orders of protection and custody orders, and should develop procedures for keeping such orders on file. All employees should be trained in such protocols. Attention to staff-client ratios is especially important in certain work environments.

2. *Provide information and assistance to victims.* Employers should actively educate their employees regarding abuse and neglect and how to access assistance if needed. Protocols must be developed to encourage employees to report incidents and potential threats, and employees should be assured of confidentiality. In addition, staff members should be designated to receive training in abuse and neglect and to serve as confidential contacts for information, support, and referral to local intervention specialists. Linkages with employee assistance programs (EAP) should be made to ensure that victims receive the proper assistance.

Additionally, employers should be as flexible as possible with victims who need medical care, counseling, legal assistance, relocation, or changes in benefits or job location. Employees should be able to attend court appearances without penalty, minimizing pay loss whenever possible. Listening to employees' needs and supporting them to the extent possible will go a long way toward assisting employees in maintaining productivity and transforming their lives. Charlene Marmer Solomon (1995, p. 72), in an article to human resources professionals regarding the role of corporations in intimate partner violence, argues:

> A company, and an HR (Human Resources) Department, in conjunction with a corporate policy and caring people, can have a role in altering the life of a victim, of an employee. It isn't the role of a company to enable the confusion and trauma of the employee, but rather be aware of the struggle and transformation that she's undergoing.

3. *Develop family friendly policies.* Employers should develop employment policies that support the family. For example, instead of creating "sick care" slots for young children who are sick and cannot attend school, efforts should be made to develop policies that allow parents to stay home from work (without penalty) to care for their sick children. Family sick leave programs or personal days, offered by many employers, allow employees the opportunity to utilize earned time off to tend to family issues without question or sanctions. Other family-friendly policies might include day care or elder care on the premises, flexible time scheduling, outsourcing work to home, flexible benefits, and so forth.

Employers could provide information and referral to employees regarding parenting and elder care. Today, it is common for employers to offer a wide range of information and services to employees for health promotion, such as weight loss programs, fitness centers, nutrition courses, and so forth. This health promotion model should be expanded from self-care to include family care. Supporting employees in their roles as family members, whether they care for children or for their elderly parents, will ultimately assist employees in maintaining their employment and performance. For example,

Liz Claiborne, Inc., instituted a series of family-stress seminars to assist employees in managing their family stress. The seminars discuss healthy and dysfunctional family environments and how to relieve stress (Solomon, 1995).

4. *Pseudo family employers.* Employers in out-of-home care environments have a number of critical concerns regarding violence in the home. Like other employers, they need to understand the dynamics of family violence and have policies in place that prevent workplace violence by family members. However, health and social service agencies, particularly those that provide residential services, are at increased risk for workplace violence perpetrated by residents, whom we have referred to as *pseudo family* members. Out-of-home care employers must delicately balance the needs of residents to be able to live in homelike environments with the safety concerns of employees.

Staff training is a critical component in reducing abuse against employees by residents, as well as in guarding the safety of the residents against abuse by employees. Training should include progressive behavior control methods, safe use of restraints, use of safety devices, and skills to deal with hostile or aggressive residents (OSHA, 1998). We also recommend that training include information regarding the particular developmental, mental, or physical issues that face residents. Employees, particularly child-care workers and health care aides, may benefit from having a deeper understanding of the issues and struggles that face residents and the behavior patterns often associated with individuals who suffer from such illnesses or developmental problems (e.g., Alzheimer's disease, schizophrenia, profound mental retardation). Education, especially for new employees, may ultimately decrease employees' levels of frustration in caring for residents who exhibit behaviors that are hostile, demanding, aggressive, forgetful, and so forth. Employers need to recognize group dynamics in determining work assignments. Burnout should be avoided by careful attention to employees' needs and workload.

A balance must be struck, however, between creating a homelike environment for residents that reduces the impact of institutionalization and creating a workplace that promotes safety and protection for employees against violence. For example, it would be challenge to create a homelike living space with furniture that is fastened to the floor. We recommend that employers in out-of-home care facilities challenge the design industry to create living spaces that can accommodate the safety needs of facilities and the environmental needs of the residents.

5. *Protect customers from abuse.* Certain industries, such as banking and insurance industries, have a responsibility to protect their customers from abuse by institutions and family members. These industries must remain vigilant in identifying financial exploitation and fraud and must develop internal mechanisms to protect their clients. In addition, these industries

should review their policies to ensure that victims are not penalized or prevented from gaining products or services because they have been victimized.

6. *Be good neighbors.* Employers can contribute to the prevention of violence in the home through a number of charitable endeavors. Donating money, equipment, or staff resources to local or national prevention and intervention programs promotes the goals of prevention. Companies can donate funds, recruit employees to serve as program volunteers, serve on boards of directors or coordinating councils for local prevention and intervention agencies, donate equipment or supplies, and so forth. Employers should collaborate with other agencies and programs to promote these goals.

A number of companies around the United States are leading the charge to prevent violence in the home through a variety of venues. Companies have yet to embrace issues of child maltreatment and elder abuse among their employees, but some have begun to take on the issue of intimate partner violence. Marshall's department stores, Blue Shield of California, Polaroid, Verizon Wireless, and Liz Claiborne are five companies worthy of mention. Their leadership, industry skill, and philanthropic spirit are demonstrated in their ongoing commitment to prevent violence in the home.

Marshall's, an off-price family retailer with more than 500 stores nationwide, has initiated a "Shop 'Til It Stops" campaign. For the past 7 years, the company has designated 1 day a year on which a percentage of their sales proceeds are donated to efforts to stop domestic violence. In addition, the company, in partnership with the Family Violence Prevention Fund, supports other programs and provides employee education regarding domestic violence (Family Violence Prevention Fund [FVPF], 2000a)

Blue Shield of California, in partnership with the Family Violence Prevention Fund and with a grant from the Corporate Citizenship Initiative of the Hitachi Foundation, has embarked on a domestic violence education program in 10 states. The program partners domestic violence advocates with businesses to help the business community in reaching out to victims and in training others about domestic violence and the workplace (FVPF, 2002).

The Polaroid Corporation has been leading the way in violence prevention through the development of personnel policies and philanthropic activities. Corporate personnel policies promote safety and protection for employees. For example, flexible leave options are available for employees who need flexible work hours to handle legal matters, attend court hearings, and take care of housing and child care issues (Fisher, 1998). Employee assistance program staff members are well trained in family violence issues. The company has also donated financial resources to shelters and batterer treatment programs. Employees have been encouraged to volunteer their time at shelters, walkathons, and agency boards. In addition, in 1991, Polaroid began the Polaroid School of Law Enforcement Imaging, a training series that educates law enforcement officials in effective field and lab photography techniques. The company also developed a program called Healthcam that improves domestic violence injury documentation in hospitals by taking photographs that illustrate the extent of injuries. In addition, Polaroid has spurred on other corporations to get involved and has partnered with the Injury Control Center of Harvard School of Public Health to measure the effects of domestic violence on the workplace (Solomon, 1995).

Verizon Wireless, following in the tradition of Bell Atlantic Mobile, utilizes its industry skills to provide protection to victims of domestic violence. Wireless technology solutions have been used to assist victims of intimate partner violence. The company sponsors the HopeLine program, which provides free voice mail services to victims who are residing in shelters, and donates cellular phones (preprogrammed to call 911). It was the first carrier to introduce a free cellular link to the National Domestic Violence Hotline (Fisher, 1998). The company has distributed awareness cards and conducted a national poster campaign to educate other corporate leaders, coworkers, and victims about domestic violence (FVPF, 2000b). In addition, the company has continuously donated funds to local intervention efforts and has encouraged employees to get involved. For example, in December 2001, the company announced a $4,000 grant to the Orange County Child Abuse Prevention Center and a $5,000 grant to the Ventura County Elder Abuse Council in California (Verizon Wireless, 2001).

Liz Claiborne, Inc., has also provided corporate leadership in the fight against domestic violence. Through public service campaigns, media events, support of the Roper Starch Worldwide, Inc., study of corporate response to domestic violence, and corporate donations, Liz Claiborne serves as a role model for other corporations. In addition, the company has an active employee assistance program (Solomon, 1995).

Mass Media

The communications industry plays a significant role in our society. News and entertainment is accessible 24 hours a day, 7 days a week, via television, radio, print, and electronic media. Mass media, through a variety of venues, are responsible for informing the public on a wide range of social issues and in many ways for framing the ways in which we understand and respond to such information. Advancements in technology have changed the ways in which we experience events and social issues. For example, Americans watched in horror as Rodney King was beaten by Los Angeles police officers on the night of March 3, 1991, and were witnesses to the infamous O. J. Simpson car chase and subsequent criminal trial.

In addition, the mass marketing of the entertainment industry makes violence a central theme in many films, television shows, "reality" programs, and magazine shows. Contemporary music helps to shape our understanding of social relationships and interpersonal violence. Surette (1998) argues that the mass media are responsible for the "social construction of reality" while simultaneously serving as a reflection of the culture of the time. More important, through its unrelenting images of violence, especially violence against women, the media may actually be a causal factor in some violent crime.

At the same time, the media provide a venue for communicating pro-social messages through entertainment and public information campaigns. For example, programs such as *Mr. Rogers' Neighborhood* and *Sesame Street* on the Public Broadcasting System have demonstrated their ability to effect prosocial behaviors among child viewers (Surette, 1998). Although the long-term effects of such prosocial programming are uncertain, there appears to be some promise. Following the success of *Mr. Rogers' Neighborhood* and *Sesame Street*, the child entertainment industry has virtually exploded. To-day, a wide range of children's programming with prosocial messages is available for children of all ages. Several successful book series, such as *Clifford*, *Arthur*, and *Little Bear*, have successfully made the transition from print to the visual media. Other shows, such as *Barney*, *Comfy Couch*, *Dragon Tales*, and *Bob the Builder*, have enjoyed tremendous popularity among young children. Similarly, shows have been created to attract ado-lescents that explore more grown-up issues such as drug abuse, dating, friendships, and family life. In fact, entire television networks have evolved to meet the entertainment needs of the younger viewer, many of which make a conscientious effort to showcase programs that have prosocial messages. Repeat exposure, in a number of media forms, is likely to increase the long-term success of such prosocial programming in influencing child and youth development.

However, what has not occurred on a large scale is prosocial program-ming for adults. Issues regarding violence in the home have appeared on numerous contemporary shows, such as *Family Law, Law and Order*, and *ER*, as well as in such news magazine shows as *20/20, Dateline*, and *48 Hours*; yet episodes tend to stop short of modeling healthy family interaction. We appear to have a fascination with the dysfunctional (the popularity of Jerry Springer and similar shows certainly proves this point); therefore, the chal-lenge exists for the entertainment industry to develop shows that can model prosocial behaviors for healthy family functioning.

The media should also contribute to the prevention of violence in the home through public information campaigns. Drunk driving, environmental protection, smoking cessation, and heart disease and cancer prevention cam-paigns are just a few examples of public health campaigns that have suc-cessfully imparted critical information to the public and called for behavior change. The key to success seems to lie in the utilization of advertising tactics in message development. Marissa Ghez (1995) outlines the strategies that have made public education campaigns successful in the past. These include crafting simple, brief messages that are action oriented, that fully understand the attitudes and beliefs of the message consumers, that utilize personal stories to send home the message (much like product testimonials), and that showcase the benefits of behavior change or communicate the consequences of not altering behavior. In addition, messages that are repeated over and over are likely to have significant impact on the behavior of the public (Rushton, 1982).

Given the influential role of the media in contemporary society, the entertainment, advertising, and news industries are positively positioned to contribute to the prevention of violence in the home. We believe that individuals in these industries have a social obligation to utilize their skills, talent, creativity, and social position to promote social change. In fact, it would be virtually impossible to transmit primary prevention messages without affiliation with the mass media.

///   The Role of Technology in Prevention

Technology has transformed the criminal justice industry in a number of important ways. Emerging technology and advancements in science have improved the investigatory power of the police, secured ample physical evidence for prosecutors, and provided new methods for monitoring and supervising offender behavior. Innovations in computer applications, forensic techniques, simulated training tools, surveillance and security equipment, DNA profiling, fingerprint analysis, and electronic monitoring devices are a few examples of the types of crime fighting tools at the disposal of police, courts, and corrections agencies. In addition, advancements in electronic media provide an additional venue in which prevention messages and information about abuse and neglect can be communicated to the public.

Technology is applied to investigate and document incidences of violence in the home. Today, technology aids in the protection of victims and the apprehension of offenders. Here we briefly discuss how technology is being applied to prevent acts of violence in the home. We provide examples of victim protection applications, crime documentation and investigatory tools, offender monitoring, and public education.

Victim Protection

Technology is being used to enhance the safety of identified victims of violence. Usually provided to families in which a violent offender has been identified, technology is applied to help victims gain immediate contact with authorities. A survey conducted by Bostaph, Hamilton, and Santana (2000) found that 84 percent of the domestic violence programs that responded to the survey indicated that they currently use some form of technology to protect battered women. The most frequently cited types of technologies used were cellular phones, surveillance cameras at shelters or safe houses, and portable panic alarms. Results also indicated that many programs applied the technology with clients who met particular eligibility requirements, for example, that the women remain in contact with the service provider. Many of the domestic programs also reported that they utilize technology in coordination with local law enforcement officials. Those programs that did not use such technology reported that lack of funding or lack of technology availability in their service areas excluded participation in such technology-based programming.

Cellular Phones

Preprogrammed cellular phones (set to dial 911) are provided to victims to ensure that they have access to the authorities at all times, especially in the case of intimate partner violence. Because many victims are isolated from friends and family, the preprogrammed phones afford potential victims a degree of comfort in knowing that the police can be summoned at any time. A national campaign is currently under way to put more cellular phones in the hands of potential victims. Community members are encouraged to donate their old cellular phones to this cause. Sponsored by the Cellular Telecommunication Industry Association and the National Coalition Against Domestic Violence (NCADV), the Wireless Foundation coordinates this national effort, titled "Call to Protect" (Wireless Foundation, 2001). In addition to the donated phones, wireless companies donate airtime to victims and victim advocacy groups.

Pagers

Pagers may also be given to victims to keep them in contact with local authorities. For example, the Domestic Violence Enhanced Response Team (DVERT) of the Colorado Springs Police Department in Colorado Springs, Colorado, distributes pagers to victims who need to have immediate contact with authorities regarding trial proceedings or who are awaiting notification of an offender's release from custody (DVERT, 2002).

Panic Alarms

Panic alarms provide another method of victim protection. Panic alarms are particularly helpful for victims in rural communities where cellular phones are unable to be accessed, in workplaces where victims can immediately summon security, or for homebound elderly or disabled people. With a touch of a button, alarms can be sounded to call authorities. Personal panic alarms can be installed in the home and are also available on wrist straps or as pendants.

Electronic Monitoring Systems

Advancements in electronic monitoring systems now provide the ability to monitor an offender's location in proximity to his victim. For example, Strategic Technologies, Inc. (Strategic Technologies, 2002), markets a curfew monitoring system to serve as a strategic domestic violence deterrent. The system provides the traditional electronic monitoring devices that are used by probation and parole officials to monitor offenders' compliance with curfews, extending the benefits to protect victims of family violence. Offenders with court restraining orders can be given a transmitter called an Offender Identification Unit. The victim is given a complimentary receiver unit. If the offender should come within a designated range of the victim's home (typically 400 feet), a violation signal is sent to a central computer that sounds a priority alarm. Because domestic violence cases can be flagged with this particular system, the proper authorities can be immediately dispatched (Strategic Technologies, 2002).

Crime Investigation and Documentation

A number of technological innovations, coupled with more old-fashioned security measures, are directed toward the documentation of abusive behavior to help in the investigation and prosecution process. Surveillance equipment, evidence collection, and the utilization of computer-based information systems have revolutionized the police industry.

Surveillance Equipment

A number of products are used to document offender behavior to aid in investigating and prosecuting family offenses. Equipment such as cameras, phone traps, caller IDs, phone bugs, and tracking systems are used by security companies, police departments, and individual citizens.

Surveillance cameras, used by hospitals, out-of-home care facilities, employers, and private residences, can provide video documentation of both an offender's behavior and location. Telephone technology also provides documentation of contact. Caller ID technology and phone bugs (wiretapping) are employed to document an offender's use of the telephone to call and threaten victims.

Global Positioning Systems (GPS) are used to locate victims in need and to track the whereabouts of offenders. For example, the Metropolitan Police Department in Nashville, Tennessee, employs a GPS tracking system called "The Shadow." Police officials attach the GPS tracker to offenders' vehicles after a court restraining order has been issued or when the vehicle is located in a public space. The vehicle's movements can then be monitored by police, providing documentation that an individual is in fact stalking a victim (Littel, Malefyt, Walker, Tucker, & Buel, 1998).

Evidence Collection

Protocols regarding proper evidence collection have been well established in policing for many years; however, applying evidence collection techniques to crimes within the family is a relatively new phenomenon. Forensic evidence, as secured through the gathering of fingerprints, body fluids, and fibers, as well as by photographing the scene and the victim's injuries, has become more commonplace in the investigation of family violence cases. For example, the Seattle Police Department in Seattle, Washington, has developed a domestic violence unit, in which officers collect necessary evidence under the assumption that some victims will not be available to testify at trial. Each patrol sergeant is provided with a camera to document injuries and to photograph the crime scene (Littel et al., 1998). Physical evidence collection will enhance the ability of prosecutors to achieve convictions in family-related crimes.

Computer and Information Systems

Information systems, computer-aided investigation software, and electronic databases are invaluable tools in the investigative process. They allow police officers the opportunity to access information regarding suspects, criminal history, active court orders, outstanding warrants, and so forth. Because many patrol cars are now equipped with computers, information regarding suspects can be retrieved in a manner of minutes. Patrol officers arrive on the scene of a family violence call with more background information. For example, in Duluth, Minnesota, the Duluth Police Department participates in the Domestic Abuse Information Network (DAIN), which shares information from incident, arrest, and investigative reports, warrant requests, and 911 watch reports. Information is shared with other criminal justice agencies (Littel et al., 1998).

Computer-aided dispatch (CAD) systems allow patrol officers to be notified when calls for service come in from homes in which repetitive violence has occurred. For example, the Colorado Springs Police Department places a "hazard alert" on both victims' and perpetrators' addresses. When patrol officers arrive at the tagged address, the DVERT team is sent into action (Littel et al., 1998). These systems will enhance victim and officer protection and offender accountability.

In addition, electronic databases, crime analysis software, and electronic filing systems provide practitioners with the ability to store, retrieve, and query information systems for improved accuracy and efficacy. For example, court orders can be placed in an electronic database and, if updated regularly, can provide practitioners with instant verification that a court order is in full force.

Family Violence Prevention Online

The World Wide Web is also becoming a prominent tool for communicating with the public regarding family violence. Primary prevention education is available online from virtually hundreds, if not thousands, of Web addresses. Police departments, government agencies, intervention specialists, victim advocate agencies, volunteer organizations, and so forth have dedicated Web pages to distribute information regarding violence in the home. Current Web sites provide a wealth of information for access by professionals, students, and the general public.

Web resources include the following types of information:

- Information about violence in the home, including types of abuse, warning signs, statistics, types of services available, and so forth.
- How and where to access local services.
- What to do if you or someone you know is being abused.
- What to do if you are an abuser.
- Updates on recent research findings.
- Government documents and other publications.
- Discussion groups.
- Databases and statistical data.
- Links to agenciesgovernment agencies, law enforcement, and so forth.
- Electronic mail addresses for contacting experts in the field.
- Participation in electronic survey research projects.
- Links to other Web resources.

Online communication will change the nature of violence prevention and education in the future. Getting information into the hands of a multidisciplinary range of practitioners, business leaders, public policy makers, school officials, the faith community, and the general public has never been easier. In addition, the multiple dimensions of Web technology will improve the multimedia formats available to transmit information, for example, through video, interactive television, videoconferencing, use of sight and sound, and so forth, in the future for little cost. We have provided numerous online resources throughout this book in an effort to provide you with access to additional information. We encourage you to "surf the Web." Be aware, though, that Web sites do come and go and that they can be developed by anyone. We have chosen Web addresses that we believe are stable and credible, and that can link you to additional resources. The future of violence prevention lies in our ability to communicate the issues, and online communication can certainly promote current efforts.

/// Chapter Summary

Building on the discussion in the previous chapter, this chapter addressed prevention by examining systemic issues, prevention ideology, the roles of various professional groups in prevention and education, and the role of technology in intervention and education. Implications for practitioners and professional practice were explored. Special emphasis was given to professional groups that are not typically considered family violence intervention specialists.

We began our discussion of prevention by highlighting systemic issues. We examined the following issues: a fragmented system of intervention that has evolved to respond to a discrete set of problems, a system that focuses on abuse and neglect after such acts have already occurred, services that focus on the pathology of families, the role of professional conflict in the delivery of services, and the need for more rigorous evaluation of policy choices and treatment methods.

Next, we reviewed prevention ideology, exploring the different levels of prevention and several types of prevention models. We also discussed the lessons learned from other, similar prevention efforts. We considered how educators, public policy makers, employers, and the mass media can specifically contribute to the prevention of violence in the home. We provided ample examples of how these professional groups can and do take responsibility for promoting social change. We applaud their efforts.

The chapter concluded with a discussion of the role of technology in abuse and neglect prevention. Here we explored the numerous ways in which modern technology is being applied to provide improved victim protection and to enhance the investigatory power of the police and how the future of violence prevention may be found online.

/// A Final Message

Family violence tends to be a hidden phenomenon, yet the responsibility for preventing violence may very well lie with all of us. As members of communities, neighborhoods, corporations, faith groups, and families, we all have a responsibility to ensure that abuse and neglect is not tolerated. Obviously, there are no simple answers. However, together we can build strong families. We must work to change the forces and circumstances that place families at risk for abuse or neglect. We should encourage family members to love and nurture each other and work to ensure that their basic needs can be met. We must argue for policies that embrace the importance of positive family experiences and search for instruction on how to be better members of our own families. To those readers who currently work with abusive families or have plans to in the future: We applaud you! We hope that you approach your positions with enthusiasm, dedication, and under-standing. Regardless of your professional discipline, embrace the long-term success of your efforts.

We offer some suggestions for professional practice:

- Continue to educate yourself. Attend professional conferences, read research publications, and network with other professionals.
- Support the evaluation of policy choices and treatment approaches.
- Dare to remove systemic barriers.
- Take time to care for yourself and your own family.
- Practice ethical behavior.

For those readers who are not likely to work professionally with the issues explored in this text, we challenge you to get involved, whether or not you make a professional contribution. We offer some suggestions:

- Donate money or goods to programs that serve families.
- Be an active participant in the discourse on public policy.
- Support the families in your life.
- Become a mentor for a child or a young parent.
- Visit out-of-home care facilities to brighten the lives of residents.
- Become a foster parent for a child or adult.
- Volunteer your time.
- Continue to educate yourself about the issues.
- Become educated about the policies, programs, and services in your community.
- Encourage your neighbors to become educated about the issues.
- Celebrate diversity, yet seek common ground.
- Treat all community members with mutual respect and realize that all individuals and families have strengths and worth.

/// References

/// Chapter 1

Alsdurf, J. M. (1985). Wife abuse and the church: The response of pastors. *Response to the Victimization of Women and Children*, 8(1), 9–11.

Asser, S. M., & Swan, R. (1998). Child fatalities from religion-motivated medical neglect. *Pediatrics*, *1001*, 625–629.

Associated Press. (2002, February 14). Utah, Colorado, New York groups campaign against religion-cloaked abuse.

Bottoms, B. L., Shaver, P. R., Goodman, G. S., & Qin, J. (1995). In the name of God: A profile of religion-related child abuse. *Journal of Social Issues*, *51*(2), 85–111.

Boyle, E. H., Songora, F., & Foss, G. (2001). International discourse and local politics: Anti-female-genital-cutting laws in Egypt, Tanzania, and the United States. *Social Problems*, *48*(4), 524–544.

Brownell, P. (1997.) The application of the Culturagram in cross-cultural practice with elder abuse victims. *Journal of Elder Abuse and Neglect*, 9, 19 33.

Bui, H. N., & Morash, M. (1999). Domestic violence in the Vietnamese immigrant community: An exploratory study. *Violence Against Women*, *5*(7), 769–795.

Cart, J. (2001, September 9). Utah paying a high price for polygamy. *Los Angeles Times*, part A, part 1, p. 1.

Children's Healthcare Is a Legal Duty. (2002). Retrieved from www.childrenshealth care.org, Feb. 13, 2002.

Congress, E. P. (1994). The use of Culturagrams to assess and empower culturally diverse families. *Families in Society*, 75, 531–540. Department of Defense Omnibus Appropriations Bill, Pub. L. No. 104-208, 110 Stat. 3009-3708 (1996).

Finkelhor, D. (1984). Child sexual abuse: New theory and research. New York: Free Press.

Finkelhor, D., Gelles, R. J., Hotaling, G. T., & Straus, M. A. (1983). The dark side of families. Beverly Hills, CA: Sage.

Gelles, R. J. (1997). *Intimate violence in families*. Thousand Oaks, CA: Sage.

Gelles, R. J., & Straus, M. A. (1979). Determinants of violence in the family: Toward a theoretical integration. In W. R. Burr, R. Hill, F. I., Nye, & I. L. Reiss (Eds.),

Contemporary theories about the family (Vol. 1, pp. 549–581). New York: Free Press.

Greven, P. (1991). *Spare the child: The religious roots of punishment and the psychological impact of physical abuse.* New York: Knopf.

Kim, J. Y., & Sung, K. (2000). Conjugal violence in Korean American families: A residue of cultural tradition. *Journal of Family Violence, 15*(4), 331–345.

Kirhofer Hansen, K. (1997). Folk remedies and child abuse: A review with emphasis on Caida De Mollera and its relationship to Shaken Baby Syndrome. *Child Abuse and Neglect, 22*(2), 117–127.

Lalich, J. (1997). Dominance and submission: The psychosexual exploitation of women in cults. *Cultic Studies Journal, 14,* 4–21.

Lasker, R. D. (1997). *Medicine and public health: The power of collaboration.* New York: The New York Academy of Medicine.

Markward, M., Dozier, C., & Hooks, K. (2000). Culture and the intergenerational transmission of substance abuse, women abuse, and child abuse: A diathesis-stress perspective. *Children and Youth Services Review, 22*(3/4), 237–250.

Nason-Clark, N. (1997). *The battered wife: How Christians confront family violence.* Louisville, KY: Westminster John Knox Press.

Pagelow, M. D. (1984). *Family violence.* New York: Praeger.

Renzetti, C. M. (1997). Violence and abuse among same-sex couples. In A. P. Cardarelli (Ed.), *Violence between intimate partners: Patterns, causes and effects* (pp. 70–89). Boston: Allyn & Bacon.

Roberts, A. R. (2002). Duration and severity of women battering: A conceptual model/continuum. In A. R. Roberts (Ed.), *Handbook on intervention strategies with domestic violence: Policies, programs, and legal remedies* (pp. 64–79). New York: Oxford University Press.

Rush, G. E. (2000). *The dictionary of criminal justice.* Guilford, CT: Dushkin/McGraw-Hill.

Schwartz, L. L., & Kaslow, F. W. (2001). The cult phenomenon: A turn of the century update. *American Journal of Family Therapy, 29,* 13–22.

Simpson, W. (1989). Comparative longevity in a college cohort of Christian Scientists. *Journal of the American Medical Association, 262,* 1657–1658.

Simpson, W. (1991). Comparative mortality in two college groups. *Mortality and Morbidity Weekly Report, 40,* 579–582.

Straus, M. A., & Gelles, R. J. (2001). Societal change and change in family violence from 1975 to 1985 as revealed by two national surveys. In H. M. Eigenberg (Ed.), *Women battering in the United States: Till death do us part* (pp. 113–128). Prospect Heights, IL: Waveland Press.

Straus, M. A., & Hotaling, G. T. (1979). *The social causes of husband-wife violence.* Minneapolis: University of Minnesota Press.

World Health Organization. (1996). *Female genital mutilation: Information Pack.* Retrieved from www.who.int/frh-whd/FGM/infopack/English/fgm_infopack.htm, Feb. 20, 2002.

/// Chapter 2

Bandura, A. (1973). *Aggression: A social learning analysis.* Englewood Cliffs, NJ: Prentice-Hall.

Belsky, J. (1980). Child maltreatment: An ecological integration. *American Psychologist, 35,* 320–335.

Berglas, S. (1998). The ties that blind. *Inc., 20*(1), 29.

Berrien, F. K. (1968). *General and social systems.* New Brunswick, NJ: Rutgers University Press.

Berry, D. B. (1995). *Domestic violence sourcebook: Everything you need to know.* Los Angeles, CA: Lowell House.

Bersani, C. A., & Chen, H. T. (1988). Sociological perspectives in family violence. In V. B. Van Hasselt, R. L. Morrison, A. S. Bellack, & M. Hersen (Eds.), *Handbook of family violence. II: Theoretical models* (pp. 57–85). New York: Plenum Press.

Browne, K., & Herbert, M. (1997). Causes of family violence. In Kevin D. Browne & Martin Herbert (Eds.), *Preventing family violence* (pp. 23–40). Chichester, England: Wiley.

Carderelli, A. P. (1997). Violence and intimacy: An overview. In A. P. Carderelli (Ed.), *Violence between intimate partners: Patterns, causes, and effects* (pp. 2–9). Needham Heights, MA: Allyn & Bacon.

Daly, M., & Wilson, M. I. (1981). Abuse and neglect of children in evolutionary perspective. In R. Alexander & D. Tinkle (Eds.), *Natural selection and social behavior: Recent research and new theory* (pp. 405–416). New York: Chiron.

deYoung, M. (1992). Traumatic bonding: Clinical implications in incest. *Child Welfare 71*(2), 165–175.

Dobash, E., & Dobash, R. P. (1978). Wives: The appropriate victims of marital violence. *Victimology, 2,* 426–439.

Dutton, D. G., & Painter, S. L. (1981). Traumatic bonding: The development of emotional attachments in battered women and other relationships of intermittent abuse. *Victimology, 6*(1-2), 139–155.

Fagan, J. A., Stewart, D. K., & Hanson, K. V. (1983). Violent men or violent husbands? Background factors and situational correlates. In D. Finkelhor, R .J. Gelles, G. T. Hotaling, & M. A. Straus (Eds.), *The dark side of families,* Beverly Hills, CA: Sage.

Finkelhor, D. (1983). Common features in family abuse. In D. Finkelhor, R. J. Gelles, G. T. Hotaling, & M. A. Straus (Eds.), *The dark side of families* (pp. 17–18). Beverly Hills, CA: Sage.

Friedrich, W., & Boriskin, J. A. (1976). The role of the child in abuse: A review of the literature. *American Journal of Orthopsychiatry, 46*(4), 580–590.

Garbarino, J. (1977). The human ecology of child maltreatment: A conceptual model for research. *Journal of Marriage and the Family, 39,* 721–735.

Gelles, R. J. (1979). Etiology of violence: Overcoming fallacious reasoning in understanding family violence and child abuse. In R. J. Gelles (Ed.), *Family violence.* Thousand Oaks, CA: Sage.

Gelles, R. J. (1993). Family violence. In R. L. Hampton, T. Gullotta, G. Adams, E. H. Potter III, & R. P. Weissberg (Eds.), *Family violence: Prevention and treatment.* Newbury Park, CA: Sage.

Gelles, R. J. (1997). *Intimate violence in families* (3rd ed.). Thousand Oaks, CA: Sage.

Gelles, R. J., & Straus, M. A. (1988). *Intimate violence,* New York: Simon & Schuster.

Giles-Sims, J. (1983). Wife battery: A systems theory approach. New York: Guilford Press.

Goode, W. (1971, November). Force and violence in the family. *Journal of Marriage and the Family, 33,* 624–635.

Hampton, R. L., Jenkins, P., & Gullotta, T. P. (1996). Understanding the social context of violent behavior in families: Selected perspectives. In R. L. Hampton, P. Jenkins, & T. P. Gullotta (Eds.), *Preventing violence in America* (pp. 13–31). Thousand Oaks, CA: Sage.

Homans, G. C. (1961). *Social behavior: Its elementary forms.* New York: Harcourt Brace.

Justice, B., & Justice, R. (1990). *The abusing family.* New York: Plenum Press.

Kalmuss, D. S. (1984). The intergenerational transmission of marital aggression. *Journal of Marriage and the Family, 46,* 11–19.

Kemp, A. (1998). *Abuse in the family: An introduction.* Pacific Grove, CA: Brooks/ Cole.

Malkin, C. M., & Lamb, M. E. (1994). Child maltreatment: A test of sociobiological theory. *Journal of Comparative Family Studies, 25*(1), 121–134.

McCue, M. L. (1995). *Domestic violence.* Santa Barbara, CA: ABC-CLIO.

Merton, R. (1967). *On theoretical sociology.* New York: The Free Press.

Mihalic, S. W., & Elliott, D. (1997). A social learning theory of marital violence. *Journal of Family Violence, 12*(1), 21–47.

O'Leary, K. D. (1988). Physical aggression between spouses: A social learning theory perspective. In V. B. Van Hasselt, R. L. Morrison, A. S. Bellack, & M. Hersen (Eds.), *Handbook of family violence* (pp. 31–56). New York: Plenum Press.

Pagelow, M. D. (1984). *Family violence.* New York: Praeger.

Phillipson, C. (1997). Abuse of older people: Sociological perspectives. In P. Decalmer & F. Glendenning (Eds.), *The mistreatment of the elderly* (pp. 102–115). Thousand Oaks, CA: Sage.

Powers, R. J. (1986). Aggression and violence in the family. In A. Campbell & J. Gibbs (Eds.), *Violent transactions* (pp. 225-248). Oxford, England: Blackwell.

Radbill, S. X. (1987). Children in a world of violence: A history of child abuse. In R. E. Helfer & R. S. Kempe (Eds.), *The battered child* (4th ed., pp. 3–20). Chicago: University of Chicago Press

Reiss, A. J., Jr., & Roth, J. A. (1993). Violence in families. In A. J. Reiss, Jr., & J. A. Roth (Eds.), *Understanding and preventing violence* (pp. 221–254). Washington, DC: National Academy Press.

Retzinger, S. (1991). *Violent emotions: Shame and rage in marital quarrels.* Newbury Park, CA: Sage.

Roberts, A. R. (1996). Introduction: Myths and realities regarding battered women. In A. R. Roberts (Ed.), *Helping battered women: New perspectives and remedies* (pp. 3–12). New York: Oxford University Press.

Roy, M. (1977). *Battered women: A psychological study of domestic violence.* New York: Van Nostrand Reinhold.

Schneider, E. (1994). The violence of privacy. In M. Fineman, M. A. Albertson, & R. Mykitiuk (Eds.), *The public nature of private violence: The discovery of domestic abuse* (pp. 36–58). New York: Routledge.

Sigler, R. T. (1989). *Domestic violence in context: An assessment of community attitudes.* Lexington MA: Lexington Books.

Skolnick A., & Skolnick, J. (1977). *The family in transition.* Boston: Little, Brown.

Steinmetz, S. K. (1977). *The cycle of violence: Assertive, aggressive and abusive family interaction.* New York: Praeger.

Straus, M. (1973). A general system theory approach of violence between family members. *Social Science Information, 12*(3), 105–125.

Straus, M. A. (1990). Ordinary violence, child abuse and wife beating: What do they have in common? In M. A. Straus & R. J. Gelles, *Physical violence in American families: Risk factors and adaptions to violence in 8,145 families.* New Brunswick, NJ: Transaction.

Straus, M. A., Gelles, R. J., & Steinmetz, S. K. (1980). *Behind closed doors: Violence in the American family.* Garden City, NY: Anchor Press-Doubleday.

Viano, E. (1992). Violence among intimates: Major issues and approaches. *Intimate violence: Interdisciplinary perspectives* (pp. 3–10). Washington, DC: Hemisphere.

Walker, L. E. (1984). *The battered women syndrome.* New York: Springer.

/// Chapter 3

Aber, J. L., & Allen, J. P. (1987). The effects of maltreatment on young children's socioemotional development: An attachment theory perspective. *Developmental Psychology, 23,* 406–414.

Administration for Children and Families. (2002). National child abuse and neglect data system (NCANDS). Retrieved June 29, 1999, from United States Department of Health and Human Services, Children's Bureau, Administration on Children, Youth, and Families Web site: www.calib.com/nccanch/pubs/factsheets/canstats.cfm.

American Psychiatric Association. (1994). *Diagnostic and statistical manual of mental disorders* (4th ed.). Washington, DC: Author.

Aries, P. (1962). *Centuries of childhood: A social history of family life* (R. Baldick, Trans.) New York: Knopf.

Arizona Department of Health Services. (2001, November). Arizona Child Fatality Review Team Eighth Annual Report. Retrieved Oct. 12, 2002, from www.hs.state.az.us/cfhs/azcf/index.htm.

Bagley, C. (1992). Development of an adolescent stress scale for use of school counsellors. *School Psychology International, 13,* 31–49.

Berlinger, L., & Barbieri, M. K. (1984). The testimony of the child victim of sexual abuse. *Journal of Social Issues, 40*(2), 125–137.

Bjorklund, D. F., & Bjorklund, B.R. (1992). *Looking at children: An introduction to child development.* Pacific Grove, CA: Brooks/Cole.

Bolger, K. E., Patterson, C. J., & Kupersmidt, J. B. (1998). Peer relationships and self-esteem among children who have been maltreated. *Child Development, 69*(4), 1171–1197.

Brown, R., Coles, C. D., Smith, I. E., Platzman, K. A., Silverstein, J., Erickson, S., & Falek, A. (1991). Effects of prenatal alcohol exposure at school age. *Neurotoxicology and Teratology, 13,* 369–376.

Charlesworth, R. (1992). *Understanding child development* (3rd ed.). Albany, NY: Delmar.

Courtois, C. A., & Watts, D. L. (1982, January). Counseling adult women who experience incest in childhood or adolescence. *Personnel and Guidance Journal, 60,* 275–279.

Cyan, J. R. (1987). The banning of corporal punishment: In child care, school and other educative settings in the U.S. *Childhood Education, 63*, 146–153.

DeMause, L. (1976). *The history of childhood.* London: Souvenir.

Dorozyaski, A. (1993). Grapes of wrath: Maternal alcoholism. *Psychology Today, 26*, 18–25.

Dubin, J. M. (1999). Constitutional law: Fourth Circuit upholds cocaine testing of pregnant women. *Journal of Law, Medicine and Ethics, 27*(3), 279–281.

Dubowitz, H. (1994). Neglecting the neglect of neglect. *Journal of Interpersonal Violence, 9*(4), 556–560.

Faulkner, N. (1996, October). Pandora's box: The secrecy of child sexual abuse [Electronic version]. *Sexual Counseling Digest.* Retrieved Sept. 22, 1999.

Ferguson v. Charleston, 186 F.3d 469 (4th Cir. 1999).

Gelles, R. (1997). Violence between intimates: Historical legacy—contemporary approval. In R. J. Gelles (Ed.), *Intimate violence in families* (pp. 123–140). Thousand Oaks, CA: Sage.

Graves, R. B., Openshaw, K. D., & Ascione, F. R. (1996, December). Demographic and parental characteristics of youthful sexual offenders. *International Journal of Offender Therapy and Comparative Criminology, 40*, 300–317.

Groth, A. N., Hobson, W. F. & Gary, T. S. (1982). The child molester: Clinical observations. In J. R. Conte & D. A. Shore (Eds.), *Social work and child sexual abusers* (pp. 129–144). New York: Haworth Press.

Houston-Harris County Child Fatality Review Team. (2002). Retrieved Oct. 12, 2002, from www.hd.co.harris.tx.us/opa/child_fatalit_review_team/home.

James, A. C., & Neil, P. (1996, June). Juvenile sexual offending: One-year period prevalence study within Oxfordshire. *Child Abuse and Neglect, 20*, 477–485.

Join Together Online. (1999, June). *Pregnant addicted women fear substance abuse treatment.* Retrieved July 26, 1999, from http://www.jointogether.org/sa/news/summaries/reader/0,1854,259135,00.html.

Jones, D. P. (1991). Ritualism and child sexual abuse. *Child Abuse and Neglect, 15*, 163–169.

Karr-Morse, R., & Wiley, M. S. (1997). *Ghosts from the nursery: Tracing the roots of violence.* New York: Atlantic Monthly Press.

Kemp, A. (1998). *Abuse in the family: An introduction.* Pacific Grove, CA: Brooks Cole.

Kempe, H. C. (1962, July). The Battered-Child Syndrome. *Journal of the American Medical Association, 181*(1), 17–24.

Lee, J. K., Jackson, H. J., Pattison, P., & Ward, T. (2002). Developmental risk factors for sexual offending. *Child Abuse and Neglect, 26*(1), 73–92.

Lefrancois, G. R. (1992). *Of children: An introduction to child development* (7th ed.). Belmont, CA: Wadsworth.

Libow, J. A., & Schreier, H. A. (1986). Three forms of factitious illness in children: When is it Munchausen syndrome by proxy? *American Journal of Orthopsychiatry, 56*(4), 602–611.

Lowenthal, B. (1999). Effects of maltreatment and ways to promote children's resiliency. *Childhood Education, 75*(4), 204–209.

Lyman, M. D., & Potter, G. W. (1998). *Drugs in society: Causes, concepts and control.* Cincinnati, OH: Anderson.

Lyons-Ruth, K., Connell, D. B., & Zoll, D. (1989). Patterns of maternal behavior among infants at risk for abuse: Relations with infant attachment behavior and infant development at 12 months of age. In D. Cicchetti & V. Carlson (Eds.), *Child maltreatment: Theory and research on the causes and consequences of child abuse and neglect* (pp. 464–493). New York: Cambridge University Press.

Meadow, R. (1977). Munchausen syndrome by proxy: The hinterland of child abuse. *Lancet, 2*, 343–345.

Morton, N., & Browne, K. D. (1998). Theory and observation of attachment and its relation to child maltreatment: A review. *Child Abuse and Neglect: The International Journal, 22*(11), 1093–1104.

National Center on Child Abuse and Neglect. (1994). *Child maltreatment 1992: Reports from the states to the National Center on Child Abuse and Neglect.* Washington, DC: U.S. Government Printing Office.

National Clearinghouse on Child Abuse and Neglect Information. (1999). *What is child maltreatment?* Retrieved June 29, 1999, from http://www.calib.com/nccanch/prevmnth/scope/childmal.cfm.

National Organization on Fetal Alcohol Syndrome (NOFAS) (1999). What is fetal alcohol syndrome? Retrieved Oct. 12, 2002, from http://www.nofas.org.

Nelson, B. J. (1984). *Making an issue of child abuse: Political agenda setting for social problems.* Chicago: University of Chicago Press.

Ontario Consultants on Religious Tolerance. (1999). Corporal punishment of children: Spanking. Retrieved from http://www.religioustolerance.org/spanking.htm.

Parks, K. (1998, Winter). Protecting the fetus: The criminalization of prenatal drug use. *William and Mary Journal of Women and the Law, 5*, 245.

Pasqualone, G. A., & Fitzgerald, S. M. (1999). Munchausen by proxy syndrome: The forensic challenge of recognition, diagnosis, and reporting. *Critical Care Nursing Quarterly, 22*(1), 1–52.

Peacock, A., & Forrest, D. (1985). Long term effects of nonorganic failure to thrive. *Pediatrics, 75*, 36–40.

Perrin, J., Theodore, A. D., & Runyan, D. K. (1999). A medical research agenda for child maltreatment: Negotiating the next steps. *Journal of the Ambulatory Pediatric Association, 104*, 168–177.

Plumb, J. H. (1972). Children, the victims of time. In J. H. Plumb (Ed.), *In the light of history* (pp. 153–165). London: Penguin.

Rathgeb Smith, S., & Freinkel, S. (1988). Adjusting the balance: Federal policy and victim services. New York: Greenwood.

Ryan, G., Miyoshi, T. J., & Metzner, J. L. (1996, January). Trends in a national sample of sexually abusive youths. *Journal of the American Academy of Child and Adolescent Psychiatry, 35*, 17–25.

Sagatun, I. J., & Edwards, L. P. (1995). *Child abuse and the legal system.* Chicago: Nelson-Hall.

Schoendorf, K. C., & Kiely, J. L. (1992). Relationship of Sudden Infant Death Syndrome to maternal smoking during and after pregnancy. *Pediatrics, 90*(6), 905–908.

Schreier, H. A. (1992). The perversion of mothering: Munchausen syndrome by proxy. *Bulletin of the Menninger Clinic, 56*(4), 421–437.

Schreier, H. A., & Libow, J. (1993). Munchausen syndrome by proxy: Diagnosis and prevalence. *American Journal of Orthopsychiatry, 63*(2), 318–321.

Sedlak, A. J., & Broadhurst, D. D. (1996). *Executive summary of the third National Incidence Study of child abuse and neglect.* Retrieved June 29, 1999, from U.S. Department of Health and Human Services, Administration for Children and Families, National Clearinghouse on Child Abuse and Neglect Information Web site: http://www.calib.com/nccanch/pubs/statinfo/nis3.cfm.

Smith, K., & Killam, P. (1994). Munchausen syndrome. *American Journal of Maternal Child Nursing, 19,* 214–221.

Straus, M. A. (1994). *Beating the devil out of them: Corporal punishment in American families.* San Francisco: Jossey-Bass/Lexington Books.

Straus, M. A., & Paschall, M. J. (1998, August). *Corporal punishment by mothers and child's cognitive development: A longitudinal study.* Durham, NH: University of New Hampshire, Family Research Laboratory.

Southall, D. P., Plunkett, M. B., Banks, M. W., Falkov, A. F., & Samuels, M. P. (1997). Covert video surveillance for life-threatening child abuse: Lessons for child protection. *Pediatrics, 100,* 735–760.

Terr, L. (1990). *Too scared to cry: Psychic trauma in childhood.* New York: Harper & Row.

Terr, L. (1991). Childhood traumas: An outline and overview. *American Journal of Psychiatry, 148,* 10–20.

Texas Department of Health. (1999). Child fatality review teams: Biennial report, 1998-1999. Retrieved Oct. 12, 2002, from www.tdh.state.tx.us/bvs/reports/99chfat/99chfat.htm.

Trickett, P. K., & Putnam, F. W. (1991, August). *Patterns of symptoms in prepubertal and pubertal sexually abused girls.* Paper presented at the annual meeting of the American Psychological Association, San Francisco, CA.

U.S. Advisory Board on Child Abuse and Neglect. (1995). *A nation's shame: Fatal child abuse and neglect in the United States.* Washington, DC: U.S. Department of Health and Human Services.

U.S. Department of Health and Human Services. (1994). *Preventing tobacco use among young people: A report of the Surgeon General.* Atlanta, GA: Public Health Service, Centers for Disease Control and Prevention, U.S. Department of Health and Human Services.

Vondra, J. I., Barnett, D., & Cicchetti, D. (1990). Self-concept, motivation, and competence among preschoolers from maltreating and comparison families. *Child Abuse and Neglect, 14,* 525–540.

Wallace, H. (1999). *Family violence: Legal, medical, and social perspectives.* Boston: Allyn & Bacon.

Whitehead, J. T., & Lab, S. P. (1999). *Juvenile justice: An introduction* (3rd ed.). Cincinnati, OH: Anderson.

Wiehe, V. R. (1992). *Working with child abuse.* Itasca, IL: Peacock.

Wolock, I., & Horowitz, B. (1984). Child maltreatment as a social problem: The neglect of neglect. *American Journal of Orthopsychiatry, 54*(4), 530–543.

Young, W. C., Sachs, R. G., Braun, B. G., & Watkins, R. T. (1991). Patients reporting ritual abuse in childhood: A clinical syndrome: Report of 37 cases. *Child Abuse and Neglect, 15,* 181–189.

/// Chapter 4

Anderson, G. (1985). Sorichette v. City of New York: Tells the police that liability looms for failure to respond to domestic violence situations. *University of Miami Law Review, 40,* 333–358.

Astin, M. C., Ogland-Hand, S. M., & Coleman, E. M. (1995). Posttraumatic stress disorder and childhood abuse in battered women: Comparisons with maritally distressed women. *Journal of Consulting and Clinical Psychology, 63,* 308–312.

Barasch, A. P., & Lutz, V. L. (2002). Innovations in the legal system's response to domestic violence: Thinking outside the box for the silent majority of battered women. In A. R. Roberts (Ed.), *Handbook of domestic violence intervention strategies: Policies, programs and legal remedies* (pp. 173–201). New York: Oxford University Press.

Browne, A. (1997). Violence in marriage: Until death do us part? In A. P. Cardarelli (Ed.), *Violence between intimate partners: Patterns, causes, and effects* (pp. 48–69). Boston, MA: Allyn & Bacon.

Browne, A., Salomon, A., & Bassuk, S. S. (1999). The impact of recent partner violence on poor women's capacity to maintain work. *Violence Against Women, 5,* 393–426.

Brownell, P., & Abelman, I. (1998). Elder abuse: Protective and empowerment strategies for crisis intervention. In A. R. Roberts (Ed.), *Battered women and their families: Intervention strategies and treatment programs* (pp. 313–344). New York: Springer.

Brownell, P., & Roberts, A. R. (2002). National organizational survey of domestic violence coalitions. In A. R. Roberts (Ed.), *Handbook of domestic violence intervention strategies: Policies, programs and legal remedies* (pp. 88–98). New York: Oxford University Press.

Bruno v. Codd. 407 N.Y.S. 2d 165 (App. Div. 1970).

Bureau of Justice Statistics. (2001). Homicide trends in the U.S.: Intimate homicide. Retrieved Sept. 16, 2001, from U.S. Department of Justice, Office of Justice Programs Web site: http://www.ojp.usdoj.gov/bjs/homicide/d_intimates.htm.

Bureau of Justice Statistics (2002). Crime and victim statistics. Retrieved October 2002 from http://www.ojp.usdoj.gov/bjs/cvict.htm.

Buzawa, E. S., & Buzawa, C. G. (1990). *Domestic violence: The criminal justice response.* Newbury Park, CA: Sage.

Campbell, J., Rose, L., Kub, J., & Nedd, D. (2001). Voices of strength and resistance: A contextual and longitudinal analysis of women's responses to battering. In H. M. Eigenberg (Ed.), *Women battering in the United States: Till death do us part* (pp. 180–195). Prospect Heights, IL: Waveland.

Canfield, K. (2000, January 27). Judge spares Thurman prison time; convicted wife-beater guilty of violation. *The Hartford* (ME) *Courant,* A3.

Carlson, B. E. (1996). Children of battered women: Research, programs, and services. In A. R. Roberts (Ed.), *Helping battered women: New perspectives and remedies* (pp. 172–187). New York: Oxford University Press.

Chaiken, J. M. (1998). *Violence by intimates: Analysis of data on crimes by current or former spouses, boyfriends, and girlfriends* (Publication No. NCJ-167237). Washington, DC: U.S. Department of Justice, Bureau of Justice Statistics.

Douglass, R. (1995). *The state of homelessness in Michigan: A research study.* Lansing,

MI: Michigan State Housing Development Authority, Michigan Interagency Committee on Homelessness.

Doyne, S. E., Bowermaster, J. M., Meloy, J. R., Dutton, D., Jaffe, P., Temko, S., & Mones, P. (1999). Custody disputes involving domestic violence: Making children's needs a priority. *Juvenile and Family Court Journal, 50*(2), 1–12.

Eigenberg, H. M. (2001). *Women battering in the United States: Till death do us part.* Prospect Heights, IL: Waveland Press.

Federal Bureau of Investigation. (2000). The structure of family violence: An analysis of selected incidents. Retrieved Sept. 28, 2001, from www.fbi.gov/ucr/nibrs/famvio21.pdf.

Finkelhor, D., Hotaling, G., & Sedlak, A. (1990). *Missing, abducted, runaway and thrownaway children in America.* Washington, DC: U. S. Department of Justice.

Fleming, J. B. (1976). *Stopping wife abuse.* Garden City, NY: Doubleday.

Gelles, R. J. (1988). Violence and pregnancy: Are pregnant women at greater risk of abuse? *Journal of Marriage and the Family, 50,* 1045–1058.

Gelles, R. J. (1997). *Intimate violence in families.* Thousand Oaks, CA: Sage.

Gordon, M., & Dutton, M. A. (2001). Validity of "battered women syndrome" in criminal cases involving battered women. Retrieved Sept. 28, 2001, from www.ojp.usdoj.gov/ocpa/94Guides/Trials/Valid/.

Harris, S. (1996). For better or worse: Spouse abuse grown old. *Journal of Elder Abuse and Neglect, 8*(10), 1–32.

Hart, B. (1996). The legal road to freedom. In N. Lemon (Ed.), *Domestic violence law* (pp. 36–47). San Francisco: Austin and Winfield.

Hathaway, C. (1986). Gender based discrimination in police reluctance to respond to domestic assault complaints. *Georgetown Law Journal, 75,* 667–691.

Herman, J. (1992). *Trauma and recovery.* New York: Basic Books.

Hilberman, E., & Munson. K. (1977-1978). Sixty battered women. *Victimology: An International Journal, 2,* 3–4.

Hoff, R. M. (1997). *Parental kidnapping: Prevention and remedies.* Retrieved Sept. 25, 2001, from American Bar Association Web site: www.abanet.org/ftp/pub/child/pkprevnt.txt.

Homes for the Homeless. (1998). *Ten cities 1997–1998: A snapshot of family homelessness across America.* New York: Homes for the Homeless and the Institute for Children and Poverty.

Hotaling, G. T., & Sugarman, D. B. (1986). An analysis of risk markers in husband and wife violence: The current state of knowledge. *Violence and Victims, 1,* 101–124.

Jaffe, P. (1995). Children of domestic violence: Special challenges in custody and visitation dispute resolution. In N. Lemon, P. Jaffe, & A. Ganley (Eds.), *Domestic violence and children: Resolving custody and visitation disputes* (pp. 19–30). San Francisco: Family Violence Prevention Fund.

Johnson, M. P. (1995). Patriarchal terrorism and common couple violence: Two forms of violence against women. *Journal of Marriage and the Family, 57,* 283–294.

Johnson, M. P., & Ferraro, K. J. (2000). Research on domestic violence in the 1990s: Making distinctions. *Journal of Marriage and the Family, 62,* 948–963.

Karmen, A. (2001). *Crime victims: An introduction to victimology* (4th ed.). Belmont, CA: Wadsworth.

Karr-Morse, R., & Wiley, M. S. (1997). *Ghosts from the nursery: Tracing the roots of violence*, New York: Atlantic Monthly Press.

Keilitz, S. (2002). Improving judicial system responses to domestic violence: The promises and risks of integrated case management and technology solutions. In A. R. Roberts (Ed.), *Handbook on intervention strategies with domestic violence: Policies, programs and legal remedies* (147–172). New York: Oxford University Press.

Kindschi Gosselin, D. (2002). Victim interviewing in cases of domestic violence: Techniques for police. In L. J. Moriarty (Ed.), *Policing and victims* (pp. 87–107). Upper Saddle River, NJ: Prentice Hall.

LAMBDA Gay and Lesbian Anti-Violence Project (2001). *Domestic violence in gay, lesbian, and bisexual relationships*. Retrieved Aug. 6, 2001, from www.lambda. org/dv background.

Lie, G. Y., & Gentlewarrier, S. (1991). Intimate violence in lesbian relationships: Discussion of survey findings and practice implications. *Journal of Social Science Research, 15*, 41–59.

Littel, K., Malefyt, M. B., Walker, A., Tucker, D. D., & Buel, S. M. (1998, February). *Assessing justice system responses to violence against women: A tool for law enforcement, prosecution and the courts to use in developing effective responses.* Retrieved Oct. 12, 2002, from Violence Against Women Office Web site. www. vaw.umn.edu.

Marrujo, B., & Kreger, M. (1996). Definition of roles in abusive lesbian relationships. *Journal of Gay and Lesbian Social Services, 4*(1), 22–33.

Martin, D. (1976). *Battered wives*. San Francisco: Glide.

McCloskey, L. A. (2001). The "Medea complex" among men: The instrumental abuse of children to injure wives. *Violence Victims, 16*(1), 19–37.

Mega, L. T., Mega, J. L., Mega, B. T., & Harris, B. M. (2000). Brainwashing and battering fatigue: Psychological abuse in domestic violence. *North Carolina Medical Journal, 61*(5), 260–265.

Miller, N. (1998). *Domestic violence legislation affecting police and prosecutor responsibilities in the United States: Inferences from a 50-state review of state statutory codes.* Retrieved April 4, 2001, from www.ilj.org/dv/dvvaw.

National Coalition for the Homeless (1999, April). Domestic violence and homelessness. Retrieved April 24, 2001, from http://nationalhomeless.org.

National Council of Juvenile and Family Court Judges. (1999). *Family violence legislative update*. Reno: University of Nevada.

National Network to End Domestic Violence. (2001). *Campaign for full funding of the Violence Against Women Act: FY 2002 Budget Briefing Book*. National Network to End Domestic Violence: Washington, D. C.

Pagelow, M. D. (1984). *Family violence*. New York: Praeger.

Pelcovitz, D., Kaplan, S. J., DeRosa, R. R., Mandel, F. S., & Salzinger, S. (2000). Psychiatric disorders in adolescents exposed to domestic violence and physical abuse. *American Journal of Orthopsychiatry, 70*(3), 360–370.

Pleck, E. (1979). Wife beating in nineteenth-century America. *Victimology, 4*(1), 60–74.

Pleck, E. (1987). *Domestic tyranny: The making of American social policy against family violence from colonial times to the present*. New York: Oxford University Press.

Raguz v. Chandler. (No. c-74-1064, N. D. Ohio, filed Nov. 24, 1976).

Rennison, C. M., & Welchans, S. (2000). *Intimate partner violence* (Publication No. NCJ 178247). Retrieved April 24, 2001, from U.S. Department of Justice, Bureau of Justice Statistics Web site: www.ojp.usdoj.gov/bjs/abstract/ipv.htm.

Reno, J. (1999). *Cyberstalking: A new challenge for law enforcement and industry. A report from the Attorney General to the Vice President.* U.S. Department of Justice. Retrieved Sept. 6, 2001, from U.S. Department of Justice Web site: www. usdoj.gov/criminal/cybercrime/cyberstalking.htm.

Renzetti, C. M. (1992). *Violent betrayal: Partner abuse in lesbian relationships.* Newbury Park, CA: Sage.

Renzetti, C. M. (1996). The poverty of services for battered lesbians. *Journal of Gay and Lesbian Social Services, 4*(1), 61–68.

Renzetti, C. M. (1997). Violence and abuse among same-sex couples. In A. P. Cardarelli (Ed.), *Violence between intimate partners: Patterns, causes and effects* (pp. 70–89). Boston: Allyn & Bacon.

Roberts, A. R. (1981). *Sheltering battered women: A national study and service guide.* New York: Springer.

Roberts, A. R. (1984). *Battered women and their families: Intervention strategies and treatment programs.* New York: Springer.

Roberts, A. R. (2002). Duration and severity of woman battering: A conceptual model/continuum. In A. R. Roberts (Ed.), *Handbook on intervention strategies with domestic violence: Policies, programs and legal remedies* (pp. 64–79). New York: Oxford University Press.

Roberts, A. R., & Kurst-Swanger, K. (2002a). Police responses to battered women: Past, present, and future. In A. R. Roberts (Ed.), *Handbook on intervention strategies with domestic violence: Policies, programs and legal remedies* (pp. 101–126). New York: Oxford University Press.

Roberts, A. R., & Kurst-Swanger, K. (2002b). Court responses to battered women. In A. R. Roberts (Ed.), *Handbook on intervention strategies with domestic violence: Policies, programs and legal remedies* (pp. 127–146). New York: Oxford University Press

Rothman, D. J. (1980). *Conscience and convenience: The asylum and its alternatives in progressive America.* Boston, MA: Little, Brown.

Rumm, P. D., Cummings, P., Krauss, M. R., Bell, M. A., and Rivara, F. P. (2000). Identified spouse abuse as a risk factor for child abuse. *Child Abuse and Neglect, 24*(11), 1375–1382.

Scott v. Hart (No. C076-2395, N. D. Cal., Oct. 18, 1976).

Silva, R. R., Alpert, M., Munoz, D. M., Singh, S., Matzner, F., & Dummit, S. (2000). Stress and vulnerability to posttraumatic stress disorder in children and adolescents. *American Journal of Psychiatry, 157*(8), 1229–1236.

Sorichetti v. City of New York. 482 N. E. 2d70 (N.Y. 1985).

Straus, M., & Gelles, R. (1986). Societal change and change in family violence from 1975–1985 as revealed by two national studies. *Journal of Marriage and the Family, 48*, 465–479.

Straus, M., & Gelles, R. (1990). How violent are American families? Estimates from the National Family Violence Resurvey and other studies. In M. A. Straus & R. J. Gelles (Eds.), *Physical violence in American families* (pp. 95–132). New Brunswick, NJ: Transaction Publishers.

Straus, M., Gelles, R., & Steinmetz, S. (1980). *Behind closed doors: Violence in the American family.* New York: Doubleday.

Thurman v. City of Torrington. 595 F. Supp. 1521 (D. Conn. 1984).

Tjaden, M. (1997). *The crime of stalking: How big is the problem?* Retrieved Sept. 6, 2001, from U.S. Department of Justice, Office of Justice Programs, National Institute of Justice Web site: www.ncjrs.org/txtfiles/fs000186.txt.

Tjaden, M., & Thoennes, N. (2000) Extent, nature, and consequences of intimate partner violence (Publication No. NCJ 181867). Retrieved April 24, 2001, from National Institute of Justice Web site: www.ojp.usdoj.gov/nij.

U.S. Conference of Mayors. (1998). *A status report on hunger and homelessness in America's cities: 1998.* Washington, DC: U.S. Conference of Mayors.

Vinton, L. (1992). Battered women's shelters and older women: The Florida experience. *Journal of Family Violence, 7,* 63–72.

Walker, L. E. (1979). *The battered woman.* New York: Harper & Row.

Walker, L. E. (1984). *The battered woman syndrome.* New York: Springer.

Walker, L. E. (1995). Understanding battered women syndrome. *Trial, 31,* 30–34.

Zorza, J. (1991). Women battering: A major cause of homelessness. *Clearinghouse Review, 25*(4), 421.

/// Chapter 5

Adler, N. A., & Schutz, J. (1995). Sibling incest offenders. *Child Abuse and Neglect, 19*(7), 811–819.

Agnew, R., & Huguley, S. (1989). Adolescent violence toward parents. *Journal of Marriage and the Family, 51,* 699–711.

American Psychiatric Association. (1987). *Diagnostic and statistical manual of mental disorders* (3rd ed., rev.). Washington, DC: Author.

American Veterinary Medical Association. (1997, October 15). AHA calls for investigation into animal/human abuse link. *AVMA News.* Retrieved June 20, 2001 from www.avma.org/onlnews/javama/oct97/s101597b.

Animal Abuse. (2001).*Statement of purpose.* Retrieved June 20, 2001, from www.petabuse.org.

Arkow, P. (1999). The evolution of animal welfare as a human welfare concern. In F. R. Ascione & P. Arkow (Eds.), *Child abuse, domestic violence, and animal abuse: Linking the circles of compassion for prevention and intervention* (pp. 19–37). West Lafayette, IN: Purdue University Press.

Arluke, A., & Luke, C. (1997). Physical cruelty toward animals in Massachusetts, 1975–1990. *Society and Animals, 5,* 195–204.

Ascione, F. R. (1998). Battered women's reports of their partners' and their children's cruelty to animals. *Journal of Emotional Abuse, 1*(1), 119–133.

Ascione, F. R., Weber, C. V., & Wood, D. S. (1997) The abuse of animals and domestic violence: A national survey of shelter for women who are battered. *Society and Animals, 5*(3), 205–218.

Baker, D. G., Boat, B. W., Grinvalsky, H. T., & Geracioti, T. D. (1998). Interpersonal trauma and animal-related experiences in female and male military veterans: Implications for program development. *Military Medicine, 163,* 20–26.

Beirne, P. (1999). For a nonspeciesist criminology: Animal abuse as an object of study. *Criminology, 37*(1), 117–147.

Bjorklund, D. F., & Bjorklund, B. R. (1992). *Looking at children: An introduction to child development.* Pacific Grove, CA: Brooks/Cole.

Boat, B. W. (1999). Abuse of children and abuse of animals: Using the links to inform child assessment and protection. In F. R. Ascione & P. Arkow (Eds.), *Child abuse, domestic violence, and animal abuse: Linking the circles of compassion for prevention and intervention* (pp. 83–100). West Lafayette, IN: Purdue University Press.

Brassard, M., & Gelardo, M. (1987). Psychological maltreatment: The unifying construct in child abuse and neglect. *School Psychology Review, 16,* 127–136.

Browne, K. D., & Hamilton, C. E. (1998). Physical violence between young adults and their parents: Associations with a history of child maltreatment. *Journal of Family Violence, 13*(1), 59–79.

Bureau of Justice Statistics. (1999). Criminal victimization in the United States: National Crime Victimization Survey. Retrieved June 20, 2001, from the U.S. Department of Justice Web site: www.ojp.usdoj.gov/bjs/cvict.htm#ncvs.

Canavan, M. C., Meyer, W. J., & Higgs, D. C. (1982). The female experience of sibling incest. *Journal of Marital and Family Therapy, 18*(2), 129–142.

Cole, E. (1982). Sibling incest: The myth of benign sibling incest. *Women and Therapy, 1*(3), 79–89.

Cornell, C. P., & Gelles, R. J. (1982). Adolescent to parent violence. *Urban Social Change Review, 15,* 8–14.

Crittenden, P. M. (1984). Sibling interaction: Evidence of generational effect in maltreating infants. *Child Abuse and Neglect, 8,* 433–438.

Dawson, J. M., & Langan, P. A. (1994). *Murder in families* (NCJ-143498). Washington, DC: U.S. Department of Justice, Bureau of Justice Statistics.

DeViney, E., Dickert, J., & Lockwood, R. (1983). The care of pets within child abusing families. *International Journal for the Study of Animal Problems, 4,* 321–329.

Dutton, D. G., & Yamini, B. A. (1995). Adolescent parricide: An integration of social cognitive theory and clinical views of projective-introjective cycling. *American Journal of Orthopsychiatry, 65*(1), 39–47.

Ewing, C. P. (1990). *Kids who kill.* Lexington, MA: Lexington Books.

Ewing, C. P. (1997). *Fatal families: The dynamics of intrafamilial homicide.* Thousand Oaks, CA: Sage.

Finkelhor, D. H. (1980). Sex among siblings: A survey of prevalence, variety, and effects. *Archives of Sexual Behavior, 9*(3), 171–193.

Flynn, C. P. (1999). Exploring the link between corporal punishment and children's cruelty to animals. *Journal of Marriage and Family, 61,* 971–981.

Garbarino, J., & Vondra, J. (1987). Psychological maltreatment: Issues and perspectives. In M. Brassard, R. Germain, & S. Hart (Eds.), *Psychological maltreatment of children and youth* (pp. 25–44). Elmsford, NY: Pergamon.

Garcia, M. M., Shaw, D. S., Winslow, E. B., & Yaggi, K. E. (2000). Destructive sibling conflict and the development of conduct problems in young boys. *Developmental Psychology, 36*(1), 44–52.

Garrett, E., & McKenzie, B. (1995). Sibling abuse: An exploratory study. *Social Worker/Le Travailleur Social, 63*(3), 102–106.

Gelles, R. J. (1997). Intimate violence in families (3rd ed.). Thousand Oaks, CA: Sage.

Goodwin, M. P., & Roscoe, B. (1990). Sibling violence and agonistic interactions among middle adolescents. *Adolescence, 25*(98), 451–467.

Graham-Bermann, S. A., Cutler, S. E., Litzenberger, B. W., & Schwartz, W. E. (1994).

Perceived conflict and violence in childhood sibling relationships and later emotional adjustment. *Journal of Family Psychology, 8*(1), 85–97.

Gully, K. J., Dengerink, H. A., Pepping, M., & Bergstrom, D. (1981) Research note: Sibling contribution to violent behavior. *Journal of Marriage and the Family, 43*, 333–337.

Harbin, H., & Madden, D. (1979). Battered parents: A new syndrome. *American Journal of Psychiatry, 136*, 1288–1291.

Hart, S., & Brassard, M. (1987). A major threat to children's mental health: Psychological maltreatment. *American Psychologist, 42*, 160–165.

Heide, K. (1992). *Why kids kill parents.* Columbus, OH: Ohio State University Press.

Heide, K. (1994). Evidence of child maltreatment among adolescent parricide offenders. *International Journal of Offender Therapy and Comparative Criminology, 38*(2), 151–162.

Heide, K., & Solomon, E. P. (1991, November). *Responses to severe childhood maltreatment: Homicidal fantasies and other survival strategies.* Paper presented at the annual meeting of the American Society of Criminology, San Francisco, CA.

High court won't hear challenge to Menendez brothers' convictions. (1998, May 28). *Metropolitan News Enterprise* (Los Angeles, CA).

Hughes, H. M., & DiBrezzo, R. (1987). Physical and emotional abuse and motor development: A preliminary investigation. *Perceptual and Motor Skills, 64*, 469–470.

Hughes, M. (1988). Psychological and behavioral correlates of family violence in child witnesses and victims. *American Journal of Orthopsychiatry, 58*, 77–90.

Jorgensen, S., & Maloney, L. (1999). Animal abuse and the victims of domestic violence. In Frank R. Ascione & Phil Arkow (Eds.), *Child abuse, domestic violence, and animal abuse: Linking the circles of compassion for prevention and intervention* (pp. 143–158). West Lafayette, IN: Purdue University Press.

Kellert, S. R., & Felthous, A. R. (1985). Childhood cruelty toward animals among criminals and noncriminals. *Human Relations, 38*, 1113–1120.

Kramer, L., Perozynski, L.A., & Chung, T. (1999). Parental responses to sibling conflict: The effects of development and parent gender. *Child Development, 70*(1), 1401.

Lockwood, R., & Hodge, G. R. (1986, Summer). The tangled web of animal abuse: The links between cruelty to animals and human violence. *Humane Society News*, 10–15.

MacKinnon-Lewis, C., Starnes, R., Volling, B., & Johnson, S. (1997). Perceptions of parenting as predictors of boy's sibling and peer relations. *Developmental Psychology, 33*(6), 1024–1031.

Miller, K. S., & Knutson, J. F. (1997). Reports of severe physical punishment and exposure to animal cruelty by inmates convicted of felonies and by university students. *Child Abuse and Neglect, 21*, 59–82.

O'Brien, M. J. (1991). Taking sibling incest seriously. In M. Q. Patton (Ed.), *Family sexual abuse: Frontline research and evaluation* (pp. 75–92). Newbury Park, CA: Sage.

Patronek, G. J. (1997). Issues for veterinarians in recognizing and reporting animal neglect and abuse. *Society and Animals, 5*(3), 267–281.

Peek, C., Fisher, J. L., & Kidwell, J. S. (1985). Teenage violence toward parents: A neglected dimension of family violence. *Journal of Marriage and the Family, 476*, 1051–1058.

Roscoe, B., Goodwin, M., & Kennedy, D. (1987). Sibling violence and agonistic interactions experienced by early adolescents. *Journal of Family Violence, 2,* 121–138.

Rowan, A. N. (1999). Cruelty and abuse to animals: A typology. In F. R. Ascione & P. Arkow (Eds.), *Child abuse, domestic violence, and animal abuse: Linking the circles of compassion for prevention and intervention* (pp. 328–334). West Lafayette, IN: Purdue University Press.

Rudd, J. M., & Herzberger, S. D. (1999). Brother-sister incest—father-daughter incest: A comparison of characteristics and consequences. *Child Abuse and Neglect, 23*(9), 915.

Sargent, D. (1962). Children who kill: A family conspiracy? *Social Work, 7,* 35–42.

Saunders, D. G. (1986). When battered women use violence: Husband abuse or self defense? *Violence and Victims, 1,* 47–60.

Schlueter, S. (1999). Animal abuse and law enforcement. In F. R. Ascione & P. Arkow (Eds.), *Child abuse, domestic violence, and animal abuse: Linking the circles of compassion for prevention and intervention* (pp. 316–327). West Lafayette, IN: Purdue University Press.

Silverstein, H. (1996). *Unleashing rights: Law, meaning, and the animal rights movement.* Ann Arbor: University of Michigan Press.

Steinmetz, S. K. (1977). *The cycle of violence: Assertive, aggressive, and abusive family interaction.* New York: Praeger.

Straus, M. A., Gelles, R. J., & Steinmetz, S. K. (1980). *Behind closed doors: Violence in the American family.* Beverly Hills, CA: Sage.

Whipple, E. E., & Finton, S. E. (1995). Psychological maltreatment by siblings: An unrecognized form of abuse. *Child and Adolescent Social Work Journal, 12*(2), 135–146.

Wiehe, V. R. (1997). *Sibling abuse: Hidden physical, emotional, and sexual trauma.* Thousand Oaks, CA: Sage.

Worling, J. R. (1995). Adolescent sibling-incest offenders: Differences in family and individual functioning when compared to adolescent nonsibling sex offenders. *Child Abuse and Neglect, 19*(5), 633–643.

/// *Chapter 6*

Administration on Aging. (1998, September). *The National Elder Abuse Incidence Study: Final Report.* Retrieved Jan. 24, 2002, from www.aoa.dhhs.gov/abuse/main-pdf.htm.

Administration on Aging. (2000a). Older Americans 2000: Key indicators of well-being. Retrieved Jan. 24, 2002, from the Federal Interagency Forum on Aging Related Statistics Web site: www.agingstats.gov.

Administration on Aging. (2000b). Elder abuse prevention. Retrieved Jan. 24, 2002, from www.aoa.dhhs.gov/factsheets/abuse.html.

Administration on Aging. (2001). The administration on aging and the Older Americans Act. Retrieved Jan. 21, 2002, from the Department of Health and Human Services, Administration on Aging Web site: www.aoa.dhhs.gov.

Administration on Aging. (2002). Elder abuse prevention. Retrieved Oct. 13, 2002, from www.aoa.dhhs.gov/may98/abuse.html.

Anetzberger, G. J. (1987). *The etiology of elder abuse by adult offspring.* Springfield, IL: Thomas.

Axinn, J., & Levin, H. (1997). *Social welfare: A history of the American response to need* (4th ed.). New York: Longman.

Block, M. R., & Sinnott, J. (1979). *The battered elder syndrome: An exploratory study.* College Park: University of Maryland, Division of Community Resources.

Booth, B., Bruno, A., & Marin, R. (1996). Psychological therapy with abused and neglected patients. In L. A. Baumhover & S. C. Beall (Eds.), *Abuse, neglect and exploitation of older people: Strategies for assessment in intervention.* Baltimore: Health Professions Press.

Bradley, M. (1996). Elder abuse: Caring for older people. *British Medical Journal, 313* (7056), 548.

Bradshaw, D., & Spencer, C. (1999). The role of alcohol in elder abuse cases. In J. Pritchard (Ed.), *Elder abuse work: Best practices in Britain and Canada.* London: Jessica Kingsley Press.

Bristowe, E., & Collins, J. B. (1989). Family mediated abuse of non-institutionalized elder men and women living in British Columbia. *Journal of Elder Abuse and Neglect, 1*(1), 45–54.

Brownell, P. (1996). Social work and criminal justice responses to elder abuse in New York City. In A. R. Roberts (Ed.), *Helping battered women: New perspectives and remedies* (pp. 44–66). New York: Oxford University Press.

Brownell, P., & Abelman, I. (1998). Elder abuse: Protective and empowerment strategies for crisis intervention. In A. R. Roberts (Ed.), *Battered women and their families* (2nd ed., pp. 313–344). New York: Springer.

Brown-Standish, M. D., & Floyd, C. W. (2000). Healing bittersweet legacies: Revisiting contextual family therapy for grandparents raising grandchildren in crisis. *Journal of Marriage and Family Therapy, 26*(2), 185–197.

Carson, D. (1995). American Indian elder abuse: Risk and protective factors among the oldest Americans. *Journal of Elder Abuse and Neglect, 7*(1), 17–39.

Choi-Namkee, G., & Mayer, J. (2000). Elder abuse and exploitation: Risk factors and prevention strategies. *Journal of Gerontological Social Work, 33*(2), 5–25.

Cohen, D., & Eisdorfer, C. (1999, August). *Clinical patterns of spousal/consortial homicide in the aged,* Paper presented at the Congress of the International Psychogeriatric Association, Vancouver, British Columbia, CA.

Collins, K., Bennett, A., & Hanzlick, R. (2000) Elder abuse and neglect. *Archives of Internal Medicine, 160*(11), 1567.

Comijs, H., Penninx, B., Knipscheer, K., & van Tilberg, W. (1999). Psychological distress in victims of elder mistreatment: The effects of social support and coping. *Journal of Gerontology, 54*(B), 240–245.

Council on Scientific Affairs. (1987). Elder abuse and neglect. *Journal of the American Medical Association, 257,* 966–971.

Daly, M., & Wilson, M. (1982). Homicide and kinship. *American Anthropologist, 84,* 372–387.

Deets, H. B. (1993). AARP study sheds some new light on elder abuse. *AARP Bulletin, 34*(3), 3.

Devons, C. A. J. (1999). Better aging starts with you. In C. K. Kassel (Ed.), *The practical guide to aging: What everyone needs to know* (pp. 3–27). New York: New York University Press.

Dobrin, A., Wiersema, B., & Loftin, C. (1996). *Statistical handbook on violence in America*. Phoenix: Oryx Press.

Elder Abuse Center. (2001). The basics: What is elder abuse? Retrieved Nov. 13, 2001, from www.elderabusecenter.org/basic/index/html.

Eisdorfer, C., & Cohen, D. (1999, August). *Homicide-suicide rates in older people*. Paper presented at the Congress of the International Psychogeriatric Association, Vancouver, British Columbia, CA.

Eisdorfer, C., & Cohen, D. (2001). *Homicide-suicide in older persons: Acts of violence against women*. Retrieved May 24, 2001, from the U.S. Department of Justice, National Institute of Justice Web site: www.ojp.usdoj.gov/nij/elderjust/elder_16.html.

Federal Bureau of Investigation. (1997). Investing in the future: Protecting the elderly from financial abuse. *The FBI Law Enforcement Bulletin, 66*(12), 1–5.

Forst, L. (Ed). (2000). *The aging of America: A handbook for police officers*. Springfield, IL: Thomas.

Frazer, J. G. (1900). *The golden bough: A study in magic and religion* (2nd ed.). New York: Macmillan.

Gesino, J., Smith, H., & Keckich, W. (1982). The battered woman grown old. *Clinical Gerontologist, 1*(1), 59–67.

Greenberg, J. R., McKibben, M., & Raymond, J. (1990). Dependent adult children and elder abuse. *Journal of Elder Abuse and Neglect, 2*(1), 73–86.

Harris, S. (1996). For better or worse: Spouse abuse grown old. *Journal of Elder Abuse and Neglect, 8*, 365–380.

Hodge, P. (2001). Elder abuse and neglect: Prosecution and prevention: Prosecutions and initiatives. Retrieved June 10, 2001, from www.asaging.org/am/cia2/abuse/html.

Hood, I. (2001). *The forensic pathologist's role in investigation of suspected abuse and neglect of care-dependent persons*. Retrieved May 24, 2001, from the U.S. Department of Justice, National Institute of Justice Web site: www.ojp.usdoj.gov/nij/elderjust/elder_16.html.

Jarde, O., Marc, B., Dwyer, J., & Fournier, P. (1990). Mistreatment of the aged in the home environment in northern France: A year survey. *Medicine and Law, 11*(7–8), 641–648.

Klaus, P. (1999). *Crimes against persons age 65 or older, 1992–1997* (NCJ 176352). Retrieved Jan. 22, 2002, from U.S. Department of Justice, Bureau of Justice Statistics Web site: www.ojp.usdoj.gov/bjs/pub/asch/cpa6597.pdf.

Kosberg, J. (1998). The abuse of elderly men. *Journal of Elder Abuse and Neglect, 9*(3), 69–88.

Kosberg, J., & Garcia, J. (1995). Common and unique themes in elder abuse from a world-wide perspective. *Journal of Elder Abuse and Neglect, 6*,(3/4), 1–11.

Kosberg, J., & Nahmiash, D. (1995). Characteristics of victims and perpetrators and milieus of abuse and neglect. In L. A. Baumhover & S. C. Beal (Eds.), *Abuse, neglect and exploitation of older persons: Strategies for assessment and intervention* (pp. 29–47). Baltimore: Health Professions Press.

Krassen, M. E., & Maxwell, R. J. (1992). Insults to the body civil: Mistreatment of elderly in two Plains Indian tribes. *Journal of Cross Cultural Gerontology, 7*(1), 3–23.

Lachs, M., Berkman, L., Fulmer, T., & Horwitz, R. (1994). A prospective community-based pilot study of risk factors for the investigation of elder mistreatment. *Journal of the American Geriatrics Society, 42,* 169–173.

Lachs, M., Williams, C., O'Brien, S., Pillemer, K., & Charison, E. (1998a). The mortality of elder mistreatment (Part 1). *Journal of the American Medical Association, 280*(5), 428A.

Lachs, M., Williams, C., O'Brien, S., Pillemer, K., & Charison, E. (1998b). The mortality of elder mistreatment (Part 2). *Journal of the American Medical Association, 280*(5), 428B.

Lachs, M., Williams, C., O'Brien, S., Pillemer, K., & Charison, E. (1998c). The mortality of elder mistreatment (Part 3). *Journal of the American Medical Association, 280*(5), 428C.

Marshall, C., Benton, D., & Brazier, J. (2000). Elder abuse: Using clinical tools to identify clues of mistreatment. *Geriatrics, 55*(2), 42.

Mayo Clinic. (2000). *Alzheimer's disease.* Retrieved Oct. 13, 2002, from www.mayoclinic.com.

Montoya, V. (1997). Understanding and combating elder abuse in Hispanic communities. *Journal of Elder Abuse and Neglect, 9*(2), 5–17.

Moon, A., & Williams, O. (1993). Perceptions of elder abuse and help-seeking patterns among African-American, Caucasian-American and Korean-American elderly women. *Gerontologist, 33*(3), 386–395.

Mui, A. (1992). Caregiver strain among Black and White daughter caregivers: A role theory perspective. *Gerontologist, 32,* 203–212.

Mui, A. (1995). Multidimensional predictors of caregiver strain among older persons caring for frail spouses. *Journal of Marriage and the Family, 57,* 733–740.

National Center on Elder Abuse. (1996). *American Public Human Services Association National Elder Abuse Incidence Study Fact Sheet.* Retrieved from www.aphsa.org Aug. 21, 2001.

National Center on Elder Abuse. (1997). *Trends in elder abuse in domestic settings: Elder abuse information (Series No. 2).* Washington, DC: U.S. Administration on Aging.

National Center on Elder Abuse. (1999). *Trends in elder abuse in domestic settings: Elder abuse information (Series No. 1).* Washington, DC: U.S. Administration on Aging.

National Center for Health Statistics. (2001). *New series of reports to monitor health of older Americans: Fact sheet.* Washington, DC: U.S. Department of Health and Human Services, Centers for Disease Control and Prevention.

National Committee for the Prevention of Elder Abuse. (2002). *Critical issues in elder abuse: Elder abuse and substance abuse.* Retrieved Jan. 22, 2002, from www.preventelderabuse.org/issues/substance.html.

National Institute on Aging. (1991). *What is your aging IQ?* Washington, DC: Department of Health and Human Services.

Paveza, G. J., Cohen, D., Eisdorfer, C., Freels, S., Semla, T., Ashford, J. W., Gorelick, P., Hirschman, R., Luchins, D., & Levy, P. (1992). Severe family violence and Alzheimer's disease: Prevalence and risk factors. *Gerontologist, 32*(4), 493–497.

Pillemer, K., & Finkelhor, D. (1989). Causes of elder abuse: Caregiver stress versus problem relatives. *American Journal of Orthopsychiatry, 59*(2), 179–187.

Pillemer, K., & Finkelhor, D. (1998). The prevalence of elder abuse: A random sample survey. *Gerontologist, 28*(1), 51–57.

Pillemer, K., & Prescott, D. (1989). Psychological effects of elder abuse: A research note. *Journal of Elder Abuse and Neglect, 1*(1), 6574.

Quinn, M. J., & Tomita, S. (1997). *Elder abuse and neglect: Causes, diagnosis and intervention strategies* (2nd ed.). New York: Springer.

Rathborne-McCuan, E. (1980). Elderly victims of family violence and neglect. *Social Casework 61*(5), 296–304.

Reinharz, S. (1986) Loving and hating one's elders: Twin themes in legend and literature. In R. Wolf & K. Pillemer (Eds.), *Elder abuse: Conflict in the family* (pp. 25–48). Dover, MA: Auburn.

Reis, M., & Nahmiash, D. (1998). Validation of the indicators of abuse. *Gerontologist, 38*(4), 471–480.

Reissberg, B., Franssen, E., Sclan, S. G., Klugar, A., & Ferris, S. H. (1989). Stage specific incidence of potentially remediable behavioral symptoms in aging and Alzheimer's Disease: A study of 120 patients using the BEHAVE-AD. *Bulletin of Clinical Neurosciences, 54*, 95–112.

Rennison, C. M. (2001). *Intimate partner violence and age of victim, 1993–1999* (NCJ-187635). Retrieved Jan. 22, 2002, from U.S. Department of Justice, Bureau of Justice Statistics Web site: www.ojp.usdoj.gov/bjs/pub/pdf/ipva99.pdf.

Salend, E., Kane, R. A., Satz, M., & Pynoos, J. (1984). Elder abuse reporting: Limitations of statutes. *Gerontologist, 24*(1), 61–69.

Sharon, N. (1991). Elder abuse and neglect substantiations: What they tell us about the problem. *Journal of Elder Abuse and Neglect, 3*(3), 19–35.

Shiferaw, B., Mittlemark, M., Woffard, J., Anderson, T., & Walls, P. (1994). The investigation and outcome of reported cases of elder abuse. *Gerontologist, 34*, 123–125.

Stearns, P. J. (1986). Old age family conflict: The perspective of the past. In K. Pillenger & R. S. Wolf (Eds.), *Elder abuse conflict in the family* (pp. 4–7). Dover, MA: Auburn House.

Steinmetz, S. (1978). Battered parents. *Society, 15*(5), 54–55.

Steinmetz, S. (1988). Dutybound: *Elder Abuse and Family Care*. Newburg Park, CA: Sage.

Center for Disease Control and Prevention. Suicide rates in the United States, 1980-1992. (1996). *Journal of the American Medical Association, 275*(7), 509.

Swagerty, D., Takahashi, P., & Evans, J. (1999). Elder mistreatment. *American Family Physician, 59*(10), 2804.

Tatara, T., & Kuzmeskus, L. (1997). Trends in elder abuse in domestic settings (Elder Abuse Information Series No. 2). Retrieved Nov. 13, 2001, from National Center on Elder Abuse Web site: www.elderabusecenter.org/basic/fact2.pdf.

United Nations. (1948). Universal declaration of human rights. Retrieved June 10, 2002, from www.un.org/overview/rights.html.

U.S. Bureau of the Census. (1993). Population projections of the U.S. by age, sex, race and Hispanic origin data: 1993-2050. *Current population reports* (Series P-25, No. 1104). Washington, DC: U.S. Department of Commerce.

U.S. Bureau of the Census. (1998). Household and family characteristics: March 1998. *Current population reports* (Series P-20-515). Washington, DC: U.S. Department of Commerce.

U.S. Department of Health and Human Services (1982). *Protective services for adults* (DHHS Publication No. OHDS 82-20505). Washington, DC: Author.

U.S. House of Representatives Select Committee on Aging (1981). Elder abuse: An examination of a hidden problem. (Comm. Pub. No. 97-277). Washington, DC: Government Printing Office.

U.S. House of Representatives Subcommittee on Domestic and International Scientific Planning, Analysis, and Cooperation (1978). Hearings of the Committee on Science and Technology, February, 1416. Washington, DC: Government Printing Office.

Wallace, G. (2001). Grandparent caregivers: Emerging issues in elder law and social work practice. *Journal of Gerontological Social Work, 34*(3), 127–136

Wolf, R. S. (1986). Major findings from three model projects on elder abuse. In K. Pillemer & R. S. Wolf (Eds.), *Elder abuse and neglect: Conflict in the family* (pp. 218–238). Dover, MA: Auburn House.

Wolf, R. S. (2000) *Emotional distress and elder abuse.* Retrieved Jan. 22, 2002, from www.elderabusecenter.org/newsletter/news25.pdf.

Wolf, R. S. (2001). The nature and scope of elder abuse. *Generations, 24*(2). Retrieved Jan. 24, 2002, from www.asaging.org/generations/gen-24-2/intro.html.

Wolf, R., Godkin, M., & Pillemer, K. (1986). Maltreatment of the elderly: A comparative analysi. *Journal of Long-Term Health Care, 5,* 10–17.

Wolf, R. S., & Pillemer, K. A. (1989). *Helping elderly victims: The reality of elder abuse.* New York: Columbia University Press.

Young, M. (2000). Recognizing the signs of elder abuse. *Patient Care, 34*(20), 56.

/// **Chapter 7**

Administration on Aging. (2001). *Ombudsmen protect lives, rights and health of long term care residents.* Retrieved Feb. 22, 2001, from www.aoa.gov/pr/Pr2000/ltcombudsman.html.

Administration for Children and Families. (2000). *HHS reports new child abuse and neglect statistics.* Retrieved fromwww.acf.hhs.gov/news/press/2000/april00.htm.

Administration on Developmental Disabilities. (2001). *State protection and advocacies FY1999 program report by age of individual clients.* Retrieved March 2, 2001, from www.acf.dhhs.gov/programs/add/P&A-age.htm.

Bartholet, E. (1999). *Nobody's children: Abuse and neglect, foster drift and the adoption alternative.* Boston, MA: Beacon Press.

Bentley, K. J., & Walsh, J. F. (2001). *The social worker and psychotropic medication: Toward effective collaboration with mental health clients, families, and providers* (2nd ed.). Belmont, CA: Wadsworth.

Besharov, D. J. (1987). Reporting out-of-home maltreatment: Penalties and protections. *Child Welfare, 66*(5), 399–408.

Bremner, R. H. (Ed.). (1970). *Children and youth in America: A documentary history: Vol. 1. 1600-1865.* Cambridge, MA: Harvard University Press.

Conwell, Y., Pearson, J., & DeRenzo, E. G. (1996). Indirect self-destructive behavior among elderly patients in nursing homes: A research agenda. *American Journal of Geriatric Psychiatry, 4*(2), 152–163.

D'Ambra, L. (1996, June). *Survey of ombudsman offices for children in the United States.* Paper presented at the National Conference of the American Bar Association, Crystal City, VA. Retrieved Jan. 9, 2001, from www.ojjdp.ncjrs.org/pubs/walls/appen-e.html.

Gibbs Brown, J. (2000a). *Annual report: State Medicaid Fraud Control Units.* Retrieved

March 2, 2001, from Department of Health and Human Services, Office of Inspector General Web site: www.oig.hhs.gov/publications/docs/mfcu/mfcuar 99.pdf.

Gibbs Brown, J. (2000b). *State oversight of residential facilities for children*. Retrieved March 2, 2001, from Department of Health and Human Services, Office of Inspector General Web site: www.oig.hhs.gov/oei/reports/oei-02-98-00570.pdf.

Goffman, E. (1961). *Asylums: Essays on the social situation of mental patients and other inmates*. Garden City, NY: Anchor Books.

Goodridge, D. M., Johnston, P. & Thomson, M. (1996). Conflict and aggression as stressors in the work environment of nursing assistants: Implications for institutional elder abuse. *Journal of Elder Abuse and Neglect, 8*(1), 49–67.

Halamandaris, V. J. (1983). Fraud and abuse in nursing homes. In J. I. Kosberg (Ed.), *Abuse and maltreatment of the elderly* (pp. 104–114). Boston: PSG.Haney, C., Banks, C., & Zimbardo, P. G. (1973). Interpersonal dynamics in a simulated prison. *International Journal of Criminology and Penology, 1*, 69–97.

Hodge, P. D. (1998). National law enforcement programs to prevent, detect, investigate, and prosecute elder abuse and neglect in health care facilities. *Journal of Elder Abuse and Neglect, 9*(4), 23–41.

Hospital 'Incident Reports' of alleged child sexual abuse are exempt from disclosure under Education Law 6527(3). (1999, December 1). *New York Law Journal*.

Karr-Morse, R., & Wiley, M. S. (1997). *Ghosts from the nursery: Tracing the roots of violence*. New York: The Atlantic Monthly Press.

Koocher, G. P. (1976). *Children's rights and the mental health professions*. New York: Wiley.

Manion, S. (2001). *Recognizing and reporting institutional abuse*. Retrieved Jan. 8, 2001, from Division of Youth and Family Services, Institutional Abuse Unit Web site: www.state.nj.us/humanservices/NJTaskForce/gtia.html.

Mercer, S. O. (1983). Consequences of institutionalization of the aged. In J. I. Kosberg (Ed.), *Abuse and maltreatment of the elderly* (pp. 68-73). Boston: PSG.

National Association of Attorneys General. (1992, January). Patient abuse statute upheld in Delaware. *AG Bulletin*.

National Association of Attorneys General. (1993, October). Patient abuse: New York. *Medicaid Fraud Report*.

National Association of Attorneys General. (1996a, February). Patient abuse: North Carolina. *Medicaid Fraud Report*.

National Association of Attorneys General. (1996b, July/August). Patient abuse: New York. *Medicaid Fraud Report*.

National Association of Attorneys General. (2000, May). Patient abuse: Arizona. *Medicaid Fraud Report*.

National Association of Protection and Advocacy Systems. (2001). The origins of P & A and CAP systems. Retrieved March 20, 2001, from *www.protectand advocate.com*.

Nelson, F. L., & Farberow, N. L. (1980). Indirect self-destructive behavior in the elderly nursing home patient. *Journal of Gerontology, 35*, 949–957.

Osgood, N. J., & Brant, B. A. (1991). Suicide among the elderly in institutional and community settings. In M. S. Harper (Ed.), *Management and care of the elderly: Psychosocial perspectives* (pp. 37–71). Thousand Oaks, CA: Sage.

Pagelow, M. D. (1984). *Family violence*. New York: Praeger.

Parent, D. G., Leiter, V., Kennedy, S., Livens, L., Wentworth, D., & Wilcox, S. (1994). *Conditions of confinement: Juvenile detention and corrections facilities.* Washington, DC: U.S. Department of Justice, Office of Justice Programs, Office of Juvenile Justice and Delinquency Prevention.

Pillemer, K., & Moore, D. (1989). Abuse of patients in nursing homes: Findings from a survey of staff. *Gerontologist, 29*(3), 314–320.

Rindfleisch, N., & Hicho, D. (1987). Institutional child protection: Issues in program development and implementation. *Child Welfare, 66*(4), 329–342.

Rivlin, L. G., & Wolfe, M. (1985). *Institutional settings in children's lives.* New York: Wiley.

Rothman, D. J. (1971). *The discovery of the asylum: Social order and disorder in the new republic.* Boston: Little, Brown.

Rothman, D. J. (1980). *From conscience to convenience: The asylum and its alternatives in progressive America.* Boston: Little, Brown.

Schneider, H. J. (1996). Violence in the institution. *International Journal of Offender Therapy and Comparative Criminology, 40*(1), 5–18.

Shore, R. (1997). *Rethinking the brain: New insights into early development.* New York: Families and Work Institute.

Sovereign immunity bars defamation action by nursing home operators. (2000). *Nursing Home Litigation Reporter, 3*(5), 5.

Stathopoulos, P. A. (1983). Consumer advocacy and abuse of elders in nursing homes. In J. I. Kosberg (Ed.), *Abuse and maltreatment of the elderly* (pp. 335–354). Boston: PSG.

Whitehead, J. T., & Lab, S. P. (1999). *Juvenile justice: An introduction* (3rd ed.). Cincinnati, OH: Anderson.

Yawney, B. A., & Slover, D. L. (1973). Relocation of the elderly. *Social Work, 18,* 86–95.

Zimbardo, P. G. (1999). *Stanford prison experiment.* Retrieved from *www.prisonexp.org.*

Zuravin, S. J., Benedict, M., & Somerfield, M. (1993). Child maltreatment in family foster care. *American Journal of Orthopsychiatry, 63*(4), 589–586.

/// Chapter 8

Administration for Children and Families. (1999). *President Clinton and Vice President Gore: Fighting to End Domestic Violence.* Retrieved Sept. 19, 2000, from U.S. Department of Health and Human Services Web site: www.acf.dhhs.gov/news/press/1999/vawa99.

Administration for Children and Families. (2000). U.S. Department of Health and Human Services. Retrieved Sept. 19, 2000, from www.acf.dhhs.gov/programs/opa/facts/majorpr.htm.

American Bar Association Commission on Legal Problems of the Elderly. (1999). *Elder abuse laws: Information about laws related to elder abuse.* National Center on Elder Abuse. Retrieved Oct. 12, 2002, from www.elderabusecenter.org.

Anetzberger, G. J. (1987). *The etiology of elder abuse by adult offspring.* Springfield, IL: Thomas.

Babcock, J. C., & Steiner, R. (1999). The relationship between treatment, incarceration, and recidivism of battering: A program evaluation of Seattle's coordinated community response to domestic violence. *Journal of Family Psychology, 13*(1), 46–59.

Baltz, T., Kelleher, K., & Shema, S. J. (1995). Factors associated with respite care use by families with a child with disabilities. *Journal of Child and Family Studies, 4*(4), 419–1024.

Bearup, R. S., & Palusci, V. J. (1999). Improving child welfare through a children's ombudsman. *Child Abuse and Neglect, 23*(5), 449–457.

Besharov, D. (1990). Gaining control over child abuse reports: Public agencies must address both underreporting and overreporting. *Public Welfare, 48*(2), 34–47.

Bishop, S. J., Murphy, J. M., & Hicks, R. (2000). What progress has been made in meeting the needs of seriously maltreated children? The course of 200 cases through the Boston Juvenile Court. *Child Abuse and Neglect, 24*(5), 599–610.

Blau, G. M., Butteweg Dall, M., & Anderson, L.M. (1993). The assessment and treatment of violent families. In R. L. Hampton, T. P. Gullotta, G. R. Adams, E. H. Potter, III, & R. P. Weissberg (Eds.), *Family violence: Prevention and treatment* (pp. 198–229). Newbury Park, CA: Sage.

Boothroyd, R. A., Armstrong, M. I., Evans, M. E., Kuppinger, A. D., & Radigan, M. (1998). Understanding respite care use by families of children receiving short-term, in-home psychiatric emergency services. *Journal of Child and Family Studies, 7*(3), 353–376.

Boudreau, F. A. (1993). Elder abuse. In R. L. Hampton, T. P. Gullotta, G. R. Adams, E. H. Potter, III, & R. P. Weissberg (Eds.), *Family violence: Prevention and treatment* (pp. 142–158). Newbury Park, CA: Sage.

Braun, K. L., & Rose, C. L. (1986). The Hawaii geriatric foster care experiment: Impact evaluation and cost analysis. *Gerontologist, 26*, 516–524.

Buttell, F. P. (1999). Level of moral reasoning among African-American and Caucasian domestic violence offenders prior to targeted professional intervention. *Journal of Offender Rehabilitation, 30*(1/2), 95–106.

Buzawa, E. S., & Buzawa, C. G. (1990). Domestic violence: The criminal justice response. *Studies in Crime, Law and Justice* (Vol. 6). Newbury Park, CA: Sage.

Calkins, C. A., & Millar, M. (1999). The effectiveness of court appointed special advocates to assist in permanency planning. *Child and Adolescent Social Work Journal, 16*(1), 37–45.

Caringella-MacDonald, S. (1997). Women victimized by private violence: A long way to justice. In A. P. Cardarelli (Ed.), *Violence between intimate partners: Patterns, causes, and effects* (pp. 144–153). Boston: Allyn & Bacon.

Cohen, R. A., Rosenbaum, A., & Kane, R. L. (1999). Neuropsychological correlates of domestic violence. *Violence and Victims, 14*(4), 397–411.

Court-Appointed Special Advocates. (2002). A powerful voice in a child's life: About national CASA. Retrieved Oct. 12, 2002, from www.nationalcasa.org.

Davis, L. V., Hagen, J. L., & Early, T. J. (1994). Social services for battered women: Are they adequate, accessible, and appropriate? *Social Work, 39*(6), 695–704.

Davis, R. C., & Smith, B. (1995). Domestic violence reforms: Empty promises or fulfilled expectations? *Crime and Delinquency, 41*(4), 541–552.

Dutton, D. G. (1988). *The domestic assault of women: Psychological and criminal justice perspectives.* Boston: Allyn & Bacon.

Dutton, D. G., Starzomski, A., & Ryan, L. (1996). Antecedents of abusive personality and abusive behavior in wife assaulters. *Journal of Family Violence, 11*, 113–132.

Epstein, D. (1999). Effective intervention in domestic violence cases: Rethinking the roles of prosecutors, judges, and the court system. *Yale Journal of Law and Feminism, 11,* 3.

Finkelhor, D., & Berliner, L. (1995). Research on the treatment of sexually abused children: A review and recommendations. *Journal of the American Academy of Child and Adolescent Psychiatry, 34,* 1408–1423.

Flint, A. J. (1995). Effects of respite care on patients with dementia and their caregivers. *International Psychogeriatrics, 7*(4), 505–517.

Hanson, B. (2002). Interventions for batterers: Program approaches, program tensions. In A. R. Roberts (Ed.), *Handbook of domestic violence intervention strategies: Policies, programs, and legal remedies* (pp. 419–448). New York: Oxford University Press.

Hobbs, G. F., Hobbs, C. J., & Wynne, J. M. (1999). Abuse of children in foster and residential care. *Child Abuse and Neglect, 23*(12), 1239–1252.

Jennings, J. (1990). Preventing relapse versus "stopping" domestic violence: Do we expect too much too soon from battering men? *Journal of Family Violence, 5*(1), 43–60.

Kitchens, H. Q. (1998). Recognition and management of elder abuse. *Physician Assistant, 22*(4), 58–66.

Lundervold, D., & Lewin, L. M. (1987). Effects of in-home respite care on caregivers of family members with Alzheimer's disease. *Journal of Clinical and Experimental Gerontology, 9*(3), 201–214.

Meadows, R. J. (1998). *Understanding violence and victimization.* Upper Saddle River, NJ: Prentice Hall.

Mignon, S. I., & Holmes, W. M. (1995). Police response to mandatory arrest laws. *Crime and Delinquency, 41*(4), 430–442.

Mills, L. (1999). Killing her softly: Intimate abuse and the violence of state intervention. *Harvard Law Review, 113,* 550–613.

National Children's Alliance. (2000). Standards for full member programs. Retrieved April 24, 2000, from www.nncac.org.

National Coalition Against Domestic Violence. (2000). *Facts on women's housing and domestic violence.* Retrieved from www.ncadv.org/publicpolicy/housing.htm.

National Network to End Domestic Violence. 2002. *On the Hill: The Campaign for full funding of the Violence Against Women Act.* Retrieved from www.nnedv.org, Oct. 12, 2002.

New York State Child Advocacy Resource and Consultation Center. (1994). Child sexual abuse public policy project and multidisciplinary response protocol: Executive summary. Retrieved Oct. 12, 2002, from www.nyscarcc.org/pubpol.htm.

Parent, D .G., Auerbach, B., & Carlson, K. E. (1992). *Compensating crime victims: A summary of policies and practices.* Washington, DC: U.S. Department of Justice, National Institute of Justice.

Parents Anonymous, Inc. (2000). About Parents Anonymous, Inc. Retrieved from www.parentsanonymous-natl.org/ABOUT.HTM?53,14.

Petit, M. R., & Curtis, P. A. (1997). *Child abuse and neglect: A look at the states. The CWLA statistics book.* Washington, DC: Child Welfare League of America.

Ragg, D. M. (1999). Dimensions of self-concept as predictors of men who assault their female partners. *Journal of Family Violence, 14*(3), 315–329.

Rathgeb Smith, S., & Freinkel, S. (1988). *Adjusting the balance: Federal policy and victim services.* New York: Greenwood Press.

Reinardy, J., & Kane, R. A. (1999). Choosing an adult foster home or a nursing home: Residents' perceptions about decision making and control. *Social Work, 44*(6), 571–585.

Rennison, C. M., & Welchans, S. (2000). *Bureau of Justice Statistics Special Report: Intimate Partner Violence* (Report No. NCJ 178247). Washington, DC: U.S. Department of Justice, Office of Justice Programs.

Rivera, J. (1997–1998). Preliminary report: Availability of domestic violence services for Latina survivors in New York State. *Buffalo Journal of Public Interest Law, 16*(1).

Roberts, A. R. (2000). *Crisis intervention handbook: Assessment, treatment and research.* New York: Oxford University Press.

Roberts, A. R., & Schenkman Roberts, B. (2002). A comprehensive model for crisis intervention with battered women and their children. In A. R. Roberts (Ed.), *Handbook of domestic violence intervention strategies: Policies, programs and legal remedies* (pp. 365–395). New York: Oxford University Press.

Rosenbaum, M. D. (1998). To break the shell without scrambling the egg: An empirical analysis of the impact of intervention into violent families. *Stanford Law and Policy Review, 9*(2), 409–432.

Rosenblatt, D. E., & Cho, K. H. (1996). Reporting mistreatment of older adults: The role of physicians. *Journal of American Geriatric Society, 44,* 65–70.

Sagatun, I. J., & Edwards, L. P. (1995). *Child abuse and the legal system.* Chicago, IL: Nelson-Hall.

Sherman, L. W. (1992). *Policing domestic violence.* New York: Free Press.

Sherman, L. W., & Berk, R. A. (1984). The specific deterrent effects of arrest for domestic assault. *American Sociological Review, 49,* 261–272.

Sullivan, C. M. (1997). Societal collusion and culpability in intimate male violence: The impact of community responses toward women with abusive partners. In A. P. Cardarelli (Ed.), *Violence between intimate partners: Patterns, causes and effects* (pp. 154–164). Boston: Allyn & Bacon.

Sullivan, C. M., Basta, J., Tan, C., & Davidson, W. S., II. (1992). After the crisis: A needs assessment of women leaving a domestic violence shelter. *Violence and Victims, 7*(3), 267–275.

Tatora, T., & Kuzmeskus, L. (1996). *Reporting of elder abuse in domestic settings* (Elder Abuse Information Series No. 3). Retrieved from National Center on Elder Abuse Web site: www.elderabusecenter.org/basic/fact3.pdf.

Tutty, L. M., & Rothery, M. (2002). Beyond shelters: Support groups and community-based advocacy for abused women. In A. R. Roberts (Ed.), *Handbook of domestic violence intervention strategies: Policies, programs, and legal remedies* (pp. 396–418). New York: Oxford University Press.

Tutty, L. M., Weaver, G., & Rothery, M. A. (1999). Resident's views of the efficacy of shelter services for assaulted women. *Violence Against Women, 5*(8), 898–925.

United States Conference of Mayors. (1999). *A status report on hunger and homelessness in America's cities: 1999.* Retrieved Oct. 12, 2002, from www.mayors.org.

Wiehe, V. R (1992). *Working with child abuse and neglect.* Itasca, IL: Peacock.

Wilson, L., & Conroy, J. (1999). Satisfaction of children in out-of-home care. *Child Welfare, 78*(1), 53–69.

Wolf, R. S. (1996). Elder abuse and family violence: Testimony presented before the

U.S. Senate Special Committee on Aging. *Journal of Elder Abuse and Neglect,* *8*(1), 81–96.

Yarborough, R. W. (1965). S.2155 of the 89th Congress: The Criminal Injuries Compensation Act. *Minnesota Law Review, 50,* 258.

/// Chapter 9

Abadinsky, H. (2001). *Drugs: An introduction.* (4th ed.). Stamford, CT: Wadsworth.

Bhalotra, S. M., & Mutschler, P. H. (2001). Primary prevention for older adults: No longer a paradox. *Journal of Aging and Social Policy, 12*(2), 5–22.

Bostaph, L. G., Hamilton, C., & Santana, S. A. (2000). *The use of security technology to protect battered women.* Paper presented at the American Society of Criminology meeting.

Chalk, R., & King, P. (Eds.). (1998). *Violence in families: Assessing prevention and treatment programs.* Washington, DC: National Academy Press.

Clayton, R. R., Cattarello, A. M., & Johnstone, B. M. (1996). The effectiveness of drug abuse resistance education (Project DARE): 5-Year follow-up results. *Preventive Medicine, 25,* 307–318.

Davis, R. C. & Taylor, B. G. (1997). A proactive response to family violence: The results of a randomized experiment. *Criminology, 35,* 307–333.

Domestic Violence Enhanced Response Team. (2001). *Vale grants.* Retrieved Jan. 21, 2002, from www.dvert.org/research/vale.asp.

Ellickson, P. L. (1995). Schools. In R. H. Coombs & D. Ziedonis (Eds.), *Handbook on drug Prevention* (pp. 93–120). Boston: Allyn & Bacon.

Family Violence Prevention Fund. (2000a). *Shop til it stops* [Press release]. Retrieved Jan. 12, 2002, from endabuse.org/newsdesk/releases.php3?Search=Article&ID= 79.

Family Violence Prevention Fund. (2000b). *National poster campaign calls for workplace support of domestic violence victims* [Press release]. Retrieved from endabuse.org/newsdesk/releases.php3?Search=Article&ID=48.

Family Violence Prevention Fund. (2002). *Corporate citizenship initiative.* Retrieved from endabuse.org/programs/display.php3?DocID=72.

Fetsch, R. J., Schultz, C. J., & Wahler, J. J. (1999). A preliminary evaluation of the Colorado RETHINK Parenting and Anger Management Program. *Child Abuse and Neglect, 23*(4), 353–360.

Finkelhor, D., Asdigian, N., & Dziuba-Leatherman, J. (1995). Victimization prevention programs for children: A follow-up. *American Journal of Public Health, 85,* 1684–1689.

Fisher, M. (1998). *Schools and early childhood development response to family violence.* Retrieved Jan. 14, 2002, from www.attorneygeneral.gov/family/schools/best. cfm.

Ghez, M. (1995). *Communications and public education: Effective tools to promote a cultural change on domestic violence.* Retrieved Jan. 12, 2002, from www. endabuse.org/programs/display.php3?DocID=24.

Harvey, P., Forehand, R., Brown, C., & Holmes, T. (1988). The prevention of sexual abuse: Examination of the effectiveness of a program with kindergarten-age children. *Behavior Therapy, 19,* 429–435.

Hazzard, A., Webb, C., Kleemeier, C., Angert, L., & Pohl, J. (1991). Child sexual abuse prevention: Evaluation and one-year follow-up. *Child Abuse and Neglect,* *15,* 123–138.

Littel, K., Malefyt, M. B., Walker, A., Tucker, D. D., & Buel, S. M. (1998). *Assessing justice system response to violence against women.* Retrieved Oct. 12, 2002, from www.vaw.umn.edu/promise/pplaw.htm.

National Network to End Domestic Violence. (2001). Campaign for full funding of the Violence Against Women Act: FY 2002 budget briefing book. Washington, DC: National Network to End Domestic Violence.

Occupational Safety and Health Administration. (2002). *Workplace violence awareness and prevention.* U.S. Department of Labor. Retrieved Jan. 10, 2002, from www. osha-slc.gov/index.html.

Occupational Safety and Health Administration. (1998). *Guidelines for preventing workplace violence for health care and social service workers.* U.S. Department of Labor. OSHA 3148. Retrieved Jan. 10, 2002, www.osha-slc.gov/index.html.

Rushton, J. P. (1982). Television and prosocial behavior. In D. Pearl, L. Bouthilet, & J. Lazar (Eds.), *Television and Behavior: Vol. 2. Technical Review.* (pp. 248-257). Washington, DC: National Institute of Mental Health.

Solomon, C. M. (1995). Talking frankly about domestic violence. *Personnel Journal,* *74,* 63–72.

Strategic Technologies. (2002). Strategic domestic violence deterrent: An innovative use of the Platinum Series Curfew Monitoring System. Retrieved Jan. from: www.strategic-tech.com/english/P_spouse.htm.

Surette, R. (1998). *Media, crime, and criminal justice: Images and realities.* Belmont, CA: Wadsworth.

Sygnatur, E. F., & Toscano, G. A. (2000, Spring). Work-related homicides: The facts. *Compensation and Working Conditions,* 3–8.

Trist, E. L. (1977). Collaboration in work settings: A personal perspective. *Journal of Applied Behavorial Science, 13*(3), 268–278.

Verizon Wireless. (2001). Retrieved Jan. 15, 2002, from www.news.verizonwireless. com.

Wireless Foundation. (2001). Donate a phone splash. Retrieved from www. wirelessfoundation.org/12give/index.htm.

Wright, K. (1999). The desirability of goal conflict within the criminal justice system. In S. Stojkovic, J. Klofas, & D. Kalinich (Eds.), *The administration and management of criminal justice organizations* (pp. 37–87). Prospect Heights, IL: Waveland Press.

/// Index

Hultman and Hultman, 200 (*see also* out-of-home care)
state Medicaid fraud control units, 205, 210–212
state units on aging, 175
stigmatization, 48
stress
  effect of chronic stress on child cognitive development, 82
  in families, 7
  and the "fight or flight" response pattern, 82
  parental, 36
  physical and psychological consequences for victims, 120–121
  stress reduction in prevention programs, 257, 267
stress theory, 34, 37–39
subculture of violence, 35, 47–48
subculture of violence perspective, 35, 47–48
subdural hematomas, 181 (*see also* elder abuse/neglect)
Substance Abuse and Mental Health Services Administration (SAMSHA), 209
"substitution effect theory," 228
Sudden Infant Death Syndrome (SIDS), 67, 69, 80
suicide, 144, 170, 182, 196, 238
surveillance equipment, 270, 272–273
symbolic interactionist theory 34, 37, 41, 46

technology, 268, 270–274
Technology-Related Assistance for Individuals with Disabilities Act, 209
Temporary Assistance to Needy Families (TANF), 234
testosterone, 36 (*see also* hormones)
therapeutic burning, 23 (*see also* folk remedies)
therapy, 238–239, 242–244, 257
Thurman, Tracey, 92–94 (*see also* wife-battering)
Title XX Social Services Block Grant, 231
token economy system, 191 (*see also* out-of-home care)
toullmos, 23 (*see also* folk remedies)
traumatic bonding theory, 34, 37–38

"underground railroad," 233
undue influence, 169,183 (*see also* elder abuse, financial abuse)

unemployment, 259
Uniform Crime Reporting, 96
United Nations Universal Declaration of Human Rights, 179 (*see also* elder abuse, individual rights)
United States Advisory Board on Child Abuse and Neglect, 80
United States Conference of Mayors, 120, 233–234
United States Department of Health and Human Services, 145, 172
United States Department of Housing and Urban Development, 103
U.S. Children's Bureau, 63

victim(s), 8
  advocacy groups for, 91
  characteristics of as predictors of abuse, 168
  "domestic violence survivor," 120
  of family violence, 8–9, 15–16
  nonambulatory, 14
  retaliation by, 111, 131, 143, 154
  role of, 36
victim compensation programs, 232–233 (*see also* victim services)
victim services, 230–241 (*see also* intervention, prevention, victim(s))
  advocacy for, 231–232, 239, 257
  barriers to, 234–235
  coalitions, 239
  community, 100, 237, 259 260, 262
  creation of, 230–232
  crisis intervention, 237–238
  funding for, 99–100, 230–232
  gay and lesbian services, 106
  grassroots advocacy for, 29–30,90–93, 99, 230
  hotlines, 210, 233, 237–238, 268
  institutionalization of, 98–99
  legal support, 92–93, 95
  for men, 109
  National Organization of Victim Assistance (NOVA), 238
  New York State Child Advocacy Resource and Consultation Center, 241
  ombudsman, 210, 212–213, 215, 239–240
  shelters and safe housing, 233–236, 257, 261–262, 268
  specialized domestic violence units, 95, 100
  technology in, 95, 270–274